Analyzing Political Change in Africa

Westview Replica Editions

This book is a Westview Replica Edition. The concept of Replica Editions is a response to the crisis in academic and informational publishing. Library budgets for books have been severely curtailed; economic pressures on the university presses and the few private publishing companies primarily interested in scholarly manuscripts have severely limited the capacity of the industry to properly serve the academic and research communities. Many manuscripts dealing with important subjects, often representing the highest level of scholarship, are today not economically viable publishing projects. Or, if they are accepted for publication, they are often subject to lead times ranging from one to three years. Scholars are understandably frustrated when they realize that their first-class research cannot be published within a reasonable time frame, if at all.

Westview Replica Editions are our practical solution to the problem. The concept is simple. We accept a manuscript in camera-ready form and move it immediately into the production process. The responsibility for textual and copy editing lies with the author or sponsoring organization. If necessary we will advise the author on proper preparation of footnotes and bibliography. We prefer that the manuscript be typed according to our specifications, though it may be acceptable as typed for a dissertation or prepared in some other clearly organized and readable way. The end result is a book produced by lithography and bound in hard covers. Initial edition sizes range from 600 to 800 copies, and a number of recent Replicas are already in second printings. We include among Westview Replica Editions only works of outstanding scholarly quality or of great informational value, and we will continue to exercise our usual editorial standards and quality control.

ANALYZING POLITICAL CHANGE IN AFRICA: APPLICATIONS OF A NEW MULTIDIMENSIONAL FRAMEWORK
edited by James R. Scarritt

Recent trends in Africa have drawn academic attention to political instability and the role of the military in unstable politics, as well as to class formation, class conflict, and prolonged economic dependency. This volume addresses these issues and others concerning national integration and institution building, using a comprehensive theoretical approach based on systems-functionalist theories. Eight diverse cases of African political change are analyzed in terms of the hierarchy of control and facilitation.

James R. Scarritt, professor of political science at the University of Colorado, has taught also at Makerere University, Kampala, Uganda.

Analyzing Political Change in Africa

Applications of a New Multidimensional Framework

edited by James R. Scarritt

Westview Press / Boulder, Colorado

A Westview Replica Edition

All rights reserved. No part of this publication may be reproduced or transmitted in any form or by any means, electronic or mechanical, including photocopy, recording, or any information storage and retrieval system, without permission in writing from the publisher.

Copyright © 1980 by Westview Press, Inc.

Published in 1980 in the United States of America by
    Westview Press, Inc.
    5500 Central Avenue
    Boulder, Colorado 80301
    Frederick A. Praeger, Publisher

Library of Congress Cataloging in Publication Data
Main entry under title:
Analyzing political change in Africa.
  (A Westview replica edition)
  Includes index.
  1. Africa—Politics and government—1960- —Addresses, essays, lectures. I. Scarritt, James R.
JQ1872.A52   320.96   80-13484
ISBN 0-89158-275-4

Printed and bound in the United States of America

TO PRUDY
*Without you, it would
have been impossible*

Contents

List of Tables and Figures xi
Contributors xiii
Acknowledgments xv

1. **Control and Facilitation: An Approach to the Analysis of Political Change,** *James R. Scarritt* 1
   - A Conceptual Framework 4
   - Propositions About Change 18
   - A Rough Causal Model 24
   - The Case Studies 25

2. **Religion and Politics in Independent Uganda: Movement Toward Secularization?** *Kathleen G. Lockard* ... 40
   - Historical Background 41
   - Religion and Politics in the Obote Regime 47
   - Religion and Politics in the Amin Regime 57
   - Conclusion 64

3. **Forecast for Political Change in Ethiopia: An Urban Perspective,** *Peter Koehn* 74
   - Significance of Urban Political Studies 75
   - Municipal Government Performance: The Pre-existing Goal Attainment System 76
   - The Process of Change: Control and Facilitation 79
   - Consequences: Urban Implications of Regime Change 84
   - Future Prospects 95

4. **Green Revolution in Ethiopia: The Politics of Rural Development in a Blocked and Inequitable Society,** *John M. Cohen* 107
   - Organizing the Study of a Rural Area 108
   - A Social Profile of Chilalo and Its Linkages to Ethiopian Society 111
   - Roles and Provincial Elites 120
   - Control, Facilitation, and the Process of Change 124
   - Conclusions in 1973 130
   - Postscript 133

5. **The Diffusion and Invention of Legislative and Party Structures in Anglophone Africa,** *James R. Scarritt* 146
   - A Review of the Literature on African Legislative and Political Party Change 147
   - Diffusion and Innovation in Legislatures 153
   - Diffusion and Innovation in Political Parties 164

6. **African Planning Failure: A Public Policy Analysis,** *Melvin J. Dubnick* 194
   Planning Failure in Africa 195
   A Framework for Analysis 197
   The Planner's Image and Planning Failure 200
   Planning System Integrative Norms and Planning Failure ... 216
   Planning System Mobilization and Planning Failure 218
   Social Conditions and Planning Failure 221
   Toward Strategies for Planning Success 225
   Summary and Conclusions 231
7. **The Significance of Sequential Ordering and Timing of Politically Induced Societal Changes in Anglophone African Party States: A Reconsideration,** *James R. Scarritt* 237
   The Analytical Problem and a Summary of the
     Original Analysis 237
   A Reconsideration of the Original Analysis 245
8. **Revolutionary Change in Mozambique: Implications for the Emerging Postindependence Society,** *Walter C. Opello, Jr.* 256
   The Preindependence Social System 258
   The Expansion of African Power and the
     Alternative Nationalist Social System 269
   The Emerging Social System of Independent Mozambique 284
9. **Prospects for Reactionary and Revolutionary Change in Zimbabwe,** *Kevin Maguire* 301
   Historical Development of the European Dominant System .. 303
   The Political Subsystems 305
   The Political Support and Legitimation Interchanges 323
10. **Conclusion: From Case Studies to Systematic Hypothesis Testing,** *James R. Scarritt* 344
Index of Authors Cited 352

Tables and Figures

Tables:
6.1 Themes of Planning: Crucial Social Subsystems 206
6.2 Themes of Planning: Strategic Use of Given Conditions . 208
6.3 Association of Physical and Demographic Factors and the Themes of Planning 210
6.4 Association of Political Structure and Process Factors and the Themes of Planning 211
6.5 Association of Political Conflict Factors and the Themes of Planning 212
6.6 Association of Economic Factors and the Themes of Planning 213
6.7 Association of Social Factors and the Themes of Planning 214
6.8 Association of Transport/Communication Factors and the Themes of Planning 215
9.1 Authority Orientations by Race 328
9.2 Regime Performance Evaluation by Race 330
9.3 Political Trust by Race: Rhodesian, Zimbabwean, and Detroit Respondents 330
9.4 Regime Ideology by Race 332
9.5 Modes of Political Obligation by Race 333
9.6 Perception of Regime Responsiveness by Race and Education 334
9.7 Perceived Intelligibility of the Political World by Race and Education 334
9.8 Rank Order of African Alienation Scores and European Legitimacy Scores 336

Figures:
1.1 Hierarchies of Control and Facilitation 13
1.2 A Rough Causal Model of African Political Change 26
4.1 Relationship of Chilalo Social System to Ethiopian Society 110
4.2 Forces of Change in Ethiopia Originating in Adaptive Subsystem and Possible Responses of Policy to the Conflict Generated 122
6.1 The Planner's Image 204
8.1 Incompatible Hierarchy of Control and Facilitation in Preindependence Mozambique 268
8.2 Compatible Hierarchy of Control and Facilitation in the FRELIMO Alternative Social System 281

Contributors

James R. Scarritt, Ph.D (1963), Northwestern University, is Professor of Political Science at the University of Colorado. He has done field research in Zambia and Zimbabwe (Rhodesia), has published numerous articles and monographs on political change in those countries, and is completing a book on Zambian Politics for Cornell University Press. He has also published several pieces on the application of theories of political change to Africa, and has taught this subject at Makerere University, Kampala, Uganda, as well as the University of Colorado. Westview Press will also publish his coedited book, *Developing Human Rights: Public Policies, Comparative Measures, and NGO Strategies.*

John M. Cohen, Ph.D. (1973), University of Colorado, is Institute Fellow at the Harvard Institute for International Development, having previously taught at Cornell University and at Haile Selassie I University, Addis Ababa, Ethiopia. He also served in the Peace Corps Lawyer Project in Ethiopia, and does extensive consulting on third world rural development. He is coauthor of two books and author of numerous monographs and articles on Ethiopia, focusing primarily on rural development.

Melvin J. Dubnick, Ph.D. (1974), University of Colorado, is currently Assistant Professor of Political Science at Loyola University of Chicago where he is Director of the Policy and Public Affairs Center and coordinator of the undergraduate public administration curriculum. His publications include articles on development planning, teaching policy studies, and standard setting in the U.S. His recent activities include research on regulatory policies and administrative reform and development of an introductory text on public policy analysis.

Peter Koehn, Ph.D. (1973), University of Colorado, is Associate Professor of Political Science at the University of Montana and does research and consultation on problems of local government in that state. He has taught in the Department of Public Administration at Haile Selassie I University, Addis Ababa, Ethiopia, and is now temporarily affiliated with the Institute of Administration, Ahmadu Bello University, Zaria, Nigeria. His many publications include a coauthored book (with John M. Cohen) and numerous articles on Ethiopian local government.

Kathleen Goodman Lockard, Ph.D (1974), University of Wisconsin-Madison, wrote a thesis based on research conducted in Uganda in 1971-72. She has taught at Northwestern University, SUNY-Buffalo, and the University of Wisconsin-Green Bay. Although her major area of research interest is East Africa, she has also done research in Malaysia and is currently preparing a manuscript on the Association of Southeast Asian Nations (ASEAN).

Kevin Maguire, Ph.D. (1969), University of Colorado, teaches political science and sociology at Waynesburg College in Pennsylvania, having previously taught at Gustavus Adolphus College, Shimer College, the University of Rhodesia, and Colorado State University. He is currently doing research on development and human needs in Greene County, Pennsylvania under a grant from the Department of Health, Education, and Welfare, and has published several articles and papers on Rhodesian politics.

Walter C. Opello, Jr., Ph.D. (1973), University of Colorado, is Assistant Professor of Political Science at the University of Mississippi, and previously taught at the State University of New York at Albany. He has done field research in Portugal and East Africa. His publications include numerous articles on political change in both Portugal and Mozambique, as well as a theoretical analysis of internal war. His current research is concerned with continuity and change in Portuguese political culture.

Acknowledgments

It would be impossible to acknowledge adequately all the people who have contributed to the writing of this book. Many of their names appear in the footnotes to various chapters. Professors E. Merle Adams, John W. Harbeson, Raymond F. Hopkins, Ronald John Hy, Kenneth Janda, John F. McCamant, William Safran, Samuel Sarkesian, and Crawford Young made valuable comments on all or parts of one or two chapters; their suggestions were greatly appreciated, although they were not always followed.

A grant from the Committee on University Scholarly Publications at the University of Colorado greatly facilitated publication of the book. Marilyn Ellis, Myra Jackson, and Terry James Rosson cheerfully performed the laborious task of typing the final manuscript and previous drafts of some chapters. Terri Albright did most of the work involved in preparing the index. Marty Powell and Sarah B.W. Shannon of Park Avenue Press competently supervised the typesetting, while doing much of the actual work, and tolerating numerous delays in the submission of manuscript. Miriam Gilbert of Westview Press ably coordinated the final stages of publication.

My wife Prudence Johnson Scarritt helped in numerous ways, of which proofreading all chapters was only the most obvious. She and my children, Susan, Ann, Katherine, and Arthur, put up with an almost constantly busy and preoccupied husband and father for many months while this book was in preparation. I am certain that the spouses and children of other contributors faced similar situations and were equally helpful in the preparation of individual chapters.

James R. Scarritt
July 1979

1

Control and Facilitation: An Approach to the Analysis of Political Change

James R. Scarritt

There is a virtually universal consensus among observers of the African scene that significant political change is taking place on that continent, but there is far less consensus on how that change can best be explained and its future extent, speed, and directions predicted. The trends away from competitive interparty politics and toward centralized executive power have been noted for some time. A logical extension of these trends which has taken place in many African countries is the weakening of even dominant or single party structures and their replacement by military regimes. Significant changes in governmental structure are by no means infrequent, even when military coups are not involved. Foreign owned enterprises, which dominated the economies of all African countries until very recently, are being nationalized or strictly controlled in some countries and allowed to strengthen their dominant position in others. The composition of ruling groups in various countries is changing, as are the broader social forces which they represent, although the exact nature of these changes is difficult to discern. Portugal has withdrawn from its former African territories, ending a protracted struggle to retain control of them, and regimes apparently committed to fundamental change have assumed power. In the white-ruled territories of Southern Africa, guerrilla warfare is on the increase and negotiations between white and black leaders are occurring with greater frequency and seriousness than ever before. In Zimbabwe and Namibia outright white rule is being replaced by regimes in which whites constitute a powerful minority. But what is the significance of these events, individually and collectively, for the overall pattern of political change and the possibilities for future change? What are the units of social and political structure in terms of which specific changes can be analyzed in order to determine their significance, and what is the nature of the crucial relationships among these units which determine the course of change? To ask these questions implies that the

James R. Scarritt

phenomena of African political change are sufficiently homogeneous to be analyzed in terms of a common theoretical approach. In fact, we believe that African political change can be analyzed in terms of an approach applicable to all political change, but we will not attempt to demonstrate this, as our substantive focus is limited to the African context.

This book analyzes eight cases of African political change, differing from one another in many respects, in terms of a common conceptual framework, a number of propositions phrased in terms of this framework, and a tentative causal model relating these propositions. Since we seek to explain and predict African political change rather than to merely describe it, we must employ some sort of theoretical apparatus, whatever its complexity and explicitness. Many social scientists believe that deductive theories equivalent to those in the physical sciences will some day be developed for the study of politics and society, but many others believe this is neither possible nor desirable. In any case, no such theories are available at the present time. The significant question for social scientists in this regard is how do we best approach building the most sophisticated theory which is possible in our fields at this time. A number of answers to this question have been suggested, and maximum over-all progress is likely to be achieved through a combination of strategies. The strategy most fruitfully employed in a given study or group of studies, however, depends heavily on the level of analysis desired and the state of theory building and data collection in the relevant subject matter area. African political change is a complex macro-level phenomenon, not fully understandable in terms of the micro-level phenomena of which it is composed, and it is a subject for which there has been limited collection of precise, quantified data, and even more limited hypothesis testing.

Given these conditions, it is useful to present our theoretical approach fully and apply it to what Arend Lijphart calls interpretive case studies,[1] thereby attempting to demonstrate the utility of this approach for explaining a wide variety of types and aspects of African political change. Although our cases do not constitute a random sample and do not comprise a test of our propositions in any rigorous sense, the book includes a brief conclusion in which the utility of these case studies for suggesting both refinements in the theoretical approach and possible data gathering techniques is examined. This is a tentative application of the comparative method, as it is defined by Lijphart.[2] In the future, we hope to test our propositions much more systematically, and thus to refine our causal model.[3] As a first step in this theory building strategy, the significance of each of the three components of our theoretical approach needs to be explicated.

A conceptual framework standing alone cannot provide explanation, but, in the absence of deductive theory, such a framework is extremely important for interrelating explanatory propositions when a broad and complex macro-level topic such as political change is to be explained. In this theoretical chapter our framework's utility in analyzing change will be compared in a general way with that of other frameworks which have been utilized by analysts of African politics, and in the subsequent case study chapters the same comparison will be made in terms of specific cases of political change. What we hope to demonstrate is that the breadth and complexity of the framework we employ, as well as the way in which it explicates the relationship between the major aspects of change, has significant pay-off in terms of the related propositions' power and completeness in explaining and predicting political change in Africa. If our interest were in a more specific topic, and/or one which did not involve conceptualizing relationships among units composed of many individuals, we could reduce the complexity of our framework to conform to the generally accepted standard of parsimony.[4] We do not believe, however, that the breadth and significance of inquiry should always be sacrificed to parsimony, and we deliberately avoid making this sacrifice, while attempting not to violate parsimony unnecessarily. These points will be examined in greater detail in the concluding chapter.

Integrated into this framework are a number of highly general propositions previously collected from the cultural and social change literature and rephrased in terms of the framework by the editor of this book.[5] The list of propositions is too long to conform to the canons of parsimony, but in the absence of a deductive theory or quantified indicators which would enable the independent effect of each variable to be tested by holding all other variables constant, it is difficult to see how the list could be significantly shortened without risking substantial loss of explanatory power. The relatively large number of concepts in the framework is in part responsible for the large number of propositions, as many of these concepts are the variables which are related in the propositions. Thus we are unparsimonious in two related ways, but for what are believed to be good reasons in each case. Dealing with a broad range of situations of political change also impels us toward propositions at a very high level of generality. Not only is there a great diversity among the cases of African political change examined in this book, but there is also the goal of saying something, and perhaps even something new, about the significant normative and empirical questions which have been and are being asked about political change in general. Where are technology and other forces of modernization leading the world's societies, and what can mankind do to control these changes? We will not deal directly with such questions in this book, but if they are to be dealt with at some future time utilizing our theoretical approach we must begin to demonstrate here that our propositions can be tested in some form on the data of African political change, and can explain and predict such change.

Given the multitude of concepts and propositions we employ, it will be useful to begin to order them in terms of a rough causal model, even though we do not have the quantified measurements which are necessary to test such a model. To relate variables in terms of sequence as well as in terms of control and facilitation is the best way to begin the process of discovering which ones may not be necessary for explanation. Investigating the fit between the causal model and various case studies will be especially useful in this regard.

A Conceptual Framework

The conceptual framework utilized in this book is called a "control and facilitation" framework to emphasize its principal thrust in explaining change. It borrows heavily from the work of Talcott Parsons, and we believe it is consistent with Parsons' overall approach.[6] However, most interpreters of Parsons' analysis of social and political phenomena believe that it is characterized by a number of faults such as assumptions of value consensus and the primacy of value determinism, a consequent disinterest in explaining the origins of values, vague and overlapping concepts adding up to a bundle rather than a system, lack of propositional content, inability to analyze conflict and change, failure to conceptualize whole individuals and their strivings for gratification, and a conservative bias.[7] To avoid debate over the correct interpretation of Parsons, we will not attempt to demonstrate that we are consistent with his analysis on every point, while acknowledging that our framework is basically Parsonian. Several commentators have noted that Parsons' work is subject to varying interpretations,[8] and, although we believe the present framework is extremely close to that of Parsons, it is not necessary to present a detailed defense of our somewhat unusual interpretation of his work. "Control and facilitation" assumes that behavior is determined by the asymmetrical interdependence of cultural and material factors and represents, we believe, a more accurately descriptive title for Parsons' concept "hierarchy of control."[9] The exact nature of this asymmetrical interdependence will be examined in detail below. We have already said that this framework is particularly suited to the analysis of change, and that propositions will be presented which are partially derived from it; we will attempt to demonstrate below that it also avoids the other alleged faults of the Parsonian framework.

Turning to a detailed presentation of our conceptual framework, the first point to be made is that the concrete suprasystem within which we will analyze political change is the society. Societies are defined as the most inclusive and relatively self-sufficient systems of interaction which can be identified. There is an all-inclusive system of interaction at the world level which is suprasocietal, but it rates quite low on self-sufficiency. African societies are by no means completely self-sufficient, especially with regard to economic relationships; they are dependent on a network of relationships with western societies and other major powers. Neither this network nor its western, capitalistic part constitute relatively self-sufficient suprasystems, however.[10] Working from society as the comprehensive unit of analysis allows changes in the political system to be related to changes in other subsystems of society, both as independent and as dependent variables, more systematically than utilizing the political system itself as the broadest unit of analysis would allow.

Since we are treating societies and political systems as systems in a technical sense, the assumptions involved in employing the latter term should be made explicit. Systems are sets of interrelated parts which persist for some period of time and are distinguishable from phenomena outside the system—i.e., they have boundaries. The boundaries of any system are not predetermined by the nature of the subject matter, but rather are determined by the definitions of concepts employed by the analyst, although there is less flexibility in manipulating the boundaries of a relatively concrete system such as society than a more purely analytic one such as the political system as we define it. Although societal boundaries shift, as exemplified by colonial conquest and neo-colonial domination, it is nevertheless possible to specify these boundaries for purposes of analysis. The interrelatedness of system parts does not imply that they are completely dependent on one another or on the system as a whole. On the contrary, there are varying degrees of independence of different parts of societies and political systems, although not so much independence that their systemic identity ceases to exist. Finally, systems tend to persist for some time, in part because the forces of change are insufficiently strong to destroy them, and in part because they include partially effective homeostatic mechanisms which will be discussed below in relation to societies and political systems. Of course, this tendency is overcome with some frequency, and all systems eventually fail to persist.[11]

It is important to discuss the various components of a society's environment and their relation to society because they can be important sources or recipients of social and political change. Societies exist within a physical environment and are somewhat affected by the biological characteristics of the human beings who populate them. More directly and powerfully influential components of society's environment, however, are culture and personality. These two components can be differentiated from societies only in analytical terms. They refer respectively to the pattern of learned behavior, symbols, and artifacts shared by some or all members of a society or several societies, and the pattern of internal orientations or predispositions of those members. A concrete society is composed of personalities who have to some degree internalized culture, but it is useful to separate out the interaction and evaluation aspects of concrete human behavior and apply the term society to them alone. This will allow exploration of the relationships between society, culture, and personality as they affect and are affected by political change. Other societies are also important parts of a society's environment, especially in Africa where dependence on the international environment is quite high.

Following Parsons, the conceptual framework employed here conceives of the internal structure of society in terms of four functionally defined subsystems, four levels of social structure, four media of exchange, and the network of relationships among these components.[12] This conception of societal structure is quite complex, but, as has been indicated, we believe that this complexity is justified by the added explanatory power which it provides.

First, society can be divided into four subsystems based on the principal function each one performs with varying degrees of success for the society as a whole. Functional subsystems are utilized in this framework to denote significant consequences produced by system units over time, and the four functions explicated below are thought to include all such consequences. Such inclusiveness is important for a complete macro-analysis. No attempt is made to explain the origin or persistence of structural units or the whole society or political system solely in terms of functional performance. Ineffective functional performance will probably lead to change, but this relationship is explained by the propositions presented below rather than accepted a priori.[13]

The pattern socialization and control subsystem[14] maintains or changes the pattern of values, norms, collectivities, and roles of which the society is composed by socializing or failing to socialize individuals into this pattern and perpetuating or failing to perpetuate their adherence to it. Pattern change can result from the successful performance of the pattern socialization and control function because the principal homeostatic tendency in society is toward the persistence of some structural pattern accepted by enough members of society to make it viable, rather than toward the maintenance of universal adherence to the prevailing structural pattern. The integrative subsystem adjusts or fails to adjust relations among all structural units of the society (as defined below), particularly with regard to the allocation of advantages and disadvantages, to keep these units working together more or less effectively. Two additional subsystems attempt to adjust the society to its environment: the goal attainment subsystem seeks to bring about valued relations with the environment, and the adaptive subsystem more or less successfully organizes and provides facilities or resources of various types for this purpose.

Employing society as the most inclusive suprasystem and analyzing it in terms of functionally defined subsystems should not be taken to indicate a lack of interest in territorially defined subsystems. There are many possible types of subsystems into which societies could be analyzed, and the undisputed significance of local communities in African societal organization dictates that our framework must include them among its units of analysis. Two of the case studies presented in subsequent chapters will deal with political change in local communities. Both functional and territorial subsystems are themselves systems and therefore have their own persistence tendencies, sometimes conflicting with the persistence tendency of society.

In this framework the political system of a society or a local community consists of the goal attainment subsystem and its interchange relationships with the other three subsystems. The primary function performed more or less effectively by the political system is the making of decisions or policies for the whole society which will result in the attainment of goals desired by at least some of its members. Many policies are binding on all members of the society, but are desired only by some. The political system must allocate rewards and costs relating to goal attainment among different classes of citizens and attempt to resolve the conflicts generated in the process. This is done in the goal attainment-integrative or political support interchange, which will be described below.[15]

Internally, the political system (and the other subsystems of society) can be divided into four functional subsystems paralleling those of society. Effective pattern socialization and control within the political system is best achieved by a widely accepted set of procedural norms—a constitution in the broadest sense, although it can be achieved for a short time by a charismatic leader. Integrative functions are performed within the political system by some combination of governmental structures and political parties, while adaptive functions center on the bureaucracy. Given the political system's primary societal function of goal attainment, its internal goal attainment subsystem, almost universally some form of "political executive," tends to be the focus of the political system's extrasocietal relations. The other three internal subsystems specialize in relating the political system to their parallel subsystem at the societal level through interchanges which will now be described.[16]

In the political support interchange the political system obtains some degree of support from the "public," organized to some extent in interest-based collectivities (part of the integrative subsystem), by the more or less successful formulation and execution of governmental policies which meet some public demands. In the resource mobilization interchange the political system stimulates and regulates the economy (adaptive subsystem) more or less effectively in exchange for the provision of some or all of the labor and material resources necessary to attain societal goals. Finally, in the legitimation interchange, the political system exchanges decisions and policies which implement prevailing values to some degree for partial or complete legitimation of political authority by the pattern socialization and control structures. Our description of these interchanges has deliberately emphasized that they operate more or less successfully in various societies, just as the major functions are performed more or less successfully. Within the political system, parallel interchanges more or less effectively relate subsystems to one another.

There are interchanges between the adaptive, integrative, and pattern socialization and control subsystems of society which do not directly involve the political system. Of these, the loyalty, solidarity, and commitment interchange is especially relevant to political change through its effects on the directly political interchanges. It involves the pattern socialization and control system legitimating or failing to legitimate the stratification system and interest-based collectivity structure of society (integrative subsystem) in exchange for support or lack of support for the prevailing cultural pattern by organized and unorganized collectivities.

At this point political change can be defined in terms of our framework. Political change encompasses changes in the political system itself and politically induced changes in the other subsystems of society. In areas such as Africa in which all subsystems tend to be changing rapidly and inducing change in one another it is especially important to examine both of these aspects of political change and their interrelations. Alternative conceptual frameworks which have been suggested as universally applicable in the analysis of African politics, such as pluralism and class analysis, often do not separate the four functional subsystems as clearly as the control and facilitation framework does, and thus do not envisage as much possible variation in the relations among them.[17] Pluralism tends to conceive of politics as dominated by a single cumulative cleavage which originates in both the pattern socialization and control and integrative subsystems, although the distinction between cultural and social pluralism suggests that either of these subsystems may be the primary source of this cleavage. Class analysis which defines classes as based entirely on the means of production combines the integrative and adaptive subsystems to create a single cumulative class cleavage and portrays politics as an instrument for furthering the interests of the dominant class. In both frameworks cumulative cleavage almost inevitably creates severe conflict.

The interchanges depicted in the control and facilitation framework, on the other hand, focus attention on the mutual dependence of the political system and each of three separate components of its social environment in relationships which may foster or impede the effective performance of each subsystem and may involve high or low levels of conflict. This added complexity allows a more realistic and exact analysis than that provided by the alternative frameworks. For example, the consequences of a political system allocating the rewards and costs of its policies extremely unequally among categories of individuals for the loss of support from relatively deprived categories will depend significantly on the total amount of resources provided by the economy, the effectiveness of the legitimation interchange in gaining acceptance of extreme inequality, and the group consciousness and organization (integrative characteristics) of the deprived categories. The separation of functional subsystems is purely analytic, and the control and facilitation framework shares a significant insight of class analysis and pluralism: that relationships among major components of society must be understood to attain adequate explanation of any of these components. Sophisticated class analysts, including some who are students of Africa, see several possible bases of class, and their analysis of the relationships between politics and other aspects of society is quite similar to the interchanges of the control and facilitation framework.[18] They differ in assuming that class processes always dominate these relationships, however, as will be elaborated below.

Structurally, societies and political systems are analyzed by our framework in terms of four levels: values, norms, collectivities and roles. "Values...are the most general statements of legitimate ends which guide social action,"[19] while norms are more situation-specific and means-related statements. Collectivities are systems of interaction among role performers, to some extent normatively regulated; and roles, which will be analyzed in detail below, are the participation of persons in such systems of interaction. Collectivities can be analyzed as systems having the same functional subsystems and tendency to persist as societies, and having values, norms, and roles specific to them. Several of the case studies presented in this book contain such an analysis.

Each structural level is found in all four functional subsystems, although values are most important in the pattern socialization and control subsystem, norms in the integrative, collectivities in the goal attainment, and roles in the adaptive. All structural levels must be taken into account to explain behavior fully. This conception of social and political structure is quite complex, but it allows a much more exact specification of sources of and mechanisms for expediting or impeding conflict and change than alternative frameworks allow. For example, members of a social class, defined in terms of either relationship to the means of production or corporate control of media of exchange (see below), are also occupants of roles and members of collectivities, only some of which are class-based. They share some values and norms with members of other classes, and have value-normative conflicts with members of their own class. Thus class membership determines some but not all of the relationships of various structural levels in the pattern socialization and control, integrative, and adaptive subsystems to recruitment to political roles and collectivities, socialization and adherence to political values and norms, and the content of governmental policies.[20]

But it may be thought that our complex conception of social and political structure has intolerably high costs. In all of this complexity where is the individual? Is his behavior so determined by social structure that he cannot make choices or seek to further his perceived interests? One concept in the framework which is close to the individual is the role, and yet the latter is shared and often largely normatively regulated behavior, and thus appears to be quite different from the calculating, choosing individual. It is significant, however, that roles are defined in our framework in terms of behavior rather than in terms of normative expectations, even though role behavior is assumed to be patterned and influenced in some more than minimal degree by normative expectations. Defining roles in terms of behavior is significant because conflicts, vagueness, and gaps in normative expectations provide the opportunity for calculation and choice on the part of individual role players. Furthermore, normative expectations regarding a single role may be perceived differently by different role players, whose behavior may thus be different. If innovative perceptions and behavior are sufficiently widespread, they may create new normative expectations and new patterns of behavior; this process has been aptly entitled "role-making."[21] Role perceptions which are related to goals which the role player or role maker wants to attain are another way of conceptualizing what have been called interests.[22] An individual plays (or makes) a number of roles and differs from other individuals with regard to the combination of roles in which he participates; both of these facts increase the autonomy of the individual from the prevailing expectations attached to any of his roles.[23]

Social structure exists in an environment, and an important component of that environment consists of the personalities of individual role players, which are themselves systems seeking to gratify need-dispositions. Personality, as well as "higher" levels of social structure, influences the way in which roles are played and made, and personality is substantially autonomous from society and culture.[24] Thus individual persons as actors enter into the control and facilitation framework in a significant way through the combination of roles and personalities, even though the individual is not one of our basic units of analysis. Persons are not made prisoners of social structure, nor are they dehumanized in the sense that human concerns are ignored. Human choice and pursuit of interests as they affect and are affected by society can, in fact, be more adequately analyzed within this framework which relates personality, role, and society than within an exchange or a symbolic interactionist framework which contains no concepts or propositions at or anywhere near the societal level.[25] Although the control and facilitation framework does not view the satisfaction of personality need-dispositions as a complete explanation of the creation or maintenance of social structures, it is certainly true that such structures are often created and maintained in an attempt to satisfy needs.

Social and political structures are not static, but rather are constantly functioning over time, and thus frequently changing. Role making is the crucial micro-level process for such change. At the macro-level where there is no direct interaction, four circulating media which are exchanged among various units of structure, both in the same and in different functional subsystems, are essential to structural operation and change.[26]

These media are commitments, influence, power, and money, and each one is most closely associated with a single level of social structure: commitments with values, influence with norms, power with collectivities, and money with roles. Since, as we have seen, there are looser associations between each structural level and a single functional subsystem, the same loose associations hold for each medium and a single subsystem.

As all four media are exchanged by and within the political system, however, they will all be explicated here and used in subsequent analyses of political change. Power, the medium most frequently exchanged by and within the political system, is the ability to affect the behavior of others by employing the threat of negative sanctions, and political power is the ability to so affect behavior with respect to the attainment of collective goals through the making of binding decisions. It is important to recognize that in this definition of political power collective goals are those of any collectivity in society and not merely those shared by the whole society.[27] Influence is "persuasion without power," employing positive sanctions or rewards rather than negative sanctions, while commitments constitute "a generalized capacity and credible promises to effect the implementation of values."[28] The medium of exchange or purchasing-power-symbolizing function of money is parallel to the other media defined above.[29]

As these media are exchanged for one another by various units of social and political structure, they are highly interdependent, as are the levels of social structure to which they are closely related. Commitments to values, for example, can be made effective only if they are exchanged for some combination of influence, power, and money which will bring about an effective normative specification of the values as well as role and collectivity behavior supportive of the values and their normative specifications. On the other side of the coin, power is not exercised in a vacuum, but needs to be exchanged for commitments and influence to give it direction, and for money to give it full effectiveness. In these exchanges of media the supply of each and all of them can be expanded or contracted. The supply of power inflates or deflates through leaders making or failing to make decisions and followers supporting or failing to support leaders, while the supply of influence inflates or deflates through leaders assuming or failing to assume responsibility for collective action and followers articulating or failing to articulate demands for collective action, and the supply of commitments is dependent on the willingness of all parties to adhere to shared values. These processes of media expansion and contraction are analogous to monetary inflation and deflation.

The control and facilitation framework gives greater emphasis than Parsons does to the distribution of media of exchange among roles and collectivities in society and the political system. There is an almost infinite number of ways in which the various media can be distributed, although the distribution of each one is usually more than slightly unequal, and there is a tendency for those who control a greater supply of one medium to also control a greater supply of the others.[30] Those who control significantly more of a medium than other individuals, regardless of the extent of their organization in collectivities or cohesion with one another, constitute the elite of the corresponding functional subsystem. The political elite controls a disproportionate supply of power and overlaps in varying degrees in different societies with other media-controlling elites. Given the previously mentioned tendency to agglomeration in the distribution of media there is usually a substantial overlap, in which case a societal elite (or, more simply, an elite) exists. Since the degree of inequality in the distribution of media varies among societies and political systems, the degree of eliteness in these systems also varies. It is thus frequently useful to distinguish between top elites and mid or bridge elites, with the latter controlling a smaller but still disproportionate supply of various media.

To the extent that there is group consciousness and concerted action among members of a societal elite in the use of media (usually all four of them) to further their corporate interests, they constitute a dominant class. These conditions are usually found when a societal elite is relatively well established, but is challenged to some degree by non-elites. Thus the formation of a dominant class takes place within the broader context of the formation of a class system, although the solidification of the dominant class usually precedes that of other classes. In this situation the dynamics of class formation and/or conflict strongly influence all levels of social structure in all functional subsystems and the interchanges among them, although the integrative subsystem and its interchanges are central to these processes. Sophisticated class analysts now recognize that the relative importance of various media (and various interchanges, as pointed out above) in class formation and conflict may vary among societies and over time, although they tend to see class relations as significant in every situation. Several of the case studies presented in this book utilize the concept of class very fruitfully in their explanations of change, but others do not utilize it because class is not highly relevant to the specific changes they seek to explain. Class analysis can be viewed as a part of the control and facilitation framework as well as an alternative to it.[31]

The dynamic aspects of our framework center on the hierarchy of control and facilitation which operates among society and the major components of its environment; within society, among the functional subsystems, structural levels (It is in this sense that they are levels.), and media of exchange; and within the political system, among the structural levels and media of exchange. The hierarchy of control and facilitation is a relationship of asymmetrical interdependence in which regulative information flows in one direction and the provision of facilities flows in the

Control and Facilitation

opposite direction. This concept, which is at the heart of our framework and thus appropriately gives the framework its name, is borrowed from cybernetics, in which: "'Control' is a special kind of relation between two machines or parts of machines, such that one part regulates the operation of the other... The essential point is that the source of energy is dissociated from the source of instructions."[32] The following diagram illustrates the operation of the hierarchy among the various units of analysis described above:

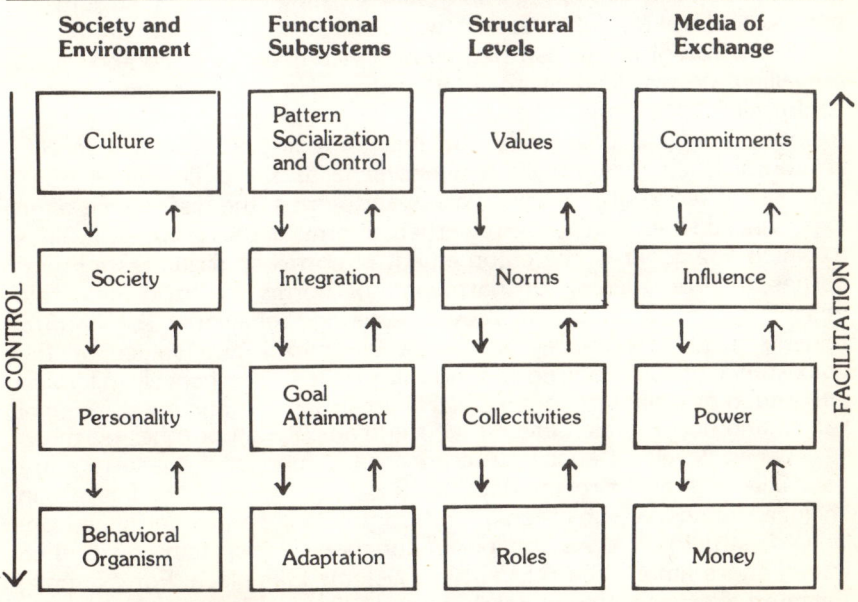

FIGURE 1.1
Hierarchies of Control and Facilitation

In the analysis of politics and society, the hierarchy of control and facilitation portrays a mutual determinism of values and interests and of the structures which specialize in their production, distribution, maintenance, and change. As Alvin Gouldner says, "To some extent...*what* [people] experience as gratifying is a function of what they believe to be desirable or moral; in turn, what they believe to be desirable or moral is a function of the gratifications produced in pursuing this."[33] This may be illustrated by several examples which refer to various aspects of the hierarchy of control and facilitation.

Among the functional subsystems of society, the hierarchy operates through the interchanges previously described. The economy provides material facilities for the political system, which, in turn, makes policies that control the level, technology, content, and distribution of economic productivity. On the other hand, the specific demands and supports produced by the integrative subsystem and the more or less legitimating values produced by the pattern socialization and control subsystem act as controls on the political system, while the policies produced by the latter provide facilities for meeting interest-based demands and implementing and transmitting values.[34]

Among structural levels in the same functional subsystem, facilitation can be exemplified by decisions to "make" roles (i.e. "play" them differently from the prevailing manner) which, if repeated sufficiently often in the same or similar ways, can modify existing collectivity structures, norms, and values, or create new ones where none had previously existed. It can also be illustrated by role incumbents' nonconformity to prevailing norms leading to modifications in those norms, or by conformity to norms due to calculation of personal advantage, membership in a collectivity, or fear of coercion. Control among structural levels includes such phenomena as the definition of one's interests in terms of prevailing values and norms, the dissonance often experienced when one is overrewarded in terms of the norms and values to which one adheres, the enforcement of norms by disinterested third parties, the broadening or narrowing of norms to cover new role behaviors or to cease to cover existing behaviors, the mutual reinforcement of identical or compatible norms and values or the coexistence of conflicting norms and values leading respectively to further integration or disintegration of collectivity structures, and the learning of values and norms which encourage the manipulation of other norms.

Specific levels of social structure in any functional subsystem are controlled by and provide facilities for "higher" structural levels in "higher" functional subsystems, and control and receive facilities from "lower" structural levels in "lower" functional subsystems only when interchanges among the relevant subsystems take place. For example, the internal organization of political collectivities such as political parties and governmental bureaucracies is controlled by values and norms specific to the pattern socialization and control or integrative subsystems only to the extent that this internal organization affects the ways in which policies enacted by these collectivities (sususally in combination with others) support or fail to support societal values, and meet or fail to meet interest-based demands. This example could be multiplied to include examples involving all functional subsystems and structural levels.

The preceding discussion has assumed, for purposes of simplification, that any specific unit at each structural level is a part of only one functional subsystem, and of course this assumption is frequently not true. If any structural unit is relevant to more than one subsystem, the number of hierarchical relationships in which it may be involved and the number of positions it can occupy in these relationships are correspondingly multiplied. When a single collectivity performs religious, political, economic, and status-determining functions, for example, it belongs to all four subsystems and its potential hierarchical relationships are much more numerous than they would otherwise be. Because of their highly general nature, values are especially likely to be relevant to more than one subsystem.

Control and facilitation among the media of exchange can be illustrated in terms of relationships between power and other media. Power can be used to facilitate escape from the obligations entailed by commitments to values, but the use of power also tends to facilitate the creation of new value-commitments which will legitimize such use; power wielders then become subject to control from commitments to these new values. Power can facilitate the exercise of influence because the ability to impose sanctions creates prestige, but influence also controls the exercise of power in relationships in which effective influence and power are both present. Inflation or deflation of each medium exerts pressure toward a similar change in the supply of other media through control and/or facilitation.[35]

As can be surmised from the above examples, the exact extent and path of control and facilitation are always empirical questions, and all units have some degree of independence from control or facilitation or both. Several possibly conflicting "higher" units (for example, values) may be relevant to a "lower" unit (for example, a norm), or a single "higher" unit may be relevant to a number of "lower" units (for example, several possible normative specifications of a commonly held value). Or there may be gaps or conflicts in the "higher" levels (for example, values and norms potentially controlling specific collectivity or role behavior) or in the "lower" levels (for example, roles and collectivities potentially implementing specific values and norms) which make hierarchical relationships in some degree inoperative. Parsons himself explicates those complexities which serve as sources of unit independence from control in the following manner:

> Cultural systems, however, are by no means fully integrated but may be regarded as varying from a pole of virtually complete integration to one of a nearly random assortment of meaning components. Furthermore, the actual behavior of individuals, their symbolically oriented action, may be to a widely varying degree congruent with the meanings of the cultural system. This applies, of course, as well to those aspects of meaning which we speak of as being institutionalized to constitute aspects of the actual structure of a social system

and those which we speak of as being internalized to constitute actual components of the structure of personality systems.[36]

What is being said in the preceding paragraphs through the explication of these various complexities is that, although we use the term hierarchy of control and facilitation in the singular to emphasize the unity of the hierarchical principle, there are in fact a number of cybernetic hierarchical relationships in society and the political system.[37] A complete and accurate dynamic analysis needs to take all of these relationships into account.

The hierarchy of control and facilitation concept has greater explanatory power and precision than other generalized conceptions of social dynamics utilized in the study of African politics and society because it makes use of the full complexity of societies and political systems, and avoids any oversimplified or single factor determinism, without falling back on the largely accurate but generally uninformative statement that everything influences and is influenced by everything else. Asymmetrical interdependence among society and environment, functional subsystems, structural levels, and media of exchange, and the relationships among these various hierarchies present a complex but clearly causal picture of social and political dynamics. The degree of interdependence among units is variable, but any unit can have some degree of independence and thus causal primacy.[38]

All of the basic elements of the control and facilitation framework have now been presented and explicated. Before listing the specific propositions phrased in terms of this framework which will be used to explain change, something should be said about the general assumptions implied by the hierarchy of control and facilitation concept in the analysis of conflict and change.

Turning first to the analysis of conflict, which is the opposite of integration, its sources may be between society and either personality, culture, or other societies; may be within or among functional or territorial subsystems of society; and may be among units at the same or different structural levels. Conflict involving value dissensus tends to be especially severe, since those holding a specific set of values usually expect generalized conformity with those values by all members of society. The severity of such conflict also depends on its concurrent manifestation at other structural levels, however, with that value conflict which is supported by conflicting norms, opposing organized collectivities, and incompatible role behaviors being the most severe. Severe conflict can also take place within the context of value consensus because of any combination of dissensus on norms, collectivity conflict, incompatible role perceptions and behavior, and personality-society incongruity. Conflict of some type and degree of severity will be present in any society or political system because it is impossible to adjust all structural, functional, and media of exchange units perfectly to one another.

The sources of change in the control and facilitation framework are the same as the sources of conflict. Change originating in other societies and transferred to the focal society is called diffusion, and change originating internally to the focal society is called invention.[39] From whatever its source, change spreads "up" and/or "down" the relevant hierarchies of control and facilitation until it meets with resistance sufficient to halt its ramification. Conflict, especially if it is severe, produces alternative structures and thus greatly expedites change, which, in turn, is likely to result in increased conflict, at least in the short run. Conflict, however, is neither a necessary nor a sufficient cause of change, and prolonged conflict may inhibit change, as is indicated in proposition A2 below.

Facilitation, or "upward" movement in the hierarchy of control and facilitation, moving from individual personality dissatisfaction or satisfaction to role making or role conformity, to expanding or retaining power through collectivity organization, to changing or maintaining norms and thus exercising influence, and finally to changing or maintaining values and commitments to adhere to them and thus changing or maintaining culture, and usually passing from the adaptive to the goal attainment, to the integrative, and finally to the pattern socialization and control subsystem in the process, provides the driving energy to sustain or block change. In any empirical instance of change all of these stages are not necessarily involved; we have attempted to present only the generalized pattern of the facilitation effect, and analyses of change situations must specify exactly which aspects of facilitation are involved. In every case, however, there is a change in the quantity and/or direction of energy flow in the system.

Control, or "downward" movement in the hierarchy of control and facilitation, moves through all or part of the same generalized pattern in the opposite direction, providing guides to behavior in the form of values and norms generated by pattern socialization structures. Such control is exercised by defining and interpreting the meaning and utility of potential changes for role players and collectivity members. Control may either foster or impede change; the former will be possible when specific changes can be legitimized by the prevailing values and norms or alternative or variant values and norms which are held by some members of the society. The control aspect of change involves changes in the quantity and/or direction of information flow in the system.

Thus the direction, extent, and speed of change vary widely from one society or political system to another, and are determined by the balance between control and facilitation. To ascertain this balance in any given society or political system at a specific point in time, the analyst must examine the distribution of control over each of the media of exchange among roles and collectivities in the various functional subsystems, and determine the degree to which specific changes are compatible with the values and norms of those potential facilitators (role players and collectivity leaders) controlling the greatest supplies of each medium—the elites or the dominant class. To examine the balance between control and facilitation over time, the analyst must also consider exchanges of media within and among subsystems, and lags in the control and facilitation process. For example, norms created to resolve collectivity conflict persist even when the conflict has been resolved, and exercise control in such a way as to stimulate new conflict. The resulting explanation of change takes into account all of the factors emphasized by other frameworks—personality dissonance, class interests, organized groups, values stressing achievement, etc.—and provides a means to relate them to one another and assess their significance. It thus provides a more complete and powerful explanation of change in societies and political systems.[40]

Propositions About Change

Within this general framework for analyzing change, the following propositions are useful for explaining the specific course of political change, whether it is initiated through diffusion or invention. The propositions are grouped into five analytical categories which are not stages in a fixed sequence[41]—state of the pre-existing system, sources and types of change, point of impact of change on the society or political system and facilitation of change, control of change, and structural and functional consequences of change. Since political change is a continuous process, although one which varies in intensity over time, the state of the pre-existing system represents merely an arbitrary starting point for analyzing a segment of this continuous process. The significance of sources and types of change, facilitation, and control have been discussed in the preceding paragraphs. The structural and functional consequences of change are the effects of control and facilitation over time; like the pre-existing system they are analyzed within an arbitrarily determined period of time, although in actual fact they are continuous.

Each of the following propositions should be read as including an implicit assumption of *ceteris paribus*. All other things are not equal, of course, and many of the significant variations are covered by other propositions on the list. As previously indicated, it is not possible to measure the interactive effects of the variables dealt with in different propositions or shorten the list of propositions because of the nondeductive nature of our approach and the nonquantitative nature of most available data. For the same reasons it is not possible to attain the desirable level of precision in many propositions, such as those dealing with degrees of concentration of power, tolerance for change, utility, and compatibility. But these admitted problems do not by any means eliminate

Control and Facilitation

the usefulness of the control and facilitation framework and the related propositions, especially since the major alternative approaches are beset by essentially the same problems.

A. State of the Pre-existing System

1. The stronger the values and norms of innovativeness in a society or political system, or a subsystem thereof, the more likely it is that change will take place.
2. The more completely integrated a society or political system, the less likely it is that change will take place within it.[42]
   a. Those subsystems which are least well integrated internally or with the remainder of the system are most susceptible to change.
   b. Extremely low levels of system integration may hinder all purposive action and thus retard change.
   c. A well-differentiated set of alternative or variant values and norms expedites change by providing a positive model in terms of which new elements can be judged.
   d. But ethnic, class, regional, and other cleavages within a society, as well as feelings of ethnocentrism toward outsiders, act as barriers which inhibit the spread of change.
3. Although the number of proposals for innovation tends to increase with the dispersion of power, the more crucial variable of the acceptance of proposals tends to increase with the concentration of power, up to quite high levels of concentration.
4. A system or subsystem which is changing is more likely to undergo further change, up to a threshold of tolerance for change, at which point recent changes will tend to have a dampening effect on future change. When change is rapid, actors in a system are more likely to anticipate further change.
5. The better a social or political system is adapted to its environment, the less the likelihood of change.

B. Sources and Types of Change

1. Important sources of change are both external to the society or political system and internal to it. Other societies are the most important external source of political change, while the major internal sources have been specified in propositions A1-4 above.
2. Units "lower" in the structural hierarchy of control and

facilitation, and thus more specific and more likely to have a material embodiment, are more easily communicable within a society or political system, and between systems, than are "higher" units.
    a. But ideas or values relatively unconnected to any other structural framework are more easily transmitted—especially between systems—than ideational elements which do have such connections, or than the other structures themselves.[43]

C. Point of Impact of Change on the Society or Political System and Facilitation of Change

    1. Given the important sources of change and the types of elements which are most easily communicable, both externally and internally induced change are likely to impinge first on the adaptive and goal attainment subsystems—the ones most closely connected with the role and collectivity levels of social structure, and the ones most closely concerned with relations between the system and its environment.
        a. Changes which impinge first on functional subsystems and structural levels "lower" in the hierarchy of control and facilitation are more easily accepted than changes which impinge directly and immediately on "higher" subsystems or structures.
        b. Changes which impinge on interchanges between functional subsystems are more easily accepted than those which impinge directly on only one functional subsystem.
    2. The mobilization of collectivities for the exercise of power and influence is the most significant development on the "lower" levels for successful change.[44] Such mobilization is more likely to take place or to take place more extensively when:
        a. it is sanctioned by variant values and norms;
        b. the values and norms of members of the collectivity being mobilized differ substantially from those held and enforced by the dominant elite(s) or class;
        c. mobilization is perceived as leading to a significant increase in the power and influence of the collectivity concerned; and

Control and Facilitation

  d. those being mobilized are in direct competition for scarce resources with the dominant elite(s) or class.
3. The mobilization of collectivities to exercise power and influence in support of change is likely to result in countermobilization to resist change.
  a. This defensive organization of power by the dominant elite(s) or class will be more likely to take place and to be more intense when:
    (1) elite values and norms sanction aggressiveness;
    (2) elite values and norms differ substantially from those of the collectivity mobilizing for change;
    (3) the elite's supply of power and influence is sufficiently small to be threatened by the change-oriented mobilization, but not so small that countermobilization appears to have little chance of success, and this supply is decreasing; and
    (4) the elite is in direct competition for scarce resources with those mobilizing for change, and the society's supply of these resources is decreasing.
  b. Vacillation between accommodation to and repression of change on the part of the political elite will tend to maximize the conflict associated with change by allowing collectivities to mobilize in support of variant norms and values and then using power against these collectivities. This policy will in many cases result in more rapid and extensive change than a constant policy of either accommodation or repression.
4. A dramatic act of power exercising can sharply accelerate or retard the process of value change, especially if it results in a substantial increase in the total amount of power available in the system.
5. Perceived utility (as defined by the values and norms of potential acceptors) sufficient to overcome the effort of adjustment (primarily a function of the degree of perceived incompatibility) tends to be the most important factor in decisions to accept change.
  a. Utility-compatibility balance calculations are usually very imperfect because any new element is likely to have advantages, disadvantages, and uncertain consequences, and some elements in a functionally interrelated complex will have different utility and

     compatibility ratings than other elements.
   b. Individuals vary in the utility they derive from the roles they play, and individuals with low or, more significantly, declining utility are more likely to accept change which offers the possibility of increasing or restoring satisfaction.
 6. Change is more likely to take place if innovators who are able to communicate effectively and to exert pressure for change are present in a society or political system.[45]
   a. Individuals who are not well integrated into a society or political system—i.e., who tend not to share many of the dominant values and norms and tend not to participate effectively in many institutionalized roles and collectivities—are the ones most likely to introduce new elements into the system; and such individuals, with the possible exception of intellectuals, are unlikely to be members of a society's dominant elite(s) or class.
   b. Once a new element is introduced, however, the prestige, power, and influence of elite members are crucial in getting it accepted.
   c. For major changes to take place, advocates need a good knowledge of the dynamics of their society and an ability to predict the consequences of their actions, although such knowledge and prediction can never be perfect.
   d. Forceful presentation by advocates, utilizing a combination of methods including both organized generation and employment of power and the invocation of dominant or alternative values, increases the likelihood that change will take place.
   e. The more advocates cooperate with one another, preferably in organized collectivities (see d above), the greater the likelihood that change will take place.
 7. Anticipation of change makes it more likely, unless the anticipated change has a definite negative evaluation. (This proposition involves both control and facilitation.)
 8. Elements which can be adopted on an individual basis are likely to be accepted more easily than those which require adoption by most or all members of a collectivity.

D. Control of Change

 1. Except in conditions of extreme systemic breakdown, a society or political system is more likely to accept new

Control and Facilitation

elements which are more compatible (more easily integrated) with pre-existing elements than those which are less compatible.⁴⁶
2. But any new element which comes into a society or political system, either by internal invention or by diffusion from external sources, is likely to be reinterpreted or modified in such a way that it will be more compatible with the existing structure of the system.
    a. If there is a close fit between new elements and variant values or norms in the existing system, the former may be reinterpreted in terms of these variant values and norms, which will then probably become dominant.
    b. Reinterpretation of a new complex of elements will be more extensive at the "higher" levels of social structure than at the "lower," except for the possible borrowing of "free-floating" ideas and values from other systems.
    c. The media of commitments and influence are especially important in this process, which may involve a substantial increase in the total amounts of these media available in the system.
3. When values are not widely shared because of ongoing change, well-established norms tend to provide the major control of behavior. Such control is often very effective in the short run.
4. Resistance to new elements introduced by invention is likely to come soon after their initial adoption, while elements introduced by diffusion are more likely to be given a longer trial.
5. Resistance is likely to be greater when existing elements must be removed or replaced than when new elements can be added without such replacement. Thus new elements may be added without the removal of very similar existing elements.

E. Functional and Structural Consequences of Change

1. Increased conflict, manifested in terms of dissension on values and norms, competition between collectivities, ambivalence of individuals concerning their roles, and lack of fit between these structural levels, is likely to be the short-run consequence of change.⁴⁷
2. Within the personalities of individual members of society, especially those who belong to one or more elites, such conflict (at the social level) will result in dissonance between cognitive and evaluative orientations.⁴⁸

a. The greater the conflict, the greater the dissonance is likely to be.
b. The greater the dissonance, the more likely it is that individuals will attempt to resolve it by changing the structure of society or the political system to make their cognitions congruent with their evaluations.
3. Eventually new values and norms will come to control behavior, and thus change will proceed in a recognizable direction, or the old values will reassume control, and thus change will be frustrated.
   a. Control of the media of power, influence, commitments, and money gives those exercising it a degree of control over life conditions, and thus can be used to change them. Changed life conditions will lead even those who were not originally dissatisfied to change their values, norms, and role perceptions in the direction of those held by the new elite(s). On the other hand, if those mobilizing power and influence in defense of the old dominant values are able to prevent significant changes in life conditions, those not immediately involved in the struggle for power will probably retain their commitment to the old values, and change will probably be frustrated.
4. The extent of change will probably be the minimum necessary to integrate the new elements into the system—i.e. to reestablish the minimum workable compatibility among the functional subsystems and levels of social structure—because this amount of change will have the highest utility for those who control the media of exchange. When pressures for change, measured in terms of the preceding propositions, are very strong, the minimum extent of change necessary to reestablish workable compatibility may be revolutionary transformation of the society.[49]

A Rough Causal Model

Given the unparsimonious nature of this list of propositions, as well as the lack of precision of most individual propositions and the absence of operational definitions for the concepts contained therein, it may appear highly premature to attempt to relate the propositions in a causal model, which often carries with it implications of parsimony, precision, and testability. But attempting to arrange a number of related propositions into a tentative causal model or diagram can serve as an important first step in increasing their parsimony, precision, and testability.[50] All that will be attempted here is to specify the variables which are included in the above propositions, to indicate which two or more variables are related by each proposition, and to suggest the relative strength or weakness and positive or negative nature of these relationships. Measurement of the actual strength, direction, and linearity of these hypothesized causal relationships will have to await the collection of quantified data.

This preliminary causal model of African political change (and perhaps of political change in general) attempts to combine control and facilitation—symbolized by the vertical dimension of the diagram, and more specifically by arrows which cross horizontal dotted lines—with causal forces operating over time—symbolized by movement from left to right on the horizontal dimension of the diagram. Each of the above propositions is represented by at least one arrow on the diagram, and in many cases by more than one. Thus, although creation of the model helps to clarify relationships among various propositions, especially by pointing to the separate variables of innovative proposals and the acceptance of innovative proposals which are not distinguished in many of the propositions, the model increases rather than reduces the complexity of the over-all theoretical approach. This is a further indication that parsimony will have to await the systematic testing of these propositions. The model will be useful, however, in organizing the following case studies and in summarizing the comparative conclusions which can be drawn from them.

The Case Studies

This purely theoretical discussion can now be concluded, and we can turn to examining how useful this model, these propositions, and the framework within which they are couched actually are in explaining a wide variety of specific cases of African political change—rapid and gradual, violent and nonviolent, fundamental and minor, pre and postindependence, in territories formerly controlled by different colonial powers, and at the international, societal, and local levels. All of these case studies utilize a variety of concepts from the control and facilitation framework to explain why change of a given type and extent, originating from some combination of external and internal sources, and involving the interaction of aspects of control and facilitation, has taken place in some pre-existing political system, and to predict possible future directions of change in this system. The emphasis given to specific concepts and propositions varies in accordance with each author's conception of the way in which the framework and propositions can best be applied to the subject matter with which he or she is dealing. Thus the reader must remember that these are interpretive case studies which do not provide a test of our propositions. When an author applies a specific proposition, its number appears in parentheses in the text. The case studies are grouped

FIGURE 1.2
A Rough Causal Model of African Political Change

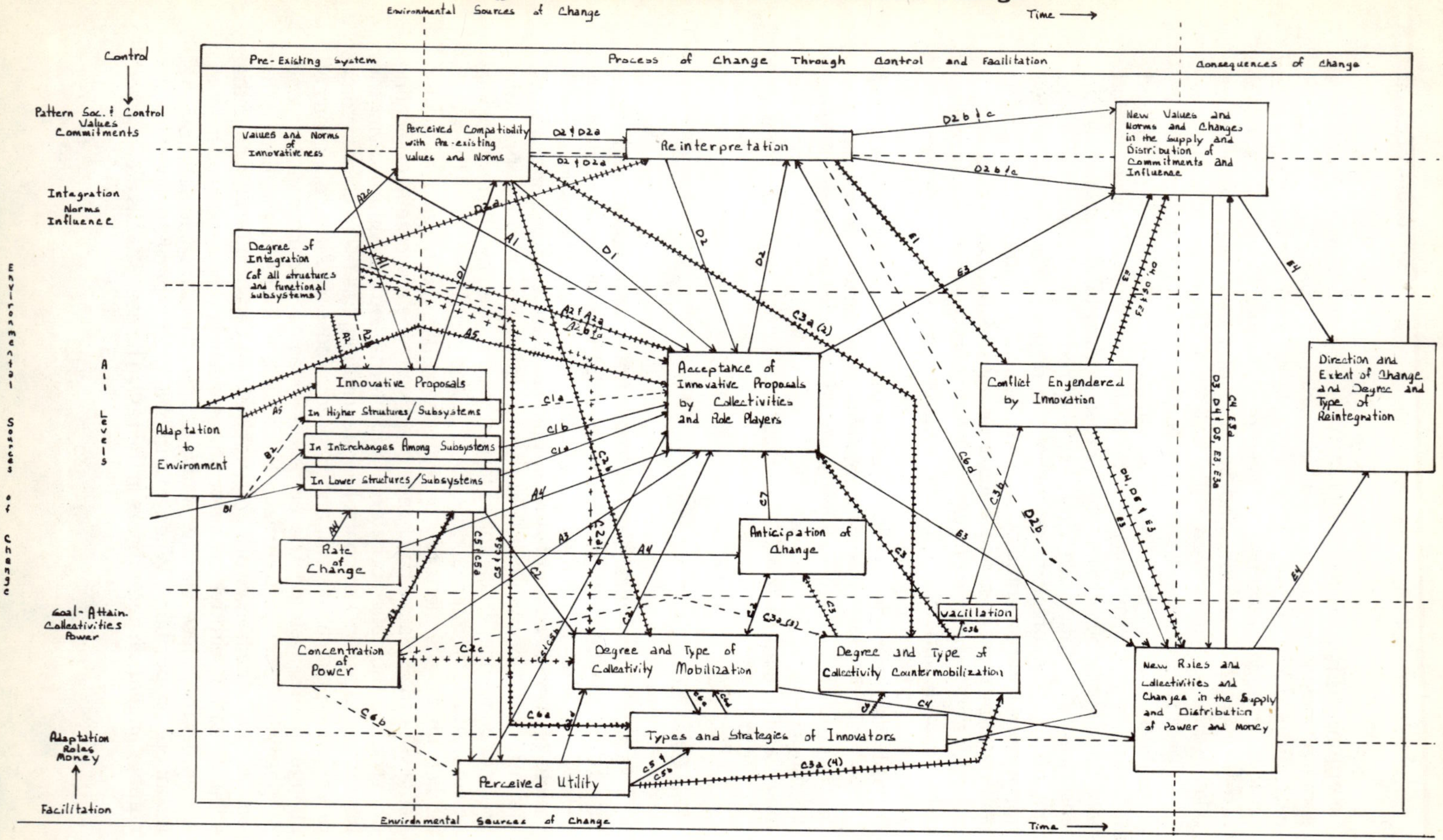

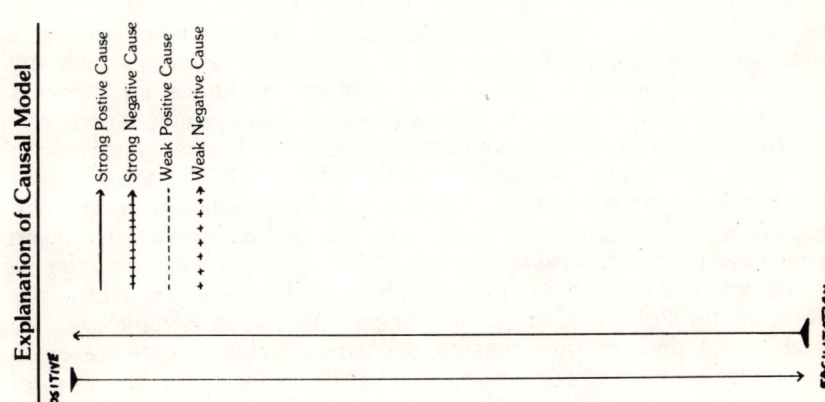

into three categories: 1) specific aspects of political change in individual African-ruled countries, 2) specific aspects of political change analyzed cross-nationally among African-ruled countries, and 3) general political change in formerly white-ruled countries which have recently undergone or are currently undergoing the transition to African rule.

The evolving relationship between religion and politics in Uganda under the colonial, Obote, and Amin regimes is examined in the first case study: "Religion and Politics in Independent Uganda: Movement Toward Secularization?," by Kathleen G. Lockard. This case study focuses at the societal level and on the gradually changing relationship between the political system and a major component of of its environment—religion, a relationship including both the control of politics by religion and the facilitation of religion by the political system. An important theme is whether this relationship has been evolving in a discernible direction— toward secularization—and whether that direction of change is likely to continue in the future. The author concludes that secularization has not been implemented successfully because of the interaction of control and facilitation, and that the balance of power has shifted away from religion toward the polity because facilitation in this direction has been effective.

The next two case studies examine change at the local level in Ethiopia. "Forecast for Political Change in Ethiopia: An Urban Perspective," by Peter Koehn, demonstrates that strong barriers to change were present in the Addis Ababa Municipality prior to 1974, especially in the form of extremely weak facilitation of change. Koehn indicates that the sources of any fundamental change had to be outside the local system at the national level; he analyzes the recent dramatic events at that level, and utilizes the control and facilitation approach to explain both the fundamental changes which have occurred in urban politics and national-local relations and the remaining obstacles to further change. "Green Revolution in Ethiopia: The Politics of Rural Development in a Blocked and Inequitable Society," by John M. Cohen, integrates land tenure into the control and facilitation framework, emphasizing the importance of land reform in the over-all process of political change. As in the previous case study, the relationship between change in the local community—in this case the predominantly rural Chilalo *Awraja* (periphery)— and change in the national political system (center) is stressed. A facilitating agent of external origin—a Swedish agricultural development project—posed a unique challenge to the control mechanisms exercised by elites in the local system, stimulating a number of role conflicts. But before the recent coup, the national government, which was responsible for the presence of the facilitating agent, frequently acted in ways which weakened this challenge. Now that land reform has been decreed and local elites have lost their control of exchange media, Cohen believes that agricultural transformation is much more likely to occur in Chilalo.

Specific aspects of political change analyzed cross-nationally are the focus of the next three case studies. In "The Diffusion and Invention of Legislative and Party Structures in Anglophone Africa," James R. Scarritt attempts to demonstrate that the propositions presented in the present chapter are useful in explaining changes in legislative and party structures and functions in former British African territories in the postindependence period. Important roles, collectivity structures, and norms present in both types of organizations at the moment of independence are identified and categorized into functional subsystems of each organization, providing a baseline against which to measure subsequent changes. Although the modified British legislative structures which were initially diffused have been very significantly reinterpreted to fit the more centralized organization of African political systems, and the functional significance of these structures—for both the legislature and the political system as a whole—has changed accordingly, some important diffused elements remain in those legislatures which have not been closed down by military governments. The path of diffusion and invention of political party structures is more difficult to trace, because borrowing has been more eclectic, but it is argued that invention has been more important in this case, and that this difference is best explained by the combination of a number of our propositions.

"African Planning Failure: A Public Policy Analysis," by Melvin J. Dubnick, discusses the failure of development planning in most African countries in terms of various components of the planning system, which includes elements of both African national political systems and their international environment. The dominant values of that system constitute an image which tends to be inflexible in its content, logic, and environmental adaptability; and many of the crucial norms in the system have been diffused from abroad with minimal reinterpretation in terms of the African context. Effective collectivity mobilization to overcome the change-resistant controls exercised by the system's values and norms does not take place, and African societies provide few material or organizational facilities to utilize in overcoming these change-inhibiting forces. Dubnick utilizes the propositions presented above to indicate how each of these aspects of the planning system might be modified so that the system as a whole would be more likely to achieve planning success.

"The Significance of Sequential Ordering and Timing of Politically Induced Societal Changes in Anglophone African Party States: A Reconsideration," by James R. Scarritt, asks whether there are significant differences among these political systems with regard to the the sequential ordering and timing of the changes they have attempted to make, and whether any such differences are related to the direction and extent of societal change. Sequential ordering and timing have usually been viewed as significant in situations in which the constraints of time and resources were much less severe than those operating in Africa today, but some of our propositions indicate that these variables may affect the possibilities of successful developmental change even when strong constraints are present. However, propositions about sequential ordering and timing need to be supplemented by propositions dealing with the role of interchanges, structural levels, and the distribution of exchange media in the determination of political goals in order to provide a satisfactory explanation of differences in the direction and extent of societal change.

Two final case studies deal with the possibility of substantial change being accomplished in Southern Africa through the use of violence. These studies focus at the societal level, and provide an interesting comparison of the operation of control and facilitation in the culturally diverse settings of unilaterally "independent" British-influenced Rhodesia and formerly Portuguese ruled Mozambique. In "Internal War in Mozambique: Implications for the Emerging Postindependence Society," Walter C. Opello, Jr. focuses on dissynchronization between the externally imposed pattern socialization and control subsystem and the other three subsystems in colonial Mozambique, the consequent failure of "lower" structural levels to implement values, the consequent personality dissonance of assimilated African and mulatto elites, and the significance of these factors for the creation of an alternative social system by the nationalist movement—FRELIMO. He then utilizes our propositions to explain the type of society and political system which is beginning to emerge in independent Mozambique, and to suggest possible directions of future change.

"Prospects for Reactionary and Revolutionary Change in Zimbabwe," by Kevin Maguire, discusses the emergence of the Rhodesian Front as a political elite and its inability to pre-empt a Zimbabwean nationalist challenge. Zimbabwe's present and future prospects are assessed in an analysis of both control and faciliation factors fostering or frustrating three possible outcomes: continued settler domination, a Zimbabwean neo-colonial solution, and a Zimbabwean revolutionary transformation. Maguire forecasts that transition to a neocolonial solution would be at most a short term outcome, while a radical regime committed, at least initially, to revolutionary transformation is most likely to emerge victorious in the continuing conflict.

A brief concluding chapter discusses how the findings of these case studies might be drawn together to guide future, and hopefully more systematic, reserach based on this approach. The explanation and predictions of various aspects of African political change presented in each case study are summarized, and the possibility of creating a data set of change events in order to test our propositions systematically is discussed.

Footnotes

1. Arend Lijphart, "Comparative Politics and the Comparative Method," *American Political Science Review* 65 (September 1971): 691-92.
2. Ibid., pp. 684-85, and "The Comparable-Cases Strategy in Comparative Research," *Comparative Political Studies* 8 (July 1975): 160. A similar definition is given in Neil J. Smelser, "The Methodology of Comparative Analysis," in *Comparative Research Methods,* ed. Donald P. Warwick and Samuel Osherson (Englewood Cliffs, N.J.: Prentice-Hall, 1973), pp. 51-52. A similar theoretical strategy is employed in Gabriel A. Almond, Scott C. Flanagan, and Robert J. Mundt, eds., *Crisis, Choice, and Change: Historical Studies of Political Development* (Boston: Little, Brown and Co., 1973).
3. Some suggestions for such testing are made in James R. Scarritt, "Culture Change Theory and the Study of African Political Change: Some Problems of Relevance and Research Design," *The African Review* 2,4 (1972): 568-71, and in the concluding chapter of this book.
4. The case for parsimony is forcefully presented in Joseph LaPalombara, "Macrotheories and Microapplications in Comparative Politics: A Widening Chasm," *Comparative Politics* 1 (October 1968): 73-74, and Lijphart, "Comparative Politics," p. 690.
5. James R. Scarritt, *Political Development and Culture Change Theory: A Propositional Synthesis with Application to Africa,* Sage Professional Papers in Comparative Politics 3, 01-029 (Beverly Hills and London: Sage Publications, 1972).
6. Parsons' approach as we understand it is not presented fully in any one place. The most important sources for the overall approach from Parsons' own writing are "An Outline of the Social System," in *Theories of Society: Foundations of Modern Sociological Theory,* Vol. I, ed. Talcott Parsons, Edward Shils, Kaspar D. Naegele, and Jesse R. Pitts (New York: Free Press of Glencoe, 1961), pp. 30-79; "The Political Aspect of Social Structure and Process," in *Varieties of Political Theory,* ed. David Easton (Englewood Cliffs, N.J.: Prentice-Hall, 1966), pp. 71-112; and *Politics and Social Structure* (New York: Free Press, 1969), Chapters 1,2, and 17. See also William C. Mitchell, *Sociological Analysis and Politics: The Theories of Talcott Parsons* (Englewood Cliffs, N.J.: Prentice-Hall, 1967); Benton Johnson, *Functionalism in Modern Sociology: Understanding Talcott Parsons* (Morristown, N.J.: General Learning Press, 1975); and Guy Rocher, *Talcott Parsons and American Sociology* (New York: Barnes and Noble, 1975).
7. Interpreters who share some aspects of this point of view include Dick Atkinson, *Orthodox Consensus and Radical Alternative: A Study in*

Sociological Theory (New York: Basic Books, 1972), pp. 9-33 and *passim.*; Walter Buckley, *Sociology and Modern Systems Theory* (Englewood Cliffs, N.J.: Prentice-Hall, 1967), pp. 23-31; Daniel Foss, "The World View of Talcott Parsons," in *Sociology on Trial*, ed. Maurice Stein and Arthur Vidich (Englewood Cliffs, N.J.: Prentice-Hall, 1963), pp. 96-126; Anthony Giddens, "'Power' in the Recent Writings of Talcott Parsons," *Sociology* 2 (September 1968): 257-72; Alvin W. Gouldner, *The Coming Crisis of Western Sociology* (New York: Basic Books, 1970); George C. Homans, "Bringing Men Back In," *American Sociological Review* 29 (December 1964): 809-18; Harold Kaplan, "The Parsonian Image of Social Structure and Its Relevance for Political Science," *Journal of Politics* 30 (November 1968): 885-909; Joseph Lopreato, "The Concept of Equilibrium: Sociological Tantalizer," in *Institutions and Social Exchange: The Sociologies of Talcott Parsons and George C. Homans*, ed. Herman Turk and Richard L. Simpson (Indianapolis and New York: Bobbs-Merrill, 1971), pp. 310-27; Marvin U. Martel, "Academentia Praecox: The Aims, Merits, and Scope of Parsons' Multisystemic Language Rebellion (1959-1968)," in ibid., pp. 175-209; Ken Menzies, *Talcott Parsons and the Social Image of Man* (London, Henley and Boston: Routledge & Kegan Paul, 1976), pp. 61, 110-14, 140; M.J. Mulkey, *Functionalism, Exchange, and Theoretical Strategy* (New York: Schocken Books, 1971), pp. 66-93; Robert F. Murphy, *The Dialectics of Social Life* (New York and London: Basic Books, 1971), pp. 53-71; Anthony D. Smith, *The Concept of Social Change: A Critique of the Functionalist Theory of Social Change* (London, Henley and Boston: Routledge & Kegan Paul, 1973), pp. 37-39, 95, 108-10, 137-56; Johathan H. Turner, *The Structure of Sociological Theory* (Homewood, Ill.: Dorsey Press, 1974), pp. 46-58; and David Walsh, "Functionalism and Systems Theory," in Paul Filmer, Michael Phillipson, David Silverman, and David Walsh, *New Directions in Sociological Theory (Cambridge: M.I.T. Press, 1973), pp. 58-71.* Szymon Chodak, *Societal Development* (New York: Oxford University Press, 1973), pp. 6-8, also makes some of these criticisms, yet in his summary variables (pp. 303-15) are very similar to some of those utilized in our approach.

8. See Buckley, *Sociology and Modern Systems Theory*, p. 24; A.L. Jacobson, "A Theoretical and Empirical Analysis of Social Change and Conflict Based on Talcott Parsons' Ideas," in Turk and Simpson, *Institutions and Social Exchange*, pp. 344-45, 360; Martel, "Academentia Praecox," p. 209; John Finley Scott, "Interpreting Parsons' Work: A Problem in Method," *Sociological Inquiry* 44, 1 (1974): 60; and Gideon Sjoberg and Leonard D. Cain, "Negative Values, Countersystem Models, and the Analysis of Social Systems," in Turk and Simpson, *Institutions and Social Exchange*, p. 213.

9. For the most complete presentation of this concept see Parsons, *Politics and Social Structure*, Chapter 1. Parsons usually uses

'conditioning" rather than "facilitation." We prefer the latter term because of its more active connotations. Parsons also uses "facilitation," particularly in regard to the adaptive subsystem. See his "An Outline of the Social System," pp. 39-40; and "An Approach to Psychological Theory in Terms of the Theory of Action," in *Psychology: A Science,* Vol. III, ed. Sigmund Koch (New York: McGraw-Hill, 1959), p. 647. Its use is also suggested in Mitchell, *Sociological Analysis and Politics,* p. 30. Perceptive commentaries on the "hierarchy of control" concept by Parsons' students can be found in Enno Schwanenberg, "The Two Problems of Order in Parsons' Theory: An Analysis from Within," *Social Forces* 49 (June 1971): 575-78; Jackson Toby, "Parsons' Theory of Social Evolution," *Contemporary Sociology* 1 (September 1972): 397-99; and Leon H. Mayhew, "Stability and Change in Legal Systems," in *Stability and Social Change,* ed. Bernard Barber and Alex Inkles (Boston: Little, Brown & Co., 1971), pp. 189-93.

10. Dependency theory speaks of a "capitalist world system," but its only fully developed subsystem is the economic, so it is not a relatively self-sufficient suprasystem. This is not to deny its significant influence in Africa. See, for example, Immanuel Wallerstein, "Dependence in an Interdependent World: The Limited Possibilities of Transformation Within the Capitalist World Economy," *African Studies Review* 17 (April 1974): 1-26. A critical evaluation of dependency theory and its assumptions concerning the world system is Tony Smith, "The Underdevelopment of Development Literature: The Case of Dependency Theory," *World Politics* 31 (January 1979): 247-88.

11. Marxist analysis shares this basic systems approach, including its interest in the performance of functions. See Harold J. Bershady, *Ideology and Social Knowledge* (New York: Halstead Press, John Wiley & Sons, 1973), p. 133; Jan J. Loubser, "General Introduction," in *Explorations in General Theory in Social Science: Essays in Honor of Talcott Parsons,* Vol. 1, ed. Jan J. Loubser, Rainer C. Baum, Andrew Effrat, and Victor Meyer Lidz (New York: Free Press, Macmillan Publishing Co., 1976), p. 18; Ralph Miliband, *Marxism and Politics* (Oxford: Oxford University Press, 1977), p. 6; and Joel Samoff, "Class, Class Conflict, and the State: Notes on the Political Economy of Africa," paper presented at the 20th Annual Meeting of the African Studies Association, Houston, November 1977, pp. 7-22.

12. Most of these points are summarized by Parsons in the appendix to "The Political Aspect of Social Structure and Process," pp. 104-12.

13. Mulkay, *Functionalism, Exchange, and Theoretical Strategy,* p. 40; and Turner, *Structure of Sociological Theory,* p. 58, indicate that Parsons intends his functional subsystems to serve the theoretical purposes described in this paragraph. Stating these purposes in this way escapes the a priori reasoning which Bershady, *Ideology and Social Knowledge,* pp. 93-97, 113-24, 135-36, 157-64, claims underlies Parsons' thought.

Miliband, *Marxism and Politics,* p. 90, attributes similar functions to the capitalist state.

14. Parsons' term is pattern maintenance and tension management, but this term seems to imply constant resistance to change, and we do not want the reader to make any such implication. See, for example, Mulkay, *Functionalism, Exchange, and Theoretical Strategy,* p. 86. Ranier C. Baum, "Introduction" [to Part IV], in Loubser et al., *General Theory in Social Science,* Vol. 2, p. 451, uses the term "pattern maintenance and modification."

15. François Bourricaud, "Penury and Deficit or the Problems of Political Underutilization," in ibid., p. 568, indicates that it may not be possible to perform the goal attainment function at all in Peru, demonstrating once again that the use of functional concepts does not imply that functions are performed effectively.

16. Parsons, "The Political Aspect of Social Structure and Process," pp. 94-96. The simplified version of the interchanges utilized here avoids problems presented by the more complex version often utilized by Parsons. See Mark Gould, "Systems Analysis, Macrosociology, and the Generalized Media of Social Action," in Loubser et al., *General Theory in Social Science,* Vol. 2, pp. 470-506.

17. Pluralism as a universally applicable framework is suggested in Michael F. Lofchie, "Political Theory and African Politics," *Journal of Modern African Studies* 6 (May 1968): 3-15. It is discussed in detail in Leo Kuper and M.G. Smith, eds., *Pluralism in Africa* (Berkeley and Los Angeles: University of California Press, 1969). An early advocacy of class analysis as a universally applicable framework is Richard L. Sklar, "Political Science and National Integration—A Radical Approach," *Journal of Modern African Studies* 5 (May 1967): 1-11. More recent advocacy of this approach is found in the sources cited in footnote eighteen.

18. For example, Richard L. Sklar, "Postimperialism: A Class Analysis of Multinational Corporate Expansion," *Comparative Politics* 9 (October 1976): 83; Stanislaw Ossowski, *Class Structure in the Social Consciousness* (New York: Free Press of Glencoe, 1963), pp. 185-86; Claude Ake, "Explanatory Notes on the Political Economy of Africa," *Journal of Modern African Studies* 14 (March 1976): 1-23; Robin Cohen, "Class in Africa: Analytical Problems and Perspectives," in *The Socialist Register, 1972,* ed. Ralph Miliband and John Savile (London: Merlin Press, 1972), pp. 237-52; Miliband, *Marxism and Politics,* pp. 20, 28, 108-9; and Samoff, "Class, Class Conflict, and the State."

19. Neil J. Smelser, *Theory of Collective Behavior* (New York: Free Press, 1962), p. 25.

20. The discussion of class power in Miliband, *Marxism and Politics,* pp. 67-74, specifies similar relationships.

21. This and related concepts are discussed in Buckley, *Sociology and*

Modern Systems Theory, pp. 145-54. Parsons indicates that he is prepared to include this type of process in his framework in "Some Problems of General Theory in Sociology," in *Theoretical Sociology: Perspectives and Developments,* ed. John C. McKinney and Edward A. Tiryakian (New York: Appleton-Century-Crofts, 1970), p. 36.

22. Parsons indicates that interests are important in his framework in "Authority, Legitimation, and Political Action," in Parsons, *Structure and Process in Modern Societies* (New York: Free Press, 1963), p. 173; and in "Comparative Studies and Evolutionary Change," in *Comparative Methods in Sociology,* ed. Ivan Vallier (Berkeley, Los Angeles, and London: University of California Press, 1971), pp. 129-30. Smith, *Concept of Social Change,* p. 124, thinks all functionalists subsume interests in values.

23. Parsons makes this point in "Systems Analysis: Social Systems," in *International Encyclopedia of the Social Sciences,* Vol. 15, ed. David L. Sills (New York: Macmillan Co. & Free Press, 1968), p. 470. For a more detailed treatment, see Brian Moris, "Reflections on Role Analysis," *British Journal of Sociology* 22 (December 1971): 395-409.

24. Gouldner, *Coming Crisis of Western Sociology,* p. 223, makes this point well, and he interprets Parsons as ignoring it. Parsons, however, makes the point explicitly in "Systems Analysis," p. 469, and sympathetic critics indicate that it is an assumption underlying all of his work. See John K. Rhoads, "On Gouldner's *Crisis of Western Sociology,*" *American Journal of Sociology* 78 (July 1972): 147-48; and Jonathan H. Turner, "Parsons as a Symbolic Interactionist: A Comparison of Action and Interaction Theory," *Sociological Inquiry* 44, 4 (1974): 285-86.

25. See the critical essays by Davis Easton on exchange theory and Rosabeth Moss Kanter on symbolic interactionism in *Perspectives in Political Sociology,* ed. Andrew Effrat (Indianapolis and New York: Bobbs-Merrill, 1972), pp. 77-92 and 129-48. Peter Blau, *Exchange and Power in Social Life* (New York: John Wiley & Sons, 1964), begins with an exchange framework, but as Mulkay, *Functionalism, Exchange, and Theoretical Strategy,* p. 244, indicates, his treatment of macro-level phenomena is not based on his micro-level exchange propositions. Blau's analysis bears many similarities to the present approach.

26. Parsons indicates that the media are crucial in providing opportunities for change in his "Commentary," in Turk and Simpson, *Institutions and Social Exchange,* p. 395.

27. Parsons makes this point clearly in "An Outline of the Social System," p. 68. Recent critical treatments of Parsons' analysis of power include Bliss C. Cartwright and R. Stephen Warner, "The Medium Is Not The Message," in Loubser et al., *General Theory in Social Science,* Vol. 2, pp. 639-60; Stephen P. Savage, "Political Power and Political Subsystems: Parsons' Analysis of Politics," *Economy and Society* 7 (May 1978): 155-74; and Giddens, "Power in the Recent Writings of Talcott Parsons."

28. Talcott Parsons, "On the Concept of Value-Commitments," *Sociological Inquiry* 38 (Spring 1968): 148.

29. David A. Baldwin, "Money and Power," *Journal of Politics* 33 (August 1971): 592-605, argues convincingly that the analogy between power and money is limited to this function of money. Mulkay, *Functionalism, Exchange, and Theoretical Strategy,* pp. 62-63, expresses this function, as it is performed by both power and money, as symbolic representation of obligations.

30. Bershady, *Ideology and Social Knowledge,* p. 131, indicates that Parsons does not deal with covariations among media. We are now suggesting one such covariation, and will suggest others below.

31. This conception of class was developed by comparing control and facilitation analysis of media distribution with the work of class analysts and their critics, including sources cited in footnote eighteen; Otwin Marenin, "Review Essay: Class Analysis in African Studies," *Journal of African Studies 3* (Spring 1976): 133-38; Robert A. Miller, "Elite Formation in Africa," *Journal of Modern African Studies* 12 (December 1974): 525-27, 533; David R. Morrison, *Education and Politics in Africa:* The *Tanzanian Case* (Montreal: McGill-Queen's University Press, 1976), p. 183; Gavin N. Kitching, "The Concept of Class and the Study of Africa," *The African Review* 2,3 (1972): 327-50; R.H. Jackson, "Political Stratification in Tropical Africa," *Canadian Journal of African Studies* 7,3 (1973): 381-400; and Szymon Chodak, "Social Stratification in Sub-Saharan Africa," ibid., pp. 401-17. Kitching, p. 332, believes that the term "elite" should be defined more narrowly than we define it; thus he finds class a more satisfactory general term for comparing a variety of stratification systems. Parsons' most recent pronouncements on class are found in "Equality and Inequality in Modern Society, or Social Stratification Revisited," in Parsons,*Social Systems and the Evolution of Action Theory* (New York: Free Press, Macmillan Publishing Co., 1977), pp. 321-80. He has a less relational definition of class, and places it more completely in the integrative subsystem, but he does point out the several possible bases of class which enter into our analysis. He believes that an unspecified degree of inequality is necessary for effective, responsible leadership.

32. G.T. Guilbaud, *What is Cybernetics?* (New York: Grove Press, 1960), p. 11.

33. Gouldner, *Coming Crisis of Western Sociology,* p. 327. Similar conceptions are found in Robin M. Williams, Jr., "Change and Stability in Values and Value Systems," in Barber and Inkles, *Stability and Social Change,* pp. 132, 136-42; and Menzies, *Talcott Parsons and the Social Image of Man,* pp. 51, 55-60.

34. Ibid., p. 140, suggests that the economy exerts control over the political system in some societies, but he combines the economy with the integrative subsystem to reach this conclusion.

35. Roland Robertson, "Societal Attributes and International Relations," in Loubser et al., *General Theory in Social Science,* Vol. 2, p. 731.

36. Talcott Parsons, "Culture and Social System Revisited," *Social Science Quarterly* 53 (September 1972): 255. See also Mayhew, "Stability and Change in Legal Systems," pp. 192-94; and Williams, "Change and Stability in Values," pp. 152-53.

37. Parsons explicitly agrees with this point in "An Outline of the Social System," p. 70.

38. Gouldner, *Coming Crisis of Western Sociology,* pp. 213-214, to the contrary notwithstanding. See also Rocher, *Talcott Parsons and American Sociology,* pp. 72, 160-61; and Bershady, *Ideology and Social Knowledge,* pp. 87, 141.

39. Diffusion also refers to the spread of innovations within a society. At this point, and at several others which follow, we explicitly mention creative change originating within society and the political system, because it has often been claimed that Parsons cannot deal with such change. See Buckley, *Sociology and Modern Systems Theory,* p. 30; Mohammed Guessous, "A General Critique of Equilibrium Theory," in *Readings on Social Change,* ed. Wilbert E. Moore and Robert M. Cook (Englewood Cliffs, N.J.: Prentice-Hall, 1967), pp. 25-27; Menzies, *Talcott Parsons and the Social Image of Man,* pp. 115-17; and Wilbert E. Moore, *Social Change* (Englewood Cliffs, N.J.: Prentice-Hall, 1963), pp. 11. On the other hand, Smith, *Concept of Social Change,* pp. 55-59, 149-54, says functionalist theories of change are endogenist. Our analysis achieves his suggested synthesis (p. 163) between endogenous and exogenous (pp. 157-62) paradigms.

40. For arguments that a Parsonian or modified Parsonian framework is quite useful for analyzing change in ways similar to that utilized in this book see Alvin Boskoff, "Functional Analysis as a Source of a Theoretical Repertory and Research Tasks in the Study of Social Change," in *Explorations in Social Change,* ed. George K. Zollschan and Walter Hirsch (Boston: Houghton-Mifflin, 1964), pp. 213-43; Johnson, *Functionalism in Modern Sociology,* pp. 33-53; Seymour Martin Lipset, "Social Structure and Social Change," in *Approaches to the Study of Social Structure,* ed. Peter M. Blau (New York: Free Press, 1975), pp. 172-84; and Rocher, *Talcott Parsons and American Sociology,* pp. 48-50, 67-70, 155-56.

41. These categories are drawn from sources cited in Scarritt, *Political Development and Culture Change Theory,* p. 14. Sources for individual propositions are also found there, pp. 15-23; more recent sources are cited below. Similar sets of analytical categories are found in Almond, Flanagan, and Mundt, *Crisis, Choice, and Change,* especially pp. 24-34; Dietrich Rueschemeyer, "Partial Modernization," in Loubser et al., *General Theory in Social Science,* Vol. 2, pp. 756-72; and Goodwin

Watson, "Resistance to Change," in *Processes and Phenomena of Social Change,* ed. Gerald Zaltman (New York: John Wiley & Sons, 1973), pp. 130-31.

42. Henry Teune and Zdravko Mlinar, *The Developmental Logic of Social Systems,* Sage Library of Social Research, Vol. 60 (Beverly Hills and London: Sage Publications, 1978), p. 83.

43. Williams, "Change and Stability in Values," p. 184. This is another example of what Mayhew, "Stability and Change in Legal Systems," pp. 207-8, calls "short circuiting" the hierarchy of control and facilitation. We disagree with his assertion that this phenomenon violates the assumptions of the model.

44. Recent studies of mobilization include David R. Cameron, "Toward a Theory of Political Mobilization," *Journal of Politics* 36 (February 1974): 138-71; Chong-do Hah and Jeffrey Martin, "Toward a Synthesis of Conflict and Integration Theories of Nationalism," *World Politics* 27 (April 1975): 361-86; and Samuel P. Huntington and Joan M. Nelson, *No Easy Choice: Political Participation in Developing Countries* (Cambridge and London: Harvard University Press, 1976). Marxist analysts' use of the concept is in many ways similar to ours. See Miliband, *Marxism and Politics,* pp. 118-25, 175-90.

45. Recent studies of leadership which contain elements of the control and facilitation approach, and which support this proposition, include Lewis J. Edinger, "The Comparative Analysis of Political Leadership," *Comparative Politics* 7 (January 1975): 253-69; Norman H. Keehn, "Building Authority: A Return to Fundamentals," *World Politics* 26 (April 1974): 331-39; and Glenn D. Paige, *The Scientific Study of Political Leadership* (New York: Free Press, 1971), especially pp. 103-4, 153.

46. Alex O. Thio, "A Reconsideration of the Concept of Adopter-Innovation Compatibility in Diffusion Research," *Sociological Quarterly* 12 (Winter 1971): 56-68, elaborates on this concept, and discusses its major types. Max Gluckman, "Social Anthropology in the Study of Developing Countries," in *Social Science and the New Societies: Problems in Cross-Cultural Research and Theory Building,* ed. Nancy Hammond (East Lansing, Mich.: Social Science Research Bureau, Michigan State University, 1973), pp. 49-51, applies this proposition to the persistence of conflict.

47. Alvin Boskoff refers to extreme forms of such conflict as "social indecision." See his "Social Indecision: A Dysfunctional Focus of Transitional Society," *Social Forces* 37 (May 1959): 305-11.

48. This proposition borrows ideas from Leon Festinger, *A Theory of Cognitive Dissonance* (Evanston Ill.: Row, Peterson, 1957); and Milton J. Rosenberg et al., *Attitude Organization and Change: An Analysis of Consistency Among Attitude Components* (New Haven: Yale University Press, 1960).

49. A careful reading of this proposition will reveal that it escapes the teleological logic frequently attributed to functionalist explanations of the extent of change which is likely to occur. See Wsevolod W. Isajiw, *Causation and Functionalism in Sociology* (New York: Schocken Books, 1968).

50. Hubert M. Blalock, Jr., *Theory Construction: From Verbal to Mathematical Formulations* (Englewood Cliffs, N.J.: Prentice-Hall, 1969), p. 29. A similar model is found in Nan Lin and Gerald Zaltman, "Dimensions of Innovations," in Zaltman, *Processes and Phenomena of Change*, p. 95.

2

Religion and Politics in Independent Uganda: Movement Toward Secularization?

Kathleen G. Lockard

Uganda has been characterized by a high level of intrusion of religious loyalties and symbols into the political process, dating back to the early colonial period and continuing up to the present. Since the achievement of independence in 1962, it has been the stated goal of successive political regimes—that of Milton Obote from 1962 through 1970 and that of the military government of Idi Amin since 1971—to bring an end to religio-political entanglements on the grounds that these have worked against nation-building goals. However, because of weaknesses in the political system which are delineated later in this chapter, both regimes eventually settled for something considerably short of the stated goal of secularization—namely the further politicization and manipulation of religious collectivities in an effort to insure that these collectivities would act in ways that would legitimize regime ideologies and programs. Even this modified political goal was not fully realized with respect to every major religious group, and variations in its impact on the several religious groups will become clear in the ensuing analysis.

Uganda is neither religiously homogeneous nor as highly fragmented religiously as many other African nations. Instead there have been, since the late nineteenth century, two major religious groups—the Roman Catholic Church and the Angelican Church of Uganda, rather evenly balanced in terms of adherents (although the former is slightly larger)—and a much smaller but nevertheless significant Muslim minority. Traditional religions declined in the wake of Christianity and Islam more rapidly then in many other African nations, and at least 70 percent of the population is now either Christian or Muslim.[1]

Because of the pluralistic religious pattern, the role of religion in legitimizing or failing to legitimize the political system (and politically induced change) has varied from one denomination to another; religion has not acted as a homogeneous force for pattern socialization and control, but it has nevertheless been extremely important. For example, until the mid 1960s formal education was almost completely under the control of religious authorities, with church-sponsored schools comprising the great majority of all educational institutions in the country; the government had remained content to rely on a system of government subsidies to church-administered schools. Political socialization through the educational system was therefore subject to pervasive religious influence, and this influence did not completely disappear even when changes were made in the educational system in 1964 and thereafter.

Religion has been a potential force for the integration of Ugandan society in the sense that the membership of each major religious group cuts across all ethnic boundaries in a nation where ethnic fragmentation and conflict are extremely important. But at the same time, intense political rivalry among religious groups has formed another line of cleavage. Although cross-cutting cleavages have often been regarded as functional for societal integration, they were not so perceived by most members of the the Ugandan political elite, who committed themselves at least verbally to the eradication of religious divisions. Furthermore, in the postindependence period the political conflict *among* religious collectivities was only one facet of a complex pattern of interaction which characterized the legitimation interchange between political and religious subsystems. Added to the intergroup political rivalry between Protestants, Catholics, and Muslims were new institutional conflicts between church and state; in addition, certain religious bodies became highly politicized internally and fell victim to severe *intra*group conflict and to manipulation by political actors.

The nature of the control-facilitation relationship differed for the three major religious groups, but there were many more similarities between the Church of Uganda and the Muslim community in this regard than there were between either of these two groups and the Catholic Church. As the ensuing analysis will demonstrate in greater detail, the potential for intragroup conflict seemed to be much greater for Anglicans and Muslims than for Catholics, because of certain historical and organizational factors. The Catholic Church was more resistant to political manipulation by government and political party actors, and the political authorities were therefore unable to make effective use of the techniques for facilitating innovation which did prove partially (but only partially) effective with respect to Muslim and Anglican collectivities. Throughout the period under consideration (1962- 1978), the Catholic Church continued to exercise a more autonomous control over the value pattern and socialization of its adherents than was true of Anglican and Islamic bodies.

Historical Background

Before attempting to delineate more fully and to explain the outcome of the pattern of control-facilitation between religious and political subsystems, it is necessary to look briefly at the historical factors which produced the conquest culture or the pre-existing system which the postindependence regimes sought to change.

The introduction of both Islam and Christianity into the area which is now Uganda coincided with, and in fact was an integral part of, a series of political upheavals which changed the course of history, first in the kingdom of Buganda (in the southern part of what became the Uganda Protectorate), and subsequently in the neighboring regions to the north, east and west. Islam reached Uganda first, brought by Arab traders who arrived in Buganda in 1844; it attracted the interest of Kabaka (King) Suna and later of his son Mutesa, and a number of Baganda at Mutesa's court were converted to Islam.[2] Christian and Muslim proselytizers arrived in Uganda during a historical era which witnessed two major political changes: first, the culmination of a process of centralization of power in the hands of the Kabaka, and secondly, the imposition of British colonial rule. The traditional religion (*lubaale*) of Buganda had become increasingly salient politically during the period of centralization because the traditional religious hierarchy of priests and mediums, allied with clan leaders, had remained the only substantial obstacle to the establishment of the full supremacy of the Kabaka and his appointees over the entire populace.[3] The struggle between *lubaale* religious leaders and successive Kabakas increased the attractiveness of Islam and Christianity in the eyes of Kabaka Mutesa, since these were religions which he might hope to control and exploit to his own advantage.[4]

The Anglican Church Missionary Society reached the Kabaka's court in 1877; the Roman Catholic White Fathers arrived two years later. Both Christians and Muslims made their first converts at the court, and this fact was of key importance in establishing a salient religio-political linkage; rivalries at Mengo (the capital) became intense, and the fact that all three new religions penetrated Buganda from the top downward meant that these rivalries became generalized throughout the population as a whole. The arrival of British agents in Buganda about 1890, led by Frederick Lugard, resulted in a situation in which the British presence became entangled with the Protestant-Catholic rivalry and in fact intensified it, as the British supported the Protestant faction. Kabaka Mwanga, the successor to Mutesa, attempted to play off one religious group against another; a series of religious wars ensued, precipitating the deportation of Mwanga and the installation of his infant son on the throne. During the next few years, and culminating with the Uganda Agreement of 1900, the British negotiated a settlement which brought an end to the period of instability and internecine warfare in Buganda, but which at the same time institutionalized the religious factor in Buganda's politics by establishing a quota system whereby certain political offices would thenceforth be held by individuals of a particular religious affiliation. As a result of this settlement, Anglicanism became in effect the established religion in Buganda, and the Anglicans received the dominant share of "Cabinet-level" posts as well as the largest number of territorial chieftaincies. It also became the informal practice to appoint civil servants who were of the same denomination as the head of the ministry in which they were to serve. Through this pattern of interchanges among the political, integrative, and pattern socialization subsystems of Buganda the Anglicans received a share of political power which was quite disproportionate to their numbers in the population, as it was estimated that by 1897 there were 155,000 Catholics and 127,000 Anglicans in Buganda.[5]

The pattern of an Anglican "establishment" in Buganda was replicated throughout most of the rest of Uganda as Christianity spread (in substantial measure through the efforts of Baganda missionaries) and as other ethnic groups sought to emulate Buganda, which was held up to them as a model of "superiority." Christianity spread rapidly and the two major denominations competed for adherents in all areas of the Protectorate. A pattern of cross-cutting cleavages was thereby created, with religious affiliation cutting across, rather than coinciding with, ethnic boundaries. The spread of Islam also cut across ethnic lines, although a much larger percentage of the conversions to Islam occurred in Buganda than was true for either of the major Christian denominations. Like Christianity, Islam owed much of its growth in Uganda to Baganda proselytizers who travelled to other parts of the Protectorate, and Baganda influence on the development of Ugandan Islam was strong.

The Christian churches formed an integral part of the new society that was emerging in Buganda and elsewhere in the Protectorate; the political and social elites, both traditional and modern, tended to be closely identified with the churches, and at the same time the churches established strong roots among the masses of the population. The mission schools were almost the only Western schools in Uganda during the colonial period, and they were thus responsible for educating and socializing the vast majority of those who were to form the nationalist and postindependence political elite. Rivalries between Anglican and Catholic schools were strong, and graduates of the elite Anglican secondary school, King's College Budo, were favored for government employment. Muslims had little opportunity to acquire Western education and were thus greatly underrepresented among the educated elite, but many Muslims entered the modern sector of the economy as traders and achieved greater economic success, and thereby greater political influence, than the average nonMuslim of equivalent educational background.

The linkage between religion and politics during the colonial period (the pre-existing system) in Uganda can be seen as having shaped that system in ways which help to explain more recent developments. The degree of integration of the social system is one crucial aspect of the pre-existing system in determining the nature of further change (A2). At first glance, it might seem that the pattern of cross-cutting religious and ethnic cleavages which first evolved during the colonial period should have produced a more highly integrated social system than would be the case in nations with a pattern of mutually reinforcing rather than cross-cutting cleavages. This prediction would be in line with the suggestions of Lewis Coser and other conflict theorists that cross-cutting cleavages can have an integrative effect. Developments in the 1950s, when political parties were first emerging in Uganda, seemed to bear this out initially. The earliest parties to emerge drew their members largely from one or the other of the two major Christian groups, and they thus had the potential of becoming truly national (i.e. trans-ethnic) parties. This was particularly true of the largely Catholic Democratic Party (DP), led by Benedicto Kiwanuka, which attracted support from all regions of the country in the first nation-wide general election in 1961. It was less true, however, of the several largely Protestant parties, which tended to be either primarily Baganda or non-Baganda in membership. Potentially integrative, cross-cutting cleavages were further weakened by the emergence of a new party in 1961—an all-Buganda party called Kabaka Yekka (KY)—which attracted Baganda of all religious faiths by its appeal to an overriding loyalty to the Kabaka.

Formation of Kabaka Yekka was a manifestation of the fact that the presence of cross-cutting lines of parochial attachments had not become a deeply rooted integrative force after all in the absence of fundamental consensus between Baganda and nonBaganda about the legitimacy of the nation's claim to ultimate loyalty. Coser has qualified his hypothesis about the integrative effects of nonreinforcing cleavages by adding that the absence of fundamental consensus can reduce or eliminate such effects,[6] and this seems to have been the case with respect to Buganda's position in the larger system. The low level of integration which characterized the Ugandan political system during the immediate preindependence period made it likely that the constitutional framework under which independence was achieved would be subject to considerable change after 1962.

Because of the links (to be elaborated upon below) between the conquest culture in Uganda and the religious bodies, it might also have been predicted that political change would create pressure for change in the religious subsystem through facilitation, and this proved to be the case. But the fact that the religious subsystem in Uganda was pluralistic (with three major religious groups and a number of smaller ones) rather than unified or homogeneous was another feature of the pre-existing system which *reduced* the likelihood of easy or rapid change within the religious sphere, despite pressures for such change. Since power was dispersed among a number of religious hierarchies, the acceptance of proposals for innovation was more difficult than in a situation of concentrated power (A3). Values and norms of innovativeness were present in the pre-existing system, but, particularly in Buganda, these values were restricted in scope and did not extend to the role of the Kabaka or the high priority which was placed on the perceived superiority of Buganda vis-a-vis her neighbors (A1). This pattern, combining flexibilty and rigidity, was characteristic not only of the Kiganda social system as a whole, but also of the religious subsystem within it. Innovation in the religious sphere was readily apparent, as is illustrated by the rapid acceptance of Christianity and Islam, but there were also inherently conservative tendencies within the new religious institutions once they developed ties to the larger Kiganda social system. For example, in the 1950s the Anglican diocese in Buganda passionately fought efforts by Anglicans elsewhere in Uganda and East Africa to create a Province of the Church which would encompass the three East African nations of Uganda, Tanganyika, and Kenya.[7] Baganda opposition to such a Province directly paralleled their opposition to plans for an East African political federation, and in both instances the underlying reason was the fear that the Baganda would lose their privileged position by being submerged in a much larger association. Similarly, in 1948 an unsuccessful movement developed among Baganda Anglicans to oppose the selection of a non-Muganda as the first African bishop in Uganda,[8] indicating their opposition to any innovation within the Church which threatened traditional Kiganda values of superiority.

Buganda was not alone in its conservatism, at least in certain respects. Although the leaders of the Uganda People's Congress (UPC), the ruling party between 1962 and 1971, held many innovative norms and values, these were frequently combined, somewhat inconsistently, with more conservative tendencies. For example, the great majority of the members of the modern elite—UPC and non-UPC alike— were mission-educated, and they tended to have difficulty in fully rejecting the norms into which they had thus been socialized. Although Obote and many others came to accept secular norms on an intellectual level, these ideas were not well integrated into a comprehensive ideology during the period leading up to independence (A2c). While proclaiming the necessity for separation of church and state, for example, a UPC policy statement in 1962 expressed satisfaction with the existing arrangements whereby education was almost entirely in the hands of church-operated schools, with government participation through a system of grants-in-aid.

It was noted above that, with respect to the political system and its subsystems, Buganda was not well integrated into the larger national system, and that this political relationship was susceptible to major change. Turning to look at the question of integration of religious subsystems, the Catholic Church was the only one of the three major religious collectivities which could be described as relatively well integrated internally. The low levels of integration in the Church of Uganda and within the Muslim community paralleled political malintegration in the sense that both derived from the problem of

Buganda. These two religious groups were each dominated by a Baganda elite during the colonial period, because both groups had put down deeper and earlier roots in Buganda than in the rest of of the country.

The Uganda Muslim Community (UMC) or New Juma sect was by far the largest of several African Muslim sects in Uganda, and it was under the leadership of Prince Badru Kakungulu, an uncle and a key advisor of Sir Edward Mutesa, the last Kabaka. Kakungulu had inherited his mantle of leadership from his father, Prince Mbogo, who had been the recognized leader of all Ugandan Muslims from the time of the religious wars until his death in 1921.[9] Although by 1948 there were three rival Muslim factions (divided over doctrinal questions as well as personal rivalries), the UMC under Kakungulu retained the allegiance of about 80 percent of all Muslims. (Asian Muslims are excluded from this calculation.) There was much resentment among nonBaganda Muslims against the UMC's tendency to use its considerable resources and landholdings largely for the benefit of Baganda Muslims. When the Buganda-centric KY was formed one year prior to independence, it was apparent that there were extremely close ties between KY and a number of the most prominent UMC leaders, and this intensified the resentment against the UMC outside Buganda. The other two African Muslim sects were also centered in Buganda, and there was similar resentment at Baganda domination on the part of their nonBaganda members.

Malintegration was similarly apparent within the Church of Uganda. Wealth was distributed very unevenly among the dioceses, with the Diocese of Namirembe (in the heartland of Buganda) and its sister diocese of West Buganda being by far the wealthiest. The Church was probably the largest owner of freehold land in the country as a result of the Uganda Agreement of 1900, and about three-fourths of this land was in Buganda.[10] Salaries for the clergy represented another issue on which there was a conflict of interest between wealthy and poor dioceses, with the latter preferring that the principle of local self-support be abandoned and a central fund created. By the 1950s, plagued by financial difficulties, a loss of morale among the clergy due to a relative decline in their standard of living, and what appeared to be the increasing success of other Protestant denominations and the Catholic Church at Anglican expense, the Church of Uganda was vulnerable to attempts to politicize it; its inadequate level of internal integration reinforced this vulnerability.

In contrast to this situation and the parallel Muslim difficulties, the Catholic Church was not characterized by extreme discrepancies in wealth between its dioceses in Buganda and those in northern Uganda. The Church was quite strong in northern Uganda and its churches, schools, and hospitals dominated the landscape there in comparison to those of the impoverished Church of Uganda. Even more important was the fact that the Catholic Church had not been intimately connected with the Buganda monarchy during the colonial period. The conquest culture was characterized by an Anglican "establishment" surrounding and including the Kabaka (and other traditional rulers) and by a Muslim community with a tradition of hereditary leadership linked to the Baganda royal family, but neither of these patterns had a counterpart in the Catholic Church. The latter church's traditions of discipline and obedience to superiors, and its international, cosmopolitan hierarchy also tended to promote internal integration and to de-emphasize the importance of subnational differences.

As the colonial period drew to a close, the Church of Uganda was experiencing problems not only of internal integration but also of integration with the larger social system. The latter difficulty was due to the pressure emanating from the political system for more rapid Africanization of church hierarchies. This pressure was also directed at the Catholic Church, but the latter body had already Africanized its highest post in Uganda—that of the Archbishop of Rubaga—prior to independence, and therefore the most prominant and visible target of the Africanization demands was the Anglican archbishop, who was still an expatriate. Although the Catholic Church actually had a higher percentage of expatriates among its clergy than did the Anglicans, the Catholic missionary priests were not clustered at the top of the Church hierarchy to the extent that was true of the Anglican expatriates, but were more evenly distributed from the parish level on up.[11] Further Africanization within the Catholic Church, to bring it into closer integration with the larger social system, would therefore presumably create less disruption and strain within the Church than would be true for the Church of Uganda, where the remaining expatriates were the "keystone of the arch," to use John V. Taylor's term.[12]

Religion and Politics in the Obote Regime

Despite the strains affecting two of the three largest religious groups, as well as a major political subsystem (Buganda), Uganda attained independence with a national political system which in many ways was resistant to change. For example, the multi-party system which developed during the nationalist period was one of the last African party systems to be transformed in the postindependence period to a single-party system. (This did not occur until 1970.) The unusually complex cleavage pattern accounts for this, at least in part (A2d). The existence of important religious cleavages in addition to, and not coincident with, ethnic and regional rivalries made it more difficult than usual to build a one-party state. This in turn was a major reason for the emphasis placed by the Obote government on the desirability of secularization or, as Obote and other UPC politicians frequently referred to it, eradication of "religionism" from the Ugandan political process. But political innovation in this and other areas was inhibited by the very existence of a relatively high degree of pluralism within the party system (A3). The continuing importance of the DP and KY during the 1962-1966 period made it difficult for the ruling UPC to effectively promote major social, economic, or political innovations because in doing so it would have run the risk of giving the opposition parties more issues on which to appeal to conservative elements in the population.

The intention of UPC policy was clearly to undermine the opposition Democratic Party by attracting Catholics to the UPC. This is not to imply that the motives behind the policy of secularization were purely manipulative; it seems likely that Obote and some of his colleagues were sincerely convinced of the desirability of eradicating religious considerations from the political process. It was recognized that the success of these efforts was contingent not only upon short-term efforts to attract Catholics to the UPC but also upon a more long-range socialization process through the educational system. It was for this reason that in 1963 the UPC abruptly changed its education policy from one which had guaranteed the continuation of the system of denominational schools to one which vigorously attacked this system and promised to secularize it as rapidly as possible. By removing supervisory and financial control of the schools from the hands of the churches, the government hoped not only to achieve control over the socialization process but also to depoliticize the role of teachers; Catholic teachers had been one of the mainstays of the DP and had used their positions to exert political influence on parents as well as students.

Both with respect to the pressure on the churches for change in the educational system, and with respect to other pressures for change in religious institutions during the post-1962 period, it was the political or goal attainment subsystem which tended to be the source of the demands for change, rather than the religious subsystems themselves. This was because the goal attainment subsystem itself was the first to experience major changes, in line with the proposition that change is likely to impinge first on the subsystems most closely connected with the role and collectivity levels of social structure (B2,C1). The changes which were occurring in the goal attainment subsystem (i.e., the movement from a federal system to a centralized, unitary system and the movement toward a one-party system) necessitated further change "higher" in the hierarchy of control—in the integrative and pattern socialization and control subsystems in which religious institutions are analytically located.

In addition to the pressures for change which were directed primarily at Catholics—encouragement to join the UPC and the demand that they relinquish control of their schools—the Church of Uganda and the Muslim community both became targets of political manipulators. The first hint of the growing politicization of the Anglican Church came as the result of a demand by the UPC Youth League shortly after independence that Archbishop Leslie Brown be replaced by an African. The Archbishop had traditionally served concurrently as Bishop of Namirembe Diocese in

Buganda, the historic and symbolic center of the Church of Uganda. The fact that an expatriate had always been Archibishop, and therefore Bishop of Namirembe, while African bishops were being appointed to other dioceses around the country, was a source of resentment for the Baganda. Baganda church leaders were therefore anxious that Brown's post be Africanized, But the possibilty that a nonMuganda might be appointed as his replacement was perceived as a threat to Baganda ambitions to maintain their dominance within the Church. Despite a threatened seccession from the Church's Uganda Province by the two Buganda dioceses, a nonMuganda, Erica Sabiti, was named Archbishop in 1966. The secession did not take place, but the political crisis of 1966 nevertheless had immediate repercussions within the Church.

Tension between the central government and the Buganda kingdom government, which had been building up since 1962, culminated in the spring of 1966 with an alleged plot by the Kabaka against the central government, and his flight from the country after an attack on the royal palace by the Uganda Army. Buganda was essentially occupied by federal troops, and a new interim constitution was promulgated, severely curtailing the Buganda government's special constitutional prerogatives. By September 1967 the federal status of the five kingdom governments of Buganda, Toro, Bunyoro, Ankole and Busoga was completely terminated, the kabakaship and other royal offices were abolished, and Uganda became a unitary republic. The ceremonial office of President, previously held by the Kabaka as part of the agreement under which Uganda achieved independence, was assumed by Obote and transformed into a strong chief executive. Baganda hostility to these changes was profound, and a state of emergency was declared in Buganda by the central government, preventing the holding of by-elections to replace those Baganda MP's who resigned from office rather than swear allegiance to the new Constitution.

While the new Anglican Archbishop Sabiti maintained apparently cordial and close relations with Obote and failed to speak out against the central government's use of force and detention without trial in Buganda, the new Muganda Bishop of Namirembe, Dunstan Nsubuga, maintained the traditionally close relations with the Baganda royal family by providing shelter in his personal residence to the exiled Kabaka's wife and other relatives. Suspicion of Sabiti's motives steadily increased in Buganda, particularly after he appointed a prominent UPC politician and close colleague of Obote, John Bikangaga of Kigezi, to head a committee which would propose far-reaching changes in the Church Constitution.

The recommendations made in the Bikangaga Report would have had the overall effect of greatly centralizing church administration by giving the dioceses less voice in the selection of their own bishops; by centralizing the management of, and revenue from, church lands; and by reducing the size and importance of Namirembe Diocese while creating a new Diocese of Kampala for the archbishop.[13] Despite the overwhelming rejection of these proposals by both Namirembe and West Buganda dioceses, a Provincial Assembly meeting was held in 1970 at which a new Church Constitution was approved, in a procedure of dubious constitutionality, by the remaining dioceses.

The atmosphere surrounding the Assembly meeting was intensely politicized; during the preceding six months it had become clear that the Obote government was taking more than a passing interest in the intra-Church conflict. Soon after the occurrence of a meeting between Obote and Sabiti, the newspaper *The People*, which was essentially a UPC party organ, published an editorial from which the following excerpt is taken:

> In a progressive, revolutionary country like ours, the Church must take part in the revolution.... The Church must be centralized; a federal Church in a centralized Uganda is a shameful anachronism.... The creation of (Kampala) diocese must be supported by all, even those not members of the Church of Uganda, but who wish to see the growth of a healthy body politic.[14]

The military coup of January 1971 took place only a month after the new Church Constitution was adopted, and the clearest evidence of the political manipulation which had surrounded the Constitution's adoption was the fact that the downfall of the UPC regime rendered the changes unenforceable; the Baganda immediately took the offensive by publicly linking Sabiti and other Provincial officials with the discredited Obote government.

As the foregoing discussion illustrates, the major concern of the UPC regime vis-a-vis the Church of Uganda was with matters of internal church organization and the internal distribution of power. This was in sharp contrast to the primary focus of the government's relations with the Catholic Church, which was in the area of education policy, in which Church activities impinged directly upon the political system. Variations in regional imbalance and Africanization within the pre-existing religious subsystems, which have already been discussed, partially explain the difference in the regime's attitude toward Catholic and Anglican intrachurch affairs. A related factor which further differentiated the two churches in the post-1966 period was the difference in the degree to which their internal organization corresponded to the pattern of organizational change within the political system—in other words, to the centralization process which gained momentum after 1966. Clearly the Catholic Church corresponded more closely to the model of centralization which the political authorities deemed desirable if ethnic and regional cleavages were to be eliminated. By promoting organizational change in the collectivity and role structure of the Anglican Church, the Obote regime was hoping to promote its ultimate goal of value and normative change away from the prevailing parochialism and toward nationalism. This strategy was in accordance with the propositions that units lower in the structural hierarchy of control (i.e., at the collectivity and role levels) are more easily communicable (in this case from the political to the religious subsystem) than are "higher" units (B2), and that changes initiated at these lower levels are more easily accepted (C1a).

The relative absence of conflict between the government and the Church of Uganda in the area of education policy can be attributed to the relative lack of opposition by the Church to the government's proposed changes; this in turn is explainable in terms of the perceived utility of these changes for the Church (C5). The Anglicans were in considerably greater financial difficulty than the Catholic Church, and were finding the operation of their schools an increasingly difficult burden to bear. At the same time, they had less invested in their education system to begin with, as the Catholic system was more extensive and had considerably more elaborate physical facilities. Furthermore, Anglican doctrine placed less importance on the necessity of maintaining parochial schools. For all of these reasons, the utility of resistance to government education policy was much lower for Anglicans than for Catholics, and the government take-over was implemented much more smoothly in Anglican schools.

Catholic resistance to the changes in the educational system was intense at the beginning of the new policy's implementation in 1964. Mass demonstrations of protest were held in Kampala and other areas, and there was resistance and lack of cooperation on the part of the church hierarchy. This mobilization by Catholics was not met by any equivalent countermobilization by the government, and this was particularly noticeable in Buganda, where a compromise resolution of the conflict left the Church with much of its control over the schools intact (C2,C3). In fact, the churches managed to retain considerable influence, especially over primary education, not only in Buganda but elsewhere. This was largely because the Ministry of Education itself was ambivalent about enforcing the changes, ostensibly because of grass-roots opposition from parents, but also probably in part because of ambivalent feelings on the part of Ministry officials themselves, given their own incompletely secularized value systems. Foundation bodies continued to have representation on school management committees, both because in most cases it was considered politically inexpedient to exclude them and because a provision for the representation of parents on the boards was utilized by the churches to send hand-picked representatives.[15] The teaching of religion in the schools was continued.[16] In short, the drive toward secularization of the schools was, in the course of implementation, substantially modified and reinterpreted to make it more compatible with the still-dominant values and norms of the population (D1,D2).

As the Obote government sought to secularize the educational system, it also sought to secularize the party system. The gradual demise of the Democratic Party and the cross-over of many of its members to the UPC in the latter 1960s seemed to indicate on the surface that this was succeeding. But two processes were at work which tended to undermine this success. Although religious nepotism was not serious at the highest levels of the central government, the strength of local (District-level) government in Uganda made it difficult for the central government to assure that its policies of nondiscrimination were observed by district party and government functionaries (A3). For example, there was almost no change toward greater representation of Catholics in appointments of *saza* (county) chiefs (a civil service post) in districts throughout the country; Catholics continued to be seriously underrepresented.[17]

The second factor undermining the UPC's ability to present itself as an all-encompassing, religiously neutral party was the growth of factionalism within the party. UPC leaders were acutely conscious of the possibility that the party could be "subverted from within" as they believed had happened in 1965-66 when large numbers of KY members joined the UPC and aligned themselves with other conservative elements in the party in a scenario which led to the detention of five cabinet members by Obote. The UPC leaders were therefore inherently suspicious of the motives of former DP supporters who joined the UPC between 1966 and 1970, perceiving them as incompatible elements (D1); factionalism developed over the question of the role which the newcomers should play in the party.[18] In addition, at lower levels of the party the goal of integrating Catholics into the party seemed to have no great utility (C5). Since personal advancement tended to be a major goal of party workers in a society where a political or civil service appointment was one of a very limited number of avenues to economic well-being, any large-scale influx of new party members created unwelcome competition. These attitudes on the part of lower-level party workers might have been effectively dampened by strong direction from the center, but the UPC had long been characterized by dispersed local power centers and considerably less power at the center than was usual for African political parties (A3).

Turning to the pattern of change experienced by the Muslim community, we find a much greater similarity to that experienced by Anglicans than to that experienced by Catholics; this was to be expected given the state of the three pre-existing subsystems outlined earlier. The UPC sought to capitalize upon the resentment among nonBaganda Muslims against Baganda royalist dominance of Muslim leadership posts and resources. Among the nonBaganda Muslims who were prominent in the UPC was Adoko Nekyon, a Langi, who was Obote's cousin and who held several ministerial portfolios culminating with that of Minister of Planning. Nekyon had long been hostile to Badru Kakungulu and the Uganda Muslim Community, and in 1965 he became the moving force behind the formation of a new organization, the National Association for the Advancement of Muslims (NAAM), which immediately challenged Kakungulu's right to leadership of Ugandan Muslims. The stated purposes of NAAM were to upgrade the status of Muslims and to promote Muslim unity and cooperation with the government. Its officers and executive board were comprised entirely of UPC politicians and a number of sheikhs. Although largely nonBaganda, the leadership did include several Baganda sheikhs, primarily men who had had long-standing personal rivalries with Kakungulu or other UMC leaders.

With the abolition of the kabakaship in 1966, the UMC was placed increasingly on the defensive; Kakungulu had lost his secular power base as advisor to the Kabaka, and increasing numbers of ambitious Baganda Muslims were attracted to NAAM because of the access they could thereby gain to government jobs and other political patronage. Obote began to speak out on the Muslim conflict, giving scarcely veiled support to NAAM.[19] Outbreaks of violence became common between members of the opposing factions as each sought to claim certain mosques and other property for itself. A new post of "Sheikh Mufti" was created under NAAM auspices and the government accorded recognition to the Mufti as the paramount Muslim in Uganda. Despite its early success in attracting members, NAAM's policies began to backfire after it took an increasingly hard line against the UMC by drawing up a new "Muslim Constitution" which provided for the incorporation in 1970 of a board of Trustees of the Muslim Religion in Uganda; the board would hold:

> "...any funds, mosques, or religious institutions, lands or other property owned by the Muslim religion...No individual or part of the community would have the right to claim ownership of such property."[20]

The threat posted to the UMC was clear: it would no longer control its extensive land-holdings and educational institutions. As in the case of the Church of Uganda, however, the "reforms" which were proclaimed in 1970 were never implemented because of the downfall of the UPC government. But prior to the coup, resistance had grown so intense that Kakungulu and the second-ranking UMC leader, Sheikh Ali Kulumba, as well as a number of lesser UMC figures, had beeen placed in preventive detention, and NAAM had begun to lose the support of some of its earlier followers.[21]

The intense resistance encountered by the advocates of change in both the Muslim community and the Church of Uganda was a function of the fact that the innovators were unable to communicate their ideas effectively and to predict the consequences of their actions (C6). The proponents of the Bikangaga reforms and the backers of NAAM were unable to present arguments in favor of the reforms which would convince most Baganda that these changes were free from political motivation. The support of the UPC for the reforms was so overt that it appeared inconsistent with the frequent UPC call for an end to the "mixing of religion and politics." The UPC ideology which had evolved by the late 1960s stressed the all-powerful role of the party in defining social values, and the duty of all other social institutions to accept and work actively to further the party's goals.[22] A sphere of autonomy for religious institutions seemed to have no place in such an ideology, and yet UPC politicians continued to say that the party stood for the separation of church and state. The norms invoked in support of the desired changes were therefore fundamentally inconsistent with other norms to which the regime paid lip service, and there was a consequent lack of credibility which made the presentation less forceful (C6d).

A second factor in the resistance to internal religious subsystem change was the apparent insensitivity on the part of the proponents of change to the consequences of their actions (C6c). The religious sector of Kiganda society was one of three social subsystems—the others being the political and the economic—in which the Baganda were simultaneously being asked to accept a reduced status or reduced benefits. The political changes were the most obvious: the abolition of the kabakaship and of Buganda's federal status, and the prolonged state of emergency in Buganda which prevented the holding of elections to replace those MPs who had resigned after 1966. In the economic sphere Baganda farmers believed that they were being intentionally and seriously discriminated against by Ministry of Agriculture policymakers in the matter of production quotas on coffee, the mainstay of Buganda's economy.[23] Working within the constraints of an export quota on coffee, the Ministry decided to restrict the production of the type of coffee grown in Buganda in favor of the higher-quality *arabica* variety which could be grown only in certain other areas of the country which had the proper climatic conditions. Although it is unlikely that the Ministry policy was intentionally discriminatory against Buganda, the serious economic blow which it dealt to Baganda farmers combined with the political changes to convince them that they were targets of persecution. A reduction of their status in the religious sphere was therefore the last straw. The advocates of change failed to comprehend this, and therefore met with greater resistance than anticipated. Proposition A4 suggested that rapid and radical political change, particularly when accompanied by changes in the economic subsystem, may reach a threshold of tolerance beyond which further change will be less likely. In Buganda a threshold was perhaps being approached, although not quite reached. (Some further change did take place.) It is likely that opposition to change in the Church of Uganda and the Muslim community would not have been so emotional and so prolonged had the demands for such change been put forward in the absence of the recent and radical political changes.

In relative terms, the proponents of NAAM were more successful in gaining support in Buganda than were the advocates of reform in the Church of Uganda. Several propositions help to account for this. Islam in Uganda had a long tradition of factionalism; several rival sects had been in existence since the 1920s. NAAM was therefore viewed as one more sect competing for adherents, and it was thus compatible with the pre-existing system (D1). On the other hand, the changes proposed for the Church of Uganda were the kinds which were least compatible with the existing pattern of organization. A possible middle ground had been rejected by the advocates of changes. For example, an alternative to the creation of a new diocese for the Archbishop was to make the post of Archbishop an executive one, eliminating the requirement that he be simultaneously a diocesan bishop. This would have been more acceptable to the Baganda because it would not involve any reduction in the size of Namirembe Diocese in order to make a Diocese of Kampala. There was some discussion of this alternative, but it was rejected without explanation in favor of the more radical, and therefore incompatible, Diocese of Kampala proposal. Another reason for the greater acceptance of NAAM than of the Church of Uganda reforms in Buganda was the factor of perceived utilty. Baganda Muslims, because of their low social status, derived less utility from the status quo than did Baganda Anglicans, and were thus more open to innovations (C5b).

The difficulties encountered by the Obote regime in promoting change within the religious subsystems, in secularizing the educational system, and in integrating Catholics into the UPC exemplify the proposition that changes impinging directly and immediately on functional subsystems and structural levels "higher" in the hierarchy of control are the least likely to be accepted (C1a). The attempts to secularize the schools preceded an effective integration of Catholics into the political system, and likewise the efforts to effect internal change in the Church of Uganda and the Muslim community coincided with the massive political changes of 1966 rather than coming after an effective reintegration of the Baganda into the new unitary political system. This raises the question of timing and suggests applicability of the hypothesis that political development will be easier if crises or problems can be solved sequentially over an extended period of time rather than simultaneously. Although the Obote government did not manifest any awareness of inconsistency in its policies, there was, as noted above, a basic incongruity in promoting secularization of the role behavior of Catholics, Protestants, and Muslims vis-a-vis one another and society, while at the same time contributing to intrachurch politicization. The effect of this pattern of government involvement could only be to reinforce the pre-existing cultural norms which had sanctioned the **absence of sharp boundaries between religious and political subsystems.**

A basic question which must be asked here is why the regime found it necessary to promote these seemingly incompatible policies. The need to attract Catholics to the UPC was a clearly understandable reason for promoting secularization. A one-party system was desirable not only because it seemed to be the trend among African nations generally (and Obote in particular looked to Tanzania as a model to emulate), but also because as long as the Baganda remained alienated from the regime the possibility of a Baganda-dominated opposition party was perceived as a serious threat to stability. Given the goal of a one-party system, Catholic support was obviously essential, considering their numbers in the population. The more difficult question is why the UPC allowed itself to become embroiled in intraAnglican and intraMuslim conflicts, thereby alienating the Baganda elite from the party and regime to an even greater degree. An answer to this must be found by examining the whole context of the regime's overall policy during the last three or four years of UPC rule. The UPC staked its reputation on an increasingly radical posture after 1967, culminating with the policies of the "Move to the Left" in 1969 and 1970. Although paying lip service to socialism, it was the centralizing, nationalistic aspects of the Move to the Left which came to predominate, because this reinterpretation of the original strongly socialist ideas represented the minimum change which had the highest utiltity for the elite (E4).[24] (Capitalist values and norms were actually becoming more important within the political elite as more politicians and civil servants had acquired business interests.) The heavy emphasis on nationalism and centralization, as opposed to socialism, necessitated the invocation of a set of values which were directly in conflict with the prevailing norms of local autonomy and support of traditional rulers within the Anglican and Muslim religious subsystems. Had the regime diverted more of its energies to the promotion of socialism or some other goal with less direct relevance to the structure of religious subsystems, the regime's preoccupation with religious organization would have been proportionately reduced. Since this was not the case, the preoccupation may have been unavoidable, given the prominent link between religion and politics in the pre-existing cultural norms, and the tendency for change to be compatible with pre-existing elements (D1).

If the UPC regime had been more effectively socialistic, of course, it might have clashed with religion over ideology and/or the class interests of some church leaders, but exactly how intense such conflicts might have become is open to question. (In the neighboring socialist country of Tanzania, for example, the major religious groups seem to have avoided any confrontation with the government serious enough to be damaging to their own status or institutional integrity.) In Uganda, the Anglican Church appeared to be ideologically more hostile to socialism than was the Catholic Church; the latter's major reservations about the Move to the Left were not based upon objections to socialism *per se*, but rather upon doubts as to whether socialist policies could be implemented effectively given the limitations on the government's administrative and economic expertise, and upon doubts about the sincerity of motivation of many UPC politicians. Furthermore, any conflict between religious bodies and the regime which might have materialized over the issue of socialism would not necessarily have produced any *intra*church conflict over matters of internal church organization and power, and therefore the government would not have had the same opportunity for manipulation which arose from the link between the centralization issue and the structure of Islamic and Anglican bodies.

Before turning to an examination of the direction of change in religio-political interaction during the post-1971 period of military rule, a brief summation of the Obote regime's balance sheet in this regard is in order. Some progress was made under UPC rule in subduing the most overt political tensions between Protestants and Catholics and in secularizing the educational system. In both of these areas, however, progress was considerably less than had been hoped, and may have been offset by the growing UPC involvement in intrachurch affairs, which weakened the regime's credibility in attempting to instill secular norms. For the most part, new values and norms had not come to control behavior, and change in the polity-religion interchange was not proceeding in a recognizable direction (E3).

Religion and Politics in the Amin Regime

The seizure of power by General Idi Amin marked a new turning point which eventually saw a resurgence of religio-political intergroup conflict, as well as the continued erosion of the internal autonomy of Anglican and Muslim institutions. The overall effect of Amin's rule has therefore been to place even greater obstacles in the way of secularization, while nonetheless paying lip service to secular political norms. Amin had involved himself in religious affairs even before coming to power—in fact his involvement can be linked to his growing alienation from the Obote government in 1970. Like other Muslims in the government, Major-General Amin had originally been a NAAM supporter and had appeared at numerous ceremonial occasions at the Kampala mosque which was the symbolic headquarters of NAAM. Amin was a Kakwa from West Nile District in northern Uganda, and therefore it had seemed natural for his sympathies to be with NAAM, whose greatest support lay in the non-Bantu areas of northern and eastern Uganda. In the summer and fall of 1970, however, he began to speak out in support of the UMC, apparently in an effort to cultivate support for himself among the Baganda. His overtures were warmly received and seemed to have the effect of restoring some of the old assertiveness to the UMC. There were some indications of collectivity mobilization on the part of the UMC, and Amin was asked to intercede on its behalf with Obote to ask for the release of

Kakungulu and Sheikh Kulumba from detention.[25] The military takeover which occurred shortly thereafter was welcomed warmly by all Baganda, but particularly by Baganda Muslims, who seemed to regard Amin almost as a messianic figure. Amin capitalized on this sentiment during his first six months in office by cultivating the UMC leaders as political allies.

However, there was no immediate indication of a desire on the part of Amin to accord favored status to Islam. Although voicing a desire to see Muslims unite and work together to upgrade their status in the community, Amin was equally concerned about Anglican divisions. His most immediate and striking departure from the previous regime's attitude toward religious institutions was his strongly proreligious bias, his cultivation of religious leaders of all faiths, and his invocation of strict moral values (particularly with regard to Western modes of dress such as miniskirts which he and many Ugandans regarded as immoral). The Obote regime, in contrast, had grown increasingly impatient with what it regarded as the reactionary tendencies of the major religious groups and their lack of enthusiasm for the Move to the Left. The early actions of Amin in paying frequent public tribute to Christian and Muslim religious institutions had the effect of restoring something of the prestige which these bodies had lost. The political or goal attainment subsystem was therefore operating to facilitate religion to a much greater extent than at any time since 1962. The religious subsystems were at the same time functioning to legitimize the military government; in this sense the prevailing values and norms in the hierarchy of control and facilitation and the positive functioning of the legitimation interchange fostered the consolidation of the political changes initiated by the new government. For a brief period during the first six months of Amin's rule, it appeared that a kind of balance had been achieved between control and facilitation in religio-political interaction, and that this might promote a certain amount of social stability. This situation was short-lived, however.

One of Amin's first innovations after assuming power had been the creation of a Department of Religious Affairs, whose functions included promoting resolutions of the intragroup disputes. Ostensibly the government was not to intervene in the disputes except to encourage the religious bodies to work toward a settlement and to provide any mediation which might be requested. But from the start it was clear that Amin was taking a more active interventionist role than he would admit. Amin's identity as a Muslim and therefore as a somewhat marginal individual in the predominantly Christian culture of the elite may have made it possible for him to introduce this innovation (the Department of Religious Affairs) with less hesitation than a Christian would have had (C6a). The emphasis placed by both the Anglican and Catholic churches on the value of religious freedom would have tended to inhibit a Christian who had been socialized into this value from creating a government agency which might appear to threaten it. Once he had announced his intention of creating such a body, however, Amin had to reassure the Christian churches of his benevolent intentions in order to gain acceptance for the new agency from the Christian elite, which still controlled the pattern socialization subsystem as well as the bureaucracy within the goal attainment subsystem (C6b). He did this by acceding to the suggestion put forth by the Catholic and Anglican churches that the new government body be established as a very small-scale department rather than as a full-fledged ministry as he had originally proposed (D2).[26] By publicly invoking Christian as well as Muslim religious values numerous times, and by appointing Christians to head the Department of Religious Affairs and all cabinet ministries except one, Amin further convinced the Christian segment of the population that his institutionalization of government participation in religious matters would be benevolent (C6d).

The first development after the coup which led to a confrontation between political and religious subsystems was the mobilization of the Baganda in 1971 in an attempt to recover some of the power and influence which they had lost in 1966. This mobilization took place simultaneously in political and religious subsystems. In the political subsystem it took the form of a campaign for the restoration of the kabakaship.[27] A certain amount of vacillation by Amin intensified the conflict which this campaign produced, because he had failed to state early enough and in unqualified terms that he would not consider a restoration of the kingdoms (C3b). In the religious sphere, mobilization took the form of a resurgence of the Anglican and Muslim conflicts as Baganda of both faiths mobilized to resist the government's efforts at mediation. Conciliation was apparently rejected because it had little perceived utility for the Baganda or the anti-Baganda Muslim and Anglican factions. Amin's frequent public pronouncements concerning his desire to see an end to the religious disputes focused the full glare of publicity on both Anglican and Muslim combatants, and they in turn began to make public statements since each of the adversaries felt that its case had been distorted. The outcome was a hardening of stands on all sides, with each faction believing that its reputation, pride, and credibility were at stake; little utility was therefore seen in any kind of compromise solution (C5). In addition, Baganda were deriving more utilty from their roles as Baganda during the postcoup period than previously, and were therefore less likely to accept change than they might have been had their utility been declining (C5b).

The military regime did not tolerate the Baganda mobilization for long, despite the early alliance between Amin and the Baganda. Retaining the unified support of the armed forces was necessarily Amin's first priority, and the military, once firmly in power, had little desire to cater to the Baganda. The Army was comprised largely of northerners and easterners, and the large Muslim contingent in the Army was primarily of Nubi[28] or West Nile/Madi origins. Their sympathies had been, and still were, with the NAAM or anti-UMC Muslim faction. The massacres of the formerly dominant Acholi and Langi soldiers in intraarmy fighting after the coup were followed by heavy recruitment in Amin's home district of West Nile, which had a much larger proportion of Muslims than did Acholi or Lango districts. As a result, the percentage of Muslim soldiers steadily increased.

The utility of asserting control over Islam in order to gain a more effective and firmer hold on the army was apparently a major factor in Amin's increasing intervention in Muslim affairs and his abrupt switch away from the role of a mediator with scarcely-concealed pro-UMC sympathies. Viewing the Anglican conflict as an exact parallel to the Muslim dispute, Amin determined in late 1971 to impose a settlement once and for all upon both religious groups, only days apart. Representatives of the conflicting factions were summoned to meetings in Kampala and were held under virtual house arrest until settlements were reached. In both cases, the Baganda were the overall losers in the agreements which were made, but enough elements of compromise were included to allow the Baganda to save face. In the Muslim case, Badru Kakungulu was forced to announce his resignation from his position of leadership in the UMC, and a Muslim Supreme Council was created which would have equal numbers of delegates from each district in Uganda. Since the Muslim population was much smaller in most of northern and western Uganda than in Buganda, the former areas would be greatly overrepresented on the Council by having equal numbers of delegates per district. The face-saving factor for the Baganda was the choice of two Baganda as Chief Kadhi and Deputy Kahdi—two newly created but largely ceremonial posts. The Muganda Chief Kadhi had been a NAAM supporter, however, and the real power apparently lay in the office of Secretary-General of the Council's Secretariat, which was held by a non-Muganda and former NAAM supporter.[29]

The Church of Uganda settlement resulted in the adoption of a new Church Constitution to replace the abortive 1970 constitution. It retained many of the innovations for which that document had provided, but modified some of them and left others intentionally vague. The major modification was the reduction in scale of the proposed new Kampala Diocese, so that it would not pose as great a threat to the stature of Namirembe Diocese; Namirembe Cathedral would remain as the Provincial Cathedral.

The religious settlements imposed by the Amin regime were undoubtedly more compatible with pre-existing elements than the changes which had taken place in 1969 and 1970 had been. The earlier innovations—the Anglican Constitution of 1970 and the Muslim Constitution of 1969 and Muslim Trustees Incorporation Act of 1970—had represented more radical departures from the status quo than did the 1971 developments, which included more elements of compromise. It therefore appears probable that the latter settlements will encounter less long-term resistance and will be more likely to endure beyond the life-span of the political regime, despite the fact that they were forcibly imposed (D1).

This is not to imply, however, that religio-political entanglement will lessen as a result. In fact, the dramatic intervention of Amin in the two cases may have operated to retard the secularization process (C4) because it set a precedent for overt, large-scale government involvement in religious affairs. It will henceforth be easier for the regime (or a subsequent regime) to intervene should any new difficulty arise within a religious institution or in that body's relations with the government. An additional factor which may have increased the potential for such intervention was the growing prestige of Islam in Uganda and the resultant greater acceptance of Islamic values, with their more theocratic bias. The army's control of the medium of power (and increasingly of money as military officers were able to take over many of the formerly Asian-owned businesses after 1972) gave it the ability to influence life conditions for large numbers of Ugandans. Because of the prominence of Muslims within the armed forces, Islam appeared to be attracting a growing number of adherents who viewed conversion as a new ladder to socioeconomic achievement. A number of Christian Army officers were said to have become Muslims.[30] Their acceptance of Islamic values could help to legitimate Amin's interventionist behavior in religious matters (E3a).

The Amin regime's education policy also had long-term implications for this continued pattern of religio-political entanglement. After the coup, the Ministry of Education took no new initiatives toward further implementation of educational secularization. To the contrary, it was decided not to implement a crucial provision of the Education Act of 1970 which had called for an end to the representation of the churches on the governing boards of secondary schools founded by them.[31] In addition, the Ministry, at Amin's urging, began a campaign to encourage greater emphasis on the teaching of religion in the schools. If these steps toward retrenchment in educational policy continued, they would be further illustrations of the tendency toward reinterpretation and modification of innovations and the pressure for compatibilty with pre-existing values and norms (D1,D2).

As the military regime's behavior grew more repressive in 1972, some politically dissident Christians, particularly several prominent Catholics, became victims of regime-inspired political murders. There was no real appearance of a persecution of Christians as Christians, however, until considerably later, and not all the targets of these early political killings were Christian. Threats were made against Catholic Archbishop Emmanuel Nsubuga and several other members of the Catholic hierarchy who opposed Amin's expulsion of the Asians, but for the most part the major effect was intimidation rather than outright persecution. The major exception to this generalization was the murder of Father Clement Kiggundu, the editor of the Catholic newspaper *Munno*. He had been a friend of Ben Kiwanuka, the Chief Justice, a prominent Catholic and former head of the DP, who was murdered by agents of Amin in 1972 after opposing Amin on several crucial issues. Kiggundu was also known as one of the most politically well-informed men in Uganda; it is likely that his death was motivated by the fear that he had knowledge of the events surrounding Kiwanuka's death. Although religion did not appear to be the motivating factor in the murders of the two men, the killings did have a profound effect on the Catholic segment of the population, particularly in Buganda, where their deaths created a strong sense of alienation.

Throughout this period, Amin's rhetoric did not become hostile to Christianity in general terms, but only to those religious leaders (and prominent laymen such as Kiwanuka who were closely identified with the Catholic Church) who were openly or semiopenly opposing his policies. In summary, Amin seemed to be making the minimum departures from his original religious policy which he deemed necessary to insure that religious leaders did not take advantage of their increased stature to oppose his regime or its policies (E4).

From early 1973 until late 1976, Amin refrained from taking any radically repressive action against the Christian churches as institutions or against Christian clergymen—at least this was true with respect to the major Christian denominations. During this period he did announce a ban against a number of much smaller Christian groups—mainly fundamentalist Protestant and syncretic sects. However, there is considerable doubt as to how effectively this ban was ever actually implemented, because in September 1977 a new ban was announced (as if for the first time) listing many of the same groups.

Amin's proArab stance had created the potential for the diffusion of change from the Arab bloc, and his original banning of the smaller Christian groups may have been in response to pressures from Muammar El Qaddafi of Libya, with whom Amin had formed a friendship in 1973. Qaddafi, a Muslim noted for his tendency toward religious fanaticism, visited Uganda and was said to have urged Amin to promote Islamic expansion at all costs. The smaller Christian denominations tended to be more avid proselytizers than the more established Catholic and Anglican churches, and thus would have been in more direct competition with Islam for converts. The original banning met with a great deal of public protest, particularly with respect to the Salvation Army and Seventh Day Adventists, and this undoubtedly accounts for the difficulty in enforcing it.

Given Amin's reputation for brutality and proIslamic leanings, and as a "man of action," it could be considered somewhat surprising that until 1977 there was no attempt to implement Qaddafi's more radical suggestion for Islamization. This was despite the occurrence of an abortive 1974 coup by Christian and Lugbara elements within the armed forces, which might have been expected to stimulate a strong countermobilization by Amin's Muslim and Kakwa supporters (C3a[3]).

The attempted coup, which was led by a Christian named Charles Arube, did produce some manifestations of stepped-up antiChristian activity, particularly the introduction of a system of government agents acting as informers on the activities of the few remaining Christian military officers.[32] But Ugandan Muslims did not mobilize as a united collectivity to confront the Christian elements of the population. Dissension and internal conflict continued to characterize the Muslim community. A shake-up in the Supreme Muslim Council resulted in the institution of tighter government control through Colonel Khamis Safi, but this reorganization was a symptom of Muslim disunity rather than a permanent solution for it. Disagreements over the handling of Muslim financial resources were cited as the cause of internal conflict, but ethnic divisions undoubtedly contributed to the cleavages, since by this time it was clear that Nubian Muslims had become an elite within an elite.

Another reason for the regime's delay in organizing a sustained drive to mobilize the Muslim community further lay in the extreme fragmentation of the opposition. The numerous unsuccessful attempts to overthrow Amin made it clear that, although opponents of the government were plentiful, they were a diverse and incohesive lot. Uganda in the 1970s appeared to be characterized by such an extremely low level of system integration that concerted purposive action to overthrow Amin was all but impossible (A2b). Former President Obote was viewed by many as the most likely figure to direct a successful coup, but many opponents of Amin, including some of his former cabinet ministers and civil servants, remained opposed to Obote as well. The division between Baganda and non-Baganda political exiles was deep and bitter. Opposition to the regime was therefore weak and disorganized, so that Amin and his supporters were under less pressure to work for Muslim unity and mobilization than might have otherwise been the case.

Furthermore, the abortive coup led by Arube was evidently not perceived by the government as a "Christian coup"; the Lugbara ethnic element was probably seen as more important. Accounts of the plot in the foreign press tended to give equal weight to the religious and ethnic elements, but Amin and his advisors were undoubtedly fully aware that the ethnic and denominational differences among Ugandan Christians would be likely to seriously hamper any large-scale Christian mobilization against him. Mobilization of Christians as a single political collectivity had never been sanctioned by the values and norms of Ugandan Protestants or Catholics (C2a).

However, the military regime's attitude towards the Christian population became much harsher by the end of 1976. Rumors of another impending coup attempt caused Amin to mount a massive purge of suspected dissidents. When the Anglican bishops and the new Archbishop Luwum spoke out publicly against the brutal tactics being used to hunt down the plotters and their weapons, Amin seems to have concluded that the plot had its origin in the Christian churches.[33] There was no evidence of this, but the outspokenness of the bishops was a factor which made the situation different from the events surrounding the Arube coup attempt in 1974, and it was apparently responsible for the different reaction by the regime. Amin was highly sensitive to criticism from the Christian clergy. His lack of formal education had resulted in an inferiority complex, and his desire for recognition and prestige placed him in a competitive position vis-a-vis the clergy, who formed a highly visible and important segment of the elite in Ugandan society. His increasingly tarnished international reputation undoubtedly heightened his sensitivity to attacks from the clergy (C3a[4]).

Within a few weeks, the Archbishop and two Christian cabinet ministers were arrested and met their deaths, allegedly in an automobile accident shortly after the arrest. The available evidence left little doubt that the deaths were far from accidental. Nationwide purges continued until March 1977, and were directed at three targets—the Christian elite, dissident soldiers, and university students and intellectuals.[34] Although the Catholic hierarchy escaped the worst of the reprisals, Catholic laymen as well as Protestants were victims, and the news editor and a reporter for the Catholic newspaper *Munno* were accused of treason.

A number of restrictions were placed on the Christian churches in 1977. Perhaps the most damaging was a cut-off of financial assistance and other kinds of donations to Christian institutions from overseas sources. According to Amin, this cut-off in foreign aid was designed to "help [the churches] be self-reliant."[35] Aid to Muslim bodies was excluded from the ban. At about the same time, Friday was declared a public holiday in Uganda—an action which other subsaharan African nations with much larger Islamic populations than Uganda had never taken.

Conclusion

In summary, it can be said that efforts during the postindependence period to set in motion a secularization process were unsuccessful. The boundaries between the political and religious subsystems did not become any more clearly defined than had been the case earlier, and in some respects—notably the autonomy of religious subsystems from political interference—the boundaries were eroded even further. In other words, the outcome of fifteen years of church-state struggle was a reversal of the balance of power, leading to a situation in which religious interference in politics became less of a threat to the principle of separation of church and state than was the increasing political interference in religious matters.

The effect of this pattern of increasing political intervention in religious affairs could only be to reinforce the prevailing dominant norms sanctioning the absence of clear-cut boundaries between religious and political subsystems. In the terminology of Donald E. Smith, such reinforcement represented a setback for attempts to bring about "polity-transvaluation secularization"[36] or secularization of attitudinal orientations toward the polity. In fact the UPC regime and, to an even greater extent the Amin regime, were taking steps toward what Smith terms "polity-dominance secularization." Polity-dominance secularization goes beyond "polity-separation secularization" (separation of church and state) and "polity-expansion secularization" (expansion of the polity's jurisdiction to include areas of social life formerly regulated by religious structures, e.g., education) to deny religion any area of autonomy whatsoever. The process of polity-dominance secularization, according to Smith, involves political authorities in the taking over of religion in order to reduce its influence or to restructure and reform it, thus bringing it into line with the modernizing program of the regime. Ironically, however, while moving toward polity-dominance secularization with respect to internal affairs of the Church of Uganda and the Muslim community, the political authorities had failed to eliminate church influence over the educational system, and had also left the churches with a sometimes reduced but still important role to play in other areas such as the provision of health services, church-sponsored mass media, church development projects and auxiliary groups—all areas in which it would be necessary to eliminate church activity, or at least establish complete control over it, if true polity-dominance secularization were to be put into practice.

Smith's model is primarily concerned with the secularization of traditional religio-political systems, whereas in Uganda the targets of the secularization efforts were relatively recently diffused religious institutions. It is likely that secularization was hindered in Uganda by the fact that Christianity has been associated with modernity in the eyes of most Ugandans, and therefore any attack on Christian institutions was not automatically justifiable in the name of modernization. Christian schools, hospitals, and newspapers were elements of modernity which it was difficult to attack, both psychologically and, at least with regard to schools and hospitals, from a practical point of view. The religious subsystems exercised a greater "control" over the goal attainment subsystem than would have been the case had they not been diffused to Uganda simultaneously with other elements of a new life style.

There was thus a mixed pattern of secularization types—combining elements of polity-dominance, polity- separation (e.g., the continued existence of church newspapers, hospitals, and auxiliary organizations), and polity-expansion (e.g., greater, although not complete, government control over the educational system). These three types of secularization deal largely with institutions, while the fourth type—polity-transvaluation—concerns psychological orientations. Presumably polity-transvaluation can therefore take place simultaneously with one or more of the forms of "institutional" secularization. But, as was noted above, polity-transvaluation secularization was hindered in Uganda by the incidence of government inference in internal religious matters—in other words, by the movement toward partial polity-dominance secularization. Whether these two types of secularization are inherently incompatible is open to question. However, in a situation such as Uganda, in which polity-dominance is far from total, attempts at partial polity-dominance rest on an inconsistent set of ideas which appears unable to form a basis for polity-transvaluation.

A number of factors must be taken into account in explaining the outcome of the Obote and Amin regimes' religious policies. Of particular importance is the use or nonuse of techniques of collectivity mobilization (C2). It could be argued that the intentional mobilization of religiously based collectivities by a political regime is by definition contrary to secularization. The major regime-inspired efforts at large-scale religious collectivity mobilization in Uganda were the creation of NAAM by UPC Muslims and the more recent attempt at mobilization of Muslims by Amin. In both of these cases the outcome of mobilization seemed to be further divisiveness rather than a generation of greater support for the regime's goals. However, it can also be argued that mobilization need not necessarily have had this effect. Smith argues that politicization of religious groups is not inherently antithetical to a secularization process, and that the two processes may proceed simultaneously, with the former process serving the function of integrating new groups into the political system as active participants for the first time, after which secularization will eventually become the overriding force.[37] This argument is in line with the theory of the integrative effect of cross-cutting cleavages which, if applied to Uganda, would suggest that the political mobilization of religious collectivities could act as a useful counterbalance to the importance of ethnic cleavages.

The acceptance of this idea by political actors would presumably call for particular attention to the mobilization of Ugandan Catholics, since they were numerically much more significant than the small Muslim community, and also tended to be alienated from the regime. However, neither the Obote nor Amin regimes made any major attempt at mobilization of Catholics as Catholics—in other words, no appeal was made to Catholics which was equivalent to that made to Muslims: a promise of facilitation of upward mobility for the group. Catholics as individuals were urged to join the UPC, but the only reference to their religion came in the form of appeals to give up their DP loyalty because the latter was based on the "mixing of religion and politics." The absence of a more positive appeal to a Catholic group identity is almost certainly explainable by the low utility which it would have for most of the Protestant UPC elite, and later for the Muslim military elite, since both Protestants and Muslims would feel threatened by a significant increase in

Catholic power, given the size of the latter group and the very limited supply of distributable resources (C3,C5).

Low regime legitimacy during the 1965-70 period was another factor which contributed to the failure of secularization and the substitution of the modified goal of political manipulation of religious collectivities. Since the Obote regime lost a great deal of its legitimacy after 1965, it needed the support that religious bodies could provide, but it could only obtain such support by insuring that Baganda critics of the regime would no longer hold positions of power within the major religious institutions. By maneuvering to achieve this the regime effectively negated any secularization process, since the net result was an intensified politicization of Anglican and Muslim institutions.

The absence of clearly defined values supportive of secularization on the part of the elite similarly caused a redefining of regime goals (D2). Although secularization was publicly espoused by most politicians, Protestant UPC politicians did not derive any immediate benefits from the entry of larger numbers of Catholics into the UPC; they merely had to share the party spoils with more members, whom they often regarded as potential subversives. The fact that the UPC was a weak, factionalized party dominated by local elites meant that, despite his commitment to ending Protestant-Catholic rivalry, Obote did not exercise enough control over district and local level developments to assure that discrimination against Catholics within the party and government would be eliminated. After the coup, the utility which Amin found in relying increasingly on a Muslim power bloc within the army made his commitment to secular values halfhearted. Amin's concept of secularization essentially meant government control of religion to an extent great enough to insure that intrachurch affairs at the very least did not work to the disadvantage of proregime factions.

A related factor which hindered the implementation of secularization specifically with respect to the educational system was the fact that the Ministry of Education was staffed by persons not fully committed to the idea of complete secularization of the schools (C6). The desirability of continued religious instruction in the schools was never seriously questioned by the great majority of Ministry officials, for example.[38]

Looking at the reasons for the modification of regime goals from a somewhat broader perspective, it seems clear that a major reason for the lack of movement in the direction of greater secularization was the difficulty in simultaneously implementing a number of major sociopolitical changes such as centralization, abolition of traditional authority, and secularization. An attack on the Baganda political elite was almost certain to have repercussions in other spheres of society, such as the major religious institutions, where Baganda were entrenched in leadership positions. It was therefore difficult to introduce changes sequentially, and the amount of change demanded within a short time span was apparently too much for the social system to absorb without intense resistance (A4,D5).

A final factor in the pattern of increasing political encroachment upon religious subsystem autonomy was, ironically, the fragility of political institutions throughout the whole period under analysis, under both the Obote and Amin governments. This fragility caused political actors to perceive the existence of other autonomous institutions, however fragile they also might be, as a challenge to the regime's effectiveness in goal attainment. Mild criticism of government policy by religious authorities, or even a simple failure to endorse government policy often triggered a government reaction which seemed (to non-Ugandan observers, at least) out of proportion to the actual seriousness of the threat (C3a[3]).

To summarize, there was change as well as continuity in the patterns of religio-political interchange in the postindependence period, and the pattern differed from one religious collectivity to another. During the first few years of Uganda's independence, the political regime received legitimation from the Church of Uganda because the UPC-KY coalition government was dominated by an Anglican elite and the Church had tacitly supported the two parties in their rivalry with the largely Catholic DP. The Church supported (or at least did not strongly oppose) major government policies during the 1962-65 period. The overall effect of the control exercised by the Church was therefore to foster the transition to independence and the new government's efforts to legitimize itself, not only in the eyes of Anglicans, but also for those other Ugandans for whom the Church was a symbol of modernity, power, and status. By 1966, however, this situation changed dramatically, as a powerful segment of the Church's membership rejected the government's continued claim to legitimacy in the face of parallel ethnic conflicts within and outside of the Church. The Church became a target of government efforts to promote wide-ranging societal change, and the new Amin government did manage to facilitate some change within the Church, but only at the collectivity level and in a less radical fashion than had been desired by the Obote regime. A new balance of power emerged within the Church by 1972 as a result of politically induced change, but there was no indication that the newly dominant role-players actually held variant values and norms with respect to the desirability of a complete disentanglement of religious and political processes and institutions.

More radical change in the pattern of control and facilitation was evident with respect to Islam as a result of the expansion of its political significance after the 1971 coup. Until the overthrow of Obote, the parallels between Muslim and Anglican religio-political processes were striking, and these parallels remained important after the coup as well, but at the same time Amin came to rely increasingly on Muslim support and on the political loyalty of Muslim army officers. As a result of the activation of this legitimation interchange the regime began to positively facilitate the emergence of Islam as a very significant political force. At the same time, the government openly intervened in Islamic religious affairs, and thereby weakened the autonomy of Islam as a controlling force. Interference in Islamic affairs, and the resultant loss of autonomous control, was even greater than was true with respect to the Church of Uganda.

The path of control and facilitation between the Catholic Church and the political system was quite different, and the differences widened during the time period under study. Although the Church was closely identified with the political party which formed the major opposition to the Obote regime, the Church nevertheless encouraged Catholic acceptance of the political rules of the game by which the UPC government had come to power in 1962, and members of the Church hierarchy and newspapers also encouraged the acceptance of a unified, relatively centralized national political system—another goal of the Obote regime. At the same time, however, the Church failed to endorse the leftward shift in regime ideology after 1968 and the imposition of a one-party system, and it opposed secularization of the schools. After an initial "honeymoon" with the new military government, the Church also lost its enthusiasm for Amin. In short, the Catholic Church legitimized existing political authority only to a limited degree; in turn the political authorities assumed a limited responsibility for facilitating Catholic values by providing religious instruction in government schools, by inviting Pope Paul VI to Uganda for the first visit by a modern Pope to the African continent, and by awarding a number of cabinet posts to Catholics. An undercurrent of contradiction characterized this policy of symbolic cooperation with the Catholic community, because at lower levels of government discrimination against Catholics (in employment, for example) continued much as it had in the past. The relative unimportance of internal divisions in the Church hindered any efforts at political manipulation which might have facilitated change in a direction that would have been compatible with the goals of either the Obote or Amin regimes. Unlike the situation in the Anglican Church and the Muslim community, the interaction between the Catholic Church and the political system was not characterized by much significant change in the nature of control and facilitation during this period; relations were at best characterized as a kind of stalemate. Amin's growing reputation for unpredictability and disregard of public opinion made the Church's position more precarious, however, and whether the stalemate could last for long remained to be seen.

What are the implications of the restratification which seems to many observers to have set in motion a reversal in the prestige and power of Muslim and Christian communities? Amin has remained in power considerably longer than many experts predicted at the outset; the longer he rules the more likely it might seem to become that Islam will attract larger numbers of opportunity-seeking converts. However, those conversions which have become publicly known thus far have mainly involved military personnel rather than civil servants. For the most part, the educated elite did not convert to Islam, but this group has been replaced in positions of power and responsibility by Muslims with little or no professional or technical competence. Initially, Muslim army officers were dependent on far better educated Christian civil servants for administrative expertise, but more recently (particularly since the purges which began late in 1976) the ranks of career civil servants have been radically thinned as such individuals have been killed or imprisoned, or have fled the country.

The extent to which Islam becomes established as a major and permanent political force will at least partially determine whether Protestant-Catholic antagonisms will remain as an important source of political cleavage, since a Christian-Muslim polarity would be more likely in the face of Muslim domination. Protestant-Catholic rivalries were less visible after the coup and the resultant ban on political parties, but there continued to be an undercurrent of conflict, particularly in Amin's home district of West Nile, which has a long history of such hostilities.

There is no available statistical breakdown on religious affiliation within the armed forces, but Catholics probably outnumbered Protestants after Amin began recruiting heavily from West Nile, where the population is disproportionately Catholic and Muslim. After 1975, however, recruitment from West Nile narrowed more and more to the Nubian and Kakwa communities there, while at the same time the military also began to recruit heavily among minority ethnic groups elsewhere in the country, such as the Karamojong, Bamba, and Bakonjo.[39] The latter peoples tended to be less heavily Christian than most of the larger ethnic groups; traditional indigenous religious beliefs remained stronger in the more remote regions of the country where most of these minorities lived. Whether nonChristian ethnic minorities would prove susceptible to Islamic proselytization while in military service remained to be seen. In any case, the decreasing numbers of Protestants in the armed forces, combined with the Church of Uganda's loss of prestige and morale as a consequence of its internal strife, may work to reduce the likelihood of any early resurgence of Anglican political dominance. Even if civilian rule is restored at some future date, the army will probably continue to play an important political role, and the religious configuration within the military will therefore remain important in any calculation of the distribution of political power.

NOTE: This chapter was in press at the time of General Idi Amin's fall from power.

Footnotes

1. Uganda Protectorate, *Uganda Census 1959: African Population* (Entebbe: Government Printer, 1963), pp. 44-76. The 1959 census is the most recent source of comprehensive religious statistics. Of the total population in 1959, 34.5 percent were Catholic, 28.2 percent Protestant, and 5.6 percent Muslim according to the census findings. There is some question about their accuracy, however, particularly with respect to the Muslim percentage, which many observers believe underestimated Muslim strength.
2. D.A. Low, *Buganda in Modern History* (London: Weidenfeld and Nicolson, 1971), p. 22.
3. Ibid., pp. 18-19.
4. Ibid., pp. 20-22.
5. B.W. Langlands and G. Namirembe, "Studies in the Geography of Religion in Uganda," Makerere University, Department of Geography, Occasional Paper No. 4, Kampala, 1969, p. 13.
6. Lewis A. Coser, *The Functions of Social Conflict* (New York: The Free Press of Glencoe, 1956), p. 94.
7. F.B. Welbourn, *East African Christian* (London: Oxford University Press, 1965), p. 74.
8. Mary Stuart, *Land of Promise* (London: Highway Press, 1957), p. 105.
9. T.W. Gee, "A Century of Muhammedan Influence in Buganda, 1882-1951," *Uganda Journal 22, 2* (1958): 144.
10. Church of Uganda, *Survey on Administration and Finance of the Church of Uganda* (Kampala: Uganda Bookshop Press, 1969), pp. 29-30.
11. John Vernon Taylor, *Growth of the Church in Buganda* (London: SCM Press, 1958), p. 92.
12. Ibid., p. 86.
13. Sabiti had retained his original position as Bishop of the Ruwenzori Diocese in western Uganda, which necessitated frequent commuting between his two offices, two hundred miles apart. For the first time, the position of Bishop of Namirembe was not held by the Archbishop, but by a Muganda, Dunstan Nsubuga.
14. *The People,* 9 May 1970. See also *The People,* 16 May 1970.
15. Apolo Nsibambi, "The Uganda Government's Efforts to Acquire Effective Control in Administering Education, 1962-1970," paper presented at the Universities' Social Science Council Conference, Kampala, December 1971, p. 58.
16. Provision was made for the instruction of each student in his own religion. Most schools remained strongly denominational in terms of the composition of their student bodies, and the "minority" students in a school, who were adherents of a religion other than that of the school's

founding body, were usually short-changed in terms of the religious instruction which they received, frequently having to rely on visits by the pastor of a neighboring church.

17. The information on *saza* chiefs comes from my own research covering the period 1965-71 and a comparison with data for 1960 found in Martin Lowenkopf, "Uganda," in *Islam in Africa,* ed. J. Kritzeck and William Lewis (New York: Van Nostrand-Reinhold, 1969), p. 220.

18. It should be noted that the issue of Catholic or former DP members who were "newcomers" to the UPC was only one of several bases for intraparty factionalism.

19. Uganda Government, National Assembly, *Uganda Parliamentary Debates: Official Report,* 80 (9 February 1968): 2784.

20. *Uganda Argus,* 12 August 1969.

21. See *Munno* (Kampala), 4 February 1970, for an illustration of this tendency in the case of one prominent Muslim in Busoga who had "given" NAAM a mosque built by his father, but who later decided to reclaim it because of his disagreement with the provisions of the new Muslim Constitution.

22. See, for example, the editorial in *The People,* 16 May 1970.

23. M. Crawford Young, "Agricultural Policy in Uganda: Capability and Choice," in *The State of the Nations,* ed. Michael F. Lofchie (Berkeley: University of California Press, 1971), p. 152.

24. James R. Scarritt, "Culture Change Theory and Post-Independence Political Change in Uganda: a Preliminary Analysis," Makerere University, Department of Political Science and Public Administration, Seminar Paper No. DSP/7/72-73, Kampala, 1972, p. 38.

25. *Munno,* 5,17,19 October 1970.

26. This request was put forward by the Uganda Joint Christian Council, a body with ecumenical aims, which had been created in 1964 by the Catholic and Anglican churches. The information on the request comes from a Council member.

27. The movement for restoring the kabakaship first emerged when the body of the late Kabaka (who died in England in 1969) was returned to Uganda for burial, at Amin's invitation, in the spring of 1971, arousing Baganda emotions to a peak of intensity. It gained momentum later that year when the Kabaka's son and declared heir returned to Uganda from his school in England and became the rallying point for numerous celebrations and meetings.

28. The term Nubi as used in Uganda refers to the descendants of Muslim Sudanese soldiers who came to Uganda as mercenaries for the British in the nineteenth century and settled permanently; their descendants have remained oriented to military careers and have always formed an important segment of the Ugandan armed forces.

29. *Uganda Argus,* 1 May 1972.

30. The most prominent of these was Col. Francis Nyangweso, who

held the post of Army Commander. See Colin Legum, ed., *Africa Contemporary Record: Annual Survey and Documents 1972-1973* (New York: Africana Publishing Company, 1973), p. B273.

31. This information comes from my interviews with Ministry officials during May and June of 1972.

32. *New York Times*, 15 April 1974; and Colin Legum, ed., *Africa Contemporary Record: Annual Survey and Documents 1974-75* (New York: Africana Publishing Company, 1975), p. B311.

33. Colin Legum, ed., *Africa Contemporary Record: Annual Survey and Documents 1976-77* (New York: Africana Publishing Company, 1977), pp. B378-83.

34. Ibid.

35. "African Update," *Africa Report* 23, 2 (March-April 1978): 31.

36. Donald E. Smith, *Religion and Political Development* (Boston: Little, Brown & Co., 1970), pp. 85-87.

37. Ibid., p. 124.

38. The bureaucracy was an obstacle not only to the secularization of the schools but to the implementation of the Move to the Left in general. See the discussion by James H. Mittleman in *Ideology and Politics in Uganda* (Ithaca, N.Y.: Cornell University Press, 1975).

39. Legum, *Africa Contemporary Record 1974-75*, p. B309.

3

Forecast for Political Change in Ethiopia: An Urban Perspective

Peter Koehn

In 1974, a committee composed of noncommissioned and junior officers representing most of the country's military units gradually assumed political power in Ethiopia through a revolutionary coup d'etat in the wake of serious famine and widespread urban unrest. The committee (called *Derg*) arrested Emperor Haile Selassie 1 on 12 September, terminating one of the longest ruling monarchical regimes in contemporary history, and formed a provisional military government. The leaders of the coup immediately sought to secure popular support for military rule by adopting radical measures designed to transform social and economic relations in a manner that would benefit the impoverished and landless rural and urban classes.[1]

The dramatic nature and scope of its political transformation make Ethiopia a particularly interesting and challenging case study for students of African political change. By identifying critical variables and propositions the control and facilitation framework provides a useful guide for the analysis of political change in contemporary Ethiopia. This chapter utilizes a control and facilitation theoretical perspective in analyzing the basic urban origins of political transformation in Ethiopia and in forecasting the impact of political change at the center on urban politics and development.[2] "Control and facilitation" assumes that behavior is determined by a complex asymmetrical interdependence of cultural and material factors. Values and norms shape behavior, while material resources and role behavior provide the energy needed to sustain or change a given social or political pattern. Finally, members of collectivities that adhere to and advocate alternative or deviant value patterns must gain power in order for radical political change to occur.

The analysis contained in this chapter is confined to the Ethiopian political system and its functional subsystems.[3] Change tends to occur at an uneven pace within the various functional subsystems of a political system, and special attention is given to leads and lags in interrelationships among the four functional subsystems of urban political systems. In the precoup period, the weakness of antisystem collectivities delayed change. Postcoup developments indicate that leaders of the new regime are willing to introduce changes in political culture and to extend governmental control over the adaptation subsystem, but are hesitant to establish strong integrative and goal attainment institutions.

Obstacles to political change could be overcome in Ethiopia once power was mobilized by urban collectivities that grew in strength and allied with one another as a result of shared deviant ideological persuasions. Change at the center of the Ethiopian political system constituted a prerequisite to progress in providing urban services to low-income city inhabitants. Significant improvement in the living conditions experienced by the vast majority of urban residents will not be actualized, however, in the absence of mass-based political institutions and the delegation of additional authority to local collectivities— changes the new military rulers have been reluctant to implement.

Significance of Urban Political Studies

Even in the case of revolutionary change involving members of the political community as well as authorities and regimes, the initiative for revolution tends to be monopolized by urban-based actors.[4] Those who control African cities speak for their countries. Even more importantly, those who control the cities speak *through* the organs of the state which they dominate.[5] Control over urban-located state media (useful for political socialization), material resources, and coercive forces enables successful revolutionary elites to carry out major transformations of social structure.

In Ethiopia, peasants did not possess revolutionary political consciousness in 1974. John Markakis shows how, in northern provinces, the absence of mechanized agriculture, the strength of patron-client ties, the *rist* system of landholding, and traditional cultural patterns inhibited the expansion of private property ownership and the growth of peasant class consciousness.[6] Even the devastating famine of the early 1970s and the callous reaction of the imperial regime to its consequences did not provoke peasant revolts—although it constituted an imporant contributing factor to the urban unrest and military intervention that led to the ouster of Emperor Haile Selassie I and the termination of monarchical rule.[7]

Therefore, scholars who focused exclusively on rural political conditions foresaw little prospect of fundamental change.[8] Students of the Ethiopian countryside reached this conclusion because political change was only indirectly related to rural conditions. The nature of *urban* economic conditions and the values, actions, and interactions of political actors in the nation's capital—particularly the military, students and workers—proved to be far more salient in shaping prospects for radical political change than rural land ownership patterns, incipient peasant class formation, and customary patterns of acquiring and distributing rural land use rights.[9] In short, the actions taken by urban-based political forces made possible the revolutionary changes in the rural as well as the urban social, economic, and legal orders which have occurred in the postcoup period.

Municipal Government Performance: The Pre-existing Goal Attainment System

The imperial government assigned municipalities a long list of local functions under national legislation. In practice, however, even the largest and wealthiest municipal governments found it impossible to perform many of these functions.[10] Major municipalities did not emphasize the provision of public services other than roads, but instead built monumental projects such as stadiums and office buildings. Only token sums were expended on social welfare, housing, health, fire protection, and sanitation, and the principal activities carried on were the maintenance of order, tax and revenue collection, and the licensing of businesses. In short, Ethiopian municipalities did little to alleviate the deplorable living conditions which prevailed throughout urban Ethiopia and included inadequate housing, transportation, water supplies, sanitary facilities, and fire and police protection, as well as widespread unemployment, poverty, and disease.[11]

A central focus of the chapters contained in this book is on overcoming barriers to change. The two most immediate reinforcing obstacles accounting for the poor urban social service performances of prerevolutionary Ethiopian municipalities involved the mobilization of local resources and central government control. Resource mobilization concerns the adaptation function of political systems. In the urban context, this involves the acquisition of money (revenues) and roles (staff and citizen) required for community development projects by government agencies and voluntary associations. Potentially, these structures and media facilitate change in urban goal attainment performance toward increased social services provision. However, the nature of the control that is exercised is crucial. Possession of the bulk of all available media of exchange (influence, power, and money) allowed the central government of Ethiopia to shape, to a large extent, the norms which municipal officials adopted when they set out to apply facilitating media and roles to urban problems.

Of course, the principal barriers to change analytically located in the political system were conditioned to some extent by performance in other functional systems. Few deployable economic resources were generated in the Ethiopian urban adaptation system, as a result of neocolonial exploitation, customary avoidance of formal savings and loan institutions, and the weak regulating and promoting performance of the state. The pattern socialization and control system greatly influenced the decisions reached by central government officials regarding which allocative values and administrative norms to encourage at the municipal level. Traditional socializing structures, including the Amhara family and the Ethiopian Orthodox Church, promoted values of hierarchical rather than egalitarian social and political relationships, obedience to authority, and acceptance and maintenance rather than change of the existing social and political order.[12]

During the precoup period, central government control over municipalities was based upon two normative predispositions which constrained rather than facilitated performance at the local level. First, rapid and fundamental urban social, economic, and political changes were not valued, and efforts to initiate change were actively discouraged. In addition, the devolution of authority to municipal governments was unacceptable to central elites.

Much of the blame for municipal nonperformance in human service areas must be borne by the central government. Emperor Haile Selassie's policy of appointing rivals to contiguous posts in the local government hierarchy and the unintegrated nature of the system insured that conflict and confusion would characterize urban administration in Ethiopia. In addition, the central government failed to provide incentives that would encourage the development of human service and popular participation orientations among municipal employees. The monarchical regime of Emperor Haile Selassie I evidenced little interest in norms of efficient administrative behavior and *public* service. The imperial government also proved unwilling to implement measures that would mobilize widespread participation in local political activity and might lead to demands for the redistribution of power and wealth in Ethiopian society. In fact, *all* associations that threatened to engage in overt political acts were deliberately and vigorously suppressed.[13] Finally, the functional performance of Ethiopian municipalities was affected adversely by financial constraints imposed at the center, and by the national government's unwillingness to delegate authority to cities and towns in the areas of taxation, zoning, and law enforcement.[14] Thus, municipal governments were beset by chronic shortages of crucial facilitating media (money and power).

Financial constraints included extended delays in central government approval of municipal tax rate increases and municipal budgets; tax exemptions for church and government lands; a central government monopoly on credit to municipalities; refusal to use the centrally controlled police force to enforce collection of unpaid taxes, which amounted to millions of Ethiopian dollars each year; central government collection of all unexpended monies from municipalities at the end of each fiscal year; and the absence of significant financial support from the central government for public services other than roads. Political pressures from both the national government and local elites kept municipal land tax rates uniformly flat at an extremely low level rather than progressive; and the substantial bribes offered by wealthy local elites and foreign businessmen induced urban administrators to place priority on the concerns of these groups, to the detriment of activities which would benefit low income urban dwellers.[15]

The opposition of the Haile Selassie regime to increased municipal autonomy over local affairs is evident from its failure to introduce municipal government reforms. In the mid-1960s, staff of the Municipalities Department of the Ministry of Interior drafted legislation that would have allowed first class municipalities (with populations of at least fifteen thousand persons) to assume all powers not prohibited by the constitution or an act of Parliament, and to establish by charter or local ordinance their own system of appointment for all executive positions other than *kantiba* (lord mayor). Candidates for the position of *kantiba* were required by this draft legislation to have resided within the municipal boundaries for at least one year prior to their nomination. Councils retained authority to nominate three candidates for the *kantiba* position, one of whom would be appointed to the office by the Minister of Interior. Municipal councils, selected without regard for the property ownership qualifications required at that time for holding municipal office and for voting in municipal elections, would have been granted power to override the *kantiba*'s veto of council enactments by a two-thirds vote. This draft legislation granting self-government powers to municipalities secured little support from Ministers of Interior or within the Council of Ministers, and was never presented to Parliament.

In sum, lack of commitment to change at the center of the Ethiopian political system and the concentration of power there constituted pervasive obstacles to social and economic progress in urban settings (A3). The central government neither inspired nor facilitated municipal efforts to mobilize revenues for, and involve people in, urban social service programs, and it blocked reforms aimed at providing municipalities with greater authority to respond to local problems. Major improvement in urban living conditions could have been effectuated by Ethiopian municipalities if central government authorities had taken steps to reshape the unintegrated prefectoral system,[16] revamp the local government bureaucracy at all levels, divert revenues into municipal coffers, grant municipalities increased authority over local affairs, and provide incentives aimed at encouraging a human service orientation among administrators and participation in development projects among urban inhabitants.

Ethiopia: An Urban Perspective

Since such actions required the commitment of the national government, *regime change at the center* posed an indispensable ingredient in any scenario for expansion and extension of the urban social services provided by municipal governments. The next section of this chapter relates precoup conditions to prospects for regime change in Ethiopia, employing the facilitation and control perspective. The focal point of this analysis is societal conditions in Addis Ababa—the center of national political activity in Ethiopia.

The Process of Change: Control and Facilitation

Most of the elements necessary for political change were present in latent form in the capital city by the early 1970s. Widespread economic dissatisfaction promised to supply the energy needed for change. An urban intelligentsia committed to pursuing strategies of rapid and fundamental social and economic transformation had articulated a clearly defined set of innovative alternative values (A1,A2c). Collectivities which possessed power to effectuate far-reaching changes in the national political system—including segments of the armed forces, labor unions, and student organizations—had increased in strength as the power of traditional forces declined in urban areas. The problem remained, however, of linking these disparate change-oriented forces into a unified movement. The most serious manifestation of this obstacle to change existed at the collectivity level, where uncoordinated radical political activities could easily be repressed by the government. Eventually, students who had learned the importance of linking alternative value orientations with mass agitation played a catalytic role in promoting political change (C6a,d).

Economic Conditions: Potential Energy For Change

As a result of inequities in the distribution of material resources Addis Ababa constituted a capital city where the vast majority of the populace suffered severe economic hardships. Industrial growth had been concentrated in the private manufacturing sector rather than among labor-intensive construction activities, and industrial operations and expansion in the capital region had been essentially confined to firms owned and managed by expatriates.[17] Inequities in the accumulation of wealth and material goods were reinforced by elite ownership of land and property,[18] lack of progressive taxation, and failure of the Addis Ababa Municipality and central government ministries in providing public services. While wealthy urbanites could purchase modern services and comforts, such material benefits remained beyond the reach of most urban dwellers in Addis Ababa as long as governmental structures did not provide them. A high rate of inflation exaccerbated economic conditions, particularly for poor persons.[19]

The Addis Ababa lumpenproletariat represented a potentially explosive nonelite segment of society in the early 1970s (C5b). However, the lumpenproletariat lacks the level of awareness and organization necessary to undertake effective action on its own. The intellectual elite plays an indispensible role in raising the political consciousness of the lumpenproletariat to a volatile level. Belief that there is nothing to lose and everything to gain by revolting against the established structure of society can provoke such a consistently frustrated nonelite group to engage in violent political acts. Where the material gap between rich and poor is vast and continuing to expand, as in Addis Ababa in the early 1970s, the role of intellectuals in raising consciousness of economic exploitation among the mass of under-and unemployed urban residents is made easier (C6d).[20] Students had encountered the abrupt frustration of raised political and social ideals as a result of the suppression of a briefly successful coup d'etat in 1960. Moreover, their personal material aspirations, encouraged by government educational policies, had been thwarted in the late 1960s and 1970s as an increasing proportion of the secondary and university graduates, as well as school leavers, proved unable to find urban jobs commensurate with their expectations (C1,C5b).[21]

Alternative Value Orientations

At the same time that the limited modernization measures permitted by Emperor Haile Selassie alienated former supporters of the traditional political system,[22] many urban dwellers exposed to modern institutions came to reject the traditional authority structure. Groups denied political participation became increasingly aware of and angered by discrimination in official circles (A2a). By the mid-1960s, most high school and university students in Addis Ababa adhered to a clearly differentiated set of alternative values that involved radical change in the social, economic, and political status quo (A2c). These intellectuals rejected the professed legitimacy of the traditional monarchical regime outright.[23] A study of university students conducted by Otto Klineberg and Marisa Zavalloni revealed that a far greater proportion of Ethiopian students than students from any of the five other African nations included in their sample opposed the continuation of traditional authority in governmental structures.[24] Most politically active students advocated land redistribution (by force, if necessary) to achieve greater equity in ownership, an end to corruption, and extensive government control of the economy along the lines of the Tanzanian socialist model (B2a).

Norms also are important for political change because they control the selection of strategies destined to shape the outcome of political events. The early 1970s marked a major shift in norms directing the Ethiopian student movement. Partly as a result of the frustrations many students experienced during national service in the provinces, the movement's emphasis upon consciousness-raising among rural peasants was gradually abandoned in favor of public demonstrations of solidarity with disaffected urban groups.

The regime of Emperor Haile Selassie did not hesitate to respond with repressive force when students organized demonstrations and strikes in Addis Ababa. Student unions were outlawed; assemblies of students were restricted and prohibited; student publications were confiscated; student leaders and protestors were arrested, beaten, and shot; and schools were closed. Later on, violent measures were moderated by official leniency. Arrested student leaders were pardoned by the Emperor and released from prison on the condition that they refrain from any further political activity. After a time, students were allowed to reorganize themselves into new associations. The central government's vacillation between force and forgiveness in dealing with student protestors grew out of a systemic contradiction between the need to educate young people to assume technical and leadership roles and the need to protect a highly traditional political system against growing criticism.[25] The vacillating pattern of repression raised the level of violent political conflict in Ethiopia (C3b). Students were allowed to mobilize in support of alternative values. They grew more intensely attached to their demands as they suffered physical injury or deprivation while promoting them. Then, shortly after the application of force, the government allowed students to reorganize and develop a more sophisticated plan of antisystem action.

Opposition to the imperial rule assumed more violent characteristics in 1971.[26] High school and university students boycotted classes, demonstrated in the streets of Addis Ababa, clashed with police, stoned buses, and protested inflated prices by overturning market stalls. The new urban-based strategy designed by students aimed at instigating violence on a wide scale and creating chaos of such dimensions that the armed forces would be compelled to intervene in order to restore order. The instigators of these acts relied upon the hope that once the army was mobilized and in position in Addis Ababa, progressive officers would move to assume political power at the expense of the Emperor.

The violent confrontation of 1971 demonstrated that students were able to generate popular support in Addis Ababa by appealing to economic issues of immediate concern to large numbers of poor urban dwellers. Workers and unemployed urbanites joined student protests against higher prices for transportation and food. However, although the armed forces were called upon to restore order, they made no overt move to overthrow the monarchy.

Peter Koehn

Urban Collectivities: The Need For Cohesive Action

The spring crisis of 1971 demonstrated that students possessed the capacity to create urban chaos by linking their ideological and leadership abilities with spontaneous mass protest activity. However, students alone among the organized collectivities in the capital city engaged in overt antisystem acts (C6b). Other groups, particularly labor unions and progressive units of the armed forces, had to be brought into the political struggle in order to sustain and channel antiregime predispositions and energies (C2,C6e).[27]

During the intermittent disturbances which plagued Ethiopia from February through September of 1974 students applied the lesson of 1971 and allied themselves with the grievances of teachers, parents, workers, civil servants, Moslems, the unemployed, and peasants experiencing famine conditions in Wollo province. The demonstrations, strikes, and protests which ensued bolstered the impression that the government was incapable of resolving the crises it faced. Much of the energy which formerly had sustained the Haile Selassie I regime was now withdrawn. Thus, student actions precipitated the military's move to arrest the Emperor and terminate the monarchical regime.

Signs of dissatisfaction within the ranks of the military surfaced in early 1974, when mutinies broke out in Neghelli (army) and Debre Zeit (air force) over employment conditions in the armed services and the government's handling of drought relief in Wollo. These revolts coincided with the sudden aggravation of already severe inflationary trends in urban areas by extraordinary price increases for fuel, and with teacher and parental resentment toward the government's plan to reorient the educational system in rural and vocational directions, limit salary increments for teachers, and restrict growth in secondary school and university enrollments.[28]

Students seized the opportunity provided by the mutinies and public unrest; they initiated demonstrations against higher prices and the government's handling of famine conditions in Wollo, and demanded wage increases, free public education, land redistribution, a secular state, and other radical changes.[29] On 18 February, a strike by teachers closed public schools throughout the empire. Taxi drivers went on strike in protest against increased gasoline costs. Violent demonstrations broke out in Addis Ababa. Striking taxi drivers and part of the Addis Ababa lumpenproletariat joined rioting students. As in 1971, the government called upon the military to restore order. The police arrested many demonstrating students and some were wounded or killed. On this occasion, however, the mobilization of the armed forces was accompanied by mutinies within the lower ranks of the army's second and third divisions (Asmara and Harar), the navy (Massawa), and the air force (Debre Zeit). Finally, rebellion spread to the fourth army division stationed in Addis Ababa.

The government reduced gasoline prices, imposed price controls on all essential goods, and announced a pay increase for privates. These actions were not sufficient to mollify the dissident soldiers, who demanded larger pay increases, the dismissal of the Cabinet of Prime Minister Aklilu Habte Wolde (because of its failure to deal effectively with the problems of drought and inflation), and social and political reforms. On 28 February, the Cabinet resigned and Haile Selassie appointed a new government, with Endalkachew Makonnen as Prime Minister.

For the next six months, reformist elements within the ranks of the military moved to consolidate their power at the expense of the monarchy. Young, educated officers began to organize dissident troops. Whether by careful design, as a reaction to unfolding events, or on the basis of compromises worked out among moderate and radical elements, the Derg succeeded in substituting military rule for ruling monarchy without resort to violence. This accomplishment was made possible by a series of piecemeal strokes that have been likened to the slicing of a salami. Foreign observers were astonished by the large (about 120 members) and anonymous nature of the military body responsible for the gradual takeover, and by the appreciation of local political conditions and skill in execution exhibited by leaders of the Derg (C6c).

After the fall of the Cabinet headed by Aklilu Habte Wolde, dissident military men recognized their potential power and the relative weakness of traditional forces. The Derg secured one concession after another from the Emperor (A4). First, the Emperor was forced to order the institution of constitutional revisions designed to make the Prime Minister and the Cabinet responsible to Parliament, and to appoint a constitutional revision commission. In an interview, he implied willingness to accept the recommendations of the commission even if they involved changing the Ethiopian system of government from a ruling to a constitutional monarchy.[30] Another commission was established to uncover corruption and the misuse of public money. Many of the most powerful figures in the previous government, in Parliament, and among the landed aristocracy were arrested (C6d). For two months, Haile Selassie reigned as a constitutional monarch while the Derg ordered Parliament called into special session and played a major role in Cabinet decisions. Then, the chief of the secret police, the Ministers of Foreign Affairs and Defense, the Commander of the Imperial Bodyguard, the Chief Justice, and the Emperor's closest advisors were detained. The Endalkachew Makonnen Cabinet was forced to resign. Finally, the Derg suspended Parliament and the Constitution, dissolved the Crown Council and the Imperial Court, disbanded the Emperor's personal military staff, nationalized his palace, and arrested Haile Selassie. The Crown Prince was declared to be the symbolic King of Ethiopia, and the armed forces formally assumed power.

In preparation for its final series of political maneuvers, the Derg, with its thorough knowledge of Ethiopian society, wisely "cultivated" the blessing of the Ethiopian Orthodox Church,[31] and widely publicized charges that Emperor Haile Selassie had illegally enriched himself at public expense and had refused to return to the Ethiopian people vast sums of money he had stashed away in foreign banks (C6c). In addition, the worker strikes, civil servant work stoppages, and unbending dedication of students to fomenting urban unrest which took place concurrently with military pressure during this period prompted the resignation of the Endalkachew Cabinet and the arrest of the Emperor (C6).[32]

Consequences: Urban Implications of Regime Change

The removal of the the upper nobility (including its reform-oriented element, which assumed power briefly under the Endalkachew Makonnen Cabinet[33]) from positions of political power and social influence constituted a dramatic political change. The arrest and subsequent death of Haile Selassie, the detainment and mass execution of landed aristocrats, and the ascent to authority of junior military personnel drastically narrowed the role of landed wealth, status, and patron-client relations in Ethiopian politics (C4).[34]

The refusal of those appointed by the Emperor to positions of power at the center to commit the Haile Selassie government to radical changes had constituted a major obstacle to social and economic progress in Ethiopia. They exercised power to facilitate the maintenance of dominant values and norms. The decimation of the most influential nobility and the upper ranks of the military establishment, coupled with the radical policy pronouncements of the coup instigators, raised the fears of the wealthy and the expectations of poorer Ethiopians that this pervasive obstacle to fundamental social and economic transformation had been removed (C5).[35]

The Derg included noncommissioned officers and enlisted men who had been recruited principally from the southern peasantry, as well as radical junior officers with ties to the intelligentsia who were committed to values of social justice which transcended their own materially privileged social position.[36] A central objective set forth by the Provisional Military Administration Council (PMAC) is a direct leap into a specifically Ethiopian socialism that minimizes private capital formation and disparities in the distribution of wealth, and averts violent class conflict (D2). Toward this end, the PMAC swiftly embarked on a course of political action designed to bring about revolution from above—that is, societal transformation facilitated and shaped by central institutions (E3).[37]

The PMAC attacked the most basic sources of disparities in urban wealth by introducing property-redistributing and income-leveling reforms at an almost unprecedented rate.[38] Shortly after the 1974 coup d'etat, the Derg imposed price and rent controls, nationalized the vast urban property holdings of the royal family and the Haile Selassie I Foundation, and nationalized or assumed majority shareholder status in more than one hundred large manufacturing and commercial firms.[39] Persons earning monthly salaries above E $250 (U.S. $125) were subjected to a special income surtax to help fund activities of the Relief and Rehabilitation Commission in the wake of the famine that affected several of Ethiopia's fourteen provinces.[40] In the face of a government threat to confiscate the property of tax defaulters, wealthy residents of Addis Ababa rushed to pay long-ignored municipal land and building taxes (C4).[41] In 1975, the PMAC instituted user fees for the operation of television sets, revised bank credit and mortgage policies in favor of low-income residents, slashed house rents below three hundred Ethiopian dollars in a graduated manner,[42] imposed and lowered salary ceilings, and denied annual salary increments at higher levels of public and private employment.

Publication of Proclamation No. 47, the "Proclamation Providing for Government Ownership of Urban Land and Extra Urban Houses," in July 1975 led to dramatic changes in urban property distribution. Article 3 nationalized all urban land without prviding compensation to former owners. In place of private ownership, a family may be granted "possessory rights" over a maximum of five hundred square meters of urban land. Tenants are freed from all land rents, debts, and other obligations to former landlords, and are authorized to claim possessory rights over up to five hundred square meters of the land they occupied on the date of the proclamation. Furthermore, the Ministry of Urban Development and Housing (MUDH) is charged with allocating nationalized land to landless urban dwellers (Article 36). All holders of urban land use rights must pay rent to the government.[43]

Proclamation No. 47 also limits a family or an individual to ownership of *one* urban dwelling house in only one city or town (Article 11). All additional or "extra" urban houses belonging to an individual or family on the date of the proclamation, as well as all multi- family dwellings, have been transferred to government ownership. House rents are now deposited with public bodies rather than paid to private individuals (Article 20). The nationalization of rented urban dwellings substantially reduces the flow of capital into the hands of propertied urban elites.

Finally, rural land nationalization constituted an integral component of the PMAC's comprehensive attack on the roots of urban income inequality in Ethiopia. Opportunities for absentee landlordism, which traditional elites thoroughly exploited under the monarchy, are precluded by provisions of Article 4 of the 1975 "Proclamation to Provide for the **Public Ownership of Rural Lands."**[44]

In contrast to the series of major radical economic measures intoduced in 1974 and 1975, the PMAC approached change in political structure more cautiously (B2). Structural remnants of monarchial rule were dismantled, Parliament was dismissed, municipal councils were suspended, and persons long- entrenched in high-level government posts were forced out of office. Although the PMAC created some new political institutions, including the *zemetcha* (student 'development through cooperation' campaign), peasant associations, and urban cooperatives, it has consistently refused to authorize the creation of a mass-based political party organization. The absence of a civilian goal-directing and support-generating political institution seriously weakened the authority and capacity of the new government. Antisystem protests have been sustained by the same urban groups that opposed Haile Selassie's monarchical regime.

Normative divisions over the right to demonstrate, military versus civilian rule, and the creation of a political party emerged immediately following Haile Selassie's arrest, and remain potent. Within days of the arrest of the Emperor, student elation over his ouster was overwhelmed by disappointment at the prospect of continued military rule. Divisions deepened when students and workers were arrested and fired upon during public demonstrations in September and October 1974.[45] Student protest demonstrations and worker strikes and unrest over political issues resumed on a wider scale in August and September of 1975.[46] The PMAC reacted by declaring a state of emergency in Addis Ababa. The decree suspended all civil rights and granted the army and police full power to maintain order in the capital city. With no need to secure warrants, the government moved quickly to detain labor leaders and workers.[47]

The frequency of violent confrontations between the military regime and the civilian left increased in both 1976 and 1977, revealing that deep divisions over political norms persist in urban Ethiopia (E1). One faction of radical intellectuals has consistently opposed military rule and categorically rejected the notion that military dictatorship imposed from the top is a necessary or even a possible transition stage to a socialist order. This group takes the position that socialism can only be achieved through a civilian "provisional people's government"; that is, through the broad political alliance of all "democratic forces" —workers and peasants, students, progressive merchants and soldiers, city beggars, and others.[48] In contrast, the PMAC contends that the creation of political parties and a move toward a representative political process at this juncture in Ethiopia's history would only serve the corporate interests of inherently antisocialist groups (including capitalists, feudalists, the bureaucratic bourgeoisie, and urban intellectuals), and thus would retard change. Therefore,the ruling council asserts, the transformation of rural and urban economic and social relations and the education of the masses under

Ethiopia: An Urban Perspective

revolutionary guidance by the military must *precede* the introduction of civilian political parties and transfer of power to a national assembly.

In early 1976, radical opponents of military rule went underground to build a clandestine organization, the Ethiopian People's Revolutionary Party (EPRP), devoted to unleashing a mass attack on the Derg. On 20 April 1976, the PMAC issued a "Programme for the National Democratic Revolution" which envisioned the conversion of the Ethiopian state into a people's democratic republic under the leadership of the proletariat and promised (without mentioning a specific timetable) the formation of a working class party. At the same time, the Derg created a civilian Provisional Office for Mass Organization Affairs (POMOA) for the purposes of assisting the masses in organizing themselves and forming a united people's revolutionary front. POMOA officials became a prime target for assassination by EPRP supporters and "the attempt to construct a political front for the military dictatorship failed."[49]

In the fall of 1976, the EPRP instigated a wave of labor strikes and launched a series of violent acts directed against government and urban association officials in Addis Ababa and other cities. Assassinations and the sabotage of government facilities became routine throughout the latter part of 1976 and 1977.[50] On 19 October 1977, the PMAC admitted that "urban terrorism...has reached a stage where concerted action to maintain peace and security for citizens is needed. Normal schooling is being disrupted, and factories are being sabotaged, as are numerous pursuits essential to the smooth functioning of our society."[51] In retaliation, the Derg and its supporters—principally urban dwellers' association officials—engaged in the summary execution of suspected EPRP members and the indiscriminate killing of young people.[52] EPRP activists suffered heavy casualties, and the frequency and scale of urban terriorism diminished substantially shortly after the conclusion of the war between Ethiopia and Somalia.

In the long run, the serious normative cleavages and violent intergroup hostilities which have characterized relations among leftist urban collectivities in the postcoup period undermine and threaten to set back irrevocably the vitally important efforts which must be made in Ethiopia to secure acceptance by urban dwellers of policies designed to benefit the rural masses[53] and support from workers and educated urban dwellers for mobilizing human energy needed to facilitate urban development schemes (A2d). Successful execution of the radical rural and urban policies of the PMAC requires a long-term commitment on the part of progressive urban groups, especially students, who must act in vital bridge elite roles (C6b). The central government's desire to promote change also focuses attention on institutions responsible for planning and executing policies in local communities. The mobilization of voluntary human energy takes on added importance in urban environs as deprived of material resources as those in Ethiopia (C2,C6e). Economic growth can be accelerated when communities participate in labor-intensive development projects supported by institutions that provide material and technical assistance.[54] But significant decision making authority must be delegated to the local level in order to secure a high rate of voluntary participation in collective action schemes. Finally, from the perspective of the citizen, increased self-determination offers valuable flexibility to develop unique and innovative responses to local problems (A3). The PMAC's decision to deploy scarce weapons and armed forces against separatist guerrillas in Eritrea, rebellious propertied elites, and students and workers engaged in urban protests has severely constrained the regime's capacity to motivate people to assume urban development roles.

The regime of Emperor Haile Selassie I had successfully resisted reforms designed to increase popular participation in local government and the authority of municipal councils. The monarchical regime discouraged widespread involvement in local political activity out of fear that participants might demand social and political changes. In contrast, the PMAC quickly initiated collective local associations, assigned important functions to the new bodies, and encouraged mass participation in their activities (C2).

Proclamation No. 47 of 1975 called for the formation of cooperative associations by local residents in urban Ethiopia. Each urban cooperative encompasses a neighborhood (kebele) of three hundred to five hundred contiguous households delineated by the Ministry of Urban Development and Housing. Although the principal initial function of the urban cooperative is to register, maintain, and collect payments for nationalized dwellings that rent for one hundred Ethiopian dollars or less, the new associations also are granted authority to adjudicate disputes over land and houses; to protect lives and property within their localities; and to set up schools, clinics, markets, roads, houses, and similar facilities in cooperation with the government. Indeed, cooperatives have been made broadly responsible for "improvement of the quality of life of urban dwellers in the area."[55] The PMAC virtually eliminated the need to elicit welfare contributions from or impose dues on association members by granting each new urban coooperative access to the substantial revenue it collects from local low-rent housing units (Article 20).[56]

Kebele associations are led by a policy committee of no less than fifteen elected members. All *kebele* associations located within an area defined by MUDH guidelines must form a higher urban dwellers' association. The policy committee of every *kebele* in the area elects one or more of its members to the executive council of the higher association, a group consisting of at least twenty-six members. Article 25 of Proclamation No. 47 made higher urban dwellers' associations responsible for coordinating the activities of lower-level cooperatives and assisting the MUDH in altering *kebele* boundaries so that cooperatives within their jurisdictions possess relatively equal land and housing holdings.

Proclamation No. 104 of 1976, the "Urban Dwellers' Associations Consolidation and Municipalities Proclamation," greatly expanded the powers and duties of higher urban dwellers' associations. Article 17 grants them broad authority "to coordinate" public safety, rent collection, and house-maintenance activities at the *kebele* level. Higher associates are also given responsibility for operating and coordinating social service programs; for establishing and supervising storage places for lost property and stray animals; for designating and supervising livestock market centers; for studying and forming cooperative societies and "people's shops"; and for assisting landless individuals, families, or organizations with applications for urban land upon which dwelling or business units will be erected. Each higher association is charged with studying and implementing ways of improving community service delivery "by coordinating the financial and manpower resources of the *kebele* associations within its boundary."

In the most populous cities, where more than one higher urban cooperative exists, such associations must jointly form a central urban dwellers' association. Each higher association elects at least two of its executive council members to serve on the congress of the central association. In chartered urban areas, all concerned ministries and government offices must send one delegate as a member of the congress. Government representatives are allowed to participate in the meetings of the congress, but cannot vote or hold any office in the central association. In nonchartered urban centers, representatives of the ministries of Urban Development and Housing and Interior participate as voting members of the congress; delegates from other ministries and government offices participate in the congress "when necessary."

Proclamation No. 104, Article 19, states that the central urban dwellers' association shall "take over the administration of the urban center." Toward this end, Article 23 confers on central associations duties and powers formerly granted to municipal governments. Section 11 states that central associations are "to perform the duties expected of municipalities," and are to assume "all powers and duties" granted to municipalities by prior laws and regulations. Specifically, central urban dwellers' associations are charged and empowered to: 1) lay out, close, and maintain main streets, squares, bridges, resorts, parks, and public gardens; 2) insure that sewerage systems and houses are built properly and according to plan; 3) organize and prepare for public use water and electric supplies, large market places, cemeteries, abattoirs, drainages, public baths, theatres, and public halls; 4) provide, in cooperation with the concerned government offices, adequate transport services throughout the urban center; 5) organize and supervise fire brigades, ambulance services, and garbage trucks; 6)take the necessary measures to ensure public health and hygiene in urban centres; and 7)operate and coordinate social service programs in collaboration with the concerned government offices and agencies. Finally, central associations are granted broad authority to coordinate development projects operated by higher authorities.

Proclamation No. 104 deals with the issue of resource allocation among urban associations at different levels through provisions that require revenue contributions from lower to higher associations and grants-in-aid from higher to lower associations. Article 9 (18) mandates that each *kebele* association contribute to the higher association at least 15 percent of the locally-derived revenues from rents and other sources it retains after paying living allowances to persons entitled to them. The higher association sets the exact amount of a *kebele* associations's contribution, taking into consideration the amount of rent it collects. Higher associations are required by Article 17 (11) to transfer one-third of the funds acquired in this manner to the central urban dwellers' association. On its part, the central association is authorized by Article 23 (14) to grant "the necessary financial support" out of municipality revenues to development projects operated by higher and *kebele* associations. Higher assocations are enjoined (Article 17 [a]) to subsidize the activities of *kebele* associations. In addition, central associations (in consultation with the Ministry of Urban Development and Housing) are charged with seeing that higher associations have "equal holdings," and higher and central associations are jointly required to ensure that *kebele* associations within the boundary of each higher association possess "as far as possible equal holdings and adequate income" (Articles 23 [12] and 17 [1]).

Proclamation No. 104 grants chartered urban centers a significant measure of local control over municipal administration. The proclamation designates the central urban dwellers' association as the principal locus of this control. New powers are to be exercised at the central association level by the congress elected from higher associations, which will sit for a maximum of four regular meetings per annum; by a full-time, salaried standing committee elected by the congress; and by a full-time, salaried mayor or head of the urban center. The mayor serves as chairman of the congress. The standing committee of the central association implements the powers possessed by the congress when the larger body is not in session.

Article 22 grants the congress of a central urban dwellers' association authority to recommend land rent charges and other local taxes and fees, and to submit a list of three nominees from among its members for appointment as mayor of the urban center. The PMAC makes the final determination regarding urban land rents, taxes, and fees; appoints the mayor from among the three nominees put forth by the congress; and may dismiss him. The congress possesses explicit authority to dismiss all other "higher officials" in the municipal administration, and to define their job descriptions. The congress is also vested with the implicit authority (Article 22 [3b]) to approve or reject the mayor's nominees for appointment to higher municipal offices. The congress is required to prescribe conditions of employment, dismissal, and promotion of municipal employees in laws and regulations issued in consultation with the PMAC. To implement these and other legislative responsibilities, the congress is granted authority to issue and amend laws pertaining to administration of the urban center, maintenance of municipal property, and local security and public health. In addition, the congress must approve the budget of the municipality and supervise its implementation, appoint auditors, and approve or reject their reports.

Article 22 (3) is labelled the "administrative section." The article grants the mayor little formal authority over municipal affairs. It provides that the mayor runs the administration of the urban center as its head, but remains responsible to the congress and the standing committee. Thus, the mayor must secure congress approval of persons nominated for appointment as higher municipal officials. The mayor is authorized to hire and dismiss all other employees on his own, however.

By 1976, urban dwellers' associations had been organized and had commenced functioning in most, if not all, urban centers. In Addis Ababa, association members had pursued the process outlined in Proclamation No. 104 through the election of a new mayor in 1977.

By first assigning critical urban development functions to newly-formed urban dwellers' associations under Proclamations 47 and 104, and then reallocating urban revenues and technical staff, the PMAC moved to circumvent and directly challenge the authority previously exercised by established associations and structures of urban government.[57] The creation of urban cooperatives introduced an institutional vehicle of change untainted by revelations or perceptions of past indiscretions, nonresponsiveness, and ineptitude. Under the monarchical regime, superior wealth and status indirectly conferred considerable political advantage on urban elites. It is well known, for instance, that absentee landlords possess ample time for political organization, interest articulation, and filling other leadership roles. Members of traditional associations elected men to leadership posts out of deference to their status in official circles, their wealth, and their local prestige.[58] A significant proportion of the leaders selected were urban landlords. In a survey of the presidents of traditional neighborhood funeral and burial associations (*edir*) in Addis Ababa conducted by the author in 1972, 37 percent of the respondents admitted to renting urban land, dwellings, or shops to others.

Traditional urban elites were quite influential during the late 1960s and early 1970s. During this period, municipal and central government officials endeavored to mobilize participation in development projects through voluntary associations, particularly *edir*. Older, conservative men dominated urban *edir*. In most *sefer*, educated persons and high-level government officials did not join *edir* associations. A great deal of rhetoric emanated from government offices concerning the importance of *edir* as vehicles for local development.[59] As a result of government initiative, one could find *edir* coordinating committees in most major Ethiopian towns by 1973. Yet, the overall record of the associations' performance in community self-help activities was unimpressive.[60] Many projects never reached fruition. Coordinating committees evidenced a preference for undertaking local activities that served the interests of more wealthy members and officers, particularly the organization of local security forces to aid police in maintaining law and order,[61] and the construction of roads to enable residents who owned automobiles to drive directly to the doors of their homes. Furthermore, allegations of corruption in the use of *edir* funds were widespread. A common accusation was that *edir* leaders loaned development funds to local merchants at high rates of interest.[62]

The military regime reacted to this situation by adopting policies designed to undermine the authority of traditional association leaders. Proclamation No. 47 of 1975 is silent concerning an urban development role for coordinating committees of *edir* associations. In addition, many traditional association officers were denied the right to vote for cooperative officials and to assume leadership positions in the new organization until October of 1977 by virtue of their former status as urban landlords (Article 23). In implementing Proclamation 47, the Ministry of Urban Development and Housing took steps to reduce the likelihood that leaders of traditional associations would exercise authority from behind the scenes: for example they drew *kebele* lines that divided the membership of traditional associations. Some students and officials who helped organize cooperatives actively promoted the candidacies of poor residents during the 1975 elections for office in the capital city. While wealth and status criteria usually prevailed in the selection of traditional urban association leaders, the PMAC sought to recruit new urban bridge elites on the basis of their ability to articulate and integrate locality needs and regime goals (C6c).

A number of potential advantages can be found in the PMAC's strategy of selectively mobilizing new bridge elites who are receptive to regime values and norms, rather than struggling to work through leaders of traditional urban associations who are corrupt, deficient in ability to prosecute development tasks successfully, and likely to resist socialist policies in order to protect their own vested interests. The PMAC's policy of controlled collectivity mobilization is intended to insure that urban cooperatives are led by individuals not elected out of deference to traditional office or status, who exhibit greater awareness of and concern for community needs, and who are grateful to the new government for the recruitment opportunities opened up as a result of official efforts to revamp the local power structure.

Serious risks also accompany the PMAC's policy of denying traditional urban associations and their leaders a meaningful role in urban development activities. For instance, the leaders of newly- established urban dwellers' associations are likely to encounter difficulty securing the sanction of traditional authority for their undertakings as a result of the PMAC's attempt to circumvent established urban structures (D1).[63] Moreover, proclamations 47 and 104 thrust immense administrative, technical, and decision making burdens onto an unfamiliar and untested system of urban cooperatives. Most urban dwellers' association leaders lack sufficient training to direct the administrative and technical staff of the municipal bureaucracy. In April of 1976, an editorial in the *Ethiopian Herald* charged some urban dwellers' association officials with failing to perform their duties, and admitted that urban residents in some Addis Ababa localities desired "new elections to change their office bearers." In all likelihood, overburdened cooperatives have concentrated on tasks involving house registration, rent collection, and maintenance, and have largely ignored the more complex and technical service functions that their members are ill-equipped to perform or supervise.[64]

While the PMAC initially appeared to recognize the opportunities which decentralization of authority to newly-created local institutions provided for controlling and facilitating urban development, by 1977 it had effectively diverted urban dwellers' associations away from service provision functions and had co-opted cooperative leaders into concentrating their energies and resources on law and order roles (D2). The Derg increasingly relied on urban dwellers' associations as one of the few institutions it could count on for political support in its efforts to suppress urban opposition to military rule. The military rulers pushed urban dwellers' associations into forming "defense squads," issuing mandatory identity cards, conducting house by house searches for "subversive literature," and arresting suspected opponents of the military regime.[65]

The Derg issued arms to *kebele* defense squads and empowered them "to administer instant 'revolutionary justice' whenever they uncovered evidence of 'counter-revolutionary activity.'"[66] In addition, the PMAC moved to establish revolution and development committees (RDCs) in Addis Ababa at the higher and central association levels to assist in mobilizing military manpower for the regime's campaigns in the Ogaden and Eritrea, and in preserving internal security. The principal charge given to the RDCs, which oversee urban dwellers' association activities, is to "crush anti-revolutionary and anti-unity forces."[67] To achieve this objective, revolution and development committees are empowered to engage in a wide variety of organizational and fund-raising tasks.

Most fundamentally, the PMAC has not demonstrated commitment to a developmental approach built upon the premise that the membership of urban cooperatives must be centrally involved in interest- articulating and policy making activities. The Ministry of Urban Development and Housing retains absolute control over preparation of comprehensive urban development plans and issuance of land use directives under Proclamation No. 47. No provision is made for local input in the setting of community development objectives. This ommission lends support to an interpretation which holds that the PMAC intends to promote centrally devised urban projects rather than respond to the local demands advanced by urban dwellers. Proclamation No. 47 further authorizes the MUDH to oversee expenditure of rents collected by urban cooperatives to ensure that funds are only utilized to provide services consistent with the "comprehensive urban development plans and directives issued by the government."[68] MUDH officials insist on reviewing each expenditure plan submitted by an urban cooperative in order to enforce conformity with specific technical and procedural guidelines. Such requirements allow expert staff in the MUDH to perform important policy determining roles during the preparation of a cooperative association's funding proposals.[69] Finally, Article 24 of Proclamation No. 47 provides that the internal regulations of urban cooperatives must be approved by the Minister of Urban Development and Housing.[70]

In sum, the PMAC created a new institutional vehicle at the local level with access to recurrent revenues from house rents. The new regime drastically curtailed the authority of established propertied elites through restrictions on political participation and radical income-leveling measures. The central government exercises strict control over vital decisions affecting community goals and over the allocation of locally-generated revenues, however, and the Derg has co-opted urban organizations into the performance of pressing law and order and military functions. At the same time, the PMAC has been reluctant to establish a mass-based political party and to decentralize governmental authority. Continued uncertainty and delay over these issues undermine the center's capacity to channel local conflict and community energies into productive endeavors, and to reduce or divert incipient hostility toward the government (C3b,C6e).

The mass-based political party offers an institutional vehicle with potential to forge a new alliance of urban and rural interests (intelligentsia, workers, lumpenproletariat, peasants); mobilize diffuse (ideological) support for social and economic changes; provide specific material benefits to members; and generate local enthusiasm for collective involvement in self-help projects (C6d,e). Failure to share policy making authority with local collectivities or their representatives thus jeopardizes a promising opportunity to secure voluntary participation by large numbers of poor urban (and rural) dwellers in self-help projects. Urban cooperatives could still become a focal point of opposition to the new

Ethiopia: An Urban Perspective

regime in the absence of political party structures capable of resolving normative conflicts at the local level. Opposition is most probable where circumstances reinforce a widely-shared preconception that the new rulers are not responsive to local concerns and are incapable of preventing serious deterioration in urban living conditions (E1).

Future Prospects

The PMAC has given ambiguous indications regarding how it intends to resolve the local self-determination dilemma in urban areas. Some central policy makers realize that constructing a highly centralized political-administrative system could impede progress in Ethiopia.[71] A highly centralized state is poorly designed for the crucial function of mobilizing local support and voluntary devotion of energy to collective activities. Nevertheless, substantial resistance to decentralization persists among high-level military and civilian officials, largely out of fear that the outcome would be increased urban conflict, opposition to the government, and support for separatist movements.[72] Meaningful local self-determination also involves risks that values and norms not shaped at the center will be articulated and pursued, and that programs antithetical to national government policies (e.g., the promotion of urban rather than rural interests) will be adopted, especially if these values and programs are more familiar to local people than those advocated by the government (D1).

There is no way out of the dilemma for the PMAC until it is willing to share policy making authority with popular local authorities. Since power is a nonzero sum political resource, centralization of the local government administrative structure and certain powers could be accomplished concomitantly with devolution of authority to urban cooperatives and/or party organs and expansion of power at the local level. The shared-powers approach seeks increases in central government control *and* local facilitation. The creation of additional roles and responsibilities at the local level can facilitate the mobilization of energy needed to attain collective goals, while central authorities work through local leaders to ensure that regime values and norms are accurately conveyed, and are interpreted in a fashion that is comprehensible and appealing to diverse urban groups (C5,C6,D1).

Ultimately, however, the capacity of the military regime to give impetus and definition to urban change is severely constrained in the absence of an institutional base of mass support (C2,C6d,e,E3). Further local self-determination requires that the center at least share authority for setting local objectives and allocating local resources with the leaders of cooperative associations. Centrally imposed prohibitions against the election of propertied elites to leadership positions and radical urban income-leveling measures have decreased the likelihood that urban cooperatives will come under the influence or control of wealthy elites (C5b). While this knowledge is reassuring, it does not *guarantee* that leaders and participants in cooperatives will hold a particular set of values and norms related to political integration, economic allocation, and collective action. In short, the military regime cannot eliminate the immediate political risks that invariably accompany increased local self-determination. Yet, the refusal to permit self-determination has forced the PMAC to rely increasingly since 1976 on violence as a substitute for popular support,[73] making it extremely unlikely that the current regime, led by Mengistu Haile Mariam, will succeed in improving urban living conditions in the face of the protracted political opposition that rigid centralization and dictatorial rule have and will continue to engender in Ethiopia (E4).

Footnotes

1. See John Markakis, "Social Transformation in Ethiopia; Prelude to Revolution," paper presented at the 20th Annual Meeting of the African Studies Association, Houston, November 1977, pp. 18-19. The stated objective of the PMAC is "to liberate Ethiopia from the yokes of feudalism and imperialism and to lay the foundations for the transition to socialism." Ethiopia, PMAC, *Programme of the National Democratic Revolution of Ethiopia* (n.p. April 1976), pp. 4-5.

2. See Mark Kesselman, "Research Perspectives in Comparative Local Politics: Pitfalls and Prospects," *Comparative Urban Research* 1 (Spring 1972): 15, 23 on the importance of investigating these relationships and the lack of attention they have received from students of local government and comparative politics.

3. Elsewhere, I have analyzed urban change from a broader, societal perspective. See Peter Koehn, "The Municipality of Addis Ababa, Ethiopia; Performance, Mobilization, Integration, and Change" (Ph.D. dissertation, University of Colorado, 1973).

4. This is recognized by Samuel Huntington and Frantz Fanon. See Samuel P. Huntington, *Political Order in Changing Societies* (New Haven: Yale University Press, 1968), pp. 290, 292; and Frantz Fanon, *The Wretched of the Earth* (New York: Grove Press, 1963), pp. 121, 126. However, both Huntington (pp. 291-93) and Fanon (pp. 126-27) view peasants as holding a key to success in revolutionary situations.

5. For these reasons, the roots of contemporary Ethiopian political organization and culture are not strictly or even primarily rural as Frederick Gamst attempts to argue. Frederick C. Gamst, "Peasantries and Elites Without Urbanism: The Civilization of Ethiopia," *Comparative Studies in Society and History* 12 (October 1970): 386, 392.

6. John Markakis, *Ethiopia: Anatomy of a Traditional Polity* (London: Clarendon Press, 1974), pp. 88-89, 101-2.

7. See Peter Koehn, "Ethiopia: Famine, Food Production, and Changes in the Legal Order," *African Studies Review* (forthcoming). Donald Crummey points out that "it was not the starving who revolted..." Instead, "the famine primarily played the political role of unmasking the benign pretensions of imperial government." Donald Crummey, "History and Revolution in Ethiopia," paper presented at the Canadian Association of African Studies Annual Conference, Vancouver, 1976, p. 17; also see Johan Holmberg, "Pricing Strategies for Agricultural Produce in a Changing Society; Rural/Urban Contradictions in Ethiopia," paper presented at the 19th Annual Meeting of the African Studies Association, Boston, November 1976, p. 16. Urban-based students effectively seized upon the issue of the government's failure to ameliorate famine conditions

in the north to generate broader dissatisfaction with the monarchical regime. See "HSIU Students Call for State of Emergency," *Ethiopian Herald*, 4 April 1974.

8. See John M. Cohen and Seleshi Sisaye, "Research Problems in Describing and Explaining Ethiopia's Socioeconomic Development: Past Failures and Future Issues in Rural-Urban Studies," paper presented at the 19th Annual Meeting of the African Studies Association, Boston, November 1976, pp. 1-2.

9. The role of urban conditions and actors is emphasized in Peter Koehn, "Forecast for Political Change in Ethiopia: An Urban Perspective," paper presented at the 16th Annual Meeting of the African Studies Association, Syracuse, November 1973; Peter Koehn and Louis D. Hayes, "Student Politics in Traditional Monarchies: A Comparative Analysis of Ethiopa and Nepal," *Journal of Asian and African Studies* 13 (January-April 1978): 33-49; and Donald N. Levine, "The Military in Ethiopian Politics," in *The Military Intervenes: Case Studies in Political Development,* ed. Henry Bienen (New York: Russell Sage Foundation, 1968), pp. 21-25. Most rural analysts overlooked these cues because they failed to link periphery studies with urban political trends. Rural land ownership patterns are emphasized in John M. Cohen, "Traditional Politics and the Military Coup in Ethiopia," *African Affairs* 74 (April 1975): 222. For a critique of oversimplified class analysis see Peter Koehn, "Selassie's Ethiopia: The Way It Was," *Africa Today* 23 (April-June 1976): 62. By permitting limited social mobility, the Amhara *rist* system divided and misled the northern peasantry. Allan Hoben shows that the *rist* system "helped commit the peasants to the political order, with its blatant inequalities of power and prestige, by holding forth the possibility [however unrealistic] that they or their children may attain office, honor, and an abundance of their hereditary *rist* land." Allan Hoben, *Land Tenure Among the Amhara of Ethiopia: The Dynamics of Cognatic Descent* (Chicago: University of Chicago Press, 1973), p. 245.

10. The responsibilities assigned to municipalities are set forth in Article 9, Part 74 of the *Administrative Regulations Decree of 1942,* "Decree No. 1," *Negarit Gazeta,* 1st year, No. 6, 27 March 1942, pp. 51-52; and in the *Municipalities Proclamation of 1945,* "Proclamation No. 74," *Negarit Gazeta,* 4th year, No. 7, 30 March 1945, pp. 39-40. The performances of the Addis Ababa Municipality and central government agencies operating programs in the capital city are discussed in Koehn, "The Municipality of Addis Ababa," pp. 127-57.

11. See the detailed analysis of urban living conditions in Ethiopia found in Peter Koehn, "Urban Origins and Consequences of National and Local Political Transformation in Ethiopia," in *The City in Comparative Perspective: Cross-National Research and New Directions in Theory,* ed. John Walton and Louis H. Masotti (New York: John Wiley and Sons for Sage Publications, 1976), pp. 155-78; John M. Cohen and Peter H. Koehn, *Ethiopian Provincial and Municipal Government: Imperial Patterns and*

Post Revolutionary Changes (East Lansing, Mich.: Michigan State University, Ethiopian Studies Center, forthcoming).

12. Asmelash Beyene, "Patterns of Authority in the Ethiopian Bureaucracy: A Study of Ethiopian Civil Servants With Respect to Their Orientation Toward Authority" (Ph.D. dissertation, Syracuse University, 1972), pp. 65-66, 68-69, 167-69, 180, 207, 216, 219; Paulos Milkias, "Traditional Institutions and Traditional Elites: The Role of Education in the Ethiopian Body-Politic," *African Studies Review* 19 (December 1976): 89.

13. These points are discussed in Markakis, *Ethiopia*, pp. 331,335.

14. See Koehn, "The Municipality of Addis Ababa," pp. 170-73, 248-51, 264; Cohen and Koehn, *Ethiopian Provincial and Municipal Government*.

15. Koehn, "The Municipality of Addis Ababa," pp. 174-79.

16. The unintegrated prefectoral system is fully described in Peter Koehn and John M. Cohen, "Local government in Ethiopia: Independence and Variability in a Deconcentrated System," *Quarterly Journal of Administration* 9 (July 1975): 369-86.

17. Duri Mohammed, "Private Foreign Investment in Ethiopia," *Journal of Ethiopian Studies* 7 (July 1969): 55,56,58.

18. Fully 90 percent of the adult (above nineteen) population of Addis Ababa owned no land in 1961. In 1967, only 30 percent of all occupied private housing units in the capital city were owned by their occupants. See Richard Pankhurst, *State and Land in Ethiopian History*, Monographs in Ethiopian Land Tenure, No. 3 (Addis Ababa: Institute of Ethiopian Studies and the Faculty of Law, Haile Sellassie I University, 1966), p. 154; Addis Ababa Municipality, *Draft Report on Housing in Addis Ababa: Results from the Census of September 1967* (Addis Ababa, March 1972), p. 192.

19. The retail prices of food and drink in Addis Ababa increased by 67.5 percent between 1963 and 1971. See United States Department of Commerce, "Ethiopia," *Foreign Economic Trends and Their Implications for the United States* (ET 72-012, 22 February 1972), p. 6.

20. For this reason, gradual degradation in material conditions cannot be excluded as a causal factor in scholarly considerations of revolutionary phenomena. For a contrasting position see James C. Davies, "Toward a Theory of Revolution," in *Anger, Violence and Politics: Theory and Research*, ed. Ivo Feierabend, Rosalind L. Feierabend, and Ted R. Gurr (Englewood Cliffs, N.J.: Prentice-Hall, 1972), pp. 68-70, 81.

21. On students' political orientations and their relationship to educational policy see Peter Koehn, "Political Socialization and Political Integration: The Impact of the Faculty of Arts, Haile Sellassie I University," paper prepared for the Interdisciplinary Seminar of Faculties of Arts and Education, Haile Sellassie I University, Addis Ababa, June 1972; and Andreas Eshete, "Some Principles of Ethiopian Education," *Challenge* 9 (December 1968): 6-21. On their job prospects see Eli Ginzberg and Herbert A. Smith, *Manpower Strategy for Developing*

Countries: Lessons from Ethiopia (New York: Columbia University Press, 1967), p. 77; and Huntington, *Political Order in Changing Societies*, pp. 186-87. According to Planning Commission estimates released in the early 1970s, roughly two-thirds of all unemployed persons in Ethiopia were under twenty-five years of age. Cited in Tekle Mariam Wolde Michael, "Progress Report on Unemployment and Migration of High School Leavers in Addis Ababa," in *Preliminary Research Progress Report on Urbanization in Addis Ababa,* comp. Asmerom Legesse (Addis Ababa: Haile Sellassie I University, Institute of Development Research, 1974), p. 5.

22. See Huntington, *Political Order in Changing Societies, p. 188.*

23. The monarchy began to be perceived as illegitimate by intellectuals following the suppression of the 1960 coup d'etat attempt. See Christopher Clapham, "The Ethiopian Coup d'Etat of December 1960," *Journal of Modern African Studies* 6 (December 1968): 500, 507.

24. Otto Klineberg and Marisa Zavalloni, *Nationalism and Tribalism Among African Students: A Study of Social Identity* (The Hague: Mouton, 1969), p. 222.

25. Huntington, *Political Order in Changing Societies,* pp. 168-69.

26. A detailed discussion of the spring crisis of 1971 can be found in Koehn and Hayes, "Student Politics in Traditional Monarchies," pp. 40-42.

27. On this point see Giovanni Arrighi and John S. Saul, "Nationalism and Revolution in Sub-Saharan Africa," in Arrighi and Saul, *Essays on the Political Economy of Africa* (New York: Monthly Review Press, 1973), p. 84.

28. See Patrick Gilkes, "Ethiopia—A Real Revolution?," *World Today* 31 (January 1975): 16; *New York Times,* 27 February 1974, pp. 1, 10; Henry Valtos, "Days of Violence Clear Way for an Educational Revolution," *London Times,* 16 November 1974; Thomas R. Knipp, "The Future of Higher Education in Ethiopia: Building on a Broken Foundation," paper presented at the 17th Annual Meeting of the African Studies Association, Chicago, November 1974, pp. 9-10, 12.

29. *Africa Research Bulletin,* Political, Social and Cultural Series 11 (15 April 1974): 3171-72; (15 May 1974): 3203.

30. *New York Times,* 12 March 1974, p. 12.

31. See Milkias, "Traditional Institutions and Elites," p. 89. In September of 1974, the Patriarch of the Orthodox Church failed to mention the Emperor's name for the first time in his New Year's message. Instead, he asked God's blessings for the revolutionary movement led by the armed forces and supported by the people. *New York Times,* 12 September 1974.

32. John Markakis and Nega Ayele, *Class and Revolution in Ethiopia* (London: Spokesman Press, 1978), pp. 93, 97. Students maintained class boycotts and periodic street demonstrations although they won major concessions in terms of their demands for changes in internal *university*

affairs (removal of the president and vice-presidents of Haile Sellassie I University; freedom of speech, assembly, and publication; restoration of the university student council; permission to re-establish the national student union) under the Endalkachew Makonnen and Mikael Imru Haile Selassie Cabinets.

33. See *Africa Research Bulletin,* Economic, Financial and Technical Series 11 (31 July 1974): 3165.

34. See Allan Hoben, "Social Stratification in Traditional Amhara Society," in *Social Stratification in Africa,* ed. Arthur Tuden and Leonard Plotnicov (New York: Free Press, 1970), pp. 209-21. The fact that such fundamental political shifts occurred rapidly and were accompanied by only token opposition is contrary to proposition D5.

35. Eighteen officers holding rank of brigadier general or above were executed on 23 November 1974. See "Ethiopia Shoots 60 Former Chiefs," *New York Times,* 25 November 1974. An early report of radical policy pronouncements is found in "Committee Announces Its Aims and Objectives," *Ethiopian Herald,* 13 September 1974.

36. See Markakis, "Social Transformation," p. 18; Levine, "The Military in Ethiopian Politics," p. 21; Patrick Gilkes, "The Coming Struggle for Ethiopia," *Africa Report* 20 (May-June 1974): 33,43; John M. Cohen, "Ethiopia After Haile Selassie: The Government Land Factor," *African Affairs* 72 (October 1973): 377-78. Prior to the events of 1974, Cohen argued that the new rulers of Ethiopia would not be committed to land reform because they had been tied into the advantages that accompanied extensive government land grants (pp. 382,379). This conclusion overlooked the possibility that value commitments would prevail over land holdings, and failed to consider the prospect that the grievances of lower-level officers might be aggravated by government land grants that were given almost exclusively to upper-level civilian and military elites. On the elite backgrounds possessed by recipients of imperial government land grants, see Michael Stahl, *Ethiopia: Political Contradictions in Agricultural Development* (Stockholm: Ruben and Sjogren, 1974), pp. 64, 67.

37. A full English text of the "Declaration of Economic Policy of Socialist Ethiopia" was published in the *Ethiopian Herald* on 12 February 1975. See Marina Ottaway, "Democracy and New Democracy: The Ideological Debate in the Ethiopian Revolution," paper presented at the 19th Annual Meeting of the African Studies Association, Boston, November 1976. Most scholars who approach the study of African politics from the perspective of class formation analysis are skeptical that social transformation can be achieved by a military regime that proclaims radical policy objectives and acts through central political institutions which it shapes or fashions. They believe that such a regime is inherently conservative because of the class interests of its leaders. See Richard L. Sklar, "Political Science and National Integration—A Radical Approach," *Journal of Modern African Studies* 5 (May 1967): 8; Addis Hiwet, *Ethiopia:*

Peter Koehn

From Autocracy to Revolution, Occasional Publication No. 1 (London: Merlin Press for *Review of African Political Economy*, 1975), pp. 112-15. Facilitation-control analysis is more open to the prospect that radical military leaders can transcend their class interests, and thus can pave the way for the transformation of social and economic conditions through political action, although a number of propositions utilized in this chapter indicate that the institutionalization of change also requires mass participation in collective action.

38. As late as 1966, urban land was not nationalized in the People's Republic of China, and landlords were receiving rent payments from tenants. Edward L. Wheelwright and Bruce McFarlane, *The Chinese Road to Socialism: Economics of the Cultural Revolution* (New York and London: Monthly Review Press, 1970), p. 104. The Tanzanian government began to convert all urban freehold land to government leasehold in 1963, and nationalized all rented buildings valued at five thousand pounds or more in 1971. See Richard Stren, "Urban Policy and Performance in Kenya and Tanzania," *Journal of Modern African Studies* 13 (June 1975): 276-77, 280.

39. *Ethiopian Herald*, 13 September 1974, pp. 1,4; *New York Times*, 2 January 1975, 4 March 1975. The armed forces mutinies in early 1974 also triggered a series of urban strikes that resulted in wage and salary increases in a number of occupations. That these benefits were secured by privileged urbanites at a time of widespread famine and starvation in rural Wollo was the subject of a critical editorial written by Tegagne Yeteshawork in the *Ethiopian Herald* on 19 March 1974.

40. Proclamation No. 36 of 1975, "Relief and Rehabilitation Temporary Surtax on Income Proclamation Amendment Proclamation," *Negarit Gazeta*, 34th Year, No. 29, 30 May 1975.

41. "Warning given to Tax Defaulters," *Ethiopian Herald*, 24 December 1974; "Many Crowd to Pay Tax," *Ethiopian Herald*, 28 November 1974.

42. *Ethiopian Herald*, 4 September 1975, 11 May 1975, 3 August 1975; National Bank of Ethiopia, Economic Research and Planning Division, *Quarterly Bulletin* 1 (June 1975): 30,32,41.

43. The MUDH collects payments for urban housing units that rent for more than one hundred *birr* (fifty U.S. dollars) per month, while urban cooperatives are authorized to receive rent payments from all other nationalized units. For details see John M. Cohen and Peter H. Koehn, "Rural and Urban Land Reform in Ethiopia," *African Law Studies* 14, 1 (1977): 3-62.

44. A helpful analysis of relationships between the early stages of urban economic expansion and absentee landlordism is found in Hans-Dieter Evers, "Urban Expansion and Landownership in Underdeveloped Societies," *Urban Affairs Quarterly* 11 (September 1975): 122-23. Markakis,*Ethiopia*, pp. 168-69, argues that absentee rural landlords in southern Ethiopia generally showed little interest in urban development.

45. *New York Times,* 17 September 1974, 25 Februrary 1975; *London Times,* 24 September 1974; *Africa Research Bulletin,* Political, Social, and Cultural Series 11 (15 November 1974): 3399; *Washington Post,* 21, 22 December 1974; Markakis and Nega Ayele, *Class and Revolution,* pp. 115-17.

46. The PMAC assigned between thirty and fifty thousand university and secondary school students to two years of work in the provinces on political education, literacy, and rural labor projects. In southern provinces, this student work force (called *zemetcha)* played a major role in the organization of peasant cooperatives and the implementation of rural land reforms in the first half of 1975. In many places, students advocated far more radical changes in rural social organization and methods of agricultural production (e.g., collective farming, arming the peasantry) than those promulgated in Proclamation 31. In several cases, violent confrontations occurred in provincial cities and towns between *zemetcha* and local police and/or local government officials. "Ethiopian Students Help Official Rural Program," *New York Times,* 11 April 1976; "Strife in Ethiopia Strains Military Rule," *New York Times,* 3 March 1976; Allan Hoben, "Perspectives on Land Reform in Ethiopia," paper presented at the 18th Annual Meeting of the African Studies Association, San Franscisco, October 1975. In Addis Ababa, roughly fourteen hundred *zemetcha* refused to complete their national work assignments in August 1975 in protest against the government's failure to respond positively to student demands. The PMAC immediately arrested the students, who had been providing assistance in the registration of urban land and houses and in the formation of urban cooperatives. David B. Ottaway, "Protesting Students Detained in Ethiopia," *Washington Post,* 25 August 1975, p. A7. The PMAC's efforts to discredit and suppress zemetcha activities in 1975 and 1976 further angered the students.

47. *Africa Research Bulletin,* Political, Social, and Cultural Series 12 (15 October 1975): 3759-61; "Ethiopia Facing Widespread Rebellion," *New York Times,* 12 October 1975, p. 1. The PMAC lifted the decree declaring a state of emergency in the capital city in December 1975. "Ethiopia Lifts Crisis Decree," *New York Times,* 7 December 1975. At the same time, the government issued a new labor law which required unions to reorganize and conduct new elections of officers, and banned strikes or lockouts in essential service industries. The new law failed to set a minimum daily wage. *Africa Research Bulletin,* Political, Social, and Cultural Series 12 (15 January 1976): 3878; Markakis and Nega Ayele, *Class and Revolution,* pp. 142-45.

48. Marina Ottaway, "Democracy and New Democracy."

49. John Markakis and Nega Ayele, "Class and Revolution in Ethiopia," *Review of African Political Economy* 8 (January-April 1977): 100-101; "Political Parties Due for Ethiopia," *New York Times,* 22 April 1976. The issues of political party formation and transition to civilian rule remain

vaguely defined in the PMAC's policy pronouncements. In a recent interview, Ethiopia's Foreign Minister stated that "there is every reason to believe that in a very short period of time a Marxist-Leninist party will soon be established within Ethiopia." Ian Goddard, "An Interview with Ethiopia's Foreign Minister,"*Horn of Africa* 1 (April-June 1978): 6.

50. Markakis and Nega Ayele, "Class and Revolution," pp. 99-101. On 8 October 1977, David Ottaway reported in the *Washington Post* that "in the past nine months, two hundred officials of the neighborhood dwellers' associations... in Addis Ababa alone have been assassinated by one or another Marxist faction and another two hundred seriously injured, according to city officials." Also see An Observer, "Revolution in Ethiopia," *Monthly Review* 29, 3 (1977): 55.

51. *Africa Research Bulletin,* Political, Social, and Cultural Series 14 (15 November 1977): 4602.

52. The Derg executed between six hundred and two thousand young people in the wake of antigovernment May Day demonstrations in Addis Ababa in 1977. One observer noted in the summer of 1977 that "dozens [of urban dwellers] were executed nightly—some for having leaflets, some by error, some to settle personal grudges. The killing was so rampant and senseless that the military leadership had to execute some local chairmen of neighborhood associations, whose excesses in carrying out personal grudges were particularly heinous." An Observer, "Revolution in Ethiopia," pp. 54-55. Also see *Africa Research Bulletin,* Political, Social, and Cultural Series 14 (15 November 1977): 4602; Markakis and Nega Ayele, *Class and Revolution*, pp. 163-68; and An American Professor, "Letter from Jeddah: An Interview with WSLF," *Horn of Africa* 1 (April-June 1978): 9.

53. See Holmberg, "Pricing Strategies," p. 17.

54. James Grant, "A Development Strategy," in *Food for People, Not For Profit,* ed. Catherine Lerza and Michael Jacobson (New York: Random House, 1975), p. 253.

55. Article 24 of the "Proclamation to Provide for Government Ownership of Urban Land and Extra Urban Houses," Proclamation No. 47 of 1975, *Negarit Gazeta,* 26 July 1975.

56. More than 90 percent of the many units occupied by tenants in Addis Ababa, for instance, rent for less than one hundred Ethiopian dollars. Addis Ababa Municipality, *Draft Report on Housing in Addis Ababa: Results From the Census of September 1967* (Addis Ababa: Municipality, 1972), pp. 192, 209.

57. On the reallocation of revenues and staff, see Cohen and Koehn, *Ethiopian Provincial and Municipal Government.* A case study of the struggle between central and municipal officials for control over urban decision making in the immediate postcoup period can be found in Peter Koehn and Sidney R. Waldron,*Afocha: A Link Between Community and Administration in Harar, Ethiopia?* (Syracuse, N.Y.: Syracuse

Univerisity, Eastern African Studies Center, forthcoming). The PMAC's critical attitude toward established structures generally elicited support from urban residents, many of whom associated municipal governments primarily with corruption, bureaucratic delay and inconvenience, inefficient technical performance, forced land and property expropriation, inattentiveness to the needs of lower-income groups, and resistance to change. Some combination of these reasons underlies the reluctance of most political leaders in Africa to delegate authority to formally constituted units of local government. United Nations, Department of Economic and Social Affairs, *Urban Land Policies and Land-Use Control Measures,* Vol. 1, *Africa* (ST/ECA 1167), 1973, pp. 37, 40.

58. See *Ye Zaritu Ethiopia*, 3 Nehassie 1967 E.C.

59. Fecadu Gedamu, "Urbanization, Polyethnic Group Voluntary Associations and National Integration in Ethiopia," *Ethiopian Journal of Development Research* 1 (April 1974): 75, 78-79.

60. Eftychia Koehn and Peter Koehn, "*Edir* as a Vehicle for Urban Development in Addis Ababa," in *Proceedings of the First United States Conference on Ethiopian Studies, 1973,* ed. Harold Marcus and John Hinnant (East Lansing, Mich.: Michigan State University, African Studies Center, 1975), pp. 422-23.

61. Peter Koehn and Sidney R. Waldron, "Afocha as a Link Between Community and Administration in Harar, Ethiopia," paper presented at the 18th Annual Meeting of the African Studies Association, San Francisco, 1975, pp. 40-41.

62. *Ye Zaritu Ethiopia*, 3 Nehassie 1967 E.C.

63. Officials in the Ministry of Urban Development and Housing expected that traditional associations would disband rather than compete with urban cooperatives (E3a), or at least would revert to an exclusive concern with funeral and burial matters and function under the direction of a "social committee" of the *kebele*. See *Addis Zemen,* 7 Nehassie 1967 E.C. But the Central Coordinating Committee of 735 Addis Ababa edir, with a membership of more than 200,000 city residents, announced its desire to assume major urban self-government and developmental functions on the eve of the publication of Proclamation No. 47 of 1975. See *Addis Ababa Municipality News,* 3 Hamle 1967 E.C. Although some traditional association leaders may have actively resisted the PMAC's efforts to eliminate their urban political roles (D5), they had demonstrated little capacity to perform such functions in the past, and therefore also lacked the sanction of mass legitimacy.

64. See *Ethiopian Herald,* editorial, 2 April 1976. No published studies exist on the leadership composition of urban dwellers' associations, or on the type and scope of the activities they have actually undertaken.

65. Amnesty International reported in December of 1977 that all 294 Addis Ababa *kebele* associations possessed their own jails, and the prisons were full. Cited in Norman J. Singer, "Legal Development in Post-

Revolutionary Ethiopia," *Horn of Africa* 1 (April-June 1978): 25-26.

66. Markakis and Nega Ayele, "Class and Revolution," p. 104.

67. This discussion is based on the partial text of and commentary on an April 1977 proclamation found in the *Ethiopian Herald*, 22 April 1977.

68. Articles 24, 36, and 37 of Proclamation No. 47 of 1975. In contrast, local planning units in Yugoslavia are independent of higher-level bodies. Local plans need not conform in every respect with national plan guidelines. Albert Waterston, *Development Planning: Lessons of Experience* (Baltimore: Johns Hopkins Press, 1965), p. 541.

69. Walsh notes that "when budget approval entails unlimited power to question the advisability of expenditures, it can, in effect, eliminate local discretion altogether." Annmarie H. Walsh, *The Urban Challenge to Government; An International Comparison of Thirteen Cities* (New York: Frederick A. Praeger, 1969), p. 148.

70. The PMAC has reserved wide latitude for central government intervention in urban affairs in numerous other functional areas. See Cohen and Koehn, *Provincial and Municipal Government in Ethiopia*.

71. In any event, the atomized nature of the central government bureaucracy in Ethiopia and the divisions which exist within the military suggest that the PMAC would find it impossible to attain the unified central control needed to operate an effective integrated prefectoral system of local government.

72. On this point see Mark Kesselman and Donald Rosenthal, *Local Power and Comparative Politics*, Sage Professional Papers in Comparative Politics 5, 01-049 (Beverly Hills and London: Sage Publications, 1974), p. 30; and Christopher Clapham, "Centralization and Local Response in Southern Ethiopia," *African Affairs* 74 (January 1975): 81.

73. Markakis and Nega Ayele, "Class and Revolution," pp. 103-8.

4

Green Revolution in Ethiopia: The Politics of Rural Development in a Blocked and Inequitable Society

John M. Cohen

Most Africans live in rural areas. The political dynamics which mark their communities and the complex linkages between them and the capital city are as crucial to the process of national change as are the more visible processes of politics that dominate the struggles for control of the central government. This is particularly the case given the now-recognized importance of agriculture to economic growth and the relationship between rural development and political stability at the center.[1]

The ecological variability of rural Africa; the range of agricultural practices and products; the diversity of land tenure rules, traditional political organizations, and voluntary associations; the complexity of cultural values and norms; the widely differing historical patterns of settlement, conquest, and rule; and numerous other differences make it extremely difficult to generalize about processes of change. Indeed, experience during the last development decade has generated several important yet distressing insights into this situation. Perhaps the most important of these is that no limited set of variables can analyze or explain rural change or the political processes that underlie it. This being the case, the narrow perspectives of some theoretical frameworks are misleading at best.[2]

Few conceptual frameworks allow for the range of analysis required. A significant advantage of the one developed in this book is that it has the scope to help the researcher organize the complexity of a rural social system in ways that facilitate the search for the critical factors that explain the process of change. Moreover, the diverse concepts and propositions encompassed by the framework facilitate the kind of broad-based analysis that is not predisposed to a single factor explanation. In the case study which follows, efforts will be made to illustrate how the control and facilitation framework provided a necessary societal-wide and multi-variable focus on a rural area in Southern Ethiopia, guided the researcher in working out its linkages with the national center that sought to control and direct it, and promoted the description and explanation of the politics of rural development in general, and the study of local elites, land tenure, and local administration in particular.

Organizing the Study of a Rural Area

The research problem underlying the study is based on the question: How can Ethiopia be one of the least developed but potentially richest agrarian nations in Africa?[3] To address this problem, the study focused on the agriculturally rich Chilalo subprovince, or *awraja,* in the south-central Ethiopian highlands.[4] Field research was undertaken between 1971 and 1973 and the analysis which follows describes and analyzes conditions which have been dramatically changed by the events following the 1974 Ethiopian revolution. A postscript on this change concludes the chapter. However, the main body of the case study *will be presented as drafted in mid-1973,* utilizing the prsent tense to refer to conditions existing at that time, in order to illustrate the kind of analysis and predictions generated by the application of the control and facilitation framework to conditions in prerevolutionary Ethiopia without the benefit of hindsight.

Research began with the goal of describing and explaining the fundamental social dimensions of Chilalo and the forces of change operating there over an extended period of time. The initial step of description was taken with no predisposition toward any particular set of behavioral or structural variables. However, the control and facilitation framework was used from the beginning. The framework led to a view of the rural social system of Chilalo as a less self-sufficient component of the larger Ethiopian society. Ethiopia is a society because it attains a higher level of self-sufficiency as a system in relation to its environment than do any of its subsystems or any suprasystem of which it is a part. That is, it has a normative order and a collectivity of organized human beings existing within a given territorial area, and is relatively independent in meeting the essential functional requisites of long-term persistence from its own resources. The social system of Chilalo is less than a society because it does not meet these theoretical requirements. The rural social system of any African state is inseparable from the larger setting of the total society of which it is a part. This situation has been somewhat narrowly characterized in both analytical and spatial terms as the relationship between the center and the periphery,[5] and the concepts of a society and its rural subsystem provide an analytically useful way of conceiving this relationship.

In spite of the intimate relationship between rural and societal change, and the fact that the rural social system constitutes in most cases the largest population segment and the potential reservoir of most of the society's wealth and power, there is a general tendency in the literature of rural change to separate the problems and processes of rural areas from those of the larger societal system. This tendency is due in part to the use of narrower paradigms than the one used here, and in part to the excessive polarization existing between the micro orientations of rural anthropology and rural sociology and the macro orientations of political development and developmental sociology. In particular, there is rarely any linkage between studies of rural anthropology and the larger social system. The anthropological focus in the rural context has been concerned mainly with the primary group as a closed social system which renders the larger societal system irrelevant. On the other hand, studies of nation-building in sociology and political science seldom link downward into what is often the most important segment of the whole society, either ignoring the process of rural change and focusing on the process of central institution-building, or viewing rural transformation processes and problems from the perspective of the national center.

When applied to the analysis of rural change, the framework developed in this book stimulates concentration on such critical issues as whether the center is committed to or careless of rural development; whether the center has the power or economic facility to implement its programs; whether the rural sector is mobilized, dispersed, participant, or withdrawn from the rural development process; and the degree to which the rural society is oriented toward the central development programs and social goals.[6]

Beyond these considerations, the ordering of data is facilitated by the framework's conception of any society or social system as divided into four subsystems performing requisite functions. As noted in the opening chapter, these are pattern socialization and control, integration, goal attainment, and adaptation. Using more familiar but essentially similar terms, these functional subsystems are the cultural system, community organization, political administration and politics, and economy of rural Chilalo. At the higher level, Ethiopian society is divided into its cultural, societal, political, and economic subsystems. Moreover, both Ethiopia and Chilalo have physical or biological environments in which they function. A summary diagram of this relationship is presented in Figure 4.1.

In the larger study from which this chapter was taken, considerable attention was given to understanding the geography, ecology, climate, resources, population characteristics, settlement patterns, town environments, transport and infrastructure patterns, and other dimensions of the rural environment in which the Ethiopian society and Chilalo social system are embedded. The cultural subsystem of these social systems was organized around data related to such topics as ethnic and religious patterns and a wide range of society-wide or local values and beliefs. Particular attention was given to patterns of rural socialization,

FIGURE 4.1
Relationship of Chilalo Social System to Ethiopian Society

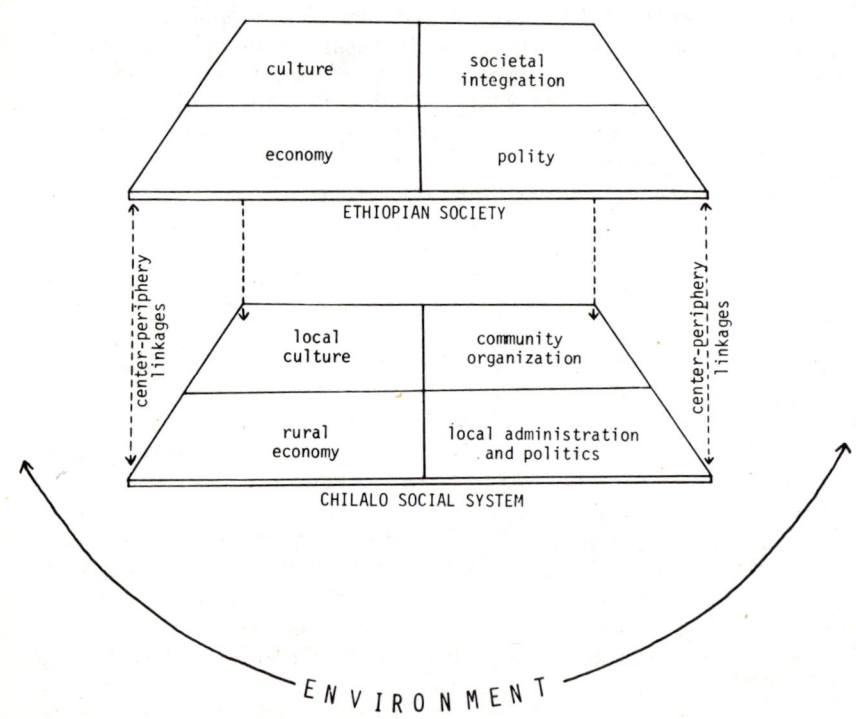

education programs, and mass media. Data gathering on community organization focused on such topics as patron-client relationships, class patterns, origins and resolution of social conflict, and such rural institutions as voluntary· associations, cooperatives, and self-help organizations. The polity subsystem contained institutions and roles of local government, administration and finance patterns, and public policy issues related to power and goals. Finally, analysis of the economy focused on data related to agricultural production patterns, the control and use of material resources, and specific factors facilitating or controlling economic growth such as markets, entrepreneurs, income, savings, government development plans, industry, and credit.

As the available data on Chilalo and Ethiopia were organized into this scheme, the conceptual richness of the control and facilitation framework helped pinpoint major gaps in the set of collected data and guided the process of filling them. The description which emerged suggested several related factors which made the critical difference[7] in explaining Ethiopia's development paradox. Before elaborating on these factors, it is necessary to present a summary of the structural patterns of rural Chilalo, their link with the Ethiopian center, and the processes of change which were occurring.

A Social Profile of Chilalo and Its Linkages to Ethiopian Society

As would be expected, the societal focus of the control and facilitation framework produced an enormously rich set of data. A lengthy description that is carefully confined to the theoretical framework is presented elsewhere.[8] What follows here is a necessarily brief presentation of the patterns of social life in rural Ethiopia as the process of change unfolds. The purpose of the section is to provide a data base for the theoretical approach used in the rest of the chapter to suggest why Ethiopia has been unable to fulfill her agrarian potential.

The Social History of Chilalo

Prior to the end of the nineteenth century, the Chilalo region was occupied by pastoral Arsi-Galla people and was outside the control of the Amhara and Tigre peoples who dominated ancient Abyssinia. It was conquered in the 1880s by the armies of Emperor Menelik II.[9] Because of Arsi resistance, Menelik's soldiers confiscated all clan lands. Although some land was returned to local chiefs to forestall opposition and win loyalty, the bulk of it was either held by the government or used to support the primarily Amhara administrators and soldiers who imposed central colonial rule. As the fertility of the region became known, Amhara and Shoa-Galla settlers arrived from the north, their migration stimulated by the granting of conquered land and by the sale of government land by the soldiers and administrators who had colonized the area. In addition, a number of large grants were made to nonresident nobles, military officers, and civil servants who lived in or near the imperial court. Many of these recipients held more land than they could farm and rented out their holdings. Most of the original Arsi-Galla became tenants on their historical tribal land, and other tenants, primarily Shoa-Galla, arrived from the north. During this colonization process, the Amharas imposed a variation of their own feudal pattern of social organization, and integrated the region into the empire with the establishment of a local government system which emphasized tax extraction and the maintenance of order.[10]

By the mid 1960s, the good soils, climate, and agrarian promise of Chilalo had attracted some 395,000 people to the area.[11] The rural population of some 65,000 households cultivated cereals on approximately 150,000 hectares through two types of production: peasant farming and small holdings under complex tenure systems, and mechanized farming of large tracts. The overall pattern for small holdings was one of plow cultivation and cattle breeding, utilizing traditional techniques. Wheat, barley, and flax were the main crops. Landownership was concentrated in a few hands; tenants constituted around 50 percent of those in agrarian production but farmed only some 20 percent of the total cultivated land. Finally, mechanization was confined to a few innovative landowners operating on a limited scale.

Aside from voluntary associations related to religious services, clan membership, and funeral functions, few inhabitants had any social ties other than kinship or the patron-client relationships that characterized Ethiopia's brand of feudalism. There were no cooperatives, and both community development and agricultural extension activities were virtually nonexistent.

Five percent of the population lived in towns, fourteen thousand living in Asella, the largest town and administrative capital. Most other towns were small periodic roadside market centers that had few permanent tradesmen. Others were local government posts as well as marketing centers. Only those towns on the poor all-weather road that runs north from Asella to Addis Ababa were linked by telephone and local bus to the national capital. The rest were connected by dry-weather tracks, and were often isolated during the long rainy season. Isolation from the national center was such that most bureaucrats in Addis Ababa were not anxious to accept a rural government post. The local administration was, therefore, largely staffed by poorly educated, locally raised civil servants, who could maintain order and collect taxes, but who had little interest in or ability to perform public service or development functions. Moreover, schools and health stations had been built in only four or five towns, of which only two had the additional amenities of electrification and rudimentary water systems.

Green Revolution in Ethiopia

The rest of the rural population lived in a traditional subsistence world. Rural habitation density was approximately forty persons per square kilometer, with 45 percent under fifteen years of age and not more than 15 percent over fifty-five. Illiteracy was at least 90 percent, and the religious distribution appears to have run 30 percent Christian and 70 percent Muslim, the Arsi-Galla being overwhelmingly Muslim and the Shoa-Galla and Amhara nearly all Christians. Perhaps 90 percent of the rural population lived outside the reach of health facilities, and rarely could their children attend distant government schools. Disease was widespread, nutrition was poor, and most Chilalo inhabitants faced early death. Agricultural production was largely consumed by the household, and what foodstuffs did reach rural markets were met by low prices. From there the chain of itinerant traders moved it upward until it reached the few major grain merchants having the storage capacity, information, and volume of trade necessary to make large profits from agricultural marketing. The purchasing power of most inhabitants was low and confined to goods essential to household survival.

The CADU Project

Into these underdeveloped but promising agrarian conditions stepped the Swedish government. Based on the assumption that in Ethiopia agricultural change was a precondition to general progress, and convinced that the "package program" concept was a proper approach,[12] the Swedish International Development Agency (SIDA) selected Chilalo as the site for such a project. The project, the Chilalo Agricultural Development Unit (CADU), began in late 1967.

CADU's objectives were to bring about economic and social development, give the population increased awareness of and responsibility for the development process, and verify methods of agricultural development. The specific aim was directed at small-scale landowners and tenant farmers, with the hope of raising not only their production levels, but also their living standards and social participation. The project's philosophy was based on the assumption that rural development is a complex process of many important and complementary parts. The strategy was to establish markets where fair prices prevailed and use extension agents and model farmers to stimulate the target population to buy and use improved seeds and fertilizers. To this end, CADU provided low-cost credit, engaged in agricultural research, developed rural water systems, improved feeder roads, provided livestock services, and participated in many community education and development activities.[13]

John M. Cohen

CADU's Effect on Economic and Social Development: Green Revolution Without Fundamental Social Change

As Swedish development experts and their Ethiopian counterparts concentrated on economic strategies, they appear to have assumed that politics and social life were dependent variables—that social change would invariably follow economic progress. In reality, however, the politics of order and continuity limited the economic effects of the project and kept it from reaching its full potential.

The project was successful in stimulating economic growth. By 1971/72, it was extending $E1,063,120 in credit to 12,624 tenants and small-scale landowners. Some twenty-five trade centers and twenty extension areas covered most of the region. Through all its activities CADU was reaching 25 percent of its target population. These farmers were buying green revolution inputs, improving livestock production, and beginning to market milk on a cash basis. Wheat, barley, and flax production expanded dramatically, and it is estimated that participating target population farmers increased their real household income by between 60 and 90 percent.

However, most of the envisioned social change did not come about, and a number of adverse side effects resulted from the operation of the project. CADU aimed directly at the small-scale farmer and indirectly influenced the large-scale farmer. It proved that imported seed and the use of fertilizer could make agriculture profitable; it did not take long before those landowners outside the target population learned this lesson by observing CADU projects and began to engage in mechanization with the resulting displacement of thousands of former tenants. Other negative results ranged from the dramatic increase in tenancy rents and land prices to the absorption of real income gains through stepped-up local government corruption and market profits by grain buyers. The cumulative effect of these developments has been to level off the growth of project activities. Specifically, 1973 project indicators make it clear that the early, rapid growth that dramatized the project has leveled off and participation has stabilized at about twelve thousand peasant households absorbing around $900,000 in credit out of a total possible target population somewhere above fifty thousand.[14] When coupled with data presented in this study, the flattening out of project growth curves suggests that no further success will result until social change and equity in Chilalo are given equal weight with production increases in the central government's formula for rural development.

From the mid 1950s until 1974, the Ethiopian government followed a policy of stimulating captial-intensive farming with little regard for social costs. In Chilalo this policy and CADU's proof that agriculture could be profitable resulted in a dramatic increase in commercial farms.[15] Larger landowners—members of the provincial elite—rapidly invested in tractors and combines. In the process they evicted their tenants and either farmed commercially themselves or rented their land on long-term contract leases with fixed, high rent schedules to other commercial farmers or elite investors whose primary profession was not farming. Some two thousand or more tenants were evicted as the message of CADU spread. No land reform legislation was passed to stop eviction, and tenants had no legal protection from it. Those not evicted faced increased tenancy rents and land prices. In addition, rising land values and accompanying mechanization led to limiting the amount of pasture available for livestock; blocking traditional easements used by peasants to herd their cattle to market, pasture, and watering places; and lowering the small-scale producer's capacity to compete with the lower prices that large-scale commercial farmers could accept with substantial profit. Since the peasant uses oxen to plow his land, his expansion and operation were jeopardized by the decline of pasture. Perhaps most importantly, even though CADU increased the incomes of participating peasants, the increase in land prices prevented them from moving toward the status of land ownership.

CADU officials tried to obtain government land for resettlement of evicted tenants. Such land was available and decrees for transferring it to them existed;[16] however, as the value of land in the area increased so did the interests of provincial elites in its acquisition. The amount of government land became a closely held secret. Local government officials either denied its existence in the *awraja* or stated that the government was studying the matter and, if there were any land, it would develop a future policy for its distribution. CADU accepted this position despite the fact that there was ample evidence in its files to support the existence of significant holdings of government land which were being distributed to national and provincial elites on a patronage basis.[17] CADU recognized that central and local government officials were not committed to goals of equitable development, and that they were not sensitive to the effects of the project on evicted tenants. Hence, CADU officials reluctantly concluded that they would be unable to obtain government land, and that government officials would continue to use it for elite patronage.

Land Tenure and Land Reform

In the traditional plow culture, a landowner using draft animals could plant only a few hectares, so most rented out their excess holdings. The same practice was followed by the religious leaders responsible for revenue from Coptic church land. While government land was held for future grants as private tenure, some of it was temporarily granted to provincial soldiers and administrators or rented to tenants. Since baseline studies are unreliable in rural Ethiopia, it is unclear how many tenants there were in Chilalo prior to the arrival of CADU. Analysis of available data leads to the conclusion that in the late 1960s 45 to 55 percent of those in agriculture were tenants. More than 90 percent of them were sharecroppers, of whom 84 percent paid between one-third and two-thirds of their production to landowners, 40 percent of whom were absentees holding an estimated 30 percent of Chilalo's measured arable lands.[18]

Of all the variables which limited the CADU strategy, the designers of the project were most aware of tenancy. As soon as CADU was established, the Swedish government began pressing for land reform. The initial SIDA survey team recognized the threat of tenant insecurity and its relationship to production and social change goals. But they underestimated the scope of the problem, or perhaps did not consider these limitations seriously. In any case, they did not initially adjust the model to the variable or think through its theoretical implications. Rather, they relied on an external solution, which was not forthcoming.

The Ethiopian government acknowledged the existence of land tenure problems, and in the initial aid agreement committed itself to submitting tenancy legislation to Parliament and implementing the resulting law in Chilalo within two years. Legislation was not enacted, and this became an issue when the first agreement expired in July 1970. Land tenure issues were given more attention at that time because the effects of the existing system were beginning to be felt. A six-month extension was signed and SIDA discussed the question in Sweden. But when the government of Ethiopia resubmitted the agricultural tenancy proclamation to Parliament in late 1970, it was taken as an act of good faith, and a second aid agreement was signed extending the project from January 1971 to July 1975.[19] As of late 1973, no such legislation has appeared.

The Local Government System

Throughout its long history, Ethiopia has been threatened by centrifugal forces of regionalism. One of Haile Selassie's main successes was the suppression of these forces and the imposition of strong central control. The price paid for this achievement has been the creation of a uniquely deconcentrated yet largely autonomous system of local government which embodies many elements currently (1973) retarding progressive change in the provinces.[20]

In Chilalo, as elsewhere, there are many territorial and functional conflicts of jurisdiction among officials governing the *awraja* through the Ministry of Interior and field agents of other ministries. None of these problems would be difficult to solve if there were a progress-oriented spirit of intergovernmental cooperation. But this spirit is rarely to be found. While the goals of Chilalo's administrative system are set by central elites who control the development ministries, there is substantial room for local administrators to impose their own interpretations on orders from above, or to resist and even suppress them. Rarely do Chilalo's officials have any conception of public service. Most merely perform their narrow order, taxation, and paper work functions while protecting their positions and seeking wherever possible to enrich themselves from the public they serve or the funds they control. If there is a response to the public, it tends to be to the vested interests of the small number of rural and urban elites who dominate social life.

Low salaries promote such corrupt behavior as misappropriation of budget funds, tax revenues, and self-help contributions, or acceptance of bribes and institutionalized extortion in return for favorable policies or government services. Such practices are stimulated by a subject political culture permissive of corruption or unable to prevent it.

Those progressive or educated civil servants who do enter the system are frequently isolated. If they seek to serve the urban poor or the peasant, fight corruption, and criticize the inefficiency of government, they eventually come into conflict with traditional sensibilities and are transferred as a result of local protest. And if they are field agents of development ministries, their positions and uncertain lines of authority often prevent them from having any real effect.

Most local government officials have few qualifications for office. Their outlook is traditional and they lack the education necessary to understand the economic strategy behind the development plans of the central government. They rarely have budgets beyond their salaries and overhead requirements. Supervision of employees is usually minimal, and they are often shifted to positions without respect for their qualifications or experience. All of these factors lower morale and lead to an emphasis on the time-consuming formality of clerical work which, given the low levels of funding for programmatic activity, is frequently time-consuming only because it must be expanded to fill a working day. Not infrequently, this situation leads to outside interests in land buying and farming. In the end, these employees rarely come to work on time, eschew innovation, and do not act.

The cumulative effect of these factors is a restrictive, self-seeking, narrowly responsive local government system. Its effects on the CADU target population will be shown in the rest of this study. For now, it is necessary to note that since Chilalo's establishment as a development center, the central government has done nothing to improve local government there.

National-Local Political Linkages

The patterns of rural change in Chilalo which led to these problems cannot be altered without the active commitment of the central government to change. It, however, is committed to growth and not to other, more sweeping changes such as development (differentiation and institutionalization) and transformation, or to such activities as social mobilization or agrarian reform.[21] This is so because it sees these sweeping changes as threats to its own survival. The relationship between land tenure and political power or social status is such that, if the government stimulates only economic growth, the constraints of the whole social system will limit the effects of such growth and give rise to substantial social costs, and if it stimulates all dimensions of change, it will eventually undermine the entire traditional rural and societal culture, power structure, and status system, in all probability destroying them. Hence, in Chilalo, the Ethiopian government has had to adopt a strategy of developing the local economy to benefit the national economy without changing the local society. This is very different from the strategy envisioned by the CADU project. This lack of mutuality of strategy is particularly clear regarding the project goal of stimulating local participation, and in the larger land tenure question. The government has not been cooperative in either area, indicating that it is resistant to basic social change.

Central governmental institutions have not given the project support where it was needed most, for no meaningful attempt was made to improve local government institutions or the attitudes of local officials. Local government employees were not encouraged to aid the project, and so acted only to advance their own interests or those of the provincial elite. In addition, grassroots political reforms that would have allowed local inhabitants greater community participation were not forthcoming, largely blocking CADU from achieving its basic social goal of giving the target population an increased awareness of and responsibility for the development process. CADU efforts to stimulate popular participation in cooperatives and farmer committees were not successful. Cooperatives got off to a slow start, in part because of the restraints of land reform and the vested interests of provincial elites, and in part because of the project's decision to let cooperatives develop slowly as social trust in CADU activities and change possibilities grew. Still, had CADU pushed cooperatives, they would have been dominated by large commercial farmers for the dual purpose of promoting economic growth and limiting social mobilization. Therefore, little rural consciousness has developed, and a subject political culture continues to predominate.

Ministerial field agents operating in Chilalo have frequently acted against the interests of the target population in other ways. In particular, the courts have refused to protect tenants from eviction or to enforce their slender legal rights against landowners; treasury officials have stepped up revenue collections from target population farmers but allowed major landowners and mechanized farmers to continue their practices of open tax evasion; land reform officials have blocked grants to landless peasants; education and health ministry personnel have made no real effort to extend their services to peasant families; road construction projects have tended more to open areas to mechanization than to improve marketing advantages of small-scale farmers; and, most importantly, many governors have increased the required levels of "voluntary contributions" by peasants to self-help funds for projects from which they rarely benefit. Most taxpayers in Chilalo are tenants and small-scale landowners. Because of the interrelation of corrupt local government officials and provincial elites, individuals of wealth, power, and status pay lower taxes or are wholly exempt, while the poorer the man and the lower his power or status, the heavier is his burden of taxation.[22] Because of CADU awareness that increased production should lead to increased tax revenues which could be used to benefit *awraja* development, local treasury officials have been forced to collect increased tax revenues. Field research indicates that this has been done by increasing revenue collection from target population farmers while trying to maintain the former tax advantages of the elites. More importantly, government expenditures based on these revenues largely benefit the local government officials, merchants, advocates, and other elites who live in towns. Schools, health stations, water systems, and electrification projects rarely touch the lives of tenants or small-scale landowners and their families. Whatever other taxes are expended in the *awraja* are consumed primarily in salaries for government employees and security forces, much of which is eventually paid to landlords as rent, or to merchants, tradesmen, and owners of bars, bus lines, and hotels in return for services.

Change has come to Chilalo through the efforts of the project, but not along lines envisioned. Unfortunately, the constraints of Ethiopian feudalism, an uncommitteed national center, and a land tenure system which concentrates the principal source of agrarian wealth in the hands of a provincial elite have limited change so that growth in yields, infrastructure, and rural amenities have principally benefited the provincial elites of the towns. Local power interests either resisted CADU programs or tried to capitalize on them. Only the determined efforts of the CADU staff prevented the project from becoming subservient to these traditional forces. And only because of CADU leadership has there been any substantial increase in the standard of living or production level of the small-scale landowner and tenant. As a result of CADU's indirect influence on the large landowner, the threat of displacement by the tractor hangs over the tenant, and the threat of inability to compete in economic production hangs over the small-scale landowner. Local participation is still nonexistent, a subject political culture predominates, political and economic power remains in the hands of those who held it before CADU arrived, and they have increased their power by riding the crest of the economic boom generated by Swedish aid.

John M. Cohen

Roles and Provincial Elites

The societal profile above is essentially structural and descriptive. By now it seems clear that the answer to the research problem rests in the relationship between land, wealth, power, and status, and in the linkages between the national center and the provincial elites. The basic hypothesis that emerges is that Chilalo is a blocked system, and to the extent that Chilalo represents other agrarian areas, so is Ethiopia. Ownership of land by a few and a social system founded on the prerogatives of Ethiopia's peculiar brand of feudalism mixed with early agrarian capitalism lead to the concentration of political power and societal influence in a conservative group of provincial elites.[23] Through the controls of Amhara culture and social organization, the power of the local polity, and the domination of energy generated by agricultural production, these elites, the big men of the little community, have the capacity to maintain the established local system and to preclude any significant change on the part of the large peasant majority—so long as their actions do not go against stronger interests of the more powerful national polity. It is further hypothesized that these elites are aided by a national center which is not committed to extensive agrarian reform because its own survival is in part dependent on the maintenance of the traditional rural system which Chilalo characterizes. The control and facilitation framework will now be utilized to explain some of the processes at work.

The major focus will be on role theory as a helpful way to link structural processes with human behavior in ways which illustrate the significance of politics in the process of change. Specifically, it is men who provide an important link between any theoretical view of society and concrete reality. Social systems and their subsystems can act only in a metaphorical sense, and to forget this is to engage in the fallacy of mixplaced concreteness.[24] As pointed out in Chapter 1, focusing on men in societal roles helps ground the conceptual framework in reality and avoid the criticisms which are so often leveled at such conceptual schemes.[25] It is useful to use the concept "role expectations" for institutionalized role behavior patterns, "role orientations" or "role perceptions" for the actual perceptions of the role held by the role player, and "role behavior" for the actual empirical actions involved in role performance.[26]

As change comes to Chilalo *Awraja*, pressure is put on men performing various roles in the social system to change their role orientations and role behavior in a manner consistent with the forces of change.[27] This creates a conflict between role expectations generally held in the community and the new behavior orientations of the involved individuals. And it is the response of these men to these pressures which provides an empirical indication of the progress of change in the area.

This study focuses on the function of the polity as the locus of decisions or policies established for the society by the various interchanges of commitments, influence, power, and land or wealth among the individual role players of the social system. In particular, it finds that the decision making function of the polity is a catalyst in the process of change, since one of its basic activities is to resolve (or attempt to resolve) conflicts introduced by the forces of change. If these forces manifest themselves empirically in the role behavior conflict of men, then the polity frequently determines, through its power to enforce negative sanctions, the resolution of that conflict and hence the nature and direction of change. Important role players, utilizing economic strength, influence, and commitments, interact with the government in an attempt to have role conflicts resolved to their mutual advantage. Sources of change can come from many places, but in the social system of Chilalo *Awraja* they come mainly from the adaptive sector. The resulting conflicts are between existing values and norms and material conditions necessary for equitable agricultural development. This conflict can be best understood by focusing on the collective goals selected, the decision making process, and the exercise of power in the polity or goal attainment subsystem.

An abstract presentation of this theoretical orientation toward change is given in Figure 4.2. Here the forces of change are located in the adaptive subsystem and are being resisted by the forces of traditionalism in the pattern socialization and control and integrative subsystems, with the conflict being decided by choices made in the goal attainment subsystem, choices which are backed by enforcement power. This diagram represents the typical pattern which the problems of change take in the **social system of Chilalo** *Awraja*.

The existence of influential minorities is one of the main characteristics of organized social life in the *awraja*. There are certain members of the social system whom the community sets aside as being part of a stratum elevated above the great majority of the area's inhabitants. These people live in both the countryside and towns, and rather than denominate them incorrectly as either rural or urban elites, they are called "provincial elites" throughout this study. There is a wide variety of definitions of the term elite.[28] In this study the term refers to those members of the community **who control a disproportionately great share of the media of exchange which** they use in the performance of the major economic, political, social, and cultural functions of the area.[29]

As the rural development takes place, roles become more differentiated. In the process, specific activities devolve on more specialized elites, and it becomes possible to delineate with some accuracy the principal functional activities of various members of this social minority. It is thus possible to classify the influential minorities of the *awraja* according to the societal subsystem in which they perform their main functions. It should be clear that in traditional rural areas there is far more multifunctional role performance than there is in modern societies. For example, a major landowner is a member of the economic elite, and

FIGURE 4.2
Forces of Change in Ethiopia Originating in Adaptive Subsystem and Possible Responses of Policy to the Conflict Generated

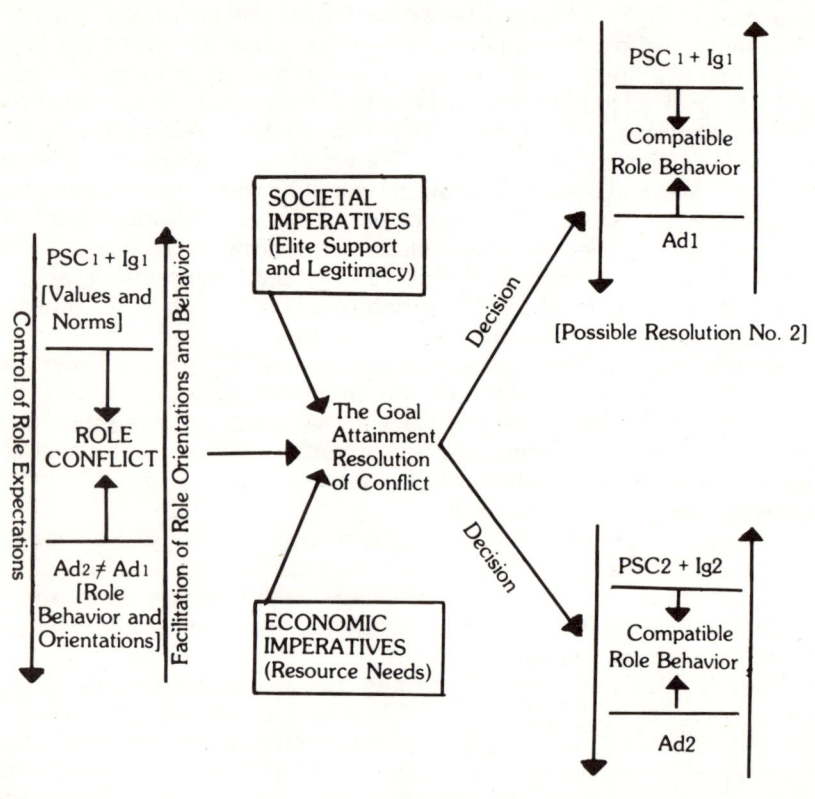

Possible Resolution 1 = Negative acceptance which leads to maintenance of old role expectations and no change in values

Possible Resolution 2 = Positive acceptance which leads to new role expectations and change in values

Where PSC = Pattern Socialization and Control subsystems (values)
Ig = Integrative subsystem (norms)
Ad_1 = Traditional Adaptive subsystem (roles)
Ad_2 = Innovative Adaptive subsystem (roles)

may also be an informal grassroots official in the political subsystem, a leader of a voluntary association in the community organization subsystem, and a religious figure in the cultural subsystem. Field research confirms the existence of this tendency toward multifunctional elites. However, the classification of such elites into their principal functional areas has proven to be very useful for analysis. Examples of these various functionally specialized elites would be: 1) landowners, mechanized farmers, grain merchants, and businessmen who would be identified with the economic subsystem; 2) local administration officials, municipality officers, members of Parliament, and field agents of the central government ministries who are primarily engaged in setting and implementing political goals; 3) elders, judges, advocates, police officers, and leaders of traditional and modern voluntary associations who maintain and affect societal order and integration; and 4) priests, sheikhs, members of leading families, and religious and secular school teachers who represent and socialize the main values of the community.

This definition of elites is situational, as is evident from the adjective "provincial". Many of these role players would not be considered elite by national elites in the capital city or by dogmatists who insist on certain rather than fruitful definitions. However, it is maintained that in terms of Chilalo *Awraja* and the basic processes of change taking place within its social system, those who meet the definitional requirements introduced above can usefully be called "provincial elites" and studied as such. The discussion which follows is based on participant observation techniques of political anthropology, secondary documents, and a detailed survey of 112 Chilalo elites through a 117 question instrument covering background variables, political perceptions, communication links, economic interests, views of change, and a number of other topics.[30]

These elites mediate between the peasant and the larger society of which he is a part. Landowners, merchants, governors, advocates, and priests stand at the junctures of economic, political, social, and cultural life which connect the rural area to the larger Ethiopian society.[31] As a result of this role, such elites provide clear points of reference which can be used to chart the ongoing social processes in the Ethiopian system. In addition, in periods of social change the orientations and choices of these elites are sharply visible, for they play an extremely influential role in the acceptance, modification, or rejection of the innovations associated with the forces of change. When the social system is relatively stable, the orientations of those elites are merged with the values, habits, and manners of the entire community. Therefore, it is only during periods of social change that their most fundamental orientations are fully revealed. The principal role conflicts in rural Ethiopia occur in situations in which provincial elites try to maintain role expectations and the forces of change try to introduce new role orientations.

John M. Cohen

Control, Facilitation, and the Process of Change

The process by which the choices of role players made in response to the forces of change have led to a blocked and inequitable social system can now be illustrated.[32] Given the heuristic thrust of this chapter, only a few role conflicts will be considered, illustrating in the process the utility of the control and facilitation framework. Each of these could be diagramed according to the format presented in Figure 4.2.

As of late 1973 only a few significant role conflicts are resulting from the processes of rural change. Those presented here relate to the introduction of new farming techniques and innovations, changes in traditional landlord-tenant relationships, cooperative activities, tax reforms, and popular participation and social mobilization. However, in general, there do not appear to be a large number of severe conflicts between role expectations and role orientations among the inhabitants of Chilalo. For this reason provincial elites face only a few major crises in the exercise of choice. And for this reason the local polity does not face many critical issues of conflict that demand resolution in terms of societal goals. This situation is due to the tremendous power and authority of the local and national polities, in combination with the control which the stratification and cultural systems exercise over role expectations and orientations in the *awraja*.

The minimization of role conflict is probably explained by the following propositions drawn from Chapter 1 and modified to apply specifically to rural change:

> The more completely integrated the rural social system, and the more in touch the functional elites of the various subsystems with each other, the less likely it is that change will take place in the rural social system, although those subsystems which are least well integrated with the remainder of the rural social system will be the most susceptible to change (A2,A2a).
>
> The better the rural social system is adapted to its environment, the less the likelihood of change (A5).

That change is taking place is indicated in the response of various farmers to agricultural innovations. One by one, landowners and rich, middle, and poor peasants have come to realize that changes in agricultural techniques can be profitable and have begun to accept innovations introduced by CADU. Originally this role behavior was at variance with traditional role expectations on farming practices. But under CADU's influence, and stimulated by its successes in yield and marketing activities, the initially deviant role orientations have become the new role expectations of the community. Both peasants and provincial elites have chosen to adopt the new techniques. The results have been both agricultural and infrastructural growth and the transformation of very specific values and norms related to the agricultural production process. Interestingly, there has been little conflict between the new technical orientations and the established value and normative system, and hence power has not been essential to the introduction of these new orientations. Still, the government played a critical role in the initial introduction of this change because it brought CADU to the *awraja* and allowed it to function in the community and to stimulate change in role performance. But it should not be forgotten that provincial elites and other interests who lend resources, support, and legitimacy to the polity were not opposed to these basic transformations in the attitudes of area inhabitants to production.

The process of positive acceptance of new role performance in farming techniques suggests that the following propositions are operative.

In regard to the state of the pre-existing system:

> The stronger the values and norms of innovativeness in the rural social or political system, or a subsystem thereof, the more likely it is that change will take place (A1).

In regard to the sources and types of change:

> Other societies are the most important source of external change in the rural social system (B1).
>
> Material innovations are more specific and are more easily communicable in the rural social system than are value innovations; however, innovations which are divisible into simpler parts rather than necessarily accepted or rejected as whole complexes are more easily transmitted from one social system to another (B2).

In regard to the point of impact and facilitation of change:

> Both externally and internally induced change are

likely to impinge first on the economic subsystem of the rural social system, since this subsystem is most closely concerned with relations between the system and its environment (C1).

Elements which can be adopted on an individual basis are likely to spread more quickly and easily than those which require adoption by most members of the given collectivity (C8).

In regard to the control of change:

Resistance is likely to be greater when existing elements must be removed or replaced than when new elements can be added without such replacement (D5).

Eventually new values and norms will come to control behavior, and thus change will proceed in a recognizable direction (E3).

Role conflict is taking place in regard to landlord-tenant relations. Here CADU's Swedish innovators have tried to introduce tenant contracts into the *awraja*. They have in effect attempted to obtain role orientations on the part of landlords which are different from expectations generally held for the role. Conflict has ocurred in the process, and the government has been either ambivalent or negative in response to this conflict. In particular it has lent none of its power and authority to the implementation of this value and normative change, and has allowed provincial elites to enforce prior expectations. The central government, which could decide the conflict through land reform legislation, has chosen to make no decisions, despite pressures from the Swedish government, while local government officials have responded in support of the traditional role expectations on landlord-tenant relationships and have used power in many ways to resolve local role conflict against the new CADU-introduced orientations. The local polity has responded willingly because of its interests in securing the resources, support, and legitimacy controlled by the elites. Furthermore, even if the central government supported contract leases, they would not be effective because landlords would treat them in bad faith, and the local court system would not enforce them, or would interpret them to favor the landlords.

Two situations can result when the government is the innovator. In the first, the government is only partially committed, and the provincial elites, including local government officials, are able to subvert the change, or modify it so that its impact is minimized. This has proven to be the case with many government attempts to introduce new orientations toward tax payment and collection. Here resistance to reform has been great, and it has proven almost impossible to convince landowners that they should bear a larger share of government operation, or that tax evasion is illegal and socially undesirable behavior. Nor have they been receptive to the idea that taxes should not be passed on to tenants. Furthermore, the provincial elites have tried to foster resistance to the attempts by the central Ministry of Finance to correct tax collection inefficiency and corruption at the local level, since the administrative reforms proposed run contrary to the vested interests of these elites. Since the central government needs the elites' support, it is allowing them to frustrate centrally introduced changes through local political pressures to continue the traditionally expected patterns of role behavior. The difference between this and the previous illustration is that with landlord-tenant relations the traditional forces will not tolerate any modernization because of their own interests, whereas with taxation the formulation of modern legislation is allowed, but its implementation is frustrated.

The other basic situation involving government innovations is one in which enforcement of new innovations is demanded by the central government, and traditional forces then try to slow down their ultimate application, but eventually fail because of central determination. This is illustrated in the abolition of *rist gult* rights in the *awraja* in 1966.[33] There was no question that the government wished to change old role expectations that *rist gult* holders would keep the taxes due on land under their control, to end the existence of that particular land tenure, and to make role behavior on the part of peasants, *rist gult* holders, and local government officials conform to this change. Under the law, peasants were to end prior orientations toward former *gult* holders and pay their taxes directly to the government. This law was ultimately implemented, but it took a long time and was resisted by former *rist gult* holders and their fellow provincial elites in charge of implementing it in the local community. Ultimately it was accepted since it became clear that other benefits would be accorded in a trade-off by the government.

A good example of a middle ground between these two situations is the enforcement of the agricultural income tax despite local resistance and evasion, and the failure to abolish the tax in lieu of tithe which most tenants continue to pay to landowners in the form of *asrat*. Part of this legislative innovation is being enforced and the other part overlooked.

A different example of role conflict is seen in cooperatives. The cooperative approach is an attempt to stimulate development, and has been coupled with the establishment of marketing or trade centers. CADU encouragement of cooperatives has led to role conflict since the provincial elites realize that cooperative role orientations can threaten their control over marketing. They also realize that, unless cooperatives are properly controlled, they can lead to new role expectations generating social mobilization which would threaten the basis of power, influence, and commitments in the local social system. On the other hand, provincial elites are well aware of the utility of cooperatives in gaining low-cost credit and green revolution inputs. Therefore, they have attempted to control the cooperative movement. Unfortunately for them, the government has passed a law on cooperatives which CADU can utilize, and thus the central government cannot decide the matter to the advantage of provincial elites. But local government officials can frustrate changes in role orientations wherever these are not in conformance with role expectations of local elites. And provincial elites can use their power, influence, and commitments to ensure that cooperatives formed operate under their control and to their advantage.

The stimulation of popular participation in the development process on the part of the local population has been a basic goal of CADU. This is an attempt to go beyond growth and stimulate development transformation. Attempts have been made to change role expectations and patterns of relationship between the rural population and provincial elites, and to involve both in the development process. It should be clear that efforts to stimulate social participation and to alter the hierarcharcial patterns of authority could not succeed without the commitment of the government, and that those provincial elites who are beginning to share more corporate perspectives of their common destiny in the face of threatening types of change would actively resist such efforts. As a result, the attempts to change elite and nonelite expectations on the issue of participation have not succeeded.

The process of acceptance or rejection of change in role performance in landlord-tenant relationships, tax reforms, cooperatives, and popular participation of peasants can be explained by the following propositions.

In regard to the state of the pre-existing system:

> A rural social system is less likely to change the greater the concentration of power in the hands of status quo elites, unless the concentrated power facilitates minor changes which act as "safety valves" by preventing major change or system breakdown, or unless pressures for change build to a point where concentrated power can be overcome, at which point change is rapid and extensive (A3,C9).
>
> A rural social system which is changing is more likely to undergo further change, up to a threshold of tolerance for change, at which point recent

changes will tend to have a dampening effect on future change (A4).

In regard to the facilitation of change:

>In calculating the advantages, disadvantages, and uncertain consequences of adopting new elements, individuals will be influenced by the perceived utility of the elements (C5).
>
>The mobilization of collectivities to exercise power and influence in support of change is likely to result in countermobilization to resist change, and such defensive organization of power is more likely when the defensive elite values and norms sanction aggressiveness, differ substantially from these of change-mobilizing individuals, and are threatened by the change-oriented mobilization (C3).
>
>In order to resist change, the status quo advocates need a good knowledge of the dynamics of their society and an ability to predict the consequences of their actions. This assumes that conscious rather than unconscious action is involved in successful resistance to innovative and threatening change. Resistance is more likely to be successful the more the advocates of status quo cooperate with each other in organizing, generating, and employing power, or invoking dominant values (C6c, d, and e).

In regard to the control of change:

>A rural social system is more likely to accept new elements if they are compatible (D1).
>
>Any new element which comes into a rural social system from external sources is likely to be reinterpreted or modified in such a way that it will become more compatible with the existing structure of the social system (D2).

In regard to the functional and structural consequences of change:

>The more the proponents of the status quo can

keep innovators from controlling money, power, influence, and commitments, the greater the likelihood that only limited and compatible change will follow (E3a).

The extent of change will probably be the minimum necessary to integrate the new elements into the system and to reestablish minimum workable compatibility among the functional subsystems and levels of the rural social structure (E4).

Conclusions in 1973

The following analysis is presented *as drafted* in 1973, unaltered by the substantial advantages of hindsight. A postscript will describe the events which overtook Chilalo beginning in 1974 and discuss the success of these 1973 projections.

It is apparent throughout the above examples that in Chilalo the polity has been resolving role conflict introduced by the process of change in favor of preserving the distribution of advantages, if not the structures, of the long-established conquest system. And it is also clear that those individuals with wealth, prestige, and status—the provincial elite—have influenced the basic decisions of those who control the polity. There does not appear to exist any extensive intraelite conflict on the maintenance of the traditional system and its dominant values.

At the surface it appears that what is taking place is the successful preservation of the status quo. Paradoxically, this is hardly the case, because there is one major aspect of change woven into everything that is happening. It is the result of decisions of the central polity to promote more modern land tenure based on freehold, along with western capitalistic agricultural development policies. And it is stimulated by the various dimensions of growth introduced by CADU. This aspect of change is the development of new economic structures which replace Ethiopia's particular brand of conquest feudalism with an early capitalism. Provincial elites currently perceive themselves as engaged in trying to support traditional values, while they are increasingly utilizing capitalistic methods of organization to do so.

What is particularly interesting is the fact that this transformation will probably strengthen the economic foundations of the provincial elites and the government, while at the same time terminating many of the unimportant cultural values and societal norms which have supported the traditional rural elites. In the trade-off it does not appear that the provincial elites' position will be eroded. For example, declining vertical patron-client relationships which characterized Ethiopian feudalism are being replaced by horizontal elite ties that are stronger because they are more open, formal, and continuous.

A number of changes are being introduced throughout the *awraja,* but the primary direction of change is toward growth and such development and transformation as are necessary to permit growth to take place. Growth is reflected in increased crop production and income over the past seven years. It is also seen in the increase of schools, teachers, health clinics, roads, telephones, markets, manpower, and other indicators. The successful implementation of growth could facilitate the occurrence of other dimensions of change, but this facilitation is carefully controlled by the polity, the stratification system, and the culture.

Development will be accepted so long as the institutional changes do not begin to threaten the vested interests of provincial elites. Markets can expand, new businesses can appear in the towns, agricultural extension can be institutionalized, and branches of various field agents of the central government can be opened. Even rationalization of the local government bureaucracy is accepted if it increases efficiency in provision of public goods or maintenance of public order. Land tenure systems can be modernized and the old requisites of feudalism terminated.[34] But the introduction of popular participation or meaningful land reforms will not be accepted.

Transformation is appearing among tenants in the move from subsistence to cash farming, and from cattle raising to plow crop production, and in a number of other changes in role expectations. Among the provincial elites, this transformation relates to the growing recognition of the capitalistic dimensions of land ownership and production, and the awareness that they and their fellow elites have a common stake in the system which they must jointly preserve through common action. Despite the future potential of this transformation, it is still not really a significant factor in the *awraja.* Where the few real changes in role orientations are taking place, they tend to be the result of outside innovators such as CADU, the arrival of particular new men from central government offices, or the spread of new ideas through the educational or communications systems. These innovations are primarily derived from western agricultural technology, and are confined almost entirely to the economic subsystem. It is clear that innovations aimed at stimulating growth do not necessarily imply the future borrowing or innovation of other more socially transformative values: the provincial elites' survival precludes such practices, and the masses are not presently inclined toward acceptance of broad innovations.

The fundamental contradiction involved in the acceptance of innovation which stimulates growth relates to whether the energy thus released can be controlled. The provincial elites who are accepting these restrictive innovations are not worried about their long-range incompatibility with the dominant core values because they believe they have the influence and commitments necessary to ensure that the polity utilizes its power and authority to control agrarian reform and rural change in accordance with established community goals. The economic growth which has resulted from selected innovation has clearly increased the strength of those who dominate the system, and has avoided extensive instability or social conflict. However, it is not at all clear whether this will be the long-run result of growth.

It should be made very clear that, because of on-going social patterns, a shift to early capitalism represents the outer possibilities of any short or medium term change in the Chilalo social system. The only real strategy which could stimulate the rapid expansion of capitalism would be to get landowners to rechannel their money into industry and to end their presently strong predisposition to invest in more land or crop marketing businesses. By late 1972 CADU was attempting to stimulate local manufacturing industries financed in part by Chilalo landowners, and the Council of Ministers was considering ending the fuel subsidies that make profits from mechanized agriculture abnormally high. But whether money can be substituted for land as the source of status and influence is as yet an unanswered question. It is quite clear that CADU cannot remain in the project area forever, but does not want to surrender its target population to domination by the provincial elite. The CADU strategy in this regard appears to be to develop cooperatives as a locus for channeling innovations and inputs into the traditional plow culture, and for stimulating social awareness and participation by the peasant. Unfortunately, the growing tendencies observed in CADU cooperatives are that they are controlled by the provincial elite, and are thus utilized to stem social mobilization among peasants and to stimulate provincial elite investment in land, with the resulting eviction of tenants. Thus the eviction of peasants by the combination of green revolution and mechanization will probably continue. When this process occurs throughout Ethiopia, pressures may develop which will force a change in either government policy or the regime itself. Under present conditions the urban sector cannot absorb those evicted tenants because of the lack of industry, and because low-land commercial agriculture, lacking capital and managerial skills, is growing too slowly to need laborers.

Until the basis of social control by provincial elites is eroded, the commitment of the government to change ignited, and social mobilization and development of rural consciousness implemented, there is little hope for sweeping change in Chilalo *Awraja*. It has been shown that land reform is the key to breaking the ability of provincial elites to control deviant role orientations. But land reform will be meaningless unless the central government is committed to meaningful change in the periphery, and is willing to support that change with economic resources, manpower, sacrifice, and perhaps most importantly, policies favorable to the great mass of middle and poor peasants.

The possibilities of such occurrences are extremely slim. The growing sense of corporate identity of the provincial elites is clear, and their ability to frustrate change is reflected in their increasingly powerful and conservative role in Parliament. The possibility of a new government appearing which would implement a meaningful land reform program is doubtful since the land grant system has effectively tied most possible military and bureaucratic sources of new governments into the land system. Furthermore, the socialization and communications system militates against the development of attitudes which would change the commitments of such groups, and the system still maintains the ability to co-opt or isolate those who might seek to implement major changes. For these reasons, the critical question of *"negus kamotu"* or when the Emperor dies, is a rather empty one for Chilalo *Awraja* in particular, and rural Ethiopia in general.[35] A military coup d'etat or the acquisition of governmental power by men of liberal orientations will not substantively affect the powers of provincial elites or eliminate their opposition to various aspects of transformation, especially land reform. It will in all probability merely mean that the possibilities for Ethiopia's following the path of early capitalism are even higher.

The answer to Ethiopia's development paradox, as derived from the Chilalo study, is not that the peasant is illiterate and fatalistic. Economic man is alive and well in Chilalo *Awraja*. Rather, it is that a group of men with narrow interests utilize their control of the local polity and their positions of high status and legitimacy to maintain a social system based on a particular form of land tenure and a particular pattern of values. Since their position is largely incompatible with more change than growth, they are carefully controlling the change process, thereby preventing Ethiopia and her large and poor agrarian population from reaching their promising potential. For the foreseeable future, as well as in long-range comparisons with the developed world, Ethiopia will remain one of the poorest yet potentially richest agrarian nations in the world.

Postscript

Far reaching and unexpected change has occurred since 1973 as a result of the gradually unfolding Ethiopian revolution.[36] This study argued that change would not occur until land reform was implemented and the controls of the provincial elite eroded. Far more than this has occurred, proving incorrect the study's conclusion that early capitalism and a compatible political regime represented the outer possibilities of long-term change in Chilalo and Ethiopia. Yet, the conclusion that Chilalo was a blocked and inequitable society has been recognized by the young Marxist-oriented military men who have seized the power of Haile Selassie. In a number of ways they have moved quickly to dismantle the controls and release the facilitating energy that could promote rapid fulfillment of the country's agrarian potential. Their policies are directed at altering the patterns of land, power, and elites that the application of the control and facilitation framework helped pinpoint.

Within months of gaining power by coup d'etat, the country's new military leaders implemented a series of radical policy measures designed to transform Ethiopian society. They began by removing, arresting, or even executing influential elites and officials in the capital city, towns, and countryside. While this purge of aristocratic and administrative systems was occurring, they removed the Emperor, abolished the monarchy, declared that Ethiopia would follow a socialist path, and subsequently issued a set of proclamations that nationalized all rural and urban land, thereby setting in motion a process of societal change that has not yet been completed.

The elements of these reforms and their effects are described elsewhere.[37] Here it need only be noted that in the southern provinces where Chilalo is located numerous important social patterns have been greatly altered. For example, no farm family can hold more than ten hectares; tenancy has been abolished and landlords have surrendered their properties without compensation; the Ethiopian Orthodox Church has lost its land and status as a state religion; the prerogatives of Ethiopian feudalism's aristocracy have been terminated; progressive, often militantly socialist administrative officials and field agents of development ministries have been assigned to the local level; and mass mobilization of the poor majority is being attempted through the formation of peasant associations and local revolution and development committees.

It would be useful to apply the role analysis developed for prerevolutionary Chilalo to these changes, but the lack of any field work in the Chilalo region since 1974 precludes this. Available evidence indicates that in 1974 events at the national center were reflected in Chilalo. They were seen in progressive, perhaps radical, employee strikes by CADU employees; the removal of the conservative and corrupt provincial governor; and the occurrence of sporadic, violent conflicts between tenants and landowners.

From the time of the first military mutiny until the removal of the Emperor, the CADU program continued to operate in a reasonably efficient way. Seven months of conflict at the center did not prevent the project from expanding or performing its functions. This was the case despite employee strikes demanding removal of the head of the Ministry of Agriculture division that oversaw the project. To CADU staff he was a conservative symbol of the numerous frustrations that plagued their ability to promote both growth and equity. Other demands relative to the blockages in the local government system were more openly voiced than ever before. Such demands were to be expected given the high educational levels and sense of commitment that generally characterized those Ethiopians who worked for CADU. Throughout this mobilization

CADU's director, a man known for his progressive ideas and commitment to reform, stood by in sympathetic agreement. The effects of this inner mobilization subsequently became evident when CADU staff came to play a very activist role in implementing land reform legislation (C2).

By mid-1974 the military was removing corrupt provincial officials. One of the first to go was the Arussi provincial governor, Sahlu Diffayei. Charges of corruption in his regime emerged very early. He was charged with collecting money illegally from the people, corrupting the judicial process, and squandering public funds during his nine-year reign. Full investigation of these charges was never undertaken because the military executed him in November 1974. His replacement was a known liberal and capable administrator. He proved to be a catalyst to the long-smoldering resentment toward CADU's progressive efforts that was held by Chilalo's provincial elites. Because of his former posts in the Ministry of Agriculture, the elites saw him as "the father of CADU," and recognized the shift of power to CADU progressives which would take place when he came to govern them.

Among the first rural disturbances to flow from the increasing liberalization of the center were those in Chilalo. These resulted from the presence of CADU, its six years of project activity, its effects on tenants, and the hostility of provincial elites toward CADU staff (E1). The disturbances began with resistance of tenants to eviction and high rents. On 17 May 1974, some tenants in the Dera area refused to give part of their harvest to the landowner in payment of rent. The landowner returned with two policemen and a violent argument ensued, resulting in the death of one policeman and two farmers. Two other farmers were taken to jail only to be seized by other policemen and shot for their part in the earlier fight. At the insistence of the provincial elites, the police force went to the governor (the new liberal) and demanded that he take strong and immediate action to stem the unruly behavior of peasants before it spread throughout the region. He refused to take such action, understanding well the new commitment of the central government, and being an outsider not linked to these powerful local men. For several days the provincial elites and police formulated their strategy; then they forced him to leave the province. Shortly thereafter CADU staff members went on strike in protest against the unlawful events. Provincial elites responded to this through the local police. CADU employees were threatened and two received nonfatal gunshot wounds. The national center quickly responded to these events and sent a special police force to Arussi to disarm the police and deal with the leaders of the conservative rebellion. The response was successful, and the governor returned.

By September 1974 these and other events had made the provincial elites uncertain about their power to control the local society and about how to respond to new and progressive policy statements coming from the national center. Some CADU staff increased this insecurity by openly distributing leaflets to peasants. While their general tenor was to raise peasant awareness of reform, some pamphlets went so far as to urge peasants to take up arms against the large landlords, drive them from the area, and take possession of their land. The creeping coup leaders were gradually consolidating power and were seven months away from declaring their sweeping reforms. Hence they did not favor these activities and the problems they were creating. Since the CADU director was looking the other way during this pamphleteering, he was arrested as a security risk.

The CADU staff responded quickly with a threat of wholesale resignation. The police backed down and the director returned to his post until his resignation in December. CADU staff mobilization efforts continued, with Asella police requesting and being denied the authority to use force to repress CADU activities in the same way that police had stopped labor union activities in Addis Ababa. Had authority to arrest and shoot been granted, much blood would have been spilled, for the provincial elites were allies of the police and both had numerous old scores to settle with CADU staff.

In early March 1975, just before Chilalo's planting season, the military government announced the nationalization of land. Internal political activity in CADU declined, for now the organization needed all the energy its staff could muster to respond to the new set of conditions that politics at the center had imposed. The principal tasks of CADU became insuring that the large farms which landowners were abandoning would be placed under cultivation, and responding to the increased demands for its basic services by former tenants and smallholders that were generated by the wave of optimism that followed the reform.

The reform was implemented quickly in Chilalo. CADU allowed students sent by the military to promote reform through the use of its extension network, marketing centers, and incipient *awraja* development committees. This established communications grid and the political consciousness which CADU generated in 1974 and early 1975 proved invaluable in the early tasks of calling peasant meetings, spreading information about the reform proclamation, and combating disruptive rumors propagated by retreating landowners to the effect that the proclamation ordered peasants not to plant until further orders, or that the government was to be the new landlord with rents being raised to 75 percent of the harvest. Together with enthusiastic peasants, CADU staff, students, and reform officers forced the rapid dispossession of large-scale landowners and the *de facto* distribution of their holdings. Earlier politicalization through CADU efforts and raised peasant anger at the thousands of evictions that had followed the introduction of mechanization created conditions conducive to rapid change (C4,C5b,C6).

Green Revolution in Ethiopia

    Despite the cumulative cleavages of Galla ethnicity and tenant status, few attacks took place against Amhara landowners or townsmen. Violence was no doubt minimized by the fact that those seizing land were generally occupants of it. Isolated and without effective organization or political support, the landowners abandoned their lands and retreated to the towns or Addis Ababa, perhaps in part because they had been investing in urban land since the attempted coup of 1961, and did not anticipate the urban reforms that were to follow. Several well known landowners took to the hills and were ultimately killed as they led their bands of supporters in antigovernment campaigns. But there was remarkably little bloodshed as the reforms were implemented. To a large extent this was because the government at the center had made its commitment quite clear, traditional local officials and the police were effectively neutralized, and the active posture of the students and CADU made it difficult for the provincial elite to develop strategies that would block or cripple the charges that had been decreed (C3a and b). By 1976 the government claimed that 113,638 people belonged to peasant associations in Chilalo. These associations were implementing the reforms in their eight hundred hectare areas, and were running a variety of rural development activities. Many students wanted to take over the large farms and turn them into collectives, and some progress was initially made in this regard. But it appears that farmers who participated did so because they lacked inputs, and when the first year was over they demanded that the farms be divided into small scale units and run on an individual basis. The peasant associations ran their own court activities and gradually succeeded in their pressure for arms. This allowed them to further neutralize those members of the police who supported the interests of the former elites.

    In short, Chilalo appears to be a very different place than it was in 1973. The economic base of the elites in land has been removed, and their support from central values and norms ended, by the emergence of a new social order. It is too soon to conclude definitively that Chilalo is no longer a blocked society, although this seems to be the case. It was argued above that Ethiopia's rural sectors would not reach their economic and social potential until the central government went beyond reform to the commitment of economic resources, manpower, and extensive technical support to creating the type of progressive infrastructure essential to rural development. Political choices at the center to expend limited state resources on the Eritrean war and problems of maintaining order in other regions have led to a present policy of rural self-help, a strategy not likely to be widely successful given the meager resources of the poor Ethiopian peasantry. Moreover, the fratracide among Marxists at the center has led to the death or forced exile of many of the skilled technocrats needed to organize the kind of research, extension, marketing, and rural infrastructure system necessary to get agriculture moving by capitalizing on the land reform and the newly established peasant associations. Hence, in terms of the research problem underlying this study, Ethiopia may still be unable to fulfill its agrarian potential.

Surely the Ethiopian experience illustrates the hazards of prediction. Few, if any, social scientists expected Ethiopia to change so dramatically in such a short period of time. This failure held true whether the scholar approached Ethiopian society as a behavioralist, structural-functionalist, or Marxist. Nevertheless, it is submitted that the control and facilitation framework functioned well in allowing the scope of theoretical and empirical vision necessary to describe and explain what proved to be the critical variables that precluded change. Failure in prediction lay in this analyst's inability to escape the accepted shibboleths that encumbered the Ethiopian literature[38] and his failure to anticipate potential control and facilitation linkages among the values and role behavior of progressive military officers, students, labor union leaders, teachers, and civil servants at the national center. That one of the only studies to anticipate the change that has occurred was done in 1973 by Peter Koehn using the control and facilitation framework testifies to this point.[39]

Footnotes

1. The critical role of agriculture in national development is set forth in Uma J. Lele and John W. Mellor, "Jobs, Poverty and the Green Revolution," *International Affairs* 48 (January 1972): 20-32; Bruce F. Johnston and Peter Kilby, *Agricultural and Structural Transformation* (New York: Oxford University Press, 1975); and Michael P. Todaro, *Economic Development in the Third World* (New York: Longman, 1977), pp. 204-32. The relationship between economic stagnation, instability, and the shift from the politics of development to the politics of order is well described in Gerald A. Heeger, *The Politics of Underdevelopment* (New York: St. Martin's Press, 1974).

2. For example, the behavioral variable of McClelland's "N-achievement" or the structural variable of Young's "differentiation" theory are too narrow either to explain rural change or analyze widely differing rural areas in useful ways. David C. McClelland, *The Achieving Society* (Glencoe, Ill.: Free Press, 1961); Frank W. Young and Ruth C. Young, *Comparative Studies of Community Growth* (Morgantown: West Virginia University Press, 1973).

3. In the 1970s more than 85 percent of the twenty-five million Ethiopians earn their livelihood from agriculture; in turn the economy is dependent on subsistence agrarian production. Total agricultural output as a percentage of gross domestic product is one of the highest in the world, probably 60 percent. Moreover, the nonmonetary sector probably accounts for 75 percent of the total agricultural contribution. The monetary sector of agriculture accounts for more than 90 percent of exports. Annual growth rate in the agricultural sector during the last decade averaged about 2.4 percent per year, an increase probably less than overall population growth. As a result, Ethiopia has one of the lowest per capita income levels in the world. The principal works on rural Ethiopia are H. Huffnagel, *Agriculture in Ethiopia* (Rome: United Nations Food and Agricultural Organization, 1961); and International Bank for Reconstruction and Development, Agricultural Projects Department, *Agricultural Sector Survey: Ethiopia*, 3 vols., (PA-143) Washington, 1972. A good discussion of agriculture and the economy is Assaffa Bequele and Eshetu Chole, *A Profile of the Ethiopian Economy* (Addis Ababa: Oxford University Press, 1969).

4. The Chilalo region is located in the western half of Arussi Province, its Northern border defined by the Awash River and its Southern by the the Webi Shebelli River. The area is approximately 140 kilometers long and varies from 20 to 70 in width. It contains 10,100 square kilometers, and its principal town, Asella, is approximately 170 kilometers from Addis Ababa. The geography, ecological environment, climate, and agricultural

resources of the area are set forth in Yelma Kabada, "Chilalo Awraja," *Ethiopian Geographical Journal* 5 (June 1967): 25-36.

5. This basic conceptual approach is taken from Dov Weintraub, "Rural Periphery, Societal Center, and Their Interaction in the Process of Agrarian Development: A Comparative Analytical Framework," *Rural Sociology* 35 (September 1970): 367-76. The analytical concept is perhaps best expressed by Edward Shils "Center and Perephery," in *The Logic of Personal Knowledge: Essays Presented to Michael Polanyi* (London: Routledge and Kegan Paul, 1961), pp. 117-30. An excellent empirical example is seen in Daniel Lerner, *The Passing of Traditional Society* (New York: Free Press, 1958). The more pedestrian spatial conception is illustrated in Harold Alderfer, *Local Government in Developing Countries* (New York: McGraw-Hill, 1964). For a general presentation of both conceptual visualizations of center and periphery see Peter H. Merkl, *Modern Comparative Politics* (New York: Holt, Rinehart and Winston, 1970), pp. 232-61.

6. Weintraub, "Rural Periphery," pp. 369-73.

7. A framework such as the one used can generate a wide range of related variables; hence it is essential to follow Robert K. Merton's rule, probably deducted from his own experience as a student of Parsons, of seeking and applying in the end only those variables that make the crucial explanatory difference. The choice should begin not from a narrow preconceived view, but from reflection on the broad range of social phenomena. Obviously, the key variables are likely to differ from area to area, and are always linked to the wider range of concepts and propositions that comprise the framework. See Merton, *Social Theory and Social Structure,* rev. and enl. ed. (Glencoe, Ill.: Free Press, 1957).

8. This brief summary is condensed from: John M. Cohen, "Rural Change in Ethiopia: A Study of Land, Elites, Power and Values in Chilalo Awraja " (Ph.D. dissertation, University of Colorado, 1973), pp. 92-616.

9. The historical background of Ethiopia and the specific relationship of Arsi Gallaland to that history are set forth in Robert L. Hess, *Ethiopia: The Modernization of Autocracy* (Ithaca, N.Y.: Cornell University Press, 1970); and Eike Haberland, *Galla Süd Äthiopians* (Stuttgart: Kohlhammer for Frobenius Institute, 1963). The territorial expansion and its effect on the Chilalo region are described in Harold G. Marcus, "Imperialism and Expansion in Ethiopia from 1865-1900," in *Colonialism in Africa,* ed. Lewis H. Gann and Peter Duignan (Cambridge: Cambridge University Press, 1969), pp. 420-61; and Arne Lexander, *The Changing Rural Society in Arussiland,* No. 7 (Addis Ababa: Chilalo Agricultural Development Unit [CADU], 1968), pp. 10-18.

10. The acquisition of the land, its conversion into government land tenure, the mechanics of its distribution, and a description of the recipients of land grants are set forth in John M. Cohen, "Ethiopia after Haile Selassie: The Government Land Factor," *African Affairs* 72

(October 1973): 365-82. The land tenure system, economic organization, hierarchical political system, and culture of provincial Ethiopia are generally summed up as feudal. The essence of this pattern in Ethiopia and Chilalo is described in Allen Hoben, *Land Tenure Among the Amhara of Ethiopia* (Chicago: University of Chicago Press, 1973); Donald N. Levine, *Wax and Gold: Tradition and Innovation in Ethiopian Culture* (Chicago: University of Chicago Press, 1965); and Frederick C. Gamst, "Peasants and Elites without Urbanism: The Civilization of Ethiopia," *Comparative Studies in Society and History* 12 (October 1970): 373-92. The differences between feudalism in traditional Amhara regions and in southern conquest areas like Chilalo are exhibited by comparing Hoben to Arne Lexander, *Land Ownership, Tenancy and Social Organization in the Wajji Area*, No. 50 (Asella: CADU, 1970).

11. For a detailed description of a broad range of demographic and social statistics on the area see Ministry of Land Reform and Administration, *Report on Land Tenure Survey of Arussi Province* (Addis Ababa: Department of Land Tenure, 1967); Central Statistical Office, *Report on a Survey of Arussi Province* (Addis Ababa: Central Statistical Office, 1966); and Central Statistical Office, *Survey of Major Towns in Ethiopia* (Addis Ababa: Central Statistical Office, 1968).

12. The project plan is described in Sweden, SIDA Project Preparation Team, *Report No. 1 on the Establishment of Regional Development Project in Ethiopia* (Addis Ababa: Swedish International Development Agency [SIDA], 1966). The concept of "package program" incorporates: 1) green revolution inputs, 2) adequate farm credits, 3) intensive educational programs, 4) individual farm plans, 5) improvement in grass roots institutions, 6) assured prices for agricultural products, 7) reliable marketing facilities, 8) rural public works, 9) coordination of all elements under a single authority.

13. The background of the CADU project, its objectives, organization, plans, programs, means of development, and results are set forth in Bengt Nekby, *CADU: An Ethiopian Experiment in Developing Peasant Farming* (Stockholm: Prisma Publishers, 1971); and John M. Cohen, "Rural Change in Ethiopia: The Chilalo Agricultural Development Unit," *Economic Development and Cultural Change* 22 (October 1974): 580-614.

14. Summary data on economic growth are set forth in CADU, Planning and Evaluation Section, *CADU Annual Reports 1971/72 & 1972/73*, revised No. 77 (Asella: CADU, 1973); CADU, Planning and Evaluation Section,*CADU Annual Report 1970/71*, No. 65 (Asella: CADU, 1971); and CADU, Planning and Evaluation Section,*Cost/Benefit Analysis on CADU for 1967/68-1974/75* (Asella: CADU, 1971). These are summarized in Cohen, "Rural Change in Ethiopia," pp. 595-601, 614.

15. The data summarized in this section are presented at length in John M. Cohen, "Effects of Green Revolution Strategies on Tenants and Small-

scale Landowners in the Chilalo Region of Ethiopia," *Journal of Developing Areas* 9, 2 (1975): 335-58.

16. Details and mechanics of the granting procedures, the concentration of land grants on central and provincial elites, and the effects of these grants on the development process are discussed in detail in Cohen, "Ethiopia After Haile Selassie," pp. 365-82.

17. Field research by the author documented the existence of approximately 40,000 hectares of government land, which findings were confirmed by a government study, "Inventory of Government Land and Arussi Province by Wereda in 1971/72," Appendix to H. Wetterhall, "Government Land in Ethiopia," internal memoradnum, Ministry of Land Reform and Administration, June 1972.

18. Based on sources cited in footnote 11 and CADU studies.

19. The new agreement stated: "Implementation of legislation on agricultural tenancy relationships shall start throughout the project area not later than one year after the promulgation of such legislation. Proposals on nationwide legislation on cadastral survey, land registration and measures aiming at optimal utilization of land shall be submitted to Parliament not later than two years after the signature of the agreement. The CADU area shall have priority in the implementation of such legislation." Sweden, SIDA, *Plan of Operation for the Chilalo Agricultural Development Unit (CADU) 1971-1974/75* (Addis Ababa: SIDA, 1971), p. 10. The history of the land reform movement is described in H.C. Dunning, "Land Reform in Ethiopia: A Case Study in Non-Development," *U.C.L.A. Law Review* 18 (1970): 271-307.

20. For a general discussion, see John M. Cohen and Peter Koehn, *Ethiopian Provincial and Municipal Government: Imperial Pattern and Post Revolutionary Changes,* Ethiopian Studies Monograph No. 8 (East Lansing, Mich.: Michigan State University, Ethiopian Studies Center, 1979).

21. On these dimensions of change see Dov Weintraub, "Developmental Change—Toward a Generalized Conceptualization of Its Basic Dimensions and the Relations Among Them," *Development and Change* 3, 1 (1971-72): 1-24.

22. This basic characteristic of the tax system is discussed in J.C.D. Lawrence and H.S. Mann, "FAO Land Policy Project (Ethiopia)," *Ethiopia Observer* 9, 4 (1966): 298-99.

23. The question of feudalism is raised in John M. Cohen, "Ethiopia: A Survey on the Existence of a Feudal Peasantry," *Journal of Modern African Studies* 12 (December 1974): 665-72; Marina Ottaway, "Social Classes and Corporate Interests in the Ethiopian Revolution," *Journal of Modern African Studies* 14 (September 1976): 469-86; Gene Ellis, "The Feudal Paradigm as a Hinderance to Understanding Ethiopia," *Journal of Modern African Studies* 14 (June 1976): 275-95; and John Markakis and Nega Ayele, *Class and Revolution in Ethiopia* (London: Spokesman Press, 1978), pp. 55-60.

24. This fallacy is effectively described by Levy who argues that society is analytical, and analytical elements cannot have causality. For causality one must move to the level of the concrete. Marion Levy, *The Structure of Society* (Princeton: Princeton University Press, 1952).

25. "The basic cause of grand theory is the initial choice of a level of thinking so general that its practitioners cannot logically get down to observation. They never, as grand theorists, get down from the higher generalities to problems in their historical and structural contexts. This absence of a firm sense of genuine problems, in turn, makes for the unreality so noticeable in their pages. One resulting characteristic is a seemingly arbitrary and certainly endless elaborating of distinctions, which neither enlarge our understanding nor make our experience more sensible." C. Wright Mills, *The Sociological Imagination* (New York: Grove Press, 1961), p. 33. Mills also criticizes the "abstract empiricist" who stays so close to the concrete that rigor and triviality are simultaneously achieved.

26. The term role has many definitional problems. Various definitions can be classified as: 1) normative culture patterns regulating behavior in social positions, 2) an individual's definition of his situation with reference to his and others' social positions, or 3) the behavior of actors occupying social positions. These lead to a common definition that "individuals 1) in social locations 2) behave 3) with reference to expectations." Neal Gross, Ward S. Mason, and Alexander McEachern, *Explorations in Role Analysis* (New York: John Wiley and Sons, 1958), p. 17.

27. It should be parenthetically noted that Levy sees a similar relationship between ideal and real roles and ideal and real structures. To Levy it is the disparity between the two which creates energy in role holders and motivates them to alter the society in which they live. This point is introduced only to show that the control and facilitation scheme is not unprecedented. Levy, *Structure of Society,* pp. 159-60, 123-25.

28. For a discussion of the concept of elite in the writing of various analysts, see: Suzanne Keller, *Beyond The Ruling Class: Strategic Elites in Modern Society* (New York: Random House, 1968), pp. 1-64. One of the best definitions of the term is that of Nadel, who defines elite as an aggregate of people with distinctive characteristics: a position of high status, some degree of corporate group character as well as exclusiveness, awareness of their pre-eminent position as a consequence of some attribute shared by right, recognition of their general superiority by society at large, and the fact that they set standards for the whole society. S.F. Nadel, "The Concept of Social Elites," *International Social Science Bulletin* 8,3 (1956): 413-24.

29. It is submitted that this definition and typology of provincial elites is more compatible with the goal of understanding these critical elites than the narrower sociological paradigms which focus on aristocracies, high estates, and ruling classes. This problem is not so great as would appear

John M. Cohen

because in rural Ethiopia in general, and in Chilalo *Awraja* in particular, there is a strong correlation between ascriptive characteristics of family, wealth, or education and the membership of an individual in any of the functional elite categories. For a similar functional categorization of elites see Keller, *Beyond the Ruling Class,* pp. 88-106.

30. Findings and cross-tabulations are set forth in detail in John M. Cohen, *Sociological Profile of Rural Elites in Chilalo Awraja,* Chialo Agricultural Unit, Special Studies Series, No. 4 (Addis Ababa: CADU, 1972); and Cohen, "Rural Change in Ethiopia," pp. 682-788. A summary of findings is presented in John M. Cohen, "Ethiopian Provincial Elites and The Process of Change," *Journal of Ethiopian Studies* 11,2 (1973): 93-111.

31. The importance of such elites to the process of change in rural areas is set forth in a series of case studies of peasant wars in E.R. Wolf, *Peasant Wars of the Twentieth Century* (New York: Harper and Row, 1970), p. xii and *passim.*

32. It is clear that the models of role behavior response to change which follow in this section are merely at the threshold of behavioral explanation. The challenge involved in actually operationalizing these models is to devise procedures by which to quantify the variables involved. This is illustrated in an area with an extensive amount of empirical data by American political science's attempt to produce a working model of judicial conversion based on role analysis. See Sheldon Goldman and Thomas P. Jahnige, *The Federal Courts As a Political System* (New York: Harper & Row, 1971), pp. 197-200. The great difficulties in establishing a working model of judicial conversion are nothing in comparison to those involved in operationalizing the model in Chilalo *Awraja.* Nevertheless, it is submitted that the models presented are correct and capable of being operationalized.

33. These are described in detail in John M. Cohen and Dov Weintraub, *Land and Peasants in Imperial Ethiopia: The Social Background to a Revolution* (Assen: Van Gorcum & Co., 1975).

34. **The question of whether this will actually occur** can be considered by comparing rural change in Ethiopia to that in the Philippines, a comparison which reinforces the conclusions presented here. In the Philippines, modern institutions and functions were superimposed on, and made to function in, an on-going social system where the old landowning elite (*illustrados*) came to constitute the political center. Using the party system, their traditional control of cultural symbols and values, and their control of the peripheral masses through a downward linking patron-client system, these elites monopolize the entire system. Further support from the conservative church hierarchy assures their monolithic control and the resulting stability. The elites disregard or misrepresent the fundamental interests of major groups, and instead of actually promoting the social processes of aggregating and articulating the fundamental economic and social interests of the periphery, they promote

political stability and their own vested interests. A strict maintenance model and a blocked society result. Those in control aim at impressions of development and change in terms of specific local conditions: loans; piecemeal projects; and general improvement of services in technology, health, education, and community welfare, but these are superficial given the problems of land and taxation reforms and land redistribution which are basic to the poverty and backwardness of the country. See Dov Weintraub, Miriam Shapiro, and Belinda Aquio, "Agrarian Development and Modernization in the Philippines in the Context of Relations Between the National Center and the Rural Periphery," research paper from the Project on Comparative Analysis of Processes of Agricultural Development and Modernization, Hebrew University and US Department of Agriculture, Jerusalem, 1971.

35. A good presentation of the dimensions of this issue is given in Hess, *Ethiopia*, pp. 240-48.

36. For a description of the general patterns of the revolution see Marina and David Ottaway, *Ethiopia: Empire in Revolution* (New York: Africana Publishing Co., 1978): Colin Legum, *Ethiopia: The Fall of Haile Selassie's Empire* (New York: Africana Publishing Co., 1975); Markakis and Nega Ayele, *Class and Revolution in Ethiopia*; Peter Koehn, "Ethiopian Politics: Military Intervention and Prospects for Further Change," *Africa Today* 22 (April-June 1975): 7-21.

37. For details on the rural and urban land reforms and their effects see John M. Cohen and Peter H. Koehn, "Rural and Urban Land Reform in Ethiopia," *African Law Studies* 14, 1 (1977): 3-61; Allan Hoben, "Perspectives on Land Reform in Ethiopia: The Political Role of the Peasantry," *Rural Africana* 28 (1975): 55-69; John M. Cohen, Arthur A. Goldsmith, and John W. Mellor, "Rural Development Issues Following Ethiopian Land Reform," *Africa Today* 23 (April-June 1976): 7-28; and Michael Stahl, *New Seeds in Old Soil; A Study of the Land Reform Process in Western Wollega, Ethiopia 1975-76*, Research Report No. 40 (Uppsala: Scandinavian Institute of African Studies, 1977).

38. These are described in great detail in John M. Cohen and Seleshi Sisaye, *Research on Socioeconomic Development in Ethiopia: Past Problems and Future Issues in Rural-Urban Studies*, Bulletin No. 84 (Ithaca, N.Y.: Cornell University, Department of Rural Sociology, 1977).

39. Peter Koehn, "Forecast for Political Change in Ethiopia: An Urban Perspective," paper presented to the Sixteenth Annual Meeting of the African Studies Association, Syracuse, N.Y., November 1973. Important points from this paper are included in Koehn's chapter in this book.

5

The Diffusion and Invention of Legislative and Party Structures in Anglophone Africa

James R. Scarritt

There is a broad consensus among students of African politics that the "Westminster Model" embodied in the British political system has not been successfully transferred to African countries formerly under British rule. Most analysts agree that the experience of British colonialism and the political structures inherited from that experience have had a significant influence on postindependence politics in these countries, although there is not a consensus on the exact nature of this influence.[1] This chapter attempts to demonstrate that the control and facilitation framework and the associated propositions and causal model can provide a more accurate description and a more powerful explanation of crucial aspects of the transformation of the "Westminster Model"—the diffusion and invention of legislative and party structures, functions, and power—than the descriptions and explanations provided in the existing literature. This demonstration will involve a brief review of the existing literature followed by an analysis of legislatures and then parties in terms of the major concepts of the control and facilitation framework, applying various propositions where appropriate.

Legislatures and political parties in ex-British Africa are usefully studied together for several reasons. They are central elements of the "Westminster Model," and are closely linked in that model, as they are in most political systems. Diffusion of Westminster type linkages to Africa and changes in these linkages through invention can be studied together with diffusion and invention of the structures themselves. Legislatures and parties both have relatively well defined external boundaries and internal units, thus providing relatively easy identification of structural elements which can be categorized as either diffused or invented. Finally, legislative structures were initially diffused involuntarily from Britain, while diffusion played a significantly smaller role in the development of African political parties, and such diffusion that did occur was voluntary. The significance of these distinctions can be explored by comparing changes in the two types of organization.

A Review of the Literature on African Legislative and Political Party Change

For legislatures in ex-British Africa the extent and path of diffusion and invention can be clearly established historically. During the colonial period the British established legislative councils in all of their African territories. These were modeled on the British Parliament in many respects, but differed from it in many others, although they became more similar to it the nearer the African territory approached to independence. As African participation in the political systems of these territories increased, legislative councils (called legislative assemblies in the terminal period of colonial rule when they had gained considerable power) evolved from appointed, advisory, and predominantly nonAfrican bodies into elected, responsible, African-dominated parliaments through a series of stages, the details of which need not concern us here. Acceptance of increasing participation in these legislative institutions was made a condition of the transfer of power to Africans, and the independence constitutions negotiated between African nationalist parties and the British Government invariably included the perpetuation of these colonial legislatures in the form of independent parliaments. This process was much more a convenient tactic of negotiation than a deliberate long range plan of preparation for independence, but it nevertheless involved deliberate and involuntary diffusion of legislative structures.[2] It was not the structure of the British Parliament itself which was diffused to Africa, but rather the terminal structure of colonial legislatures. The more significant ways in which the latter differed from the former will be explicated in the course of the detailed analysis presented in the following section.

In 1968 Newell Stultz made the first significant attempt to generalize about postindependence legislatures in formerly British-ruled black African countries.[3] He identified eleven "structural and performance characteristics" of these legislatures: unicameralism, popular election of legislators, presidentialism, constitutional supremacy, impotence of those second chambers that did exist, absence or ineffectiveness of a formal parliamentary opposition, independence of government party backbenchers, absence of lobbying, parochialism of demands and inexpertness of debate, and functional ambiguity. These were then grouped under two more general and basically contradictory characteristics: commitment to popular government and isolation and concentration of decision making power. Stultz gave specific explanations for some of the characteristics he identified, but the two more general characteristics constituted implicit explanations of the others, and Stultz predicted that future changes would be heavily influenced by the working out of the contradiction between the articulated value of popular government and the extant situation of isolated, concentrated power. This situation was seen as the primary source of changes in the legislative characteristics inherited at the time of independence.

In an unpublished paper written in 1974, Malcom Jewell attributed legislative change in Africa away from the "Westminster Model" to the political elites' desire for a structure which would contribute more effectively to national integration, and to the establishment of one-party systems.[4] Other recent general discussions of legislatures in formerly British-ruled African countries are descriptive and legalisitc, or extremely brief.[5] Virtually all commentators agree that while many "forms" or "structural details" of the inherited parliamentary system have been retained, the "reality" or "deeper structures" have been changed substantially, and the power of African legislatures has declined sharply. These phenomena can be described and explained more completely utilizing the control and facilitation approach.

Attempts to generalize about changes in African political parties have been more numerous and more contradictory. The path of diffusion and invention of political party structures is more difficult to trace because borrowing has been more eclectic. Groups more or less closely affiliated with the British Labor Party influenced the structure of African parties,[6] but the structure of the Labor Party was not diffused in *toto* to Africa, especially with regard to that party's trade union base. Structures were also borrowed from other European leftist parties. Because African parties were organized by emerging educated elites in response to grievances they felt against specific aspects of colonial rule, they had greater freedom to invent structures than did legislatures, whose development was under British control, and they thus reflected more extensively the diverse social structures of various territories. Because the masses shared many of the elites' grievances, parties gained broad popular support, and in some cases utilized this support to create an apparently strong organization. In order to demonstrate their strength, and thus exert pressure on the British government to grant African majority rule and then independence, nationalist parties vigorously contested elections. Upon winning these elections, they participated in, and eventually came to dominate, the legislatures whose structures they had helped to create through negotiations with the British. On the surface, then, at least some aspects of the "Westminster Model" of party organization and party-legislative relationships appeared to have been successfully diffused to British African territories.

Observers of postindependence changes in parties first noticed the decline of interparty competition and the rise of the one-party system, involving various degrees of authoritarian measures such as restricting or outlawing opposition parties, controlling nonparty associations, and manipulating elections. James Coleman and Carl Rosberg explained this phenomenon in terms of the heavy functional load placed upon governing parties at the time of independence; the authoritarian-bureaucratic-centralizing ethos of colonial rule; the high legitimacy granted to parties, which were seen as having brought about independence; and the elitism, statism, and nationalism which were prominent characteristics of African elite political culture.[7] The same authors divided African parties into two broad types: revolutionary-centralizing and pragmatic-pluralistic, with the former rating higher on ideology, organization, and popular participation. The one-party tendency was present in both types of parties.[8]

The same study also noted that dominant parties became weaker in some respects at the same time that they were increasing their dominance, and this tendency was explicated in greater detail by Immanuel Wallerstein and Michael Lofchie.[9] The former attributed it to mass interest in private affairs, the party leadership's assumption of government jobs, the internalization of societal conflicts within the party as former opposition party members and various auxiliary organizations were incorporated into it, and the increasing strength of government as performer of some functions previously carried out by the party; while the latter attributed it to the simultaneous presence of a high level of mass political participation, widespread demands for welfare services, extensive unemployment, problems of managing a technologically sophisticated economy, and a poorly developed sense of national unity—a set of characteristics quite similar to Coleman and Rosberg's heavy functional load—combined with the strength of the bureaucracy as an alternative dominant structure. The fusion of many party and government roles, which was sometimes termed a merger of party and government, was intended to strengthen party control over government, but its actual effect was almost always the reverse. These developments raised the possibility that African one-party states were becoming no-party states.[10]

It was not long before Aristide Zolberg suggested that mass parties had never, or only very briefly, been as well-organized as their own propaganda and previous studies had claimed, thus raising doubts about the significance of the distinction between revolutionary-centralizing and pragmatic-pluralistic parties. He felt that party state rather than no-party state was the appropriate term for African single-party regimes because parties continued to exist in the form of political machines, emphasizing local autonomy and the provision of jobs and material rewards.[11] This theme received considerable elaboration from Henry Bienen and James C. Scott, who pointed out a number of differences as well as similarities between American urban political machines and African national political machines, especially the much greater significance of elections in the former case; Scott also suggested that African political machines were not very successful in maintaining themselves because of a combination of scarce rewards available for distribution, traditional resistance, and bureaucratic-military opposition.[12]

Giovanni Sartori notes the resemblance of African parties to both no-party systems and political machines, but suggests that, as parts of "formless" or "fluid" (undifferentiated and diffuse) political systems, they are fundamentally different from western, communist, and some other third world parties which exist within "formed" political systems. He and others doubt that the functional performance of one-party systems is significantly superior to, or even as good as, that of other types of regimes.[13] Roberta McKown and Robert Kauffman found that one-party or one-party dominant systems were superior to multi-party and no-party systems in controlling turmoil and communal instability in the mid-1960's, but were not superior in controlling elite conflict or in fostering economic development. These authors concluded that "party system" was not a very useful concept in the analysis of African politics, a conclusion reinforced by the fact that a number of countries with various types of party systems have experienced military coups.[14]

Most observers agree that the trends toward authoritarianism and the weakening of party structure are closely related. Nelson Kasfir includes both in the broader concept of "departicipation," a phenomenon which he believes is caused by elites' desire to stay in power, their authoritarian habits, and their belief that economic development requires central direction; and by mass acquiescence, which is partly habitual and partly a response to coercion.[15] Claude Ake and other class analysts see departicipation as a technique utilized by sections of the dominant class to protect their class interests against challenges from other sections of that class and from subordinate classes.[16] There is considerable overlap between these types of explanation, including the prediction that African political parties are likely to remain both poorly organized and oligarchic in that organization which they do possess.

Zolberg's analysis of the structural weakness of almost all parties at almost all times and the various assertions in the literature cited above which are compatible with his analysis constitute what may be called the first revisionist interpretation of African political party change. More recently, there has been a second revisionist interpretation which has questioned the structural and functional uniformity attributed to African parties by the first revisionists, although the variations emphasized by this interpretation are quite different from the typologies criticized by the first revisionists.

Mary Welfling measured the institutionalization of African party systems from 1945 to 1970 in terms of thirteen indicators, and found that institutionalization was not strongly related to the number of parties, the Coleman-Rosberg typology, recency of independence, or length of experience with party activity. Highly institutionalized one-party systems, however, were all ones in which interparty competition had always been relatively insignificant, and thus minimal coercion had been employed against opposing parties. When level and trend of institutionalization scores were combined in a two-dimensional graph, all formerly British African countries which have not had military coups were found to have more institutionalized and/or institutionalizing party systems than all such countries which have had coups. This same distinction held true for almost *all* African countries. Although Welfling detected a trend toward convergence among African parties in their level of institutionalization, she also found that the more nationally oriented a party system was at the time of independence, the more likely it was to become more institutionalized between independence and 1970, and that party system institutionalization reduced elite conflict.[17]

Jay Hakes' finding that, in formerly British African countries which have not had coups, the percentage of contested seats in postindependence elections increased or remained constant in comparison with the last election prior to independence, while in such countries which have had coups, the percentage of contested seats decreased, is consistent with Welfing's findings.[18] Sang-Seek Park suggests that these studies be expanded by utilizing various indicators of institutionalization, scope of popular support, and separation of party and government to classify African political systems under civilian rule into four categories: party-dominant, government-dominant, party-government balanced, and party-government fused.[19]

Most recently, Ruth Collier has argued that "...African countries, starting with different preindependence experiences with mass political participation and party dominance during the period in which democratic institutions were introduced, followed different sequences of events in dismantling these institutions and in setting up different subtypes of authoritarian rule in the first decade and a half of independence." She points out that elections played a different and more significant role in British Africa than they did in French Africa. In the former they tended to be competitive, in the latter, plebiscitary. There were two patterns of electoral and party system development in formerly British countries, differing sharply from the patterns found in formerly French territories. First, those countries with high interparty competitiveness before independence also had high electoral participation, and retained these characteristics for a while after independence, but have since experienced military coups. Second, those countries with low interparty competitiveness had lower electoral participation, formed one-party regimes soon after independence, usually with a low or moderate level of coercion, and in most cases have since instituted competitive elections within the one-party framework. In these countries the political power of the European settler population kept Africans united in a single party for most of the preindependence period, and this relative unity has had lasting consequences for party system development.[20]

The common themes running through all of these studies are that: 1)

James R. Scarritt

There are significant differences among African parties and party systems in terms of at least some components of structural institutionalization and at least some aspects of functional performance, although these differences are small in comparison to those found in global comparisons. 2) The most institutionalized and functionally effective party systems tend to be those in which a single party which had the support of a substantial majority of voters prior to independence eliminated opposition parties with relatively little coercion and established competitive intraparty elections after independence. It is not claimed that such parties are mass parties in the European sense, or that they are a guarantee against military coups, but only that they have been relatively strong and successful up to the present time. Finally, it should be noted that these studies rely more heavily than did the previous literature on systematic comparisons utilizing relatively precise data on numerous specific characteristics of African parties and party systems.

This last point suggests the potential utility of an even more detailed examination of political party change employing the functional, structural, and media of exchange categories of the control and facilitation framework. Such an examination will help to demonstrate the relative validity of the contradictory trends presented in the literature and the somewhat contradictory explanations given for them, and to assess the relative importance of invention and diffusion, even though quantified or even reasonably precise data on many of the variables included in the framework are not available, and we have not attempted to measure variables quantitatively even where appropriate data are available. The general way in which structural, functional, and media concepts will be applied to legislatures and political parties can be summarized briefly here, prior to the detailed discussion presented in subsequent sections. Although legislatures and political parties have been terminated by military coups (twice in the case of Ghana), the following analysis will use the present tense as a matter of convenience, except where specific reference is made to organizations which no longer exist.

Within any societal political system organized collectivities such as legislatures and political parties can be a part of any one or more functional subsystems, and can command varying amounts of each medium of exchange. A number of scholars have suggested a variety of functions which both legislatures and political parties may perform.[21] The framework employed in this book suggests that one important set of questions to be asked about the diffusion and invention of legislative and party structures concerns continuities and changes in their functional performance and the subsystems of the societal political system to which they consequently belong. To the extent that legislatures and parties are engaged in socializing and legitimizing activities they are part of the pattern socialization and control subsystem of the societal political system; to the extent that they attempt to represent interests, support or

Legislative and Party Structures

oppose other political structures, or resolve conflicts they are part of the integrative subsystem; to the extent that they engage in policy making they are part of the goal attainment subsystem; and to the extent that they affect the provision of material resources or services they are part of the adaptive subsystem. Their ability to employ some combination of exchange media in the performance of each of these functions is the primary determinant of their functional effectiveness.

Internally, diffusion and invention of legislative and political party structures can be analyzed in terms of continuity and change in both structural levels and internal functional subsystems. Values generally pertain to societal political systems or, in the case of variant values, to elites seeking to change the system, rather than to specific collectivities such as legislatures or political parties. The latter do have their own specific norms, collectivity structures, and roles, however, which can be diffused or invented, and these are analyzed extensively in the relevant case study literature. With regard to internal functional subsystems, on the other hand, this chapter will have to be inventive because the theoretical literature from which relevant ideas can be diffused is extremely sparse, and the case study literature without exception fails to categorize data in this fashion. Norms, collectivity structures, and roles within legislatures and political parties in formerly British African territories will be categorized as belonging to various functional subsystems on the basis of their performance for the legislature or political party of the same functions which have been described for societal political systems. Thus, a norm or role may be diffused from one legislature or political system to another, but a new function invented for that norm or role in the borrowing system. It may also control more or less of various exchange media than is the case in its system of origin.

Diffusion and Innovation in Legislatures

Although there were numerous differences of detail in the structure of terminal colonial legislatures in British Africa, they were even more similar to one another than to the metropolitan Parliament, and thus they can be described in terms of a common pattern of roles, collectivity structures, and norms. This will enable changes in all of these structural levels to be described systematically and comparatively, and explained in terms of our propositions. Since independence, some piecemeal diffusion of legislative structures has taken place, mainly among the ex-British African countries, but also from sources outside the British-type parliamentary system. Such diffusion and the significant invention which has also taken place create differences as well as new similarities among the legislatures of ex-British Africa. Thus the following analysis will describe how and explain why unique characteristics of individual legislatures differ from the common structural pattern present at the time of independence.

Turning first to roles, we may identify the following significant ones for terminal colonial or postindependence legislatures: speaker, deputy speaker, head of state, prime minister, leader of government business, minister, junior minister, whip, leader of the opposition, opposition front bencher, government party backbencher, opposition backbencher, party member, committee member, nominated or specially elected member, member, civil service advisor, and clerk or administrative staff member. Significant collectivity structures within the legislature include: the cabinet, the government (including cabinet and junior ministers), the opposition, parliamentary parties, standing committees, and in some cases the second chamber which, because of its relative unimportance, will be analyzed as a single collectivity structure.

Legislative norms are quite numerous, and our treatment of them must be highly selective, attempting to identify both the major formal rules and the major informal norms. The list presented here was developed from the general legislative liturature and that on the British Parliament,[22] in addition to the Africanist literature. From these sources we can identify significant sets of norms relating to: the selection of members of the legislature through election or appointment; the frequency of legislative sittings; procedures for dissolving the legislature; various aspects of legislative debate such as the head of state's annual message to the legislature, the number of stages in debating a bill and the time and attention devoted to each stage, the introduction and debate of government and private members' bills and motions, the budget debate, adjournment debates, limitations on debate, divisions, and questions; party discipline, crossing the floor, and the legitimate bases and tactics of opposition; constituency and special interest representation; substantive specialization and expertise; and the privileges of members of the legislature.

After discussing changes in these structures, we will examine their significance for changes in internal functional subsystems and the distribution of power and influence in Anglophone African legislatures, and will discuss the consequent changes in the functions which these legislatures perform for the societal political systems of which they are a part.

The role of speaker is one which has been diffused in a relatively unaltered form from the British Parliament and colonial African legislatures. As in the latter, the person elected speaker usually need not be a sitting member of the legislature. His role as impartial master of legislative debate and proceedings off the floor remains essentially the same as in the British model. Although speakers have occasionally had difficulty maintaining their rapport with opposition parties because of rulings unfavorable to these parties, as was the case in Zambia in 1969, such instances have been far outnumbered by instances of speakers bending over backward to be fair to opposition legislators.[23] Several of the propositions presented in Chapter 1 are useful in explaining the successful diffusion of this role. It is a specific role (B1) which can be adopted separately from other structural elements, and thus requires minimal reinterpretation (D2). Speakers performed effectively for a long time in colonial legislatures, and during the latter part of that period established a reputation for giving fair treatment to African nationalist legislators, many of whom were inexperienced in legislative procedures; thus the continuance of this role after independence was compatible with positively evaluated tradition (D1). Given the frequent conflicts and low level of expertise which are, as we will see, typical characteristics of African legislatures, the presence of a neutral expert parliamentarian in control of legislative proceedings has high utility for government, government party backbenchers, and the opposition (C5). Since this utility and compatibility continue to be perceived over time, in spite of other changes in legislative stucture, the government, which exercises the predominance of power in African legislatures, favors the continuation of the role of speaker in relatively unmodified form (E4).

What has been said concerning the role of speaker also applies to some extent to the role of deputy speaker. This is a newer role in most African legislatures, however, and some incumbents have not played the role very effectively, and have certainly not engaged in role making, often because their tenure in office has been quite brief.

In sharp contrast to the role of speaker, the role of head of state in African legislatures changed fundamentally both before and after independence. British colonial governors were both the local embodiment of the monarch and the effective chief executive. After the early years of the colonial period, they did not participate in the legislative councils except to deliver annual addresses outlining the major events of the past year and policies to be implemented in the coming year. During the period of self-government immediately prior to independence, as well as the first few years after independence, the governor or governor general was a primarily symbolic head of state, while effective executive powers were wielded by the prime minister. Within a few years of independence, however, most ex-British African territories had adopted a presidential structure of government, which essentially returned the position of the head of state in the legislature to that of the effective colonial governor. [24] Even in Ghana and Kenya, where the president was entitled to a regular seat in the legislature, this privilege was rarely used.[25] The form and significance of the head of state's annual message have remained constant in spite of these changes in other aspects of his role, although during the period of a British-type parliamentary system messages were delivered for the effective executive. The same pattern of continuity can be observed in the head of state's possession and effective use of power to dissolve the legislature, in the head of state's independence of legislative votes of confidence, and in the head of state's extensive use of emergency powers

James R. Scarritt

with very little legislative oversight. The concomitant election of presidents and legislatures, combined with legal provisions guaranteeing that the legislative majority will be committed to supporting the president, and presidents' extraparliamentary sources of power, tie legislatures to presidents even more closely than their legislative council predecessors were tied to colonial governors. Change in this role clearly involved diffusion among ex-British countries; most of those attaining independence at a later date switched to a presidential head of state at the time of independence.

Continuity and change in this role and the norms associated with it can be explained by a combination of several propositions. The initial change to a British-type role for the head of state was a part of the involuntary diffusion of legislative structure discussed above; it is the further change to the presidential role which needs explanation at this point. Presidentialism represented a well-differentiated set of alternative norms (A2c) diffused from various political systems outside the British sphere of influence. The role of a separate ceremonial head of state, although well integrated into the involuntarily diffused parliamentary system, was poorly integrated and incompatible with the strong personal leadership which pervaded African political systems (A2, D1). An effective head of state possessing a high degree of power, on the other hand, was well integrated with this type of political leadership and compatible with traditions established by the preindependence role of governor. The strength of negative evaluation attached to the latter role by politically conscious Africans was insufficient to retard adoption of a similar head of state role with the title of president. More important than compatibility, however, was the high utility which a presidential head of state appeared to have for maintaining political stability and fostering development (C5). This utility was highest for those who were in an excellent position to act as innovators—the top political leadership (C6) who exercised extensive control of power and other media of exchange (E4), and for whom playing roles in the split executive had low utility (C5b). Specific norms such as the form of the annual address and the power of dissolution could be more easily diffused once the complex role of head of state was broken down into its component parts (B2). Thus the role of head of state diffused involuntarily from the British political system was reinterpreted to be more compatible with other aspects of the extensively different African political systems into which it was introduced (D2), although specific norms related to this role have been accepted virtually unchanged. This reinterpretation took place over time as this role complex interacted with other elements of political structure (C4).

With the abolition of the role of prime minister and the absence of the president from legislatures in ex-British Africa, leadership in those bodies tended to fall to the collectivity structure of government as a whole—the cabinet and junior ministers, although the role of leader of government business was diffused from Britain in modified form, or the role of vice president was invented to more or less effectively centralize leadership in one person in some countries. Governments in ex-British African countries which still have legislatures do act with a very high degree of unity in the legislature, and it is government acting as a whole which wields the predominance of power in those legislative bodies. Governments are larger in proportion to the total size of the legislature than is the case in Britain or most other countries with parliamentary systems, frequently approaching half of the membership, and the size factor alone augments government's power. This collectivity's greater unity, prestige, and expertise relative to other legislators further augment its power and influence. Working through its civil service advisors, who are usually seen by backbenchers as appendages of government in the legislature, government drafts virtually all of the bill considered by these legislatures, and other members are almost never consulted in this process.[26]

The role of individual ministers within the government is one which is or was played differently in different ex-British countries and by different individuals in the same country. At one extreme is the case of Ghana under Kwame Nkrumah in which all ministers were completely overshadowed by the president.[27] More frequently, however, ministerial position is closely related to overall political power and influence, with powerful politicians occupying key ministerial roles and engaging in some degree of role making, and shifts in the occupants of these roles following closely upon shifts in overall political standing. Yet there is no doubt that criteria of administrative competence have also frequently influenced ministerial appointments. Ethnic and factional balance in the government have been more important criteria in the selection of junior ministers, and incumbents of these positions have had much less opportunity for significant role making. They have also occasionally failed to support the government in all of their speeches.[28]

Norms closely related to government and the roles of which it is comprised include the frequency of legislative sittings, the number of stages in debating a bill and the time and attention devoted to each stage, and the significance of government bills and motions. Because of government's deliberate decisions, ex-British African legislatures meet relatively infrequently, and in some cases with declining frequency over the years.[29] The process of considering bills has also been significantly speeded up, again deliberately. The third reading is a mere formality even more frequently than is the case in the British Parliament, and it has been eliminated altogether in Tanzania.[30] Certificates of urgency are commonly used to avoid delays between the date bills are published and the date they are introduced in the legislature, and all stages of debate are frequently carried out in one day. Finally, virtually all bills debated are government bills, and the same is true for a greater proportion of motions than is the case in the British Parliament.

James R. Scarritt

There are common tendencies toward centralization of power and increasing the compatibility of legislative structure with the structure of the broader societal political system in all of these changes in government and related roles and norms. Thus the same propositions can be used to explain this entire set of related changes. Governments in formerly British African countries were initially composed of a relatively cohesive group of nationalist political party leaders who were committed to the actualization of a number of innovative norms (A1, C6, C6e) in the structure of the political system itself, but more importantly in policy programs which required changes in political structure for their successful implementation (C5). They believed that successful policy implementation required greater concentration of power (A3). Some aspects of the increased concentration of power in the government, such as rapidity in debating bills and the predominance of government bills, were compatible with preindependence legislative traditions (D1). Changes of this type were anticipated by most relevant political actors, both inside and outside the legislature, at least after they had taken place in Ghana, the first British African territory to attain independence (C7). Thus reinterpretation of some aspects of the complex collectivity structure of government and its associated roles and norms, combined with the diffusion of other aspects—usually quite specific ones—in relatively unmodified form, established a direction of change which, interacting with changes in other legislative and nonlegislative components of these African political systems, provided a reintegration of political structure highly satisfactory to the political elites of these systems (B2, D2, E3, E4).

The opposition as a collectivity and its associated roles and norms have significantly eroded or disappeared altogether in all ex-British African territories since independence. As was noted above, this phenomenon—essentially an aspect of political party change, but also affecting legislatures—sometimes occured peacefully and sometimes only after bitter and often violent confrontations between government and opposition. The failure to recognize an official leader of the opposition has sometimes been a signal for the opposition's demise. Oppositions were usually poorly disciplined and beset by leadership conflicts. Thus they were often poorly prepared to perform the functions of constructive criticism, formulation of alternative policies, and facilitation of legislative control over the executive traditionally assigned to oppositions.[31] The opposition, however, has not always been ineffective or totally opposed to the policies of governing parties. In the case of Zambia, where a relatively strong opposition existed in the legislature for eight years after independence, and where relations between government and opposition have been studied in depth,[32] opposition support for government bills as measured by favorable speeches was high (averaging close to two-thirds) and rising during the life of the First National Assembly (1964-68). Opposition support for government motions was mixed, however, and

Legislative and Party Structures

the existence of substantial tension was indicated by the total failure of government to support motions made by the African opposition party, and by several suspensions of opposition members from the legislature. In the Second National Assembly (1969-73) the African opposition party became more active in debate in the absence of most of the European independents who had been extremely active in the First Assembly, but government-opposition relations became even more conflictual, ending in the banning of all opposition parties in 1972.

In most ex-British African countries, however, government party backbenchers provide or provided more effective opposition than did the official opposition. In many cases some of the former had at one time belonged to the latter, as crossing the floor to the government side was strongly and successfully encouraged in most of the countries under consideration.[33] In cases such as Zambia and Kenya where crossing the floor in the opposite direction became a significant factor, changing party allegiance was made grounds for losing one's seat in the legislature, and the same is true in *de jure* one-party systems.[34] These and other changes designed to strengthen party discipline and increase the significance of government parties in the legislature have met with some success, as opposition from government party backbenchers has generally been less basic or bitter than that from opposition parties.

Although in a stronger position than opposition parties, government party backbenchers suffer from the same disabilities in milder form. They usually lack discipline, effective leadership, civil service advisors, and other sources of information and expertise which are available to government members. All of the above factors have contributed to a pattern of backbench behavior which has generally combined a very high level of support on virtually all basic policy questions with considerable opposition on a number of specific questions of implementation, and has sometimes resulted in getting the details of policy changed. Although there have been relatively frequent exhortations from presidents and other leaders for backbenchers to be more active in constructively criticizing government policies and representing the interests of their constituencies, there have also been threats of disciplinary action and a smaller number of instances of its actual exercise, which have served to discourage backbench activism.[35] Rather than any continous trend toward increasing or decreasing backbench opposition, the available data indicate increasing opposition both before and after elections when backbenchers feel a special need to impress their constituents or when new legislators are adjusting to their roles. Norms of limited backbench opposition seem to be gaining substantial effectiveness in those ex-British territories which still have legislatures.[36] Only in Kenya do they include substantial voting against government in divisions, which have been rare in most legislatures except when constitutionally required, and even in Kenya such voting has usually been on nonessential private member motions.[37] Nigeria did not deviate significantly from most of the above generalizations, although it had a two-party coalition government.[38]

Parliamentary parties exist or existed in all legislatures in ex-British Africa; they have sometimes served as a forum for the exercise of party discipline, and less frequently as the forum in which backbenchers could most effectively influence government. Measures aimed at increasing party discipline have already been discussed, as has their partial success in engendering backbench support. Yet party discipline has been insufficiently strong to allow parliamentary party caucuses to enforce anything like complete unity, and backbenchers have certainly not exercised enough power to have the caucus serve as an instrument through which they could consistently influence major policy decisions. Departure from the British but not the colonial model is substantial in this regard, although adaptation to the realities of external party structure rather than deliberate invention is the primary cause of these changes. With the establishment of a one-party state, the parliamentary party loses its significance, and in some cases is abolished, although party organs outside the legislature often assume a role in the approval of proposed legislation. It follows from the weakness of parliamentary parties that the role of whip has been both less powerful and less intimately bound to government than in the British Parliament. African whips have been known to join rebellious backbenchers.

The principal devices offered by the British parliamentary model for government party backbenchers or opposition members to initiate debate on topics of their own choice are private members' bills and motions, questions, adjournment debates, and the budget debate. As we have mentioned, private members' bills have been extremely rare in British-influenced African legislatures, if for no other reason than the lack of access to qualified draftsmen. The frequency and significance of private members' motions has varied widely among these legislatures, but this is due mainly to their frequent use and relatively frequent success in Kenya, where the legislature makes the most effective use of all the devices discussed in this paragraph, and in Ghana from 1963 to 1966, where more time was spent on debate of private members' motions than on debate of government motions.[39] In all other countries such motions have been infrequent and/or on minor constituency matters. Analyses of questions asked in these legislatures are generally very incomplete, the primary exception being a detailed study of the Tanzanian Bunge from 1965 to 1969.[40] What seems to be indicated by these studies, however, is that the form of the question period has been diffused relatively intact from the British Parliament, in spite of some leaders' belief that it is inappropriate to the African context, but that questions are asked with much less frequency in African legislatures. In most of these legislatures, however, questions have been asked with sufficient frequency to be considered a significant form of backbench/opposition participation in debate. The same pattern

Legislative and Party Structures

of relatively unaltered diffusion of form combined with less frequent use for initiating major debates can be observed in adjournment and budget debates. Because these and other opportunities for prolonging debate have not been utilized with great frequency in British-influenced African legislatures, norms for limiting debate through closure have little significance in these legislatures.

Changes have take place in the overall role of member in the legislatures of ex-British Africa and in the norms asssociated with that role which have generally tended to weaken the role and reduce the opportunities for role-making by its occupants. Members usually lack expertise in both legislative procedures and the substance of policy, and collectivity structures within either parties or standing committees which foster such expertise in the British Parliament are generally absent in Africa.[41] Although many privileges continue to be associated with the role of member of the legislature, and individuals compete vigorously to fill this role where it still exists, there has been some diminution of legislative privileges through methods ranging from the enactment of leadership codes in Ghana, Tanzania, and Zambia requiring members to renounce some of their property and outside income and reducing their legislative pay, to the subjugation of legislators to preventive detention in several countries, including Kenya which has increased rather than reduced financial privileges. Although no member of the legislature in any of these countries has been detained because of remarks made on the floor of the house, several have been suspended for such remarks.[42] Legislators are frequently encouraged to occupy various administrative roles concurrently with their role as member of the legislature, thus reducing the prestige of the latter role in and of itself. Finally, British colonial African legislatures, unlike the British parliament, contained nominated and specially elected members as well as regular elected members. After initially rejecting this practice as undemocratic, most ex-British African governments have reintroduced it as a technique for giving added support to executive leadership, and have thereby reduced the prestige and influence of regular elected members. Like their colonial predecessors, nominated and specially elected members are relatively inactive, but they provide extra votes for governments and occasionally represent interests which would otherwise be ignored.[43]

In their constituencies African legislators are forced in varying degrees to defend government's policies, including the unpopular ones, and are faced with relatively powerful rivals in the local representatives of the civil service and/or party hierarchies. The high rates of defeat encountered in several countries by legislators seeking re-election indicate their relative weakness in this aspect of their role. Compared to their counterparts in other formerly British African countries, Kenyan legislators are expected by the regime and by their constituents to devote substantial effort to obtaining specific benefits for their constituencies, including development projects, and the more successful among them conform to these expectations. They are not viewed by their contituents as important policy makers, however, so constituents do not waste time attempting to influence them in this regard.[44] Furthering specific group interests is officially discouraged in African legislatures, although virtually all legislators come from relatively highly privileged strata in their societies, and in varying degrees consciously or unconsciously work for the advancement of elite or dominant class interests. Very few data are available on the specific mechanisms of elite or class influence on legislators.

Changes in opposition, partisan, backbencher, member, and representative roles and the collectivity structures and norms associated with them are clearly related to one another and to changes in the governmental-ministerial roles and norms previously discussed. Thus the former changes can be explained by the same propositions that were utilized to expalin the latter changes. Once again, these changes reflect the effects of centralized, organized power (A3, C6e), the relatively complete diffusion of specific structural elements (B2) judged in terms of compatibility (D1) and utility (C5), and the eventual reinterpretation of more complex diffused elements (D2, D3), as they interact within African legislatures over time, to create a new workable integration of legislative systems controlled by elite values and norms (E4). Ghana once again led the way, and crucial political actors in countries which adopted these changes at a relatively late date correctly anticipated that some aspects of the model provided by Ghana and other early adopters would be diffused to their legislatures (C7).

Other examples of diffusion and invention through this process include the successful diffusion of the form but not always the effectiveness of the Public Accounts and Standing Orders or Business Committees; the insignificance of most other committees in legislatures which handle the committee stage of most bills in Committee of the Whole, and even in Tanzania where an effort has been made to revitalize standing committees; the relative weakness of legislative staff even though the role of clerk has been effectively diffused; and the weakness and demise of second chambers.[45]

As indicated above, most commentators on the diffusion of the British parliamentary model to Africa conclude that this process has been a virtually unqualified failure, aside from the acceptance of mere "forms." Our analysis of specific roles, collectivity structures, and norms gives some support to such a conclusion, but also points out necessary modifications to be made in it. The significance of continuities as well as changes in legislative structure can be more clearly comprehended by reinterpreting these structural changes in terms of the internal functional subsystems of legislatures in formerly British African territories, and by examining the functions these legislatures perform for the societal political systems of which they are a part. Government is clearly central in the performance of the internal goal attainment function and the exercise of power in African legislatures, and we have seen that government has been significantly strengthened. This does not mean, however, that the legislature has been strengthened in the performance of goal attainment for the societal political system, because government in the legislature is only a part of the societal political executive which has gained goal attainment significance and power at the expense of the legislature. The complex set of norms which gives the British Parliament a restricted but at times significant goal attainment capability has not been successfully diffused to Africa because it is incompatible with both the authoritarian, centralizing character of African executives and the trends in political party organization described in the previous and following sections of this chapter, to say nothing of the economic, stratification, and cultural differences between Britain and African societies which underlie these political differences. In fact, this complex of norms was never fully established in the terminal colonial legislative structures which were the vehicles for the diffusion of parliamentary practices to Africa.

Collectivities central to the performance of internal integrative functions in most British-influenced legislatures—the parliamentary party of the governing party, committees, the opposition, and second chambers where they exist— are all weaker in Africa than in Britain, and African legislatures have consequently had more internal conflict. In those legislatures which still exist, conflict is kept at a tolerable level by the strength of government in the legislature, combined with either the strength of the governing party outside the legislature, as in Tanzania, or a patronage system which has high utility for many legislators and at least some of their constituents, as in Kenya. In the latter case but not the former the legislature plays a relatively significant integrative role for the societal political system and exercises significant influence within that system.[46] Both of these patterns involve some degree of conscious invention.

Legislatures are of little importance in the performance of the adaptive function in most societal political systems, and this is certainly true of the countries under consideration, where mechanisms for day-to-day control of the political executive and the bureaucracy are virutally nonexistent. African legislatures have adequate money for their own maintenance, but committees and administrative staff, which are also important for the performance of internal adaptive functions, are relatively weak.

Pattern socialization and control is performed by most collectivities within African legislatures, and much evidence indicates that it is performed relatively well. The vast majority of African legislators remain committed to the legislature as an institution, although some of them undoubtedly have even stronger commitments to potentially competing institutions. It is not surprising that this is the function to which legislatures contribute most significantly in the societal political systems of ex-British Africa.[47] Those African legislatures which continue to exist are highly significant in legitimating societal political systems because of their symbolic status, and in some cases because of their performance of limited integrative functions. And when civilian rule has been restored after a period of military government in formerly British African countries, there has never been any debate about re-establishing the legislature. Thus the diffusion of the concept of a legislature is significant for pattern socialization and control and the exercise of commitments in these societal political systems, although invention of new ways to link the legislature to the president and the ruling party further enhances the former's legitimating capacity. To a lesser extent, the invention of national symbols to replace British robes, wigs, and mace, and the change in seating arrangements away from the crossbenches symbolizing opposition, which have occurred in most countries, have had the same effect.

Both the present internal functional performance and distribution of power and influence within legislatures, and their present external functional performance, relative powerlessness, greater influence, and high commitment are compatible with the broader characteristics of societal political systems in formerly British African countries and have high utility for existing elites and emerging dominant classes in those countries (C5, D1). Thus these characteristics of legislatures are not likely to change significantly until significant changes take place in the broader societal political systems of which they are parts (E4). The contradiction between the articulated value of popular government and the extant situation of isolated, concentrated power pointed out by Stultz more than a decade ago has yet to be resolved, although the preceding analysis indicates that isolation is by no means total. Legislatures help to minimize the conflict-engendering effects of this contradiction by providing a basis of legitimacy which is both compatible with popular government and supportive of executive power, and by performing minor integrative functions with regard to constituents, party factions, and civil servants. Thus the successful diffusion of some parliamentary "forms"—among African countries as well as from Britain—is not without substantive functional significance.

Diffusion and Innovation in Political Parties

The more diverse paths of diffusion and the greater significance of invention in African political party structures (in comparison with legislative structures) make the identification of roles, collectivities, and norms in terms of which parties can be compared more open to the danger of ethnocentrism—i.e., forcing the characteristics of African party systems into a model based on one African country or on Britain. This danger has been minimized by using works on political parties in individual ex-British African countries as well as works on comparative political parties, African political parties in general, and British political parties to construct our lists of structural characteristics, [48] and by giving greater emphasis to differences among the countries under consideration than was given in the preceding discussion of legislative change.

The following significant political party roles can be identified from the sources consulted: leader, secretary general, central committee member, national executive committee member, legislator, regional/provincial chairman, regional/provincial secretary, district chairman, district secretary, branch chairman, branch secretary, sub-branch/cell leader, militant/activist, and member. Significant collectivities include: head office, central committee, national executive committee, national conference, parliamentary party, regional/provincial organization, district/constituency organization, branch, sub-branch/cell, faction, auxiliary group, and ideological institute. Among the many norms which could be specified, the most important are those relating to: leadership selection procedure, party official selection procedure, legislative candidate selection procedure, control of legislators/parliamentary party, methods/sources of finance, membership participation, patronage, level of internal conflict favored/allowed, discipline, centralization of power, interest representation/control of auxiliary groups, ideological/issue orientation, tactical orientation, tolerance of external opposition, and degree of organization.

The role of party leader is crucial in all African political parties. The leader of the single or dominant party is inevitably head of state, and he plays a dominant role in the party as its leader for the same reasons that he plays a dominant role in the legislature and the broader society as head of state. The role of party leader entails great control of power and functional significance in British and other European political parties from which African parties borrowed most of their initial formal structure, and it has been reinterpreted to have even greater power and functional significance in order to meet the challenges which the political elite perceive to be facing African societies (C5, C6, D2, E4). All leaders have the dominant voice in their parties' structure, personnel decisions, and policies, and have had primary responsibility for such ideology formation as has taken place. There have been extensive opportunities for role making in the exercise of leaders' powers, however, especially in the case of founder-leaders who created their parties before independence and shaped their initial postindependence characteristics.[49]

While all leaders have attempted to place themselves above factional conflicts and above criticism, there have been great variations in their success in doing so. Julius Nyerere of the Tanganyika African National Union (TANU) in Tanzania, Kenneth Kaunda of the United National

James R. Scarritt

Independence Party (UNIP) in Zambia, Kwame Nkrumah of the Convention People's Party (CPP) in Ghana, and Jomo Kenyatta of the Kenya African National Union (KANU) in Kenya are or were relatively successful leaders in this respect, but they differed dramatically in the means by which they attained this success, the attention they paid to party organization, and the functional significance they attributed to their parties.

Kenyatta was at one extreme, paying virtually no attention to party organization, and using the party only as an arena in which conflicts among subordinates could be worked out and individuals could prove themselves worthy of consideration for national political roles by creating local political bases. His role as party leader was almost purely nominal, and he exercised power almost entirely as head of state, interpreting his role as that of Mzee, the respected elder who made all final decisions on the basis of his own wisdom, after hearing all views. Nyerere is at the opposite extreme, devoting more attention to party organization and placing more functional significance on the party than any other leader in ex-British Africa. Resigning his position as prime minister shortly after independence, he devoted almost a year to building up TANU's sense of purpose and base of popular support, although not its organization.[50] Interpreting his role as that of Mwalimu (teacher) and power wielder combined, he has maintained his position as unchallenged party leader while leading TANU and the nation toward gradual adoption of equalitarian and socialist policies. It is frequently difficult to separate Nyerere's roles of party leader and head of state in this process, but he makes certain that the party leader component remains sufficiently differentiated and significant to give some degree of credence to the claim that TANU, now merged with the Afro-Shirazi party of Zanzibar into Chama Cha Mapinduzi (CCM), is superior to the government in the formulation of general policies.

Although Nkrumah was the first African leader to adopt the model of a well-organized single party leading the political system and society toward fundamental change, and Nyerere and others sought to emulate the Ghanaian model, at least in part, [51] Nkrumah did not give first priority to his role as party leader. He continued to make changes in party organization until shortly before he was deposed by a military coup in early 1966, but some of these weakened the party while strengthening his own position as balancer among factions, many of whose members he feared as potential competitors for supreme power. Kaunda's perception of the role of party leader is quite similar to Nyerere's (as was that of Apolo Milton Obote of Uganda),[52] but the higher level of conflict within UNIP has involved Kaunda more directly, and thus he has not been able to devote as much attention to strengthening the organization and increasing the functional significance of the party. This problem was even more severe in Obote's Uganda's People's Congress (UPC). These examples suggest that internal conflict tends to place serious restraints on the leader's ability to use the party to facilitate change (A2b, C6e).

There have been too few instances of leadership selection in the postindependence period to generalize very extensively about this process, except to say that the choice is always made by some organ of the party outside the legislature. This is compatible with the extraparliamentary origins of these parties, the selection of original leaders through the mobilizing activities involved in the founding of nationalist movements, and the continuing control of most power and influence (other than that controlled by the leader himself) by extraparliamentary organs (D1).[53]

Most political parties in the countries under consideration incorporated the role of secretary general into their structure with the initial assumption that its occupant would control day-to-day affairs of the party, and be the second most powerful person in it. But, given the importance of the leader in all parties, and the challenges to his authority which have arisen with varying frequency in every party, the role of secretary general has been reinterpreted to have considerably less power and functional significance, has been occupied by the party leader himself, or has been abolished (D2). There have also been trends toward having the secretary general appointed by the party leader rather than elected by a national party organ, and towards having the role filled on a part-time rather than a full-time basis.[54] The weakness of this role has limited the effectiveness of party head offices, which are usually under the direction of the secretary general. This collectivity is also hampered in most parties by small size, lack of skilled personnel, and limited financial resources. In some parties, however, the head office appears to be growing somewhat stronger.[55]

There are most commonly three collectivities which are formally empowered to make policy at the national level in African political parties: the central committee, the national executive committee, and the national conference, in order of increasing size and decreasing frequency of meetings.[56] Only the latter two exist in British parties, although the central committee is found in many European parties. In the majority of African parties the central committee, which is either elected by one of the larger bodies or appointed by the party leader, is the most powerful decision making collectivity, although it has less power in most circumstances than the party leader. While party constitutions usually assign to the central committee the task of implementing policies formulated by the national executive committee and the national conference, those bodies rarely formulate policies because of their large size, infrequent meetings, and the dominant role of the leader in policy formation (A3). The central committee, which is smaller, more frequently in session, and closer to the leader is thus in a better position to at least give him significant advice in policy formulation. There is considerable variation among parties in the power and functional significance of the central committee, however. The extent of factionalism in the party, the organizational norms held by the leader, and the relationship of the central committee to the cabinet are the most important factors for explaining this variation (C5). When the level of intraparty conflict is high, the central committee is more likely to be a principal arena for this conflict than an effective policy making body. If the party leader does not want continuous consultation with a specific collegial organ, and does not feel that the balance of power within the party requires such consultation, the central committee will have little power. Finally, if the party is weak and/or sharply divided, the leader tends to rely on the cabinet rather than the central committee, although these two bodies often have largely overlapping memberships.

The body which we label with the generic term "national executive committee" is or was called the national council in UNIP and in the UPC, and its size and composition diverge widely among parties. In every case it is comprised of a combination of elected members, usually representing party regions, and those who are members by virtue of the party or government office they hold. The National Executive Committee of TANU (CCM) constitutes a significant exception to the generalization that such bodies are less powerful and functionally significant than central committees, and its power and significance have increased over the years since independence as the party has striven to become more important in the political system. The NEC does not initiate policy, but provides the principal sounding board for party reaction to policies initiated by the leader; its discussions have resulted in substantial modifications of these policies in a number of cases, although these modifications have not changed the over-all direction of policy. In addition, the NEC is the body which has final say in approving the two TANU candidates in each constituency for the single-party parliamentary elections (while the Central Committee has final say in approving candidates for party offices).

National conferences, originally held annually in most parties, following the British practice, are now held at most every other year, and in some parties, such as KANU and (until 1966) the CPP, very infrequently and irregularly. They have ranged in size of membership from less than two hundred to several thousand. In all parties the conference functions primarily to ratify decisions made by the leader or the other central party organs, although when factional conflicts are intense, the conference can become an arena for attempting to resolve them. African party structures are too fragile to withstand many close votes on important questions at party conferences, and party leaders always attempt to return conflict to narrower arenas as soon as possible after such a vote has occurred (A2b, C5). Thus the integrative functions of national conferences are also quite limited. Nevertheless, the continued holding of conferences on a regular basis in some parties, and the relatively open representation of various elements of the party which they provide, indicate the continuing viability of some parties as legitimating organizations at the present time and as potential performers of other functions in the future, and differentiate these parties from those in which the conference does not meet regularly.

In opposition parties there is a tendency for power to be more concentrated in the hands of the leader, and for representative collectivities to be less important. Given the pressure for elimination of all opposition parties, they are usually too preoccupied with fighting for survival and too poverty-stricken to organize strong local and regional units from which effective national representative collectivities could be elected, or to conduct such elections.

Because of the relative unimportance of legislatures, the power and influence of party leaders, and the influence which the national party collectivities just discussed have on leaders, the power and functional significance of parliamentary parties as such within African political parties are considerably less than in British parties (D2). In most parties all or most legislators are members of both the national conference and the national executive committee; ministers are frequently central committee members in addition. They may have some influence in party affairs through occupying these roles, or through informal relationships with the party leader and his immediate subordinates, such as the patron-client relationships which have been shown to be so important in KANU. The parties in which legislators are or were most powerful were those which had least formal organization and/or depended almost entirely on chiefs for their local bases of support: KANU, the Sierra Leone People's Party (SLPP), the Northern People's Congress (NPC) of Nigeria, and the Progress Party (PP) of Ghana (1969-72).[57] But legislators were also relatively important in the other two major Nigerian parties, the National Convention of Nigerian citizens (NCNC) and the Action Group (AG), because interparty competition for both the regional and federal legislatures focused party activities on electing legislators to a greater extent than in other countries under consideration. TANU (CCM) appears to be the party in which legislators are least powerful, since it is the party in which both the NEC and regional and local party structures are most significant, and legislators play a minor role in all of these structures.

Although their power in both party and governmental arenas may be quite limited, legislators have high symbolic status and good incomes. Thus competition for nomination to candidacy for seats in national legislatures is often intense, and the same is sometimes true for seats on local councils as well. There are substantial differences among parties, and within the same party in different geographical areas and time periods, in the degree to which central and local organs participate in the candidate selection process.[58] The most common pattern is local selection, with national organs occasionally exercising a veto or acting as referee. Where national organs function more regularly and effectively, as in TANU, one of them is generally empowered to approve nominations. Finally, where national organs formally exercise such power, but are torn by intense internal conflict, nominations may be made by the party leader, although party leaders generally prefer to avoid engaging in this potentially controversial activity.

There are important contrasts among political parties in ex-British Africa with regard to the financial resources they possess, the sources from which these resources are derived, and the methods used for procuring them. Most parties were initially poor, but few remained so for more than a few years after independence. Membership dues are formally required in every party, but are rarely collected from more than a small minority of the membership; thus they cannot make a party wealthy. In sharp contrast to the British Labour Party's heavy reliance on trade union contributions, a substantial majority of the funds possessed by most African parties comes from contributions by wealthy individuals or institutions in the private sector, or from various forms of requisitions from government. Once substantial amounts of such contributions have been made, party funds can be invested in the private sector to generate even greater income. TANU (CCM)'s leadership code prohibits wealthy contributors, who were important sources of funds until recently, from being party leaders or members, and the party rejects private sector investments, although it does receive funds from government. At the opposite extreme were the NCNC, the AG, and the CPP, which attracted many supporters but alienated even more potential supporters by their vast and corruptly acquired wealth.[59]

In all British African territories the basic administrative unit was the district, and districts were usually grouped into provinces. Given their extraparliamentary origins, it was natural for most nationalist parties to base their intermediate levels of organization on these administrative areas, rather than on parliamentary constituencies as in Britain (D2). Although there have been some boundary and name changes since independence, especially the division of larger districts and provinces, and the change of the title "province" to "region" or "state," contemporary administrative units remain similar to those of the late colonial period, and are still the bases for intermediate units of organization in most parties (D1). The importance of district councils in the local government systems of most of these countries and the common practice of fusing the top positions in both party and government at these levels into the powerful role of regional or district commissioner or governor reinforce the long-standing adherence of parties to these intermediate organizational levels (C5).

Representative party structures in the regions and districts often parallel those found at the national level, and have the similar titles of working committees, executive committees, and conferences. In addition to the elected officials staffing these structures, who are led by the regional or district chairman, these levels of party organization have appointed secretaries. The regional or district commissioner may be the party secretary, or may be his superordinate.[60]

The power of these various individuals and the tasks performed by them differ greatly from country to country, and sometimes among regions in the same country, although commissioners generally command the greatest amount of power. Regional commissioners are often ministers or members of the central committee of their party. Where the party as a whole is inactive and the commissioner is a strictly governmental role, as in Kenya, there is little for provincial party officials to do. District officials are occupied with maintaining control of the machine politics of their districts, or are also inactive.[61]

On the other hand, where the party is active and the commissioners' party role is important, as in Tanzania, the commissioner/secretaries at both regional and district levels are crucial agents for implementing party policy, while the chairmen and the elected conferences and committees which they chair are crucial agents for furthering local/regional interests. While central control is greater in the latter case, it is far from complete. Appointed officials responsible to the national party leader and organization must accommodate to local interests to some degree if they are to accomplish anything. Furthermore, they are transferred frequently, while most locally responsible elected officials remain in the same areas permanently unless they are elected or appointed to higher party or government positions. In addition, while the role of the party as a decision making, integrative, and legitimating organization is also greater in this case than in parties like KANU, the party's decision making functions in particular remain constrained. The fusion of party and government roles in regional and area commissioners strengthens government's goal attainment or decision making power. Since day-to-day and year-to-year policies are made and implemented primarily by government, commissioners emphasize the governmental aspect of their role in their goal attainment activities, using the party for resolution of some of the conflicts inherent in policy implementation, and for legitimating policies and implementation activities.

The greatest variety in political party structure in the countries under consideration is found at levels below the district, where local party structure must adapt to both national structure and local conditions (A5, C5, D2). The number of subdistrict levels of organization varies from one to three, and their activities vary from highly significant and continuous to nil. Immediately below the district is found the branch, which is frequently the lowest level of party organization. Branches differ extensively in size and functions. They may be based on chiefdoms, villages, groups of villages, electoral wards, or various other geographical units.[62] In TANU (CCM) branches also exist at places of work, and this was also true of the CPP for a few years before its overthrow. Branch chairmen, secretaries, and other officers are officially elected, except in TANU (CCM) where secretaries are appointed. In many cases, elections do not actually take place, however; individuals sometimes simply assume the roles of branch officials, and district party officials sometimes appoint people to fill these roles. This happens because the branch membership, if it exists at all, is too inactive and poorly organized to protest effectively. But because they are often elected, and are always permanent local residents with limited prospects for advancing to higher political roles, branch leaders tend to be responsive to their membership, or segments of it, rather than to pressures from above, at least unless the latter pressures are very strong (C5). Thus the greatest gap in parties' organizational communications networks tends to be between the branch and the district.

Beneath the branch in more effectively organized parties there may be one or more levels of party structure, called sections, wards, villages, etc.[63] These are generally tied very closely to branches, both organizationally and in terms of political values and norms. Like branches, they vary greatly in their level of activity. Those that are active are engaged in both providing services and attempting to exercise political control. Even more than branches, they are responsive to perceived local interests, and thus tend to be extremely unreliable as agents of central control. Either branches or units beneath them may be partially fused with government structures in village or ward development committees, and this relationship increases the potential for central control slightly.

TANU (CCM) differs from all other political parties in formerly British African territories in having the ten-house cell as the lowest level of party organization.[64] The cell system is designed to increase the party's contacts with ordinary Tanzanians, to stimulate popular participation in party decision making and local development projects, and to increase party control over the entire population (with an emphasis on the collection of taxes). The kinds of people selected as cell leaders and the functions they perform differ widely among and even within districts. Cell leaders tend to be similar in many ways to cell members, and to adhere to the same values and norms. Thus, in areas with more educated populations and greater economic development, cell leaders usually conform more closely to the ideal model of leaders encouraging development and participation, while cell leaders in other areas tend to be more apolitical and "traditional," focusing their activities to an even greater extent on the settlement of disputes, which is an important activity for all cell leaders (D2). A number of cell leaders of both types do not conform to the principles of the leadership code regarding property ownership and sources of income. As of the time that research on them was carried out, cells were more a reflection of local community and kinship structures than of TANU's effectiveness in changing such structures, and this is probably still true today (D1). Nevertheless, the potential for change through mobilization which the cell system provides is clear (C2), and the existence of this unique structure differentiates TANU significantly from

Legislative and Party Structures

other parties under consideration. Although TANU (CCM) cells bear some resemblance in name and size to units found in communist parties, their actual operation is quite different, and they constitute the outstanding example of invention in African political party structure.

Given the operation of various collectivity structures within African political parties, what can be said about the roles of ordinary party member and activist, and norms of membership participation? Data on the size of party membership are extremely limited and unreliable. Membership means very little in the parties under consideration, in terms of privileges, duties, constraints, or behavior, except perhaps in TANU (CCM), in which cells make membership a more active role, and in which the constraints imposed by the leadership code are now being applied to all party members.[65] But membership does not have much meaning in most political parties in various types of societies, including British parties. Many postindependence African parties differ more substantially from the European parties from which their structure was partially borrowed in having lower participation by party activists or militants. This contrasts sharply with their significance as agitators in the nationalist period. After independence many party activists either received jobs as a reward for their activism or became politically alienated because they expected jobs or material rewards and did not receive them. They have not been replaced by activists mobilizing for development because it is more difficult to create intense feelings and activity for such a long-run diffuse goal, especially among people with little education, and because party leaders fear that such activists would turn their activity against the party leadership if development were not quickly achieved (C5).[66]

The preceding discussion demonstrates that departicipation has occured in a number of roles and collectivites within all African political parties, but this change has been more extensive in some parties than in others, and some forms of participation remain available to fairly large numbers of people wherever parties continue to exist.[67] While the official norms found in party constitutions indicate that participation takes the form of membership control of all party structures through election of officials at various levels culminating in the national conference which has final authority in all issues; the informal norms which actually control behavior provide for much more limited and circumscribed membership participation, one prominent form being the receipt of patronage.[68] The degree of effective participation varies rather directly with the number of active party structures (C2).

Factionalism is a prominent feature of the political parties under consideration. While it is difficult to measure the magnitude of factionalism on the basis of available data, its overt manifestations appear to be greater in most of these parties than in the British parties on which they are partially modeled. Factionalism in ruling parties is usually a mixture of all types: ideological, issue, leadership, and strategic-tactical,[69] although the relative importance of each type varies among countries, and among time periods and parties within a given country. Factionalism in opposition parties is usually less severe and based on leadership rivalries and/or tactical differences. The increase in factionalism which usually follows incorporation of opposition parties into a dominant or single party, or exists within such a party even if it has emerged naturally without any oppposition, indicates that the attempt to include all elements of poorly integrated, rapidly changing societies is one cause of factionalism (A2, E1). This is compounded by the fear that losers in the intraparty conflicts of the moment may not get another chance to become winners tomorrow (C5b). In this situation "party discipline" becomes "intraparty diplomacy," among factions as well as between central and local party organs.[70]

Centralization of power in all of these parties is thus less than in British parties, and efforts to assert more extensive central control, although sometimes successful, are more likely to cause tension (E1). Once again, formal norms—in this case norms rejecting internal conflict and stressing the overriding need for unity—are in conflict with informal norms which actually control behavior—in this case norms sanctioning a relatively high level of factional conflict. In KANU the informal norms may be on the way towards attaining formal status through the institutionalization of controlled factional competition.

Beginning as nationalist movements seeking to win political independence, political parties in ex-British Africa were extremely diffuse ideologically. After independence, many upper and middle level party leaders felt the need for greater ideological specificity, and, as has been pointed out, inevitably turned to the top leader to provide ideological guidelines. These guidelines have, for the most part, added to rather than substituted for pre-existing norms of party structure (D5). In the post-independence period such tactical norms have centered on gaining or retaining power, maintaining national unity, and achieving specific economic development goals. Even though the ideological guidelines of most of these parties are themselves relatively diffuse, there are conflicts between ideological and tactical norms which vary in intensity from party to party, but which are relatively intense in those parties whose ideologies encourage substantial change in a socialist direction (E1, E4).[71] Some of these parties have established ideological institutes as collectivities within the party structure to produce party officials and militants committed to actualizing the ideology. Up to the present time, such collectivities, with the possible exception of Kivukoni College in Tanzania, have had very little impact on party structure or policies.

A set of collectivities which often contribute substantially to intraparty factionalism is auxiliary groups. Some, such as women and youth, were organized in the process of nationalist political mobilization, and are typically incorporated as sections of the party. Others, such as workers and farmers, were usually organized separately from and often prior to the nationalist movement, and were typically incorporated into the party after independence as affiliated organizations. These organizations, especially trade unions, usually resisted incorporation, and continued to pursue their specific interests within the party framework after being incorporated (C5). Youth wings have also frequently attempted to work for policies which differed from those selected by party leaders, who have sometimes responded by denying the party youth league separate organizational status, or at least restricting its autonomy.[72] Ethnic associations, especially important in southern Nigeria, but also of some importance in several other countries, have not usually been official party auxiliaries, but have actually performed some or all of the functions of party branches or district organizations, including nomination of candidates.[73] Attempts to exert party control over auxiliaries have met with varying degrees of success, but the fact that most of them retain some degree of independence is another aspect of power decentralization within these parties. Opposition parties usually experience great difficulties in maintaining auxiliary groups.

Factionalism and opposition are closely related in all political party systems, but especially in Africa, where today's faction is tomorrow's opposition party and vice versa. Studies of specific African party systems confirm the findings of the general literature that interparty opposition has declined substantially since independence (D2), and that this decline has involved varying degrees of coercion. These studies also demonstrate that tolerance of opposition parties began to develop in some countries—Sierra Leone, Zambia, and Southern Nigeria are probable examples—before it was overcome by events, while such tolerance never even gained a toe hold in other countries. The explanations given in the general literature for the decline of opposition are all supported by the studies of specific party systems, although many of the latter appear to place greatest emphasis on the lack of mutual trust and the desire of elites to remain in power (C5).[74]

The preceding analysis of party norms, collectivities, and roles supports the second revisionist interpretation in the generalizing literature, which finds significant differences among party systems in formerly British African countries with regard to structural institutionalization or decay, internal authoritarianism, and functional performance. TANU (CCM) has become substantially better organized since independence, in terms of all or most of Kenneth Janda's criteria of articulation (number of national organs, prescriptiveness of selection procedures, and specificity of functions), intensiveness (smallest unit), extensiveness (geographical spread), frequency of meetings, maintenance of records, and pervasiveness (extensiveness of auxiliary groups),[75] and has significantly decreased some of its authoritarian characteristics. In other parties, of which UNIP is a good example, trends in organizational strength and internal authoritarianism have differed sharply among criteria, geographical areas, and time periods. [76] Even KANU does not present a uniform pattern of continuous and comprehensive organizational decay or increased authoritarianism.

Neither characterizing all parties as machines nor noting the relative strength of government provides an adequate explanation of these divergent trends, because these factors are constant. Comparing the history of electoral participation, conflict and coercion, and party dominance in party systems is also inadequate. It is easier for parties which have little opposition to strengthen their organization, but such change also requires a committed and competent leadership (A2c, C6) which wields sufficient power (A3) to mobilize various national, regional, and local party organs and auxiliary groups (C2) at the optimum rate (A4, C4, C7) to instill innovative values and norms (A1) and a sense of the utility of organization-building (C5) in party activists and a substantial portion of party members, innovating new structural elements and reinterpreting borrowed ones (D2), without evoking a strong sense of either incompatibility (D1, D5) or violation of class-ethnic interests (C5) and thus provoking countermobilization (C3) on the part of substantial segments of the party. Some resistance is almost inevitable, creating a degree of factionalism (E1), but this will be mitigated by the initially low level of organization (A2), and if organizational goals become widely accepted and organizational strength widely valued, this resistance will be overcome (E3, E4). The detailed analysis of party norms, collectivities, and roles presented above shows that many of these things have not happened in most parties, and that organizational decay has consequently taken place.

Variations in parties' internal and external functional performance correspond closely but not perfectly to variations in their organizational strength. There is a low level of structural differentiation in the performance of internal functions. The party leader is extremely powerful and crucial for pattern socialization and control, integration, and goal attainment in all parties. Depending on their organizational strength, various national and local party collectivities may share in the exercise of power and the performance of these functions in accordance with institutionalized procedures. Thus, these collectivities and role players within them also tend to be multifunctional, except that only central committees play a role in the *selection* of basic *national* party goals.

Maintaining legitimacy is probably the most important societal function performed by African political parties, and its performance varies least with organizational strength. Weak parties can use patronage, symbolism, and elections to maintain legitimacy, but inefficiency and corruption will weaken this capacity. Even here, organizational strength is by no means irrelevant. Patronage may also serve as an effective integrative device in the short run, but organizational strength greatly facilitates the performance of various integrative activities, especially those which also involve the attainment of developmental goals, as many do.[77] Even the strongest parties in ex-British Africa remain subordinate to governments in the performance of purely goal attainment, policy making functions; but these parties' continued performance of integrative functions connected with policy implementation will strengthen their significance for goal attainment, as well as for adaptation, since there is considerable overlap among functions in these activities.

In summary, recent literature on African political party change—which we have called the second revisionist position—has adequately described and partially explained variations in the direction and extent of change in the political parties of formerly British African countries. Application of the control and facilitation framework has resulted in a more complete description and a more adequate explanation of these variations. Party change has been more varied than legislative change because invention has been more important in the former case. Diffusion among African countries has also taken place, but reinterpretation of diffused elements of party structure has been extensive (D2), blurring the distinction between diffusion and invention. As of October 1979, if plans for the return to party government in Ghana, Nigeria, and Uganda are carried out, and if no further coups take place, all ex-British African countries will once again have functioning party systems. Although this situation may not be permanent, it probably indicates that the party system as an institution has been more completely diffused to ex-British Africa than to the remainder of the continent.

James R. Scarritt

Footnotes

1. See, for example, J.E. Goldthorpe, *The Sociology of the Third World: Disparity and Involvement* (Cambridge: Cambridge University Press, 1975), pp. 254-55; Onésimo Silviera, *Africa South of the Sahara: Party Systems and Ideologies of Socialism* (Uppsala: Political Science Association in Uppsala, 1976), pp. 17, 27-30; and numerous sources cited below in reference to more specific aspects of these general points.

2. A succinct and perceptive discussion of legislative change in the terminal colonial period and its significance in the overall decolonization process is found in B.B. Schaffer, "The Concept of Preparation: Some Questions about the Transfer of Systems of Government," *World Politics* 18 (October 1965): 42-67. Academic and official thinking at that time about the diffusion of the parliamentary system can be understood from Hansard Society for Parliamentary Government, *What Are the Problems of Parliamentary Government in West Africa?* (London: Hansard Society, 1958); and Sir Alan Burns, ed., *Parliament as an Export* (London: George Allen and Unwin, 1966). Two of the many general studies of decolonization in British Africa which place legislative change in this broader context in a sophisticated manner are J.M. Lee, *Colonial Development and Good Government: A Study of the Ideas Expressed by the British Official Classes in Planning Decolonization 1939-1964* (London: Clarendon Press, Oxford University Press, 1967); and Crawford Young, "Decolonization in Africa," in *Colonialism in Africa 1870-1960*, Vol. 2: *The History and Politics of Colonialism 1914-1960*, ed. L.H. Ganr and Peter Duignan (Cambridge: Cambridge University Press, 1970), pp. 450-502.

3. Newell M. Stultz, "Parliaments in Former British Black Africa," *Journal of Developing Areas* 2 (July 1968): 479-93.

4. Malcolm E. Jewell, "Transformation of the Westminster Model: Legislative Systems in the New Independent States of Africa," paper prepared for the Conference on Legislative Origins at the University of Hawaii, Honolulu, April 1974, pp. 16-32.

5. In the former category are J.F. Maitland-Jones, *Politics in Africa: The Former British Territories* (New York: W.W. Norton & Co., 1973); and B.O. Nwabueze, *Presidentialism in Commonwealth Africa* (New York: St. Martin's Press, 1974), pp. 255-97. In the latter category are Dorothy Dodge, *African Politics in Perspective* (Princeton: D. Van Nostrand Co., 1966), pp. 112-19; Ruth First, *Power in Africa* (New York: Random House, 1970), pp.51-54; and Ali A. Mazrui, *Cultural Engineering and Nation-Building in East Africa* (Evanston: Northwestern University Press, 1972), pp. 111-17. Mazrui attempts to explain "parliamentary vigor" in terms of cultural pluralism and precolonial political values, but his explanation is not convincing.

6. See David Goldsworthy, *Colonial Issues in British Politics 1945-1961: From 'Colonial Development' to 'Wind of Change'* (London: Clarendon Press, Oxford University Press, 1971), pp. 113-64, 254-78, 321-60; and Young, "Decolonization in Africa," pp. 465-67.

7. James S. Coleman and Carl G. Rosberg, Jr., "Conclusions," in *Political Parties and National Integration in Tropical Africa*, ed. Coleman and Rosberg (Berkeley and Los Angeles: University of California Press, 1964), pp. 655-64. Also see Martin L. Kilson, "Authoritarian and Single-Party Tendencies in African Politics," *World Politics* 15 (January 1963): 262-94.

8. Coleman and Rosberg, "Introduction," in *Political Parties and National Integration*, pp. 1-12. This distinction is very similar to that between mass and cadre parties made by Thomas Hodgkin, *African Political Parties* (Baltimore: Penguin Books, 1961), pp. 68-75; and by Ruth Schachter Morgenthau, *Political Parties in French-Speaking West Africa* (London: Oxford University Press, 1964), pp. 336-41.

9. Coleman and Rosberg, "Conclusions," pp. 672-80; Immanuel Wallerstein, "The Decline of the Party in Single-Party African States," in *Political Parties and Political Development*, ed. Joseph La Palombara and Myron Weiner (Princeton: Princeton University Press, 1966), pp. 201-14; and Michael F. Lofchie, "Representative Goverment, Bureaucracy, and Political Development: The African Case,"*Journal of Developing Areas* 2 (October 1967): 40-47. See also William J. Foltz, "Political Opposition in Single-Party States of Tropical Africa," in *Regimes and Oppositions*, ed. Robert A. Dahl (New Haven: Yale University Press, 1973), pp. 154-65.

10. See Robert I. Rotberg, "Modern African Studies: Problems and Prospects," *World Politics* 18 (April 1966): 571; Coleman and Rosberg, "Conclusions," p. 676; and Wallerstein, "The Decline of the Party in Single-Party African States," p. 214.

11. Aristide R. Zolberg, *Creating Political Order: The Party-States of West Africa* (Chicago: Rand-McNally & Co., 1966), pp. 9-12, 122-27. The theme that parties were always relatively weak is also found in Jean-Yves Calvez, *Politics and Society in the Third World*, trans. M.J. O'Connell (Maryknoll, N.Y.: Orbis Books, 1971), pp. 96-101; and Martin Staniland, "Single-Party Regimes and Political Change: The P.D.C.I. and Ivory Coast Politics," in *Politics and Change in Developing Countries*, ed. Colin Leys (Cambridge: Cambridge University Press, 1969), pp. 135-40.

12. Henry Bienen, "One-Party Systems in Africa," in *Authoritarian Politics in Modern Society: The Dynamics of Established One-Party Systems*, ed. Samuel P. Huntington and Clement Henry Moore (New York: Basic Books, 1970), pp. 99-127; Bienen, "Political Parties and Political Machines in Africa," in *The State of the Nations: Constraints on Development in Independent Africa*, ed. Michael F. Lofchie (Berkeley, Los Angeles, and London: University of California Press, 1971), pp. 195-213 [both of which are also found in Bienen, *Armies and Parties in Africa*

(New York and London: Africana Publishing Co., 1978), pp. 38-77]; and James C. Scott, "Corruption, Machine Politics, and Political Change," *American Political Science Review* 63 (December 1969): 1144-45, 1157-58.

13. Giovanni Sartori, *Parties and Party Systems: A Framework for Analysis*, Vol. I (Cambridge: Cambridge University Press, 1976), pp. 244, 253-54. A few years after his previously cited work was written, Aristide Zolberg, "The Structure of Political Conflict in the New States of Tropical Africa," *American Political Science Review* 62 (March 1968): 72, suggested that using the word "party" for African parties involved "a dangerous reification." S.E. Finer, "The One-Party Regimes in Africa: Reconsiderations," *Government and Opposition* 2 (July-October 1967): 491-509, strongly disputes one-party systems' claimed superiority in functional performance. In reply Benyamin Neuberger, "Has the Single-Party State Failed in Africa?," *African Studies Review* 17 (April 1974): 173-78, only claims that their functional performance has not been demonstrated to be inferior to that of other types of regimes.

14. Roberta E. McKown and Robert E. Kauffman, "Party System as a Comparative Analytic Concept in African Politics,"*Comparative Politics* 6 (October 1973): 47, 59-62, 64-68.

15. Nelson Kasfir, *The Shrinking Political Arena: Participation and Ethnicity in African Politics, with a case Study of Uganda* (Berkeley, Los Angeles, and London: University of California Press, 1976), pp. 237-51, 270-78. A similar explanation is given in Crawford Young, "Political Systems Development," in *The African Experience*, Vol. I: *Essays*, ed. John N. Paden and Edward W. Soja (Evanston: Northwestern University Press, 1970), pp. 459-69. Scott, "Corruption, Machine Politics, and Political Change," pp. 1154-56, sees machine politics as a conservative response to change.

16. Claude Ake, "Explanatory Notes on the Political Economy of Africa," *Journal of Modern African Studies* 14 (March 1976): 9-15. See also Richard Harris, "The Political Economy of Africa—Underdevelopment or Revolution," in *The Political Economy of Africa*, ed. Harris (New York, London, Sydney, and Toronto: Schenkman Publishing Co., Halstead Press Division, John Wiley & Sons, 1975), pp. 32-33; and numerous studies of specific parties cited below.

17. Mary B. Welfling, *Political Institutionalization: Comparative Analyses of African Party Systems*, Sage Professional Papers in Comparative Politics 4, 01-041 (Beverly Hills and London: Sage Publications, 1973), pp. 18-26, 34-37, 43-45, 47, 51; and Raymond Duvall and Mary Welfling, "Social Mobilization, Political Institutionalization, and Conflict in Black Africa: A Simple Dynamic Model," *Journal of Conflict Resolution* 17 (December 1973): 691-92. Sartori, *Parties and Party Systems*, p. 261, attacks Welfling's findings on two grounds: that coups which have occurred since the publication of her work have greatly weakened the relationship between party institutionalization and

persistence, and that her concept of institutionalization does not take into account the differences between authoritarian and nonauthoritarian party systems. However, his first criticism would be weakened if he had utilized Welfling's two dimensional measurement of level and trend in institutionalization rather than her data on level alone. His second criticism may have more validity, but the fact that his classification of specific parties on the authoritarian-nonauthoritarian dimension (pp. 262-64) is highly questionable suggests that he has not hit upon exactly the right point. Ruth Collier's distinction among types of relatively authoritarian party systems, presented below, is probably more valid.

18. Jay E. Hakes, *Weak Parliaments and Military Coups in Africa: A Study in Regime Instability,* Sage Research Papers in the Social Sciences, Comparative Legislative Studies Series 1, 90-004 (Beverly Hills and London: Sage Publications, 1973), p. 30.

19. Sang-Seek Park, "Political Systems in Black Africa: Toward a New Typology," *Journal of African Studies* 4 (Fall 1977): 302-10.

20. Ruth Berins Collier, "Parties, Coups, and Authoritarian Rule," *Comparative Political Studies* 11 (April 1978): 64, 68-74, 76-77, 80-84. Collier found that among former French colonies participation and competitiveness were negatively correlated, and that, although one-party systems were sometimes established with relatively little coercion, elections have remained plebiscitary.

21. Possible legislative functions are suggested in G.R. Boynton and Chong Lim Kim, "Introduction," in *Legislative Systems in Developing Countries,* ed. Boynton and Kim (Durham, N.C.: Duke University Press, 1975), pp. 15-28; Alan Kornberg, Samuel M. Hines, Jr., and Joel Smith, "Legislatures and the Modernization of Societies," *Comparative Political Studies* 5 (January 1973): 476-80; Gerhard Loewenberg, "Comparative Legislative Research," in *Comparative Legislative Behavior: Frontiers of Research,* ed. Samuel C. Patterson and John C. Wahlke (New York: Wiley-Interscience, 1972), pp. 3-21; Robert A. Packenham, "Legislatures and Political Development," in *Legislatures in Developmental Perspective,* ed. Alan Kornberg and Lloyd D. Musolf (Durham, N.C.: Duke University Press, 1970), pp. 521-82; Samuel C. Patterson, "The Emerging Morphology of the World's Legislatures," *World Politics* 30 (April 1978): 469-81; Fred W. Riggs, "Legislative Structures: Some Thoughts on Elected National Assemblies," in *Legislatures in Comparative Perspective,* ed. Alan Kornberg (New York: David McKay Co., 1973), pp. 85-92; and preliminary drafts of papers by various members of the Consortium for Comparative Legislative Studies. Possible political party functions are suggested in Gabriel A. Almond and G. Bingham Powell, Jr., *Comparative Politics: System, Process, and Policy,* 2nd ed. (Boston and Toronto: Little, Brown & Co., 1978), pp. 97-99, 205-24; David E. Apter, *The Politics of Modernization* (Chicago and London: University of Chicago Press, 1965), pp. 179-222; William J.

Crotty, "Political Parties Research," in *Approaches to the Study of Political Science,* ed. Michael Haas and Henry S. Kariel (Scranton: Chandler Publishing Co., 1970), pp. 295-300; Maurice Duverger, *Political Parties: Their Organization and Activity in the Modern State* (New York: John Wiley & Sons, 1954), pp. 352-421; Kay Lawson, *The Comparative Study of Political Parties* (New York: St. Martin's Press, 1976), pp. 136-42, 162-69; Peter Merkl, *Modern Comparative Politics* (New York: Holt, Rinehart, and Winston, 1970), pp. 272-84; Myron Weiner and Joseph La Palombara, "The Impact of Parties on Political Development," pp. 399-435; and W. Howard Wriggins, *The Ruler's Imperative: Strategies for Political Survival in Asia and Africa* (New York and London: Columbia University Press, 1969), pp. 113-24.

22. Kenneth Bradshaw and David Pring, *Parliament and Congress* (Austin: University of Texas Press, 1972); A.H. Hanson and Malcolm Walles, *Governing Britain: a Guide-Book to Political Institutions* (London: Fontana/ Collins, 1970), pp. 68-85; Inter-Parliamentary Union, *Parliaments: A Comparative Study on the Structure and Functioning of Representative Institutions in Fourty-One Countries* (New York and London: Frederick A. Praeger, 1961); R.M. Punnett, *British Government and Politics* (New York: W.W. Norton & Co., 1968), pp. 215-52; Peter G. Richards, *The Backbenchers* (London: Faber and Faber, 1972); Frank Stacey, *The Government of Modern Britain* (Oxford: Clarendon Press, Oxford University Press, 1968), pp. 66-209; and Roland Young, *The British Parliament* (London: Faber and Faber, 1962).

23. Nwabueze, *Presidentialism in Commonwealth Africa,* p. 275. The Zambian Speaker's refusal to recognize an official opposition in 1969 is discussed in John Leonard Helgerson, "Institutional Adaptation to Rapid Political Change: A Study of the Legislature in Zambia from 1959 to 1969" (Ph.D. Dissertation, Duke University, 1970), pp. 144-45.

24. This phenomenon is examined in great detail, although primarily from a legalistic point of view, in Nwabueze, *Presidentialism in Commonwealth Africa.*

25. Cherry Gertzel, *The Politics of Independent Kenya 1963-8* (Evanston: Northwestern University Press, 1970), p. 140; and J.M. Lee, "Parliament in Republican Ghana," *Parliamentary Affairs* 16 (Autumn 1963): 378.

26. Ibid., pp. 376-93; G.F. Engholm, "The Westminster Model in Uganda," *International Journal* 18 (Autumn 1963): 468-87; Gertzel, *Politics of Independent Kenya,* pp. 125-43; Jay E. Hakes, "The Parliamentary Party of the Kenya African National Union: Cleavage and Cohesion in the Ruling Party of a New Nation" (Ph.D. Dissertation, Duke University, 1970), pp. 231-318; Helgerson, "Institutional Adaptation to Rapid Political Change," pp. 254-86; Helge Kjekshus, "Parliament in an One-Party State—the Bunge of Tanzania, 1965-70," *Journal of Modern African Studies* 12 (March 1974): 21-22, 28-29; Jon Kraus, "Ghana's New

'Corporate Parliament'," *Africa Report* 10, 8 (August 1965): 6-11; J.P.W.B. McAuslan and Yash P. Ghai, "Constitutional Innovation and Political Stability in Tanzania: A Preliminary Assessment," *Journal of Modern African Studies* 4 (December 1966): 493-501; Nwabueze, *Presidentialism in Commonwealth Africa,* pp. 268-69, 276-77; and William Tordoff, *Government and Politics in Tanzania* (Nairobi: East Africa Publishing House, 1967), pp. 2-15.

27. Lee, "Parliament in Republican Ghana," p. 382.
28. Hakes, "Parliamentary Party of the Kenya African National Union," p. 188; Helgerson, "Institutional Adaptation to Rapid Political Change," pp. 170-72; Raymond F. Hopkins, "The Kenyan Legislature: Political Functions and Citizen Perceptions," in Boynton and Kim, *Legislative Systems in Developing Countries,* p. 218; and S.D. Tansey and D.G. Kermode, "The Westminster Model in Nigeria," *Parliamentary Affairs* 21 (Winter 1967-68): 29-34. That similar criteria are involved in the selection of ministers in Britian is indicated in Richard Rose, *The Problem of Party Government* (London and Basingstoke: Macmillan Press, 1974), pp. 363-64.
29. Hakes, *Weak Parliaments and Military Coups,* p. 15.
30. Kjekshus, "Parliament in a One-Party State," p. 22.
31. David E. Apter, "Some Reflections on the Role of a Political Opposition in New Nations," *Comparative Studies in Society and History* 4 (January 1962): 154-68.
32. Helgerson, "Institutional Adaptation to Rapid Political Change"; William Tordoff and Robert Molteno, "Parliament," in *Politics in Zambia,* ed. Tordoff (Berkeley and Los Angeles: University of California Press, 1974), pp. 197-241; and James R. Scarritt, *Zambia: The Search for Humanism* (Ithaca, N.Y.: Cornell University Press, forthcoming).
33. The significance of this phenomenon in Kenya, Tanzania, and Uganda is discussed in G.F. Engholm and Ali A. Mazrui, "Crossing the Floor and the Tensions of Representation in East Africa," *Parliamentary Affairs* 21 (Spring 1968): 137-54.
34. Nwabueze, *Presidentialism in Commonwealth Africa,* p. 284, indicates that this rule originated in Ghana in 1965, at which time that country was a *de jure* one-party state.
35. Engholm, "Westminster Model in Uganda," p. 480; Gertzel, *Politics of Independent Kenya,* pp. 130-43, 148-52; Hakes, "Parliamentary Party of the Kenya African National Union," pp. 186-230; Helgerson, "Institutional Adaptation to Rapid Political Change," pp. 92-105; Raymond F. Hopkins, *Political Roles in a New State: Tanzania's First Decade* (New Haven and London: Yale University Press, 1971), pp. 146-49, 162-75; Newell M. Stultz, "The National Assembly in the Politics of Kenya," in Kornberg and Musolf, *Legislatures in Developmental Perspective,* pp. 313-17; Tordoff, *Government and Politics in Tanzania,* pp. 13-15; and Tordoff and Molteno, "Parliament," pp. 224-25, 228, 235-40.

36. Hopkins, *Political Roles in a New State,* pp. 190-95.
37. Hakes, "Parliamentary Party of the Kenya African National Union," pp. 190-200.
38. John P. Mackintosh, *Nigerian Government and Politics: Prelude to the Revolution* (Evanston: Northwestern University Press, 166), pp. 104-18.
39. On Kenya, see Gertzel, *Politics of Independent Kenya,* p. 130; Hakes, "Parliamentary Party of the Kenya African National Union," pp. 190-94; and Jay E. Hakes and John L. Helgerson, "Bargaining and Parliamentary Behavior in Africa; A comparative Study of Zambia and Kenya," in Kornberg, *Legislatures in Comparative Perspective,* p. 350. On Ghana, see Trevor Jones, *Ghana's First Republic 1960-66: The Pursuit of the Political Kingdom,* Studies in African History 14 (London: Methuen & Co., 1976), p. 40.
40. Helge Kjekshus, "The Question Hour in Tanzania's Bunge," *The African Review* 2, 3 (1972): 351-79.
41. Engholm, "Westminster Model in Uganda," p. 485; Gertzel, *Politics of Independent Kenya,* p. 131; Helgerson, "Institutional Adaptation to Rapid Political Change," p. 181; Hopkins, *Political Roles in a New State,* p. 165; and Oluwole Idowu Odumosu, *The Nigerian Constitution: History and Development* (London: Sweet and Maxwell, 1963), p. 164.
42. Nwabueze, *Presidentialism in Commonwealth Africa,* p. 292.
43. Hopkins, *Political Roles in a New State,* p. 154; and J. Harris Proctor, "The National Members of the Tanzania Parliament: A Study of Legislative Behavior," *The African Review* 3, 1 (1973): 1-19.
44. These characteristics of Kenyan legislators are discussed in Joel D. Barkan, "Bringing Home the Pork: Legislator Behavior, Rural Development and Political Change in East Africa," Occasional Paper No. 9, Comparative Legislative Researh Center, University of Iowa, 1975, pp. 7-34; Barkan, "Legislators, Elections and Political Linkage," *in Politics and Public Policy in Kenya and Tanzania,* ed. Barkan with John J. Okumu (New York, London, Sydney, and Toronto: Praeger Publishers, Praeger Special Studies, 1979), pp. 65-74. Barkan and Okumu, "Political Linkage in Kenya: Citizens, Local Elites, and Legislators," paper prepared for the 70th Annual Meeting of the American Political Science Association, Chicago, September 1974, pp. 8-21; Hopkins, "The Kenyan Legislature," pp. 215-17, 220-27; Jeffrey A. James, "Legislatorial Decision-Making Role Perceptions in Kenya," paper presented at the 15th Annual Meeting of the African Studies Association, Philadelphia, November 1972, pp. 17-28; Malcolm E. Jewell and Chong Lim Kim, "Sources of Support for Legislative Institutions: Kenya, Korea, and Turkey," paper presented at the 48th Annual Meeting of the Southern Political Science Association, Atlanta, November 1976, pp. 10, 12-16, 19-22, 30; and M. Tamarkin, "The Roots of Political Stability in Kenya," *African Affairs* 77 (July 1978): 317-18. Barkan contrasts Kenya to Tanzania, where constituents often want

legislators to provide them with specific benefits, but where legislators are unable to do so. Weak legislator-constituent ties in Zambia are described in Tordoff and Molteno, "Parliament," pp. 208-17.

45. Gertzel, *Politics of Independent Kenya*, pp. 127-29, 153; Helgerson, "Institutional Adaptation to Rapid Political Change," pp. 255-58; Jones, *Ghana's First Republic*, p. 42; Kjekshus, "Parliament in a One-Party State," p. 21; W.J.A. Macartney, "African Westminster? The Parliament of Lesotho," *Parliamentary Affairs* 23 (Spring 1970): 121-40; Mackintosh, *Nigerian Government and Politics*, pp. 118-23; J. Harris Proctor, "The Role of the Senate in the Kenyan Political System," *Parliamentary Affairs* 18 (Autumn 1965): 389-415; Proctor, "The House of Chiefs and the Political Development of Botswana," *Journal of Modern African Studies* 6 (May 1968): 59-79; and Tordoff and Molteno, "Parliament," pp. 200-201.

46. That this occurs in Kenya is suggested by Barkan, "Legislators, Elections and Political Linkage," pp. 88-91; Hopkins, "The Kenyan Legislature," pp. 215-17, 228-29; Newell M. Stultz, "Parliament in a Tutelary Democracy: A Recent Case in Kenya," *Journal of Politics* 31 (February 1969): 104-11, 116-18; and Tamarkin, "Roots of Political Stability," p. 305. Jones, *Ghana's First Republic*, pp. 37, 39; Jon Kraus, "Political Change, Conflict, and Development in Ghana," in *Ghana and the Ivory Coast: Perspectives on Modernization*, ed. Philip Foster and Aristide R. Zolberg (Chicago and London: University of Chicago Press, 1971), pp. 49-50; Kraus, "Ghana's New Corporate Parliament," pp. 6-9; and Lee, "Parliament in Republican Ghana," p. 390, suggest that the legislature performed minor integrative functions in the last years of Nkrumah's Ghana. A good case study of the difficulties faced by Tanzanian legislators attempting to perform either integrative or goal attainment functions is James R. Finucane, *Rural Development and Bureaucracy in Tanzania: The Case of Mwanza Region* (Uppsala: Scandavian Institute of African Studies, 1974), pp. 143-69.

47. Barkan, "Legislators, Elections and Political Linkage," p. 89; Helgerson, "Institutional Adaptation to Rapid Political Change," pp. 277-80; Hopkins, "The Kenyan Legislature," pp. 214-15; Stultz, "Parliament in a Tutelary Democracy," pp. 101-3; and Stultz, "Parliaments in Former British Black Africa," p. 156.

48. Works on political parties in specific countries used in constructing the lists were Margaret Rouse Bates, "UNIP in Postindependence Zambia: The Development of an Organizational Role" (Ph.D. Dissertation, Harvard University, 1971); David E. Apter, *Ghana in Transition*, 2nd rev. ed. (Princeton: Princeton University Press, 1972), pp. 206-18, 338-52; Henry Bienen, *Kenya: The Politics of Participation and Control* (Princeton: Princeton University Press, 1974), pp. 66-130; Bienen. *Tanzania: Party Transformation and Economic Development*, expanded ed. (Princeton: Princeton Unversity Press, 1970), pp. 60-202, 431-47; Dennis L. Cohen, "The Convention People's Party of Ghana:

Representational or Solidarity Party?," *Canadian Journal of African Studies* 4, 1 (1970): 173-94; Akiki B. Mujaju, "The Role of the UPC as a Party of Government in Uganda," *Canadian Journal of African Studies* 10, 3 (1976): 450-67; Joel Samoff, *Tanzania: Local Politics and the Structure of Power* (Madison: University of Wisconsin Press, 1974), pp. 175-220; Richard L. Sklar, *Nigerian Political Parties: Power in an Emergent African Nation* (Princeton: Princeton University Press, 1963), pp. 379-473; and William Tordoff and Ian Scott, "Political Parties: Structures and Policies," in Tordoff, *Politics in Zambia*, pp. 111-41. Works on comparative political parties used were Crotty, "Political Parties Research," pp. 304-7; Duverger, *Political Parties,* pp. 1-202; Kenneth Janda, *A Conceptual Framework for the Comparative Analysis of Political Parties*, Sage Professional Papers in Comparative Politics 1, 01-002 (Beverly Hills: Sage Publications, 1970), pp. 83-112; Janda, "Comparative Political Parties: A Cross-National Handbook," Department of Political Science, Northwestern University, Evanston, 1974, Chapters 3-12; Lawson, *Comparative Study of Political Parties*, pp. 77-187; and Avery Leiserson, *Parties and Politics: An Institutional and Behavioral Approach* (New York: Alfred A. Knopf, 1958), pp. 133-279. Works on African parties in general which were used were Collier, "Parties, Coups, and Authoritarian Rule"; Hodgkin, *African Political Parties,* pp. 63-124; and Welfling, *Political Institutionalization*, pp. 18-26. Finally, works on British parties which were used were R.T. McKenzie, *British Political Parties: The Distribution of Power Within the Conservative and Labour Parties*, 2nd ed. (New York and London: Frederick A. Praeger, 1963); and Rose, *Problem of Party Government.*

49. Studies of African party leaders have been far too numerous to cite here. Those which are especially useful in describing leaders' roles in determining and changing party structure and functions include: Apter, *Ghana in Transition*, pp. 303-24, 358-86; Guy Arnold, *Kenyatta and the Politics of Kenya* (London: J.M. Dent, 1974); Bienen, *Kenya*, pp. 73-81; Henry L. Bretton, *The Rise and Fall of Kwame Nkrumah: A Study of Personal Rule in Africa* (New York, Washington, and London: Frederick A. Praeger, Publishers, 1966), although his interpretation is oversimplified; John R. Cartwright, *Political Leadership in Sierra Leone* (Toronto and Buffalo: University of Toronto Press), 1978, pp. 89-115; A.G.G. Gingyera-Pinycwa, *Apolo Milton Obote and His Times* (New York, London, and Lagos: NOK Publishers, 1978), pp. 51-75; John Hatch, *Two African Statesmen: Kaunda of Zambia and Nyerere of Tanzania* (Chicago: Henry Regenry Co., 1976); Jones, *Ghana's First Republic*, pp. 6-25, 58-91; Jan Pettman, *Zambia: Security and Conflict* (Lewes, Sussex: Julian Freidmann Publishers, 1974), pp. 37-46, 51-65; Cranford Pratt, *The Critical Phase in Tanzania 1945-1968: Nyerere and the Emergence of a Socialist Strategy* (Cambridge, London, New York, and Melbourne: Cambridge University Press, 1976), pp. 63-89, 114-21, 172-215, 237-64;

Selwyn Ryan, "The Theory and Practice of African One-Partyism: The CPP Re-examined," *Canadian Journal of African Studies* 4, 1 (1970): 145-72; and Sklar, *Nigerian Political Parties,* Part II.

50. Pratt, *Critical Phase in Tanzania,* pp. 114-21; Hatch, *Two African Statesmen,* pp. 179-85; and Bienen, *Tanzania,* pp. 160-68.

51. Opoku Agyeman, "Kwame Nkrumah's Presence in A.M. Obote's Uganda: A Study in the Convergence of International and Comparative Politics," unpublished paper, York University, Toronto, April 1974; Lionel Cliffe, "The Political System," in *One Party Democracy: The 1965 Tanzania General Elections,* ed. Cliffe (Nairobi: East African Publishing House, 1967), p. 8; Gingyera-Pinycwa, *Obote and His Times,* pp. 6, 89; David C. Mulford, *Zambia: The Politics of Independence 1957-1964* (London: Oxford University Press, 1967), p. 80; Joseph S. Nye, Jr., "TANU and UPC: The Impact of Independence on Two African Nationalist Parties," in *Boston University Papers on Africa: Transition in African Politics,* ed. Jeffrey Butler and A.A. Castagno (New York, Washington, and London: Frederick A. Praeger, Publishers, for the African Studies Center of Boston University, 1967), p. 230; Pettman, *Zambia,* pp. 22-23; and Young, "Decolonization in Africa," pp. 459-60.

52. Bates, "UNIP in Postindependence Zambia," pp. 248-49; Gingyera-Pinycwa, *Obote and His Times,* pp. 6, 59, 89; Pettman, *Zambia,* pp. 220-24; T.V. Sathyamurthy, "The Social Base of the Uganda Peoples' Congress, 1958-70," *African Affairs* 74 (July 1975): 443; and Tordoff and Scott, "Political Parties," pp. 127, 152-53.

53. A case study of party officials seeking to assure that the party leader selected by them would become head of state without facing a general election, and a leader seeking popular election to assure some independence from these party officials, is the debate over new electoral proposals in the Uganda People's Congress (UPC) in 1970. See D.L. Cohen and J. Parson, "The Uganda Peoples Congress Branch and Constituency Elections of 1970," *Journal of Commonwealth Political Studies* 11 (March 1973): 52-54; James H. Mittelman, *Ideology and Politics in Uganda: From Obote to Amin* (Ithaca, N.Y. and London: Cornell University Press, 1975), pp. 126-30; Norman W. Provizer, "The National Electoral Process and State Building: Proposals for New Methods of Election in Uganda," *Comparative Politics* 9 (April 1977): 319-21; and Peter Willetts, "The Politics of Uganda as a One-Party State," *African Affairs* 74 (October 1975): 291-98.

54. For the rise and fall of ambitious secretaries general, see Jones, *Ghana's First Republic,* pp. 92-101, 133-39, on Tawia Adamafio of the CPP; and Mujaju, "Role of the UPC," pp. 458-63, on John Kakonge of the UPC.

55. Lionel Cliffe, "Tanzania—Socialist Transformation and Party Development," *The African Review* 1, 1 (1971): 132, suggests that the head office of TANU has grown stronger since Bienen conducted the

research on it reported in *Tanzania,* pp. 190-98. Cohen, "Convention People's Party of Ghana," pp. 183-84, suggests that the head office of the CPP was stronger than many observers, including Jones, *Ghana's First Republic,* pp. 79-82; and Ryan, "Theory and Practice of African One-Partyism," pp. 154-55, thought it was.

56. The structure and functions of these collectivites in various parties at various times are discussed in David E. Apter, *The Political Kingdom in Uganda: A Study in Bureaucratic Nationalism* (Princeton: Princeton University Press, 1961), pp. 310-36; Bates, "UNIP in Postindependence Zambia," pp. 57-64, 309-12; Bienen, *Kenya,* p. 82; Bienen, *Tanzania,* pp. 169-90, 198-202; Cliffe, "Tanzania," pp. 131-32; Cohen, "Convention People's Party of Ghana," p. 185; B.J. Dudley, *Parties and Politics in Northern Nigeria* (London: Frank Cass & Co., 1968), pp. 125-30, 171-73; Helgerson, "Institutional Adaptation to Rapid Political Change," pp. 264-71; Martin Kilson, *Political Change in a West African State: A Study of the Modernization Process in Sierra Leone* (Cambridge: Harvard University Press, 1966), pp. 243-48; Mujaju, "Role of the UPC," pp. 453-54; Nye, "TANU and UPC," pp. 226-27, 233-43; Pratt, *Critical Phase in Tanzania,* pp. 210-15; Ian Scott, "Middle Class Politics in Zambia," *African Affairs* 77 (July 1978): 332; Sklar, *Nigerian Political Parties,* pp. 382-84, 395-99, 426-30; Tordoff, *Government and Politics in Tanzania,* pp. 15-19; and Tordoff and Scott, "Political Parties," pp. 120-24.

57. On KANU see Kenneth Good, "Kenyatta and the Organization of KANU," *Canadian Journal of African Studies* 2, 2(1968): 122-24; and Hakes, "Parliamentary Party of the Kenya African National Union," pp. 64-68. On the SLPP see Walter Barrows, *Grassroots Politics in an African State: Integration and Development in Sierra Leone* (New York and London: Africana Publishing Co., Holmes & Meier Publishers, 1976), pp. 120-33, 232-38; and John R. Cartwright, *Politics in Sierra Leone 1947-67* (Toronto: University of Toronto Press, 1970), p. 140. On the NPC see Dudley, *Parties and Politics in Northern Nigeria,* pp. 125-38, 199-209; Sklar, *Nigerian Political Parties,* pp. 382-84; and C.S. Whitaker, Jr., *The Politics of Tradition: Continuity and Change in Northern Nigeria 1946-1966* (Princeton: Princeton University Press, 1970), pp. 363-69. The PP had parliamentary origins (the constituent assembly which approved the 1969 constitution). See Yaw Twumasi, "The 1969 Election," in *Politicians and Soldiers in Ghana 1966-1972,* ed. Dennis Austin and Robin Luckham (London: Frank Cass, 1975), pp. 158-60.

58. Barrows, *Grassroots Politics,* pp. 143-96; Cartwright, *Politics in Sierra Leone,* pp. 140-44; Cliffe, *One Party Democracy,* pp. 30-34, 230-33, 257-60; Election Study Committee, University of Dar es Salaam, *Socialism and Participation: Tanzania's 1970 Elections* (Dar es Salaam: Tanzania Publishing House, 1974), pp. 141-61, 243-46, 265-68, 301-5; Robert Molteno and Ian Scott, "The 1968 General Election and the Political System," in Tordoff, *Politics in Zambia,* pp. 168-71; K.W.J. Post,

The Nigerian Federal Election of 1959: Politics and Administration in a Developing Political System (London: Oxford University Press for the Nigerian Institute of Social and Economic Research, 1963), pp. 230-60; K.W.J. Post and Michael Vickers, *Structure and Conflict in Nigeria 1960-66* (Madison: University of Wisconsin Press, 1973), pp. 162-70; Audrey C. Smock, *Ibo Politics: The Role of Ethnic Unions in Eastern Nigeria* (Cambridge: Harvard University Press, 1971), pp. 160-62, 167-68, 174-75; and Herbert H. Werlin, *Governing an African City: A Study of Nairobi* (New York and London: Africana Publishing Co., Holmes & Meier Publishers, 1974), pp. 256-59.

59. See Cohen, "Convention People's Party of Ghana," pp. 185-87; Finucane, *Rural Development and Bureaucracy*, p. 64; Kilson, *Political Change in a West African State*, pp. 248-50; Post, *The Nigerian Federal Election of 1959*, pp. 150-56; Sklar, *Nigerian Political Parties*, pp. 158-89, 388-89, 414-18, 440-41, 446-60; and Tordoff and Scott, "Political Parties," pp. 124-26.

60. Valuable descriptions of regional and district party organization, spanning a time interval extending from before independence up to the early 1970s, are found in Bienen, *Tanzania*, pp. 84-157; Cohen, "Convention People's Party of Ghana," pp. 176, 179-82; Finucane, *Rural Development and Bureaucracy*, pp. 62-66, 110-17; Cherry Gertzel, *Party and Locality in Northern Uganda, 1945-1962* (London: Althone Press for the Institute of Commonwealth Studies, University of London, 1974); Clyde R. Ingle, *From Villiage to State in Tanzania: The Politics of Rural Development* (Ithaca, N.Y. and London: Cornell University Press, 1972), pp. 113-38; Jones, *Ghana's First Republic*, pp. 68-78; Kraus, "Political Change, Conflict, and Development," pp. 55-57; Maxwell Owusu, *Uses and Abuses of Political Power: A Case Study of Continuity and Change in the Politics of Ghana* (Chicago and London: University of Chicago Press, 1970), pp. 170-94, 205-95, 308-21; Samoff, *Tanzania*, pp. 195-220; Ian Scott, "Party Functions and Capabilities: The Local-Level UNIP Organization During the First Zambian Republic (1964-1973)," *African Social Research* 22 (December 1976): 107-29; and Whitaker, *Politics of Tradition*, pp. 363-68.

61. Joel D. Barkan with John J. Okumu, "'Semi-Competitive' Elections, Clientilism, and Political Recruitment in a No-Party State: The Kenyan Experience," in *Elections Without Choice*, ed. Guy Hermet, Richard Rose, and Alain Rouquié (New York: Halstead Press, John Wiley & Sons, 1978), pp. 93-96; and Bienen, *Kenya*, pp. 81-83.

62. Generalized discussions of the structure and functions of branches in any political party are necessarily brief because of limited data. Valuable case studies of specific branches include Pauline H. Baker, *Urbanization and Political Change: the Politics of Lagos, 1917-1967* (Berkeley, Los Angeles, and London: University of California Press, 1974), pp. 135-48; Peter Harries-Jones, *Freedom and Labour: Mobilization and Political*

Control on the Zambian Copperbelt (New York: St. Martin's Press, 1975), pp. 51-57, 123-30, 216-23; Ingle, *From Village to State*, pp. 145-54; Norman H. Miller, "The Rural African Party: Political Participation in Tanzania," *American Political Science Review* 64 (June 1970): 548-70; Tony Seymour, "Squatters, Migrants, and the Urban Poor: A Study of Attitudes Toward Inequality with Special Reference to a Squatter Settlement in Lusaka, Zambia" (Ph.D. dissertation, University of Sussex, 1976), pp. 388, 398-405, 416-35; and Smock, *Ibo Politics*, pp. 161-69.

63. See Harries-Jones, *Freedom and Labour*, pp. 57-62, 68-95; Ingle, *From Village to State*, pp. 154-69; Miller, "Rural African Party"; and Seymour, "Squatters, Migrants, and the Urban Poor."

64. Cells are described in Bienen, *Tanzania*, pp. 442-44; Finucane, *Rural Development and Bureaucracy*, pp. 65-66; Ingle, *From Village to State*, pp. 169-84; Katherine Levine, "The TANU Ten-House Cell System," in *Socialism in Tanzania: An Interdisciplinary Reader*, Vol. 1, *Politics*, ed. Lionel Cliffe and John S. Saul (Nairobi: East African Publishing House, 1972), pp. 329-37; Jean F. O'Barr, "Cell Leaders in Tanzania," *African Studies Review* 15 (December 1972): 437-65; J. Harris Proctor, ed., *The Cell System of the Tanganyika African National Union* (Dar es Salaam: East African Publishing House, 1971); and Samoff, *Tanzania*, pp. 135-52, 233-34.

65. Differing conclusions about the significance of membership in TANU are found in Göran Hydén, *Political Development in Rural Tanzania: TANU Yajenga Nchi* (Nairobi: East African Publishing House, 1969), pp. 218-19; and Jon R. Moris, "The Voter Level Surveys," in Election Study Committee, *Socialism and Participation*, p. 359, both of which are based on survey data. The issue of utilizing economic criteria to limit membership in TANU is discussed in Bismarck U. Mwansasu, "Commentary on *Mwongozo Wa TANU, 1971*," *The African Review* 1, 4(1972): 22-24; and Helge Kjekshus, "The Ruling Party: Essays on TANU," in *The Party: Essays on TANU,* University of Dar es Salaam Studies in Political Science No. 6, ed. C.R.S. Muzo et. al. (Dar es Salaam: Tanzania Publishing House, 1976), pp. vii-x. Rejection of a similar proposal in Ghana is discussed in Ryan, "Theory and Practice of African One-Partyism," pp. 159-61.

66. Similar explanations are given in Kasfir, *Shrinking Political Arena,* pp. 270-78; and Miller, "Rural African Party," pp. 567-69.

67. Electoral participation—both attending campaign meetings and voting—in Tanzania is high by world standards, and has increased form each election to the next. See Lionel Cliffe, "The Campaigns," in Cliffe, *One Party Democracy,* pp. 236, 241-42; Helge Kjekshus, "Socialism and Participation: Some Concluding Remarks," in Election Study Committee, *Socialism and Participation,* p. 372; and Denis Martin, "The 1975 Tanzanian Elections: The Disturbing Six Percent," in Hermet *et al.*, *Elections Without Choice,* p. 110.

68. Barkan with Okumu, "Semi-Competitive Elections, Clientilism, and Political Recruitment," pp. 96-99; Barbara Callaway, "National-Local Linkages in Ghana," *The African Review* 4, 3(1974): 415; Owusu, *Uses and Abuses of Political Power*, pp. 222-24; Scott, "Party Functions and Capabilities," pp. 119-26; and Sklar, *Nigerian Political Parties*, pp. 446-53.

69. These types are discussed in Janda, "Comparative Political Parties," Chapter 11, pp. 5-15.

70. Lionel Cliffe and John S. Saul, "The District Development Front in Tanzania," in Cliffe and Saul, *Socialism in Tanzania*, Vol. 1, p. 309. Factionalism has been rife in the ruling or dominant parties of Ghana, Kenya, Eastern and Western Nigeria, Uganda, and Zambia. On Ghana, see Dennis Austin, *Politics in Ghana 1946-1960* (London, New York, and Toronto: Oxford University Press under the auspices of the Royal Institute of International Affairs, 1964), pp. 402-14; Cohen, "Convention People's Party of Ghana," pp. 174-76, 188-91; Jones, *Ghana's First Republic*, pp. 92-140; Martin Kilson, "Cleavage Management in African Politics: The Ghana Case," in *New States in the Modern World*, ed. Kilson (Cambridge and London: Harvard University Press, 1975), pp. 75-88; Owusu, *Uses and Abuses of Political Power*, pp. 230-35, 317-21; and Ryan, "Theory and Practice of African One-Partyism," pp. 149-54. On Kenya, see Bienen, *Kenya*, pp. 82-89, 101-21; Gertzel, *Politics of Independent Kenya*, pp. 39-72, 155-66; and Hakes, "Parliamentary Party of the Kenya African National Union," pp. 37-62. On Nigeria, see Mackintosh, *Nigerian Government and Politics*, pp. 441-50; Sklar, *Nigerian Political Parties*, pp. 190-230, 261-83; and Sklar, "Nigerian Politics: The Ordeal of Chief Awolowo, 1960-65," in *Politics in Africa: Seven Cases*, ed. Gwendolen M. Carter (New York, Chicago, and Burlingame: Harcourt, Brace & World, 1966), pp. 126-40. On Uganda, see Mujaju, "Role of the UPC," pp. 450-63; and Sathyamurthy, "Social Base of the Uganda People's Congress," pp. 451-56. On Zambia, see Bates, "UNIP in Postindependence Zambia," pp. 293-96; Robert Molteno, "Cleavage and Conflict in Zambian Politics: A Study in Sectionalism," in Tordoff, *Politics in Zambia*, pp. 65-68; Pettman, *Zambia*, pp. 51-61; Scott, "Middle Class Politics," pp. 327-33; and Tordoff and Scott, "Political Parties," pp. 112-20, 151.

71. TANU has generally been considered to have a low level of factionalism; see, for example, Cliffe, "The Campaigns," p. 252. The existence of ideological factionalism, increasing with the more vigorous implementation of socialist measures since 1967, is suggested in Bienen, *Tanzania*, pp. 221-25; Raymond F. Hopkins, "Political Opposition in Tanzania: Containment v. Coercion," in *Political Opposition and Dissent*, ed. Barbara McLennan (New York and London: Dunellen Publishing Co., 1973), pp. 276, 297-300; Martin, "1975 Tanzanian Elections," pp. 114-16; Pratt, *Critical Phase in Tanzania*, pp. 108-14, 182, 203, 237-43; Joel and Rachel Samoff, "The Local Politics of Underdevelopment," *Politics and Society* 6, 4(1976): 418-19; and John S. Saul, "Tanzania's Transition to

Socialism?," *Canadian Journal of African Studies* 11, 2(1977): 320.

72. Valuable discussions of the role of auxiliary groups and resistance to incorporation are found in David E. Apter, "Ghana," in Coleman and Rosberg, *Political Parties and National Integration*, pp. 293-99; Robert H. Bates, *Unions, Parties, and Political Development: A Study of Mineworkers in Zambia* (New Haven and London: Yale University Press, 1971), pp. 126-200; Björn Beckman, *Organizing the Farmers: Cocoa Politics and National Development in Ghana* (Uppsala: Scandanavian Institute of African Studies, 1976), esp. pp. 179, 239-44; Elliot J. Berg and Jeffrey Butler, "Trade Unions," in Coleman and Rosberg, *Political Parties and National Integration*, pp. 340-81; Foltz, "Political Opposition in Single-Party States," pp. 158-61; William H. Friedland, *Vuta Kamba: The Development of trade Unions in Tanganyika* (Stanford: Hoover Institution Press, 1969), pp. 116-29, 148-49; Gingyera-Pinycwa, *Obote and His Times*, pp. 153-61; Anirudha Gupta, "Trade Unionism and Politics on the Copperbelt," in Tordoff, *Politics in Zambia*, pp. 288-319; Jones, *Ghana's First Republic*, pp. 219-53; Kilson, *Political Change in a West African State*, pp. 242, 259-65; Akiki B. Mujaju, "The Demise of UPCYL and the Rise of NUYO in Uganda," *The African Review* 3, 2(1973): 291-307; Samoff, *Tanzania*, pp. 69, 179-95; Sklar, *Nigerian Political Parties*, pp. 453-60; Tordoff, *Government and Politics in Tanzania*, pp. 137-58; Twumasi, "The 1969 Election," pp. 145-56; and Wallerstein, "Decline of the Party," pp. 208-9.

73. Sklar, *Nigerian Political Parties*, pp. 460-67; and Smock, *Ibo Politics*, pp. 159-66, 173-74.

74. On opposition as both a norm and collectivity and role behavior in Ghana, see Dennis Austin, *Ghana Observed: Essays on the Politics of a West African Republic* (Manchester and New York: Manchester University Press and Africana Publishing Co., Holmes & Meier Publishers, 1976), pp. 90-101; Austin, *Politics in Ghana*, pp. 28-48; and Sanjeeva Nayak, "An Analytical Model of Hegemonical Tension Among Ghanaian Elites," in *Political Decision-Making Processes: Studies in National, Comparative and International Politics*, ed. Dusan Sidjanski (Amsterdam, London, and New York: Elsevier Scientific Publishing Co., 1973), pp. 55-81. On opposition in Kenya, see Gertzel, *Politics of Independent Kenya*, pp. 73-124, 144-48; and Suzanne D. Mueller, "Statist Economies and the Elimination of the KPU: A Critique of Political Party Analysis and the 'Center-Periphery' Argument," paper presented at the 15th Annual Meeting of the African Studies Association, Philadelphia, November 1972, pp. 15-33. On opposition in Nigeria, see B.J. Dudley, *Instability and Political Order: Politics and Crisis in Nigeria* (Ibadan: Ibadan University Press, 1973), pp. 40-83; Mackintosh, *Nigerian Government and Politics*, pp. 508-609; Post and Vickers, *Structure and Conflict in Nigeria*, pp. 63-236; Sklar, *Nigerian Political Parties*, pp. 87-140, 321-76; Sklar, "Ordeal of Chief Awolowo," pp. 119-62; and Whitaker,

Politics of Tradition, pp. 384-414. On opposition in Sierra Leone, see Cartwright, *Politics in Sierra Leone,* pp. 103-37, 167-81, 210-38. On opposition in Uganda, see Donald Rothchild and Michael Rogin, "Uganda," in *National Unity and Regionalism in Eight African States,* ed. Gwendolen M. Carter (Ithaca, N.Y.: Cornell University Press, 1966), pp. 355-60, 389-94. On opposition in Zambia, see Pettman, *Zambia,* pp. 60-69; Thomas Rasmussen, "Political Competition and One-Party Dominance in Zambia," *Journal of Modern African Studies* 7 (October 1969): 407-24; and Tordoff and Scott, "Political Parties," pp. 134-43.

75. Janda, "Comparative Political Parties," Chapter 9.

76. On geographical and temporal variations in the strength of UNIP, see Bates, "UNIP in Postindependence Zambia," pp. 87-88, 128, 187-88, 320-26; Scott, "Middle Class Politics," pp. 322, 331-33; Scott, "Party Functions and Capabilities," and Seymour, "Squatters, Migrants, and the Urban Poor," pp. 437-38. Cohen, "Convention People's Party of Ghana," pp. 188-91, suggests that the CPP was changing from a "party of representation" to a "party of solidarity" in its last years, rather than decaying organizationally as has been commonly assumed.

77. Barrows, *Grassroots Politics,* p. 232; Scott, "Party Functions and Capabilities," pp. 108-28; Samoff, *Tanzania,* p. 202. The importance of TANU in performing integrative, conflict-resolving functions is indicated in ibid., pp. 202-3, 216-19, 230-31; Bienen, *Tanzania,* pp. 334-49; Election Study Committee, *Socialism and Participation,* p. 343; Ingle, *From Village to State,* pp. 186-95; Miller, "Rural African Party," p. 551; and Samoff and Samoff, "Local Politics of Underdevelopment," pp. 424-25.

6

African Planning Failure: A Public Policy Analysis

Melvin J. Dubnick

In the opening pages of this volume the claim is made that the control and facilitation framework will have significant pay-off in terms of its power and completeness in explaining and predicting political change in Africa. In this chapter we consider that claim in light of a specific political phenomenon: public policies.

For political science the concern with public policies is a relatively recent development. For decades there has been an emphasis on the institutional and behavioral dimensions of political life. Many analyses of these dimensions have without doubt been extremely valuable; and, as is demonstrated in other chapters of this volume, the control and facilitation framework suits such approaches well. Nevertheless, it has become increasingly evident that institutional and behavioral foci do not constitute the entire picture. Political analysis is no longer restricted to answering questions relating to what the political system is and how those in it carry on their tasks. Instead, political scientists are more frequently exposed to inquiries about public policy making and the products of that process: What is the policy? How was it determined? Why was policy "x" chosen and not policy "y"? Was the policy selected a "good" one in the sense that it will allow the system to attain its goals? If the answer is yes, why has the policy selected succeeded? If no, why has it failed?[1]

How useful is the control and facilitation framework as a basis for answering such questions? In order to answer that query we will analyze an important example of public policy in African states: development planning policies. Following a brief introduction to planning in Africa and the third world, we will attempt to apply the control and facilitation model to explain planning policies, and to develop strategies for overcoming problems found in them. At the heart of this approach is the concept of the planning system. Although the impact of all four subsystems in determining planning policies will be considered, special attention will be given to the role of the pattern socialization and control subsystem since this matter is generally unexplored in the literature.

Planning Failure in Africa

In sub-Saharan Africa, economic development planning is commonplace. "Africa is a continent of economic plans," states Andrew M. Kamarck. "Every country in Africa (except South Africa) has had at least one [plan] since World War II, and most have had several."[2] The urge to plan has been so strong that there has never been any question for most countries in the area regarding whether or not to plan, at least not since the period immediately preceding independence. In fact, planning is more or less regarded as an integral part of the exercise of sovereignty in most African states.[3] If there is any debate taking place regarding planning, it concerns the question of why planning in Africa has failed to promote the development of this, the poorest of the third world areas.

Since it is debatable whether "development" is a measurable concept, doubts can be raised concerning *any* judgment of planning success or failure.[4] Such doubts cannot be put aside easily. Yet even in the absence of some specific and accurate means for determining plan "success" or "failure", the verdict of failure permeates evaluations conducted by analysts of and leaders in the planning profession. A perusal of the relevant literature will uncover many judgments similar to that offered by Albert Waterston, a leading authority in the field. To him it is obvious that third world development programs in general

> are falling short of what is reasonable to expect. The record is so poor—it has been worsening in fact—that it has sometimes led to disillusionment with planning and the abandonment of plans. Even in India, a citadel of planning, planning has been under unprecedented attack. Indeed, participants in the United Nations Meeting of Experts on Administrative Aspects of National Development Planning held in Paris in June, 1964, went so far as to suggest that national development planning was in crisis.[5]

Since that time the situation has not seemed to improve. The literature of planning has become increasingly a literature of discouragement and failure. While most development planning "textbooks" avoid evaluations of actual plan performance,[6] those books and articles which assess planning programs present a dismal picture of the results. United Nations documents are most revealing in this respect. One Eastern European planner, Jozef Pajestka, notes that the "experience of developing nations that have resorted to planning in recent years" reveals a great discrepancy between plan targets and achievement.[7] *The 1970 Report on the World Social Situation* (published by the U.N.) is highly critical of third world development plans and planners for their inability to obtain desired objectives.[8] In addition, at a September 1969 meeting of planning experts at Stockholm, top authorities from around the world accused themselves and their colleagues of narrowness in approaching the problems of development and of relying too heavily upon rather "simplistic" models which resulted in poor plan performance.[9] Still another organ of the United Nations states the problem as follows: "...there is a great deal of dissatisfaction with the results of the planning process. In some quarters the dissatisfaction had even reached the point where the value of planning as an instrument of development has been questioned".[10]

This attitude of failure seems to have been magnified by the results of the U.N.'s First Development Decade which reduced any optimism that remained in the late 1950s. Not only is failure admitted in several official documents, but also in the records of major conferences on development planning. The results of one gathering were published in a volume edited by Colin Legum, and reflect the feeling of failure that has permeated other sources.[11] Another conference, at the University of Sussex in June 1969, was attended by a World Bank official whose comments are relevant in this regard. Having noted that since World War II "more than 1200 development plans have been prepared, over 125 central planning offices have been established [and] about 100 training centers giving courses in planning have been created," C.J. Martin expressed the expectation that "planning should have gained in stature and have received a secure place of importance in the development sphere." To his dismay, however, development planners were being called to Sussex for a conference on "The Crisis in Planning."[12] Paraphrasing Martin's lament, Guy Benveniste noted that, "with twenty-five years of experience behind them, national planners talk more about failures than about successes."[13]

In focusing on the experiences of economic planning in Africa, professional judgments are not different. Both Soviet and western analysts and planning experts agree. "The independent African countries plunged into the fight for economic development with new ideas and bright hopes for a quick and decisive change for the better; but many of them failed to make even the slightest change."[14]

There have been more optimistic assessments, of course, but even these have judged the overall results as poor. Most positive evaluations of development planning in Africa tend to concentrate on the "side benefits" derived from planning efforts. G.K. Helleiner, for instance, begins his analysis of development planning in the 1960s by noting that during that decade plans were essentially symbolic exercises through which "lip service" was paid to social and economic development. Helleiner points out that, despite this fact, some good has been derived: plans have failed while *planning* has improved: "While the elaborate national plans...have typically been forgotten shortly after their production, and have had limited effect upon subsequent governmental investment allocations and policies, there has been steady improvement in the quality of economic decision-making."[15]

There seems to be little opposition to the position that economic planning has to some extent failed in almost every African country. The basic debate is concerned with the question of why development programs have failed. What causes development planning failure?

A Framework For Analysis

The search for those causes can begin with the premise that planning policies are the product of processes and actions taken within a specific social subsystem we will designate the *planning system*. As an analytic construction, the planning system includes all social system interactions motivated by the desire to formulate and/or implement a development plan.

The primary purpose of any plan is to reduce uncertainty, and there is much evidence that a form of planning occurs in all individuals and organizations.[16] Our specific interest, however, is in *development planning*, which is defined as "the conscious effort of a central organization to influence, direct, and, in some cases, even control changes" in the principal social variables "...of a certain country or region over the course of time in accordance with a predetermined set of objectives."[17] This planning process can be seen as functioning at two levels, one qualitative and the other quantitative.[18] At the qualitative level, development plans involve the search for and attainment of the "optimum social order" which best serves all concerned. On the more specific quantitative level, development planning seeks to manipulate certain key factors; e.g. production, educational achievement, national identity, etc. These latter objectives are the operational goals for which action is undertaken in the planning system.

The structural organization of this planning system can be described in terms of the framework outlined in Chapter 1. At the top of the hierarchy of control and facilitation is the pattern socialization and control subsystem, in which are found the system's dominant values and commitments. The visions of the future manifested in a development plan have their roots in these values, and those who determine the values of the system have a considerable impact on the form and content of official plans. In the planning system the determination of those values is left primarily to *planner experts:* "men of knowledge" or social architects commissioned by those who claim a political mandate to do so. Guy

Melvin J. Dubnick

Benveniste views these professionals as

> ...first and foremost staff people with a concern for policy research and planning. They are devoted to certain ways of conceptualizing policy issues. Their professional ideology is apolitical. The canons of their approach include teamwork, interdisciplinary research, a penchant for problems that can be quantified, and continued long term improvement in policy and planning.[19]

In a prescriptive statement, Jan Tinbergen offers the following view of development planning experts in terms of their backgrounds:

> Because of the comprehensive nature of the tasks undertaken by a planning office, its staff will have to include experts with widely different educational backgrounds, training and experience. The two most important groups will be economists and engineers, and within each of these groups there must be specialists in many different fields. Among the economists, there will be experts in statistics, in national accounting, in public finance, in econometric and mathematical techniques, in the theory of international trade and in agriculture and other branches of industry. The engineers on the staff...should also have specialized in the most There will also be specialists in the fields of education, social relationships, government and administration. Their specialized knowledge will be the result partly of their university training and partly of their previous practical experience.[20]

It is the value system of these planner experts which we examine in the next section as a possible cause of development planning policy failure. The impact of these values on the official plan will depend on their acceptance by other relevant actors, especially the political executives described below; but while the values of other actors in the planning system may contradict those of the planners, sufficient deference is given to the latter that their values usually prevail.

At the second level of the hierarchy of control and facilitation is the integrative subsystem, in which are found the norms and influence patterns which determine the integration of the planning system. Here we again find the planner expert as the central actor, but in this case as an object related to by others. The quality of deference paid to the planner and the expectations held in regard to his/her behavior by others in the planning system are examined in the section on planning system norms and integration with an eye toward viewing them as sources of plan failure.

The most crucial collectivities, roles (aside from that of planner expert), and power relationships relevant to the planning system are those involved in the actual decision making processes—the goal attainment subsystem. Planner experts are "policy recommenders," not decision makers.[21] Those involved in decision making are left with the task of officially formulating planning policies (i.e., setting policy goals) and then implementing them through the mobilization of available resources. For present purposes we will focus on two sets of collectivities and roles which take part in this process: political executives and administrators.

Political executives constitute the politically responsible actors in the planning system. Acting as more or less legitimate agents of the total political system, the political executives contract for the services of the planning experts. It is the political executive who is being advised by the various planning professionals, and it is that same official (or officials) who initiates the mobilization of resources for purposes of carrying out a plan strategy. The political executive also plays a major role in the formulation of plans by formally supplying and officially sanctioning what Herbert Simon has called the "ought-sentences," i.e. the value imperatives upon which substantive planning is based.[22] In determining these imperatives political executives generally defer to planner experts.

Several caveats regarding this particular collectivity and the roles of which it is composed are in order. First, the political executive may be either a single individual or a collectivity on whom the responsibility for planning falls. Second, relevant political executives will not necessarily be *top* authority figures in the political system. They may be lower-level appointees of a top official or extremely powerful individuals with sources of influence all their own. Third, that political executives do have some power does not indicate they will be the most powerful actors in the planning system.

Administrators are those in the planning system who organize, coordinate, and direct the mobilization of resources. It is with the necessary help of administrators that information and other resources are gathered for the use by planning experts; it is through the administrators' efforts that plans are implemented and evaluations are undertaken. Their activities in the planning system are thus related to adaptation and integration as well as goal attainment, but they do contribute significantly to the latter subsystem.

There are, of course, other collectivities and roles to be considered in regard to decision making processes. Those mobilized either for or against proposed development plans constitute a potentially important factor in determining development policy failure. Pressure groups, interested legislative leaders, heads of opposition political parties, revolutionary counterelites, etc., can all develop into major sources of support and opposition. While we will take these actors into account as possible determinants of plan failure, our main concern in the section on goal attainment and mobilization will be with political executives and administrators and their impact on planning policy outcomes.

At the foundation of the hierarchy of control and facilitation is found the adaptive subsystem of the planning system, i.e., the relationships between crucial planning system actors and the *subject society* of development plans—the social system which is to be affected by the designs of planner experts as manifested in the decisions of the political system. In the section on social conditions we will examine those hypotheses which consider the cause of plan failure to lie in the subject society's values, norms, collectivities, or roles, and their incompatibility with equivalent structures in the planning system.

Using this general framework of the planning system we will be able to view planning policy failure from a broad perspective that other analysts have failed to use. From such an analytic base we will then consider possible strategies for corrective actions where these are deemed necessary.

The Planner's Image and Planning Failure

Development plans are human creations, and as such they are guided by the "social values, visions and interests" of those who compose them. In almost all cases the "composers" are planner experts— professional policy recommenders commissioned to draw up development plans by a country's "legitimate" political rulers. In contracting for these experts, third world leaders are getting more than functional expertise; they are also purchasing sets of assumptions about what constitute desirable social conditions for a "modern" society and how these are to be attained in a reasonable amount of time. These assumptions—values and commitments—are purchased for the subject society as a whole and the planning system in particular. Should these values and commitments be relevant to and demonstrate a high utility for the subject society, plans will tend to be successful; if not, then we have pinpointed one possible source of planning failure.

The relationship between plan failure and planner experts' values is neither often discussed nor well researched. Several comments related to this topic can be found in the general literature of planning,[23] but these are usually little more than brief commentaries with no substantial empirical evidence to support them. In this section we will attempt to indicate how planner expert values influence planning policy by demonstrating the generally inflexible nature of their value systems in the face of conditions which demand open and malleable assumptions.

We begin by developing a framework by which we can analyze the expert's value system. For this purpose the concept of the "image," extrapolated from Kenneth Boulding's work, will be used. Defined as "subjective knowledge" which is largely responsible for an individual's behavior, the image has as its source "all past experience of the possessor of the image itself." The image has several functions, two of which are relevant at this point. First, it is the repository of an individual's values and commitments. Second, it acts as a constantly adapting filter for present and future actions and experiences. Viewed within the context of a systems framework, the image is located between the individual and his/her environment. The image acts as a screen or control apparatus through which incoming information is processed (or not processed) in accordance with the image's form at the time of contact (D1,D2). In its role as a filter, the image can respond to incoming messages in three ways: 1) not at all, i.e., by rejecting or ignoring the input; 2) by accepting the input in some "regular and well-defined" way which, at the most, can lead to a gradual modification of the image itself; and 3) by accepting certain messages which will change the image "in a quite radical way," thus causing some degree of intellectual revolution.[24]

Every image configuration is unique in its responses to inputs from the environment. The particular form of an image is strongly influenced by what Boulding calls the "process of testing." This process exposes the image in its current form to "reality" (i.e., incoming messages) which tests the image's ability to give its holder relevant and useful data. Having delivered relevant and useful information, an image verifies itself. If it fails to deal with reality it is open to challenge and change. In this sense, then, much depends on the image's ability to be tested. An easily tested image will be a flexible one, open to challenge and change as "reality" warrants such adjustments. But as Boulding notes, not all images are easily tested, and some might even be impossible to verify.[25] In such cases we can talk of *inflexible images*.

One can expect some degree of inflexibility in all images. A completely flexible image would, in fact, be no image at all. Similarly, some degree of flexibility would be necessary if an image were to be of any use to its holder. There remains a wide range between the poles of flexibility-inflexibility within which any particular image can be located. That location constitutes an important factor in determining an image's utility for its holder, such as a planner, or those who depend on that holder, such as other actors in a planning system.

In order to further facilitate this analysis, we will consider the image itself as characterized by four basic qualities which may be viewed as its four functional subsystems. First, images have *content* (pattern socialization and control): an abstract and theoretical portion which negatively relates to alternative abstractions and theories. Each image contains values which reflect a choice among various value alternatives. Planner experts have a considerable number of views about desirable societal forms to choose from, and in making their choice and internalizing it as their value they have given content to their image, i.e., they have adopted a bias which is then used by the planning system. The question of image flexibility in regard to content should be viewed as the extent to which a particular bias is held. The greater the bias toward one particular view of a "desirable" societal form for the subject society, the more inflexible the image.

The second quality of an image is its internal consistency—its *structural logic* (integration). We can attribute to images the same tendency Leon Festinger attributes to their holders: the drive for consonancy and congruity in the cognitive realm.[26] Images are organized entities that are continually exposed through the testing process to entropic forces which seek to disorganize structured patterns.[27] To ward off such forces, images continually strive for an internal logic which can withstand dissonance creating pressures (D1,E2,E4). This logic, to be effective for the image, must also be open enough to permit the empirical realities of the environment some role in determining the image's form. Here again we see the need for a mixture of flexibility and inflexibility. The image of planner experts must therefore contain a structural logic closed enough to give it a relatively persistent form and internal consistency, and at the same time be open enough to allow for adjustments of the structural logic to variations in environmental conditions.

A third quality of an image is its *strategical logic* (goal attainment). This characteristic reflects an image holder's perception of the means by which it is to be applied in given situations. As with structural logic, strategical logic can be either open or closed. A closed strategical logic is necessary to the extent that it instructs the holder in definitive terms about what must be done and how. Yet, excessive specificity breeds excessive inflexibility. Strategies must also be open and flexible in light of the realities of environmental variations. Planner experts must therefore have a strategic logic which helps them direct the application of their expertise while leaving the door open to adjustments in methods mandated by unique or changing circumstances.

Finally, an image is characterized by its *adaptability,* i.e., its capacity to relate to specific environmental conditions that are relevant for the image holder's purposes. An image which relates to one set of conditions is useful only when faced with that set or a closely related set. This is a sign of a maladaptive inflexibility which should be avoided. On the other hand, one finds images which are so adaptable that they lose all value for their holders. Completely adaptable images lack the capacity to select certain features of the environment as keys to bringing about specific changes. Such images would lack any guiding logic—structural or strategic. All four qualities of the image are related to one another in terms of control and facilitation. The planner expert's image will be relevant and useful where its content is adaptable to the environmental conditions of the subject society without being so adaptable that it has no structural or strategic logic. This system of mutual determinism (see Figure 6.1) indicates several points at which the planner experts and their value system can cause planning failure.

The empirical evidence useful for an analysis of planner expert images is extremely scarce. However, the present writer recently undertook a limited analysis of planner images, and the results of that study will be used here where applicable.

Content Bias

A thematic content analysis of introductory chapters to thirty national development plans (including twelve sub-Saharan Africa plans) revealed very little in terms of the type of society advocated by planner experts. The analysis sought to determine the number of times these documents mentioned *Gesellschaft,* atomistic social systems as desirable objectives as opposed to the more organistic, *Gemeinschaft* societal forms. The results of this attempt were meager, with the content almost always being "not ascertainable." Of the 317 "plan objectives" in sub-Sahara African documents, all but sixteen were not ascertainable in regard to this theme.[28]

The lack of any indication of preference in this area can be interpreted in two ways. First, we could hold that there was in fact no preference. Such a conclusion cannot stand, however, in light of the obvious fact that development planners constantly deal with the question of changing societies. They are commissioned for the purpose of converting one societal condition into another; thus it would seem absurd for them to disavow any preference in societal form.

A second interpretation would hold that the lack of a stated preference for societal form is actually an indication that such a preference is widely held and taken for granted. When clarification of the content analysis is sought in other studies, this interpretation seems to stand up. For instance, a study by Warren Ilchman and others involving interviews with thirty-three "middle range planners" indicated a strong desire for social relationships closely associated with *Gesellschaft*-type society: individualism, materialism, capitalism, and other attributes common to modern western society. The interviewees reacted negatively to "traditional values" and "ascriptive" attitudes which they perceived as constraints to development planning—another indication of a pro-*Gesellschaft* view. When asked to cite countries they saw as "models" of development, their choices were basically oriented toward modern,

FIGURE 6.1
The Planner's Image

Functional Components

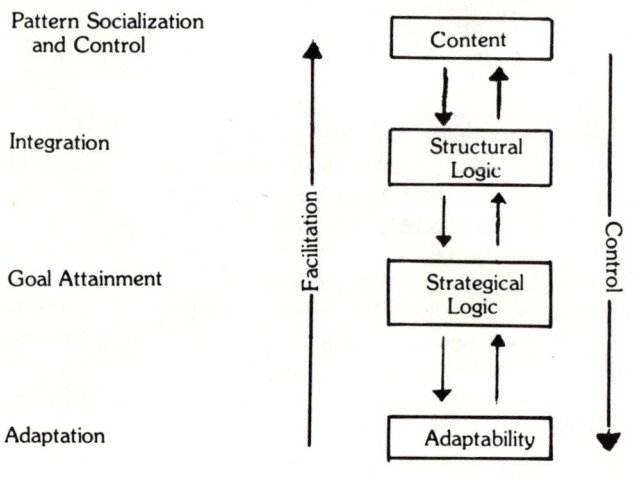

westernized examples like Japan, the United States, and Western Europe. The *Gesellschaft* bias was clearly evident.[29] Any perusal of the general literature of planning will indicate the same strong bias.

Structural Logic

The same thematic content analysis attempted to uncover the orientation of planners toward development by determining which social subsystem they held to be most crucial for purposes of attaining desired ends. Uncovering this orientation is important in two respects: first, it indicates the operational direction of the content bias; and second, it offers the analyst some insight into the specific form of the structural logic. In regard to the former, one can see the four functional subsystems of society as four different yet interrelated directions from among which the image holder chooses his/her particular point of emphasis. The choice, once made, becomes a base upon which the structural logic is formed. Thus, in regard to the second reason for investigating this orientation, once there is some indication of the general direction or emphasis of the content bias, there is also some hint as to the specific form the structural logic will take. For example, if the analyst were to find an emphasis on the pattern socialization and control subsystem as a focal point for the content bias, then his/her attention must be turned to the theoretical literature and conventional wisdom related to that area. An examination of that literature and wisdom can be undertaken for the purpose of determining its logical openness or closedness which, in turn, will indicate the image flexibility in this regard.

Using the four functional subsystems of the control and facilitation framework as the thematic alternatives, 826 "plan objectives" were surveyed for the thirty national development plans, including the twelve sub-Sahara African ones. As shown in Table 6.1, about 70 percent of the African plan objectives focused on the adaptation subsystem, thus indicating a strong emphasis on a subject society's economic sector for purposes of bringing about development. It would follow that development plans concentrate on economic policies (which they obviously do), and that the planner expert's image is based on economic theories and models. An in-depth review of the literature of development planning supports this finding, and also gives us some insight into the structural logic of the image itself. An economic determinism seems to permeate this image, with considerable weight being given to economic growth as a key to attaining "modernity." Among planner experts there exists a substantive controversy relating to which economic factor is the *primum mobile* for development, but overall there is little debate regarding the primacy of economic variables. In fact, the structural logic involved in these theories is basically a closed and inflexible one which tends to deny

Melvin J. Dubnick

the relevance of variables which do not "fit" into its general economic framework.[30] The result is reflected in development studies that fail to take advantage of alternative models and approaches,[31] thus limiting the applicability of such studies and the official plans which build upon them.

Strategical Logic

The strategic orientation of planner experts is an extension of the structural logic with an added emphasis on eliminating perceived constraints. Strategy in development plans which heavily emphasize the adaptation subsystem will, of course, concern itself primarily with the

TABLE 6.1
Themes of Planning: Crucial Social Subsystems

Social Subsystem	Botswana (N=32)	Burundi (N=12)	Central African Republic (N=22)	Chad (N=19)	Dahomey (N=31)	Ethiopia (N=16)
Pattern Socialization and Control N=	0	0	1	0	0	0
%=	0	0	4.5	0	0	0
Integration N=	9	0	3	5	2	3
%=	28.1	0	13.6	26.3	6.5	18.7
Goal Attainment N=	1	1	3	0	3	0
%=	3.1	8.3	13.6	0	9.7	0
Adaptation N=	22	11	15	14	26	13
%=	68.8	91.7	68.2	73.7	83.9	81.3
Not Ascertainable N=	0	0	0	0	0	0
%=	0	0	0	0	0	0

manipulation of economic factors. Planning documents are, in many cases, little more than statements about which production factors (land, labor, capital, technology, etc.) are to be adjusted and how. As shown in Table 6.1, rarely does one come across strategies related to the political subsystem or the integrative subsystem of the subject society. Even less frequent are references to the need for modifying the pattern socialization and control subsystem as a means for bringing about development objectives. Such tendencies are continually reinforced by the historical traditions of development planners which seem to equate all planning with economic planning, and the pressures of a professionalism which defines theories and models that planners should follow if they are to be accepted by their professional peers.[32] These determinants of strategy are thus

Themes of Planning: Crucial Social Subsystems

Gabon (N=20)	Kenya (N=46)	Nigeria (N=33)	Tanzania (N=36)	Togo (N=32)	Zambia (N=21)	Sub-Sahara (N=320)	All Regions (N=826)
0	0	0	0	1	0	2	15
0	0	0	0	3.1	0	.6	1.8
1	15	11	8	3	4	64	171
5.0	32.6	33.3	22.2	9.4	19.0	20.0	20.7
0	1	0	5	6	2	22	50
0	2.2	0	13.9	18.7	9.5	6.9	6.0
19	30	18	23	22	15	288	582
95.0	65.2	54.5	63.9	68.8	71.4	71.3	70.5
0	0	12.1	0	0	0	1.2	.9
0	0	4	0	0	0	4	8

Melvin J. Dubnick

related more to factors outside the truly relevant environment (that is, the subject society) than to factors in that environment. The result is a high degree of strategical logic inflexibility in the image of planner experts.

An indication of this inflexibility was uncovered in the thematic content analysis. For each of the 826 plan objectives found in the thirty plans, this writer sought to determine the strategic orientation advocated vis-a-vis current conditions in the subject society. Strategic flexibility would be indicated by strategies which oriented to specific conditions on the basis of their individual utility for achieving given plan objectives. Inflexibility would manifest itself as strategies which failed to consider utilities of individual conditions and instead perceived *all* current conditions as either useful or not solely on the basis of their identification with the present state of "underdevelopment." The strategic choices involved either the *maintenance* of current conditions, thereby implying their possible use in the development plan; or the *change* of such conditions, implying that their elimination would best facilitate development efforts. The results, shown in Table 6.2, point to the overwhelming concentration on *eliminating rather than utilizing* given subject society conditions; on imposing a new social system rather than modifying the old one to fit

TABLE 6.2
Themes of Planning: Strategic Use of Given Conditions

Strategic Approach	Botswana (N=32)	Burundi (N=12)	Central African Republic (N=22)	Chad (N=19)	Dahomey (N=31)	Ethiopia (N=16)
N= Change	19	12	22	19	31	15
%	59.4	100.0	100.0	100.0	100.0	93.8
N= Maintenance	5	0	0	0	0	0
%	15.6	0	0	0	0	0
N= Not Ascertainable	8	0	0	0	0	1
%	25.0	0	0	0	0	9.3

African Planning Failure

contemporary conditions. The most effective stance for successful planning in regard to this particular strategic question would be one which calls for the evaluation of current subject society conditions in terms of their potential utility for development planning efforts. The evidence, however, indicates a tendency for planner experts *to assume* condition-change to be of greater value. This reflects a considerable inflexibility in the image of planner experts.

Adaptability

The adaptability of planner expert images is very difficult to analyze. Some indication was obtained in the previously mentioned study when this writer attempted to uncover what relationship, if any, there was between the frequency of the planning themes found during the content analysis and the environmental conditions of the thirty countries whose development plans were used.[33] That analysis, involving six categories of environmentally relevant factors (physical and demographic factors, political structure and process factors, political conflict factors, economic variables, social factors, and transport/communications variables), indicated little if any association between environmental conditions and planning themes. Using Goodman and Kruskal's *tau beta* as a measure,

Themes of Planning: Strategic Use of Given Conditions

Gabon (N=20)	Kenya (N=46)	Nigeria (N=33)	Tanzania (N=36)	Togo (N=32)	Zambia (N=21)	Sub-Sahara (N=320)	All Regions (N=826)
20	34	26	28	32	21	279	762
100.0	73.9	78.8	77.8	100.0	100.0	87.2	92.2
0	2	0	2	0	0	9	21
0	4.3	0	5.6	0	0	2.8	2.5
0	10	7	6	0	0	32	43
0	21.7	21.2	16.7	0	0	10.0	5.2

associations were determined between the frequency of planning themes and variables derived from Arthur S. Banks' *Cross Polity Time Series Data*. The results, displayed in Tables 6.3 through 6.8, reflect low levels of association between the frequency of planning themes and each of the forty-eight variables used to represent environmental variations among the thirty countries examined.[34] While it is impossible to draw definitive conclusions from such limited evidence, the implication of the study is obvious: planner expert images tend not to adapt to given environmental conditions.

While much more investigation is needed in this area, the evidence presently available leaves little doubt that the values and commitments which guide the planning system, as manifested in the images of planner experts, reflect an inflexibility which can only limit the applicability of planning efforts in third world states in general, and in African states in particular.

TABLE 6.3
Association of Physical and Demographic Factors and the Themes of Planning

Enviornment Factors 1966	Maintenance/ Change	Gemeinschaft/ Gesellschaft	Adaptation/ Goal Attainment/ Integration/ Pattern Socialization and Control
Area	.0957	.0381	.0246
Population	.0631	.0320	.0338
Population Density	.0267	.0086	.0010
Percentage of Population in Cities of Over 100,000	.0384	.0041	.0119

TABLE 6.4
Association of Political Structure and Process Factors and the Themes of Planning

Environment Factors 1966	Themes		
	Maintenance/ Change	Gemeinschaft/ Gesellschaft	Adaptation/ Goal Attainment/ Integration/ Pattern Socialization and Control
Regime Type	.0116	.0028	.0062
Head of State	.0164	.0059	.0048
Effective Executive Type	.0168	.0055	.0041
Legislative Selection Process	.0108	.0024	.0055
Effective Executive Selection Process	.0017	.0121	.0014
Nomination Process	.0258	.0088	.0072
Party Legitimacy	.0055	.0088	.0061
Parliamentary Responsibility	.0073	.0063	.0029
Legislative Effectiveness	.0148	.0047	.0067

TABLE 6.5
Association of Political Conflict Factors and the Themes of Planning

Environment Factors 1964-1966	Themes		
	Maintenance/ Change	Gemeinschaft/ Gesellschaft	Adaptation/ Goal Attainment/ Integration/ Pattern Socialization and Control
No. of Coups	.0093	.0179	.0053
No. of Major Constitutional Changes	.0212	.0280	.0038
No. of Major Cabinet Changes	.0244	.0066	.0076
No. of Changes in Effective Executive	.0084	.0250	.0131
No. of Legislative Elections	.0142	.0144	.0012
No. of Assassinations	.0112	.0006	.0037
No. of General Strikes	.0406	.0075	.0096
No. of Government Crises	.0278	.0006	.0065
No. of Political Purges	.0440	.0068	.0124
No. of Anti-Government Demonstrations	.0853	.0307	.0235

TABLE 6.6
Association of Economic Factors and the Themes of Planning

Environment Factors 1966	Themes		
	Maintenance/ Change	Gemeinschaft/ Gesellschaft	Adaptation/ Goal Attainment Integrations/ Pattern Socialization and Control
Gross National Product (GNP) Per Capita	.0565	.0108	.0138
Gross Domestic Product (GDP) Per Capita	.0387	.0063	.0114
GDP Per Capita Originating in Industrial Sector	.0375	.0252	.0119
Energy Production Per Capita	.0285	.0080	.0072
Energy Consumption Per Capita	.0353	.0104	.0118
Imports Per Capita	.0154	.0100	.0163
Exports Per Capita	.0156	.0082	.0133
Proportion of World Trade	.0546	.0281	.0190

Melvin J. Dubnick

TABLE 6.7
Association of Social Factors and the Themes of Planning

Environment Factors 1966	Themes		
	Maintenance/ Change	Gemeinschaft/ Gesellschaft	Adaptation/ Goal Attainment/ Integration/ Pattern Socialization and Control
Primary School Enrollment Per Capita	.1019	.0412	.0216
Secondary School Enrollment Per Capita	.0350	.0131	.0249
University Enrollment Per Capita	.0379	.0238	.0176
Total School Enrollment Per Capita	.0739	.0207	.0192
Percentage of Population Literate	.0616	.0349	.0208
Physicians Per Capita	.0303	.0052	.0189

TABLE 6.8
Association of Transport/Communication Factors and the Themes of Planning

Environment Factors 1966	Themes		
	Maintenance/ Change	Gemeinschaft/ Gesellschaft	Adaptation/ Goal Attainment/ Integration/ Pattern Socialization and Control
Railroad Mileage Per Square Mile	.0146	.0039	.0224
Rail Passenger-Kilometers*	.0244	.0445	.0089
Passenger Cars Per Capita	.0366	.0252	.0155
Commercial Vehicles Per Capita	.0394	.0252	.0126
All Highway Vehicles Per Capita	.0309	.0248	.0115
Telegrams Per Capita	.0419	.0063	.0091
Telephones Per Capita	.0380	.0248	.0141
Radios Per Capita	.0400	.0240	.0128
Newspaper Circulation Per Capita	.0422	.0270	.0299
Book Prod. By Titles Per Million Pop.	.0322	.0045	.0203
All Mail Per Capita	.0358	.0133	.0092

*Number of kilometers traveled by rail passenger in given year.

Melvin J. Dubnick

Planning System Integrative Norms and Planning Failure

Somewhat less obscured in the discussion about planning failure are those hypotheses which place the blame on planning system norms and resulting patterns of influence. Normative orientations serve to integrate various actors into the planning system, or at least offer a set of expectations by which behavior (particularly that of the planner expert) may be evaluated by other actors (D1,D2).

The predominant sources of third world policy makers' norms are the colonial inheritance and current pressures imposed by professionalism. This normative pattern emphasizes the positive (and one must add, assumed) relationship between "objectivity" and rational (and therefore, "most likely to succeed") decision making. To be apolitical and nonideological—these are the standards set forth by the many analysts who focus on corruption and the politicization of the bureaucracy as the primary causes of planning failure. The decolonization period set the stage for these developments, as is described by Irving Louis Horowitz:

> In the transition from colonial to native political rule, relations between politicians and bureaucrats pass through a highly fluid stage during which no agreed-upon normative patterns exist to guide interaction....The political-civil service tensions and conflicts...produce varying degrees of non-cooperation, sabotage and reprisal until eventually some form of modus vivendi emerges.
>
> Discredited in the eyes of the public and lacking formal power, the civil service is in a weak position to defend its inherited ideal of political and ethnic neutrality, technical competence and efficiency...Given the propensity of politicians in power to place highest value on loyalty and nationalistic zeal, it is inevitable that the conflict should be resolved in complete politicization of the bureaucracy...
>
> Transformation of the civil service into a political forum makes it unable to resist other forms of particularism. It becomes permeated with family, ethnic, regional, and religious divisions, aggravated by the ever present conflict between generations.[35]

The end results are a breakdown in the internal communications system which the bureaucrats formerly supplied; the erosion of impersonality standards; and the overall impairment of the bureaucracy's ability to function effectively. The remedy is implied in such explications of the cause: depoliticization of bureaucracies or, in more positive terms, the professionalization of them.[36] As applied to planners and the planning system specifically, this normative order has continually emphasized the need for the experts to be apolitical and to guard the planning system against such potential dangers as partisan interference or power politics. Such apoliticism, states Guy Benveniste, is part of the "ideology of planning," and has a considerable impact on the behavior of planner experts and others in the system.

> A planner is supposed to elaborate a plan; he is supposed to find the "best" solution, i.e., the most rational use of scarce resources which will help achieve modernization. It seems always to be assumed that once this "best" solution is made known, it will be endorsed spontaneously by all those who are to implement the plan.[37]

This ideology is deeply rooted in an antipolitical tradition which is reflected in an article by John Friedmann. Friedmann views planning as a "certain manner of arriving at decisions and actions the intention of which is to promote the social good of a society undergoing rapid change." Characteristically, planning is regarded as objective, analytic, integrative, projective, experimental, utopian (in a "practical" sense), and aesthetic—but not political. Planning "represents the work of reason in history." The serious constraints on planning are "two powerful forces at play within society which are opposed to the use of reason": power and ideology. In light of the constant presence of such potentially disturbing factors, "the planner must be quite clear in his own mind that his primary responsibility is to work for the interest of the whole; he must be courageous enough to lay all the evidence before the judges, to make it perfectly clear just what is being chosen." This is "imperative" for the planner to do "if reason is not to be abandoned altogether."[38]

Such are the norms imposed on planner experts, and for Benveniste, such are the *causes* of planning failure. The "reality" of planning would not lead to an apolitical or antipolitical set of norms, but rather, to norms that emphasize the place of and need for political role-taking by planners and others in the process. If planners are to be at all successful, they must obtain power. "A powerless planner can only elaborate trivial or nearly trivial plan. . ."[39] The need for political activism by planners is also stated by Bertram Gross, who regards it as a necessary response to the problems of plan implementation.[40] These analysts suggest that an increased potential for planning success would result if planner norms were adjusted. In this way, the blame for planning failures has been placed on the apolitical normative subsystem of the planning system.

Planning System Mobilization and Planning Failure

To plan is to make policy; and to make policy involves the mobilization of available resources for use toward a goal (C2). Goal attainment is a major aspect in the planning system, one which some analysts feel is crucial in the determination of planning success or failure in developing states. Those who regard planning failure to be rooted in the goal attainment subsystem generally discuss the procedural and organizational weaknesses of the policy making (decision making) entities of the planning system. Although the argument is made in a number of ways, the conclusion is generally the same: the procedures and organizations used in formulating and implementing development planning policies are insufficient to accomplish the successful determination and execution of such programs (C6).

The basis for such evaluations is found in the literature of decision making. No policy making system is perfect. As Charles Lindblom and others have noted, all decision making processes include some inherent obstacles to achieving policy perfection. Five are especially relevant to planning. First, policy problems must be defined into existence; thus the stated problem necessarily reflects the biases and concerns of the definer. Second, to develop rational solutions to any problem, total knowledge of the general situation is necessary—a prerequisite which is "beyond the capacity of the human mind" to fulfill. Third, the priorities and methods of approaching a problem should be agreed upon, but are usually not due to the almost inevitable conflict of values which plagues decision makers. Fourth, decisions are made in a human environment which always provides resistance, no matter how valid a policy may seem. And finally, policy making involves organizations which themselves bias and distort information and decisional activities.[41]

All of these procedural barriers are found in planning efforts. For instance, Albert Waterston has observed that while a clearly defined set of objectives is necessary as a sound foundation for planning, in most cases this is not supplied. This is apparently due to the political executive's inability or unwillingness to specifically state and identify the problems at hand and the goals sought.

> Incongruous mixing of primary and secondary, long- and short-term, and qualitative and quantitative objectives with aims which are not really objectives, but are essentially means for obtaining the basic objectives of a development plan, is generally an indication about what they expect from their plan.... In lieu of facing up to difficult decisions, political authorities frequently prefer to list objectives which, although mutually inconsistent, will include something for everybody.[42]

Thus, even the basic prerequisites for planning—unambiguously defined problems and objectives—are neither clearly nor frequently fulfilled. While this obstacle is partially rooted in developing social structures (that is, in the instability of their political institutions, etc.), it is also a problem inherent to the policy making process of all contemporary societies. There are no known procedures which could eliminate this problem.
knowledge which is already possessed) are as pervasive in the developing world as in the developed. The only difference is that, in the third world, the problem is magnified by societal conditions. "Even the most advanced countries may lack many of the statistical series which planners require," note Watson and Dirlam; "but the shortage is much more serious in an underdeveloped nation: some countries attempt comprehensive plans without even tolerably reliable estimates of population or national income and no information on their past rates of growth."[43] Information-gathering facilities are inadequate or totally lacking in developing societies, and the time and financial expenditure necessary for correcting this situation seem out-of-reach for those who wish to correct it.[44] Thus, while no society's planning organization can hope for perfect awareness of all relevant variables, third world planners have even more difficulty in attempting to overcome the information-gathering problem (C6c).

The third process problem involves competition among specific norms which guide planning formulation and implementation. Such competition takes place within the confines of the broad consensus among planner experts which has been previously delineated. Explanation by example will be the most useful approach. In country "X," a hypothetical African nation, three actors are involved in the process of planning—each regarded as an "expert" in the planning field. Planner "A" is the director of the planning organization; in order to help him in his efforts, the government has contracted with planner "B" who is from Eastern Europe; and, in order to protect their investment in the program, the World Bank has sent planner "C" to aid these professionals. "C" is a planning expert educated in the United States. "A" 's education was accomplished in England during the early 1950s, while "B" was trained in Yugoslavia.

Melvin J. Dubnick

"A" feels that an aggregate model of development best suits his country's situation. He perceives that problems must be considered on a macroeconomic level where factors such as production, investment, etc. take primacy. Expert "B," however, feels that development is a matter of sector manipulation, using varying strategies in order to create a balanced situation in the economy. Planner "C" counters with an emphasis on inter-industrial planning, which is concerned with the relationships among productive, i.e., industrial, sectors. These individuals—all planners by profession and all well trained and highly qualified— have a basic dispute among themselves in regard to those factors which are crucial in making the plan work. Each perspective is theoretically correct in its own right and, perhaps, can be used in similar circumstances.[45] The mutual exclusiveness of each approach, however, breeds a conflict among those involved in the formulation process. That this is not an infrequent occurrence can be seen in the notes of planning conferences and the literature on development, which seem marked by a continuous competition among various schools of thought. The obstacles posed by such competition plague numerous planning attempts in the third world.

Fourth, the barriers imposed by human resistance to the planning process are described in almost every work on the subject. The irrational responses of clientele groups, the reluctance of administrators, the reasoned objections of some economists and politicians, the ideological and dogmatic demands of political elites and counterelites—each of these hinders attempts to analyze, formulate, and implement development policies (C3). Inability to adjust procedurally to these human obstacles may result in planning failure.

A final category of obstacles inherent in the planning process involves organizational barriers. Organizational form is given to planning efforts for a number of reasons, the primary one being that many of the previously mentioned procedural obstacles can be overcome only through a coordination of resources and roles (C6e). This is especially true as most planners are concerned with the implementation as well as the formulation of plans. In both processes the role of organizations is crucial. Formulation, for example, is a task given to planning organizations because political executives feel that, by structuring a distinct plan organization, they are decreasing the usual waste of more decentralized policy formulation procedures. While a plan organization may not meet its established objectives for the subject society, it can ease the path toward these goals. In this light, political leaders expect the planning officials to conduct themselves in an efficient manner which will not only reduce waste in the policy making process, but will also offer the rest of society an example to be followed. The potential result of such efficiency is an increased "trust" which the political executive, the administrator, and others give the planner. And for many, trust is half of the battle! Richard Meier has argued that the planner, through his or her organized efforts, must make others "believe" in his attempts to develop the society.[46]

So far as implementation is concerned, one need only peruse recent planning literature to see how much weight is given to efficient and effective planning organizations. For some, planning failure has become synonymous with "non-implementation,"[47] and this is considered by many to reflect the poverty of implementation organizations. Thus, in the case of both plan formulation and implementation, organization is deemed crucial. This has been reflected in an increasing emphasis among planning experts on organizational reform. As far as they are concerned, improving the organization means eliminating more procedural inefficiencies which, in turn, will produce more successful planning attempts.[48]

Yehezkel Dror's analysis of public policy making in developing states is perhaps the most relevant summation of this particular approach to explaining policy (i.e. planning) failure. After ascertaining the input, output, procedural, and structural qualities of policy making of an "avant-garde developing state," Dror notes that "most developing states lack both the necessary knowledge and the necessary behavior patterns for realistic planning, which is more often imposed from abroad as a condition for financial assistance than practical because of local initiative."[49] Lacking in those functional and structural attributes which promote successful planning, development planning systems in the third world generally, and Africa specifically, have been frustrated. From this point of view, the rearrangement of procedural and/or organizational patterns can increase the chances of planning success. Such modifications call for the cooperation of those who function within the decision making system: planner experts as policy recommenders; political executives as policy makers (or agents of policy makers); and administrators as policy implementors. The ideas presented below concerning organizational weaknesses in the subject society generally also apply to the goal attainment subsystem of the planning system.

Social Conditions and Planning Failure

Bertram Gross has defined planning as a process by which certain individuals called "planners" commit themselves or others to some "representation of future action."[50] Planners deal in commitments and value structures. They attempt to develop what Benveniste calls "images of the future" for use by their clientele.[51] In this regard the planner is faced with various limitations imposed by the structure of the subject society.

Adaptive structures form the facilitation base in the control and facilitation framework. They are the environmental "givens" of all social systems including the planning system. As such, they determine to a great extent how successful a plan will be. Incongruities between an abstract plan and concrete conditions in a society will present the planning system with its greatest obstacles to success. Thus, a plan which calls for ten billion dollars in expenditures in one sector of the economy is unrealistic or impractical for a social system that cannot or will not generate more than five billion dollars in tax or aid revenues. *Planning must be in tune with the realities of the social system* and its environment. The subject society may not have the resources—physical, financial, material, or human— necessary for a certain type of plan to be implemented. The result will be plan failure.

Many explanations of development planning failure have been based on this approach. The most direct explication is found in the works of David E. Apter. In *The Politics of Modernization,* Apter touches upon the subjects of "professionalism" and the "ideology of science" as these are associated with the modernizing process. He notes four ideological tendencies which are relevant for that process: socialism, nationalism, national socialism, and science. The last, science,

> is not merely a style of thinking about problems, nor is it solely a derivation from the functional significance of science in an industrialized world, although this is clearly the origin of its power. Rather, it is the application of rational methods and experimentalism to social affairs.

The ideology of science is manifested in "professional roles and norms" usually associated with manpower experts, social survey teams, management experts, *and planners,* among others. While these professionals might exist within a modernizing social system, there are limits to their respective utility in the development process. It is Apter's contention that the professional's ideology of science "functions only in a period of practical realism, and is ultimately antagonistic to any other ideology...," while the alternative ideologies of nationalism, socialism, and national socialism are more likely to predominate in the early stages of modernization. The overall result is a societal context which, at least ideologically, works against professional efforts such as development planning. The early stages of development call for an emphasis on "identity" and "solidarity" functions which create the foundations for future collective action. "For these purposes the ideologies of nationalism, socialism, and possibly, national socialism are more satisfactory than the ideology of science."[52]

If this is the case, what is the role played by planners and other professionals found within political and administrative systems during those early stages of modernization? Which functions do they perform which make them valuable enough to keep? For Apter they are "a kind of exhibit; they are formally consulted, but their advice is not followed."[53] For Benveniste, who regards the planner's primary task as the "reduction of uncertainty," a number of secondary functions are also attributable to their roles: legitimization of the regime; acting as a private staff for the political leaders; and supplying the political leaders with a means of obtaining secrecy in policy formulation, thereby enhancing the leaders' political power.[54] In other words, the ability of professional planners to perform functions in addition to their primary task may give them a role within the political and/or administrative structure of a developing social system. However, this role is not of a nature that will lead to planning success, which can only occur, according to the Apter hypothesis, when societal conditions permit the dominance of the ideology of science.

At what point in the modernization sequence does the ideology of science become useful? When can planners and other professionals expect to have some impact relevant to their main task of aiding development? Apter's implied answer is that this will occur only when the modernizing nation "develops" sufficiently to permit the exercise of this ideology. For this to occur, three conditions are deemed necessary: first, there must be "a general acceptance of common membership in the society, with the result that nationalism has become internalized and implicit"; second, "sufficient development" has already occurred so that societal dislocations require fine adjustments rather than gross "solutions"; and, third, "a consensus prevails about the roles that are functional to the continuous process of development." In other words, for development planners to have any impact in development processes, development must already have taken place to a considerable extent.[55] As an explanation of plan failure, this hypothesis suggests, first, that the planner accept as a "fact of life" that the conditions necessary for the fulfillment of his primary task are absent and, second, that he or she also realize that no professionally sanctioned (i.e., planning) action he or she might take or suggest will change the situation until the facilitating circumstances are present.

This same argument is made on what Apter terms the structural level. Not only can the value environment of planning lead to failure, but the stratification and role systems can impose themselves as barriers as well. In a later work—*Choice and the Politics of Allocation*—Apter accomplishes a transition between normative and structural levels. In his theory, Apter posits a correlation between the degree of development and the structure of the stratification system. As development passes from one stage to the next (always becoming progressively more and more "modern" at each successive stage), the stratification system changes from a rather simple to a complex structure. At various stages new classes appear and new stratification relationships are formed, the most recently developed class tending to dominate and grow as time goes on. The normative and structural characteristics of these classes vary. As in his exposition of the ideological barriers to professionalism, Apter's argument vis-a-vis stratification is that, until the correct circumstances arise—that is, until "functional status elites" (professionals) are dominant—there will be little possibility for the effective utilization of professional expertise. In summary, where the society is sufficiently developed the planner will have the opportunity to aid in the development process. Until then, it is implied, the planner must fulfill other functions while awaiting the appropriate moment.[56]

While not oriented toward the specific consideration of the role of planners and/or other professionals in developing countries, numerous analysts besides Apter have commented about the societal prerequisites for facilitating development and modernization efforts. Dankwart Rustow cites nationalism as such a prerequisite, while Edward Banfield cites corporate organization and an "ethos" which permits such corporate forms of action to develop. Banfield's outlook for creating such an "ethos" is not very optimistic. "Changing the ethos, if it could be done deliberately, would entail...dangers."[57]

At a more general level, there is that school of thought which sees the prime deficiency as a society's lack of "institutionalization." Defined in various ways—as change absorbing, conflict managing, or valued and stabilizing[58]—institutions are regarded by many analysts to be a key variable which will determine the success or failure of development policies. A lack of such institutions means, according to these writers, that a necessary prerequisite for the use of planning expertise is missing.

The political environment within which planning occurs is also regarded as having an impact on whether attempts at planning are even worthwhile. Certain types of political institutions might develop into barriers with which the planner cannot contend. For example, what if the role of the political opposition is too powerful? Planning, by its very nature, involves collective choices which will benefit some sectors and present costs to others. To be effective, planning must not only attract the attention and commitment of important policy makers; it must also take account of those whose opposition will be aroused.[59]

Even more common is the view that economic development planning cannot succeed unless some "minimal political conditions" are present. J.J. Spengler summarizes these conditions as minimal public services; growth-supporting and stimulating policies; public personnel development; and viable political instruments such as parties and welfare state machinery.[60] Development planning will fail due to the absence of these prerequisites.

Still another explanation of this genre concerns the lack of the bureaucratic talent so necessary for development planning. With few exceptions (e.g., India), the third world has not had the "reservoir of bureaucratic skills" that development programs require.

> In Africa, where the Congo would be an extreme but not untypical example, the situation

is...desperate. Colonial administration, which emphasized the services of police and law and which did not recruit large numbers of Africans to positions of policy responsibility, has been replaced by public administration that is closely tied to goals of national development. African administrators whose responsibilities until recently were characterized by routine are catapulted to the top of the hierarchy, where they are expected to advise ministers and politicians regarding major programs of economic and social development. As J. Donald Kingsley aptly observes, the inexperience and other limitations of unseasoned public administrators necessarily set limits to the dreams of politicians. How much the state can accomplish in a setting that manages to steer clear of administrative chaos, to say nothing of just plain inefficiency, is clearly circumscribed by the nature of the bureaucratic talent available.[61]

Thus, from its general structural and normative configurations down to its pool of available bureaucratic talent, the subject society is regarded as a major obstacle to planning success. The exigencies of the situation render the planning system ineffective according to those analysts who adhere to these explanations, the implication being that until such societies have the prerequisites necessary for planning, any attempts will inevitably fail.

Toward Strategies for Planning Success

We have seen how the control and facilitation framework can be used to indicate possible causes of planning failure. From the planners' value system at the top of the hierarchy of control and facilitation within the planning system to the subject society and its "energy" generating roles at the base, we are presented with potential causes of planning failure which challenge those who seek development in African societies. What can be done in the face of such challenges? Is the control and facilitation framework helpful in developing strategies for planning success? In this section we will attempt to answer that question by applying the framework and relevant propositions to the problems indicated by our previous analysis.

We begin our analysis by assuming we are faced with a planning system characterized by: 1) an inflexible planner expert's image which is accepted as the guiding value set for the system; 2) a normative pattern which emphasizes the necessity of planner expert objectivity and apoliticism; 3) policy-making and administrative machinery that is unstable, inefficient, and ineffective: i.e., generally incapable of fulfilling the formulation and implementation functions assigned to it; 4) a subject society which lacks the basic prerequisites deemed necessary for the development of a successful planning policy. Viewing this as the "pre-existing" planning system and applying propositions relevant to such a system (A1-A4), we draw the following conclusions:

First, the bias of the planning system's values and norms works against the innovativeness or flexibility necessary for policy changes that can increase the chances for plan success (A1). As we saw above, some of the blame for planning failures can be placed on the obstinacy of professionally sanctioned belief and behavior patterns found among planners.[62] While these patterns are not completely inflexible, innovativeness is limited to only those minor variations in values and norms which are considered acceptable.

Second, the integration of the planning system is, in one crucial respect, very high. Planner experts are highly integrated with each other; that is, as a "community of experts" which knows no national boundaries, professional planners relate to and interact with each other with considerable frequency. Working with a common pool of knowledge and seeking to substantiate each other's "professionalism," this community has been an important force in third world policy making. Those who are regarded as radicals within the profession are seldom approached to serve as planner experts. This integration further strengthens the planning system's resistance to new or challenging ideas that are not within the range of acceptable notions (A2).

In a different respect, however, there is potentially weak integration in the planning system. Planner experts are not so much "citizens" of the subject society as they are members of an international community.[63] Thus they are regarded as "outsiders," men of knowledge who follow a "different drum." They have overcome this distinctiveness to a considerable extent by using the legitimacy of their claims to be different and their demands for deference. In this sense, the differences among the actors in a planning system are not so much causes of conflict as they are the basis of an integration that is perceived as legitimate and therefore sanctioned by the entire planning system. The political executive and the administrator do not attempt to challenge the ideas and knowledge of the planner, for he or she is considered *the* expert. It is expected that the planner professional will return such respect in-kind, the overall result being a planning system well integrated enough to apparently supercede most attempts at substantial change.[64] Nevertheless, this integration is dependent to a considerable extent on those who grant it legitimacy. In light of massive examples of planning failure, it is possible that this integration can easily be weakened by means discussed below (A2a).

Third, in the planning system power is highly concentrated in some respects while well dispersed in others. According to proposition A3, an appropriate distribution of power for purposes of facilitating policy innovation would be a dispersion of power among different planners (thereby promoting a proliferation of proposals) and a high concentration of power among policy makers and implementors. However, in the typical planning system just the opposite situation exists. Power is very concentrated at the source of policy proposals—among planner experts—since these professionals usually follow a common line as defined by fellow members of the community of experts; and such "lines" are reinforced by the few major external sources of funding (the World Bank, the U.N., and foreign ministries of "developed" nations which make large grants of aid) which typically engage planner experts as consultants. At the same time, and despite the view that power is highly concentrated within African subject societies, power at the policy making and implementing end is often extremely dispersed.[65]

Finally, the planning system—like all social systems—undergoes constant changes; but the changes currently underway are not significant in terms of what is "necessary" for converting plan failure to plan success. The planner expert's image of development is constantly changing, but only within a limited range of ideas defined by the current paradigm of economic and social progress. Planners are constantly trying new approaches in terms of normative behavior patterns for themselves and others involved in the system, but only to the extent that their objectivity and apoliticism are not compromised. And as for the political, administrative, and social subsystems, their changes seem to be increasingly away from rather than toward development. The planning system is undergoing change, but not of the type which will facilitate a more flexible and thus a more successful planning effort (A4).

Given the pre-existing planning system (and assuming that changes are possible in planning policies) where will we be most likely to find sources of changes that will result in more successful planning policies? Among potential internal sources are the actors involved in the system itself: planner experts, political executives, administrators, active supporters and opponents, and the subject society in general. Relevant external sources might be other societies, various international funding organizations, the planning profession (as an international community of experts), and general environmental conditions which can have an impact on the planning system.

Any of these sources, both internal and external, may be useful. But which will have the greatest impact? That is an empirical question not answered in proposition B1. Some indication of which sources would be of greatest value is found in proposition B2 which indicates that within the planning system the adaptive subsystem—relations with the subject society—is most susceptible to change. Therefore, those sources of change which can potentially have the greatest impact on the subject proposition even further, the subject society itself is susceptible to being influenced through the "lower" levels of its functional hierarchy: through its economic and political subsystems. In short, the best source of change for the planning system will be that which most effectively mobilizes the subject society's economic and/or political subsystems for such change (C1).

Put in structural terms, the way to adjust the inflexble image of the planner expert, the norms which add to plan failure, and the ineffectual decision making apparatus is through the manipulation of the basic resources with which the planning system must work as defined by the political and economic conditions of the subject society. We will thus be considering strategies which deal with the mobilization of relevant collectivities in the subject society and the manipulation of its available resources.

Let us assume, for the moment, that the sources of change will be external, and that there will be an attempt to change the planning system by manipulating the subject society's available resources. The manipulation of available resources is not a simple task, for there are some resources more vulnerable to external influence than others. Perhaps the most important variable in this regard is development plan funding, a factor which determines the availability of other resources to a considerable extent. The capacity of a social system in fiscal and monetary terms is an important consideration for planners and others in the planning system. Most African states are severely limited in this regard. Much reliance is placed on external sources of financing: foreign countries, international organizations, foreign private investors, etc. Currently funds from these sources are in short supply, and their use is usually tied to numerous "strings" which determine who will use the funds, for what purposes, and in what manner. The standards currently reflected in such "strings" tend to substantiate the values and norms of present planning systems, not challenge them. Money "talks," and if international institutions such as the World Bank or national agencies such as the United States' Agency for International Development can be convinced of the damage being perpetuated by dominant planner images and behavior patterns, much can be done to improve the chances for planning success.[66]

Of course, money is not the only resource open to manipulation. Certainly many other factors in the subject society will be malleable. The important question is, how malleable and at what costs? We would postpone planning altogether if we accepted David Apter's argument that successful planning necessitates an appropriate social environment, and thus that we must develop a country before we can plan development! If there were some means for injecting a subject society with new resources or more well-developed ones, our problem would be a minor one. However, such opportunities are rare. The discovery of oil or some other valuable resource can certainly spark a reaction from the planning system. A mass education system that increases the potential of available human resources can do the same, but its creation involves a long-term policy based on planning. As an access point for changing the planning system, innovative role-making by major actors in that system seems viable but somewhat limited for reasons discussed above. The best hope for change using these innovative actors also seems to rely on the manipulation of financial resources.

We next turn to the potential for mobilizing relevant collectivites and thereby involving segments of the subject society in the policy making subsystem of the planning system. The planner, it must be remembered, is dependent upon the structures and processes by which plans are formulated and implemented. Through the selective mobilization of certain collectivities and their biases, one can have a great impact on the success or failure of planning efforts. The problem is to determine which collectivities to mobilize and how to do so most effectively.[67] External sources of change are again very important, especially as they stimulate actions and reactions among the citizens of a country. This does not mean that a country must submit to external controls, but rather that it should selectively avail itself of external influence. Such influence can be used as either a positive force to aid in collectivity mobilization or a scapegoat upon whom one can count for a "useful" threat: one that will mobilize previously indifferent and dormant populations. But regardless of whether one is to rely on external or internal sources of change, attention must be paid to the factors brought out in propositions C2 through C6. Care must be taken to mobilize those whose orientations will have a *corrective* impact upon the planning system (C2). There is always the chance that those being mobilized are not against the type of planning that failed, but rather see no utility in planning whatsoever (C5). Similarly, one must calculate how to manage the countermobilization that will inevitably occur (C3). And, most importantly, those mobilized must have a relatively good chance of influencing the planning system and those in it so as to stimulate innovativeness and flexibility at the control levels of the hierarchy (C6). The roles played by specific collectivities in stimulating, supporting, or opposing planning system change will vary among societes; thus it is virtually impossible to generalize about the most fruitful strategy to employ with regard to such collectivities.

Assuming the planning system has been sufficiently stimulated, the next problem indicated by our propositions concerns control of the changes that are to take place. We are not seeking just change, but change which will further planning system success. For the planning system this means: making the planner expert's value system more flexible and open to the conditions in the subject society; establishing planning system norms which make the attainment of goals more important than the perpetuation of professional objectivity and apoliticism; and improving the policy making and implementation systems so that they are capable of formulating and carrying out plans appropriate to the subject society. The key to our approach will be to orient the planning system to its subject society (which will be changing at the same time in response to collectivity mobilization and resource manipulation). This strategy is based on proposition D1 which holds that "a society...is more likely to accept new elements which are compatible with pre-existing elements that those which are less compatible." This does not mean that planning systems will not be change-oriented. Quite the contrary, the planning system under this strategy will attempt to achieve very fundamental changes. What this type of approach does is assume that change begins with and uses as many current conditions as possible. What seems to be inherent in present day planning systems is the misconception that change begins when previous conditions are eliminated: when tradition is exchanged for modernity, nomads are settled, old crops are replaced by new, farmers are placed in factories, ox-power is exchanged for electric-power, and so on. The successful planner will be one who injects change into the present system, not one who attempts to establish an entirely different society atop the ruins of the "underdeveloped" one (D5). The successful planner will calculate resistances and means to use rather than destroy them. The successful plan creates, not destroys.[68]

Assuming our strategy for planning is undertaken, what will our creation look like? One cannot expect the emergence of a world economic and political power overnight, especially given an approach in which "compatibility" plays such an important role. Rather, one should expect the planning system to create a society in motion, a social system in the process of change toward a more "developed" state. What is a "developed" state? For our purposes, to be developed is to be increasingly capable of contending with a turbulent and often inhospitable environment. This type of environment does not call for a stable, mechanical social system, but one which is mobile and organic, constantly interacting both positively and negatively with its surroundings. Thus, one should not be surprised when planning policies result not in smooth transitions to new social states, but instead create "short-run" conflict, dissonance, ambivalence, and other forms of uncertainty (E1,E2). Eventually the dust will settle and the planning system will have succeeded or failed in its task of moving the subject society one step closer toward the objective of a "developed" social system (E3). If successful, the planning effort will probably not have manifested many dramatic changes (E4).

The results may in fact seem minor, although their overall impact will be major. Such is the type of planning which can be successful in sub-Saharan Africa and the rest of the third world as indicated by our framework.

This sketch of a strategy for planning success has been accomplished at a high level of abstraction. More specific suggestions using the propositions presented in Chapter 1 must await an attempt to apply this overall framework to a particular instance of planning policy failure. Nevertheless, it is obvious that the control and facilitation framework and the associated propositions can be utilized not only to assess and analyze development planning failure, but also to prescribe a means for turning that failure into success.

Summary and Conclusions

In this chapter we have considered the usefulness of the control and facilitation framework generally as a tool for the analysis of public policy, and specifically as it might be applicable to the examination of planning policy failures in Africa. For that purpose we developed the concept of a planning system along lines similar to the social system construct used in the control and facilitation framework. At each level of that planning system we found possible causes of planning failure. The framework and relevant propositions were then applied in an attempt to develop strategies for overcoming some of the problems of the planning system which might cause plan failure.

While we have not proven the utility of the control and facilitation framework as an analytic and strategic tool, some indication was given of its potential for performing both functions. As political science moves increasingly into the area of problem-solving through policy analyses, it will have to rely more and more on conceptual frameworks which are not only consistent and complete, but also "useful" as tools for the application of knowledge to given problems.[69] The control and facilitation framework has considerable potential in this regard.

Melvin J. Dubnick

Footnotes

1. For an introduction to the public policy approach, see Austin Ranney, ed., *Political Science and Public Policy* (Chicago: Markham Publishing Co., 1968); Charles O. Jones, *An Introduction to the Study of Public Policy*, 2nd ed. (North Sciatuate, Mass.: Duxbury Press, 1977); Richard I. Hofferbert, *The Study of Public Policy* (Indianapolis: Bobbs-Merrill, 1974); and Thomas R. Dye, *Understanding Public Policy*, 3rd ed. (Englewood Cliffs, N.J.: Prentice-Hall, 1978).

2. Andrew M. Kamarck, *The Economics of African Development*, rev. ed. (New York: Praeger Publishers, 1971), p. 264.

3. Reginald H. Green, "Four African Development Plans: Ghana, Kenya, Nigeria, and Tanzania," *Journal of Modern African Studies* 3 (August 1965): 249. This is not to say questions have not been raised in regard to planning. See, for example, P.T. Bauer, *Dissent on Development: Studies and Debates in Development Economics* (Cambridge: Harvard University Press, 1972).

4. See the discussion regarding this point in Chapter 1 of Melvin Jay Dubnick, "The Planner's Image: The Role of Expertise in Development Planning and Policymaking" (Ph.D. dissertation, University of Colorado, 1974).

5. Albert Waterston, *Development Planning: Lessons of Experience* (Baltimore: John Hopkins Press, 1965), p. 4..

6. See, for instance, W. Arthur Lewis, *Development Planning: The Essentials of Economic Policy* (New York: Harper and Row, 1966); and Jan Tinbergen, *Development Planning*, trans. N.D. Smith (New York: World University Library, 1967).

7. Jozef Pajestka, "Planning Methods and Procedures and Plan Implementation," in United Nations, Department of Economic and Social Affairs, *Planning and Plan Implementation* (ST/ECA/102), 1967, p. 2.

8. United Nations, Department of Economic and Social Affairs, *1970 Report on the World Social Situation* (ST/SOA/110), 1971.

9. Meeting of Experts on Social Policy and Planning, "Social Policy and Planning in National Development," in United Nations, Department of Economic and Social Affairs, *International Social Development Review, No. 3: Unified Socioeconomic Development and Planning; Some New Horizons* (ST/SOA/Ser.X/3), 1971, p. 4.

10. Centre for Development Planning, Projections and Policies of the United Nations Secretariat, "Employment Strategies and Poverty-Reduction Policies of Developing Countries: Problems and Issues in the Light of Experience in Development Planning," *Journal of Development Planning* (ST/ECA/165) 5 (1972): 3-4.

11. Colin Legum, ed., *The First U.N. Development Decade and Its Lessons for the 1970's* (New York: Praeger Publishers, 1970).

12. C.J. Martin, "A Conference Note: Crisis in Planning," *International Development Review* 11 (March 1969): 40-41.
13. Guy Benveniste, *The Politics of Expertise* (Berkeley: Glendessary Press, 1972), p. 6.
14. V.C. Vignad, "Africa—The Time of Choice," *Journal of Modern African Studies* 7 (April 1969): 35.
15. G.K. Helleiner, "Development Policies for Africa in the 1970's," *Candian Journal of African Studies* 4 (Fall 1970): 285, 301.
16. See George A. Miller, Eugene Galanter, and Karl H. Pribram, *Plans and the Structure of Behavior* (New York: Henry Holt and Co., 1960); and Herbert A. Simon, *Administrative Behavior: Study of Decision-Making Processes in Administrative Organizations*, 3rd ed. (New York: Free Press, 1976).
17. This definition is a modification of one given in Michael Todaro, *Development Planning: Models and Methods* (Nairobi: Oxford University Press, 1971), p. 1.
18. Tinbergen, *Development Planning*, pp. 64-78, discusses the two levels of planning vis-a-vis economic development.
19. Benveniste, *Politics of Expertise*, p. 6. He calls planner experts "pundits," political executives "Princes," and administrators "implementors."
20. Tinbergen, *Development Planning*, p. 186.
21. This important distinction is brought out by Raymond Apthorpe in "Development Studies and Social Planning," *Journal of Development Studies* 6 (July 1970): 4.
22. Simon, *Administrative Behavior,* Chapter 3.
23. See Ruth Glass, "The Evaluation of Planning: Some Sociological Considerations," *International Social Science Journal* 11, 3 (1959): 393-409; David C. Ranney, *Planning and Politics in the Metropolis* (Columbus: Charles E. Merrilll Publishing Co., 1969), especially Chapter 2; Apthorpe, "Development Studies and Social Planning," p. 4; and Gunner Myrdal, *Asian Drama: An Enquiry into the Poverty of Nations* (London: Penguin Books, 1968)
24. Kenneth E. Boulding, *The Image: Knowledge in Life and Society* (Ann Arbor: University of Michigan Press, 1956), pp. 5-10. For a discussion of the reasons why the image concept is adopted, see Dubnick, "The Planner's Image," pp. 55-62. See also Peter L. Berger and Thomas Luckmann, *The Social Construction of Reality: A Treatise in the Sociology of Knowledge* (New York: Anchor Books, Doubleday and Co., 1966), pp. 44; and Leon Festinger, *A Theory of Cognitive Dissonance* (Stanford: Stanford University Press, 1957), p. 3, with regard to the first possible response of the image; and Thomas S. Kuhn, *The Structure of Scientific Revolutions,* 2nd ed. (Chicago: University of Chicago Press, 1970), with regard to the third.

25. Kenneth E. Boulding, "Verifiability of Economic Images," in *The Structure of Economic Science,* ed. Sherman Krupp (Englewood Cliffs, N.J.: Prentice-Hall, 1966), p. 132.

26. Festinger, *Theory of Cognitive Dissonance.*

27. Boulding, *The Image,* p. 19; see also Norbert Wiener, *The Human Use of Human Beings: Cybernetics and Society* (New York: Avon Books, 1954), Chapter 1.

28. A "plan objective" is "a somewhat coherent and complete statement regarding the goals being sought by the statement's authors." Dubnick, "The Planner's Image," p. 94. For a summary of the research strategy used for this analysis, see ibid., pp. 82-98. For a summary of the results, see Chapter 3 of that work.

29. Warren Ilchman, Alice Stone Ilchman, and Philip K. Hastings, *The New Men of Knowledge and the Developing Nations: Planners and the Polity; A Preliminary Survey* (Berkeley: Institute of Governmental Studies, University of California, 1968).

30. On the primacy of economic variables see Dubnick, "The Planner's Image," pp. 147-74. On the closed nature of economic development logic, see ibid., pp. 168-71.

31. Apthorpe, "Development Studies and Social Planning," pp. 4-5.

32. See Dubnick, "The Planner's Image," pp. 188-205, 206-14.

33. For a discussion of the methods and measures used, see ibid., pp. 102-14.

34. See ibid., pp. 175-87 and Appendix C (pp. 289-332); and Arthur S. Banks, *Cross-Polity Time Series Data* (Cambridge: M.I.T. Press, 1971).

35. Irving Louis Horowitz, *Three Worlds of Development: The Theory and Practice of International Stratification,* 2nd ed. (New York: Oxford University Press, 1972), pp. 416-17.

36. Lucian W. Pye, *Politics, Personality, and Nation Building: Burma's Search for Identity* (New Haven: Yale University Press, 1962), p. 289.

37. Guy Benveniste, "Towards a Sociology of National Development Planning," *Journal of Developing Areas* 3 (October 1968): 29. This theme is repeated in Benveniste, *Politics of Expertise.*

38. John Friedmann, "Introduction" to Symposium on "The Study and Practice of Planning," *International Social Science Journal* 11, 3 (1959): 328-36.

39. Benveniste, "Towards a Sociology of National Development Planning," p. 36; and Benveniste, *Politics of Expertise.*

40. Bertram M. Gross, "Activating National Plans," in *Action Under Affairs, International Social Development Review,* No. 3, pp. 32-40. is viewed as a necessary evil by Richard L. Meier, *Development Planning* (New York: McGraw-Hill, 1965), pp. 114-17.

41. Charles E. Lindblom, *The Policy-Making Process* (Englewood Cliffs, N.J.: Prentice-Hall, 1968), Chapter 3; and David Braybrooke and Charles

E. Lindblom, *A Strategy of Decision* (New York: The Free Press, 1963), Part 1.

42. Waterston, *Development Planning*, pp. 146-47, 149.

43. Andrew Watson and Joel B. Dirlam, "Planning Problems," in *Economic Development: Challenge and Promise*, ed. Stephan Spiegelglas and Charles J. Welsh (Englewood Cliffs, N.J.: Prentice-Hall, 1970), p. 52.

44. See Waterston, *Development Planning*; also Pajestka, "Planning Methods and Procedures."

45. United Nations, Department of Economic and Social Affairs, "Use of Models in Programming," *Industrialization and Productivity Bulletin* 4 (April 1961): 7-15; reprinted in Gerald M. Meier, *Leading Issues in Development Economics: Selected Materials and Commentary* (New York: Oxford University Press, 1964), pp. 465-76; see also Todaro, *Development Planning*.

46. Meier, *Development Planning*, pp. 114-17.

47. Marshall Wolfe, "Between the Idea and the Reality: Notes on Plan Implementation," in United Nations, Department of Economic and Social Affairs, *International Social Development Review*, No. 3, pp. 32-40.

48. Gross, "Activating National Plans," pp. 186-232; Waterston, and Procedures"; and Zdeneka Vergener, "On the Relationship between Objective Conditions and Adopted Forms of Planning: The Problem of Adequate Planning," in United Nations, Department of Economic and Social Affairs, *Planning and Plan Implementation* (ST/ECA/102), 1967, pp. 10-18.

49. Yehezkel Dror, *Public Policymaking Reexamined* (Scranton: Chandler Publishing Co., 1968), Chapter 10 and Appendix A, Table 3.

50. Bertram M. Gross, *The Managing of Organizations: The Administrative Struggle* (New York: Free Press, 1964), pp. 775.

51. Benveniste, *Politics of Expertise*, pp. 24, 30-34.

52. David E. Apter, *The Politics of Modernization* (Chicago: University of Chicago Press, 1965), pp. 343, 317, 328.

53. Ibid., p. 318.

54. Benveniste, *Politics of Expertise*, Chapter 3.

55. Apter, *Politics of Modernization*, p. 344.

56. David E. Apter, *Choice and the Politics of Allocation: A Developmental Theory* (New Haven: Yale University Press, 1971), pp. 1-71.

57. Dankwart A. Rustow, *A World of Nations: Problems of Political Modernization* (Washington: Brookings Institution, 1967), p. 31; see also W.W. Rostow, *Politics and the Stages of Growth* (London: Cambridge University Press, 1971), p. 283; Edward C. Banfield, *The Moral Basis of a Backward Society* (New York: Free Press, 1958), Chapter 9.

58. S.N. Eisenstadt, *Modernization: Protest and Change* (Englewood Cliffs, N.J.: Prentice-Hall, 1966); John P. Powelson, *Institutions of*

Economic Growth: A Theory of Conflict Management (Princeton: Princeton University Press, 1972); and Samuel P. Huntington, *Political Order in Changing Societies* (New Haven: Yale University Press, 1968).

59. Watson and Dirlam, "Planning Problems," p. 51.

60. See J.J. Spengler, "Economic Development: Political Preconditions and Political Consequences,"*Journal of Politics* 22 (August 1960): 387-416.

61. Joseph La Palombara, "An Overview of Bureaucracy and Political Development," in *Bureaucracy and Political Development*, ed. La Palombara (Princeton: Princeton University Press, 1967), p. 17.

62. For an excellent overview of the conservative tendencies of professions and the restraints they impose on their practitioners, see Wilbert E. Moore, *The Professions: Roles and Rules* (New York: Russell Sage Foundation, 1970).

63. For specific evidence in this regard, see Ilchman, Ilchman, and Hastings, *New Men of Knowledge;* and Warren Ilchman, "Productivity, Administrative Reform, and Anti-Politics: Dilemmas for Developing States," in *Political and Administrative Development,* ed. Ralph Braibanti (Durham, N.C.: Duke University Press, 1969), pp. 472-526.

64. Benveniste has given much of the credit for this integration to the planner's use of the systems approach. See Benveniste, *Politics of Expertise,* Chaper 4.

65. The cultural, racial, and ethnic divisions which facilitate power dispersion in Africa are exemplified in Leo Kuper and M.G. Smith, eds., *Pluralism in Africa* (Berkeley: University of California Press, 1971).

66. Albert O. Hirschman discusses the role of foreign capital and aid as a means of starting "unbalanced growth" in the final chapter of *The Strategy of Economic Development* (New Haven: Yale University Press, 1958). That the World Bank can be used to adjust development strategies is indicated in Escott Reid, "McNamara's World Bank," *Foreign Affairs* 51 (July 1973): 794-810. Some substantive suggestions in this regard are presented in Robert L. Ayres, "Development Policy and the Possibility of a 'Livable' Future for Latin America," *American Political Science Review* 69 (June 1975): 507-25.

67. For examples of how this can be done, see Warren F. Ilchman and Norman Thomas Uphoff, *The Political Economy of Change* (Berkeley: University of California Press, 1971).

68. A classic exposition of this approach to planning is found in Robert A. Dahl and Charles E. Lindblom, *Politics, Economics, and Welfare: Planning and Politico-Economic Systems Resolved into Basic Social Processes* (New York: Harper Torchbooks, 1953); see also E.F. Schumacher, *Small is Beautiful: Economics as if People Mattered* (New York: Harper and Row, 1973).

69. See Austin Ranney, "The Study of Policy Content: A Framework for Choice," in Ranney, *Political Science and Public Policy,* pp. 13-18.

7

The Significance of Sequential Ordering and Timing of Politically Induced Societal Changes in Anglophone African Party States: A Reconsideration

James R. Scarritt

Six years ago this author wrote a paper in which the control and facilitation framework and propositions phrased in terms of it were utilized to demonstrate that variations among five Anglophone African party states in the sequential ordering and timing of politically induced societal changes in the direction of development significantly affected the successful implementation of these changes, even though the variations were minor by world standards because of the constraints operating on all African political systems.[1] During the intervening years there have been numerous additions to the literature on various aspects of development in those African party states—Ghana, Kenya, Tanzania, Uganda, and Zambia. Further reflection, based in part on that literature, has convinced me that some aspects of the control and facilitation framework were not fully utilized in the original analysis. Thus a reconsideration of the original conclusions, based on a complete application of the framework, is in order. First, the analytical problem under consideration will be clarified and the original analysis summarized. Then ways in which that analysis should be enhanced and modified will be discussed.

The Analytical Problem and a Summary of the Original Analysis

The prevailing scholarly attitude toward the prospects for political development or politically induced economic, stratification, or cultural development in Africa has recently been described as "qualified pessimism."[2] Emphasis is placed on the constraints on development which stem from the history, the economic, sociocultural, and international environments, and the fragile structures of contemporary African polities. The occurrence of African independence at the historical

James R. Scarritt

moment of the 1960s means that African countries are confronted with enfranchised masses adhering to a welfarist political culture before they have a chance to even attempt to strengthen the fragile and unsuitable political structures which they inherited from the later colonial period, or to develop their weak economies. These difficulties are further intensified by pressures for governments to assume new functions, particularly entrepreneurial ones, combined with economic dependence on more developed, primarily capitalist countries, which severely constrains the performance of all economic functions. This dependence includes the export of primary products as the dominant activity of the money economy; the dominance of foreign trade by one or a few industrialized countries; chronic balance of payments deficits; extensive direct foreign investment; unbalanced growth; and pressure to adopt the highly sophisticated technology which is a part of current world culture, but which, if adopted, minimizes the number of people who will be employed to produce a given amount of goods and services. In all of these respects, Africa in the 1960s and 1970s differs profoundly from Europe during its industrial revolution a century or two earlier.

It is not the purpose of this chapter to question the general validity of the current pessimistic mood. It is rather to examine the applicability of propositions concerning the sequential ordering and timing of various aspects of developmental change to five similar African polities in order to discover whether or not pessimism is uniformly pertinent. The difficulties faced by African countries are undoubtedly great, and the structures available for coping with them are undeniably weak, but perhaps strategies or tactics of sequential ordering and timing, or other types of strategies and tactics, can make a significant difference in the prospects for overcoming these difficulties.

It may seem at the outset that much of the literature on the sequential ordering and timing of politically induced, or at least politically controlled, change is inapplicable to comparisons among African polities for the very same reasons that cause many observers to be pessimistic about African development. Problems must be faced now, and all at once, and it is not possible to decide the sequence or timing of attempted solutions to them. Universal franchise, welfarist culture, and sophisticated technology cannot be made to go away until the time has come in terms of a deliberate strategy of sequential ordering and timing to reintroduce them. Dependence can only be overcome by comprehensive revolutionary change, and the control and facilitation factors necessary for such change—ideology and organization—do not appear to exist in most African countries. Discussions of sequential ordering and timing in the literature rely heavily on European, and to a lesser extent Asian and Latin American examples, in which the same constraints of time and environment were not present, although political structures were (and in some cases still are) also weak in these polities.

Two major propositions which come out of this literature are that development will be easier if various problems or crises can be dealt with one by one over a fairly long period of time, and that national unity should be created before the attempt is made to tackle other basic problems.[3] These propositions are major in terms of their high level of generalization, as well as in terms of the number of authors who present them and the relative wealth of evidence they cite in support of them. As presented by most authors, these propositions are imprecise in several respects. One imprecision in the first proposition which is of great concern in the present context is the failure to specify how much time is needed between various steps in the sequence of change in order to significantly facilitate development. A comparison of similar political systems faced with similar and severe constraints on their development strategies and tactics allows us to examine whether small time intervals between steps make a difference, and whether, given these small time intervals, any one sequence facilitates development more than any other sequence.

Imprecision is found in the second proposition with regard to the extent of national unity which must precede attempted solutions to other problems. It is not possible to create a high level of national unity in African polities before tackling changes in political, economic, and stratification structures. Comparing similar African polities should help us to understand whether slight increases of unity at low levels facilitate development, and to discover what is the next best sequence if it is not possible to create unity first.

Differing and vague definitions of development constitute the most significant imprecision in these propositions. The original analysis sought to avoid the highly controversial issues surrounding the definition of development by taking the perspective of the actors being studied. Leaders of all five Anglophone African party states under consideration have articulated at some point essentially the same broad goals which they ostensibly desire to attain: politically they desire greater capacity and institutionalization while maintaining a high level of participation; economically they desire to increase per capita income and reduce international dependence; culturally they desire to weaken subnational identifications and to Africanize their culture-maintaining structures; and in terms of stratification they desire greater equality. It was assumed that shared commitment to these broad goals was sufficient to justify their use as a definition of development, even though it was recognized that leaders differ significantly in their interpretation of and emphasis on various goals.

It was acknowledged that this approach left some problems unresolved. Sidney Verba points out that sequential models should answer the following questions as specifically as possible: 1) Sequences in relation to what?; 2) Sequences of what?; 3) What is the relationship among the items in the sequence?[4] The first of these questions concerns the specification of an underlying dimension along which development can be said to be

James R. Scarritt

taking place in order to eliminate the possibility of conflicting consequences of a particular sequence or stage in a sequence, which might arise if several dimensions were being examined simultaneously. Such an underlying dimension is not specified in this chapter. Since we do not employ a unitary definition of development, the explicit recognition of conflicting consequences of various sequences or stages is all that is possible, and this recognition will play a part in the evaluation of any tentative conclusions reached.

Verba's second question concerns the precise specification of the items or stages which appear in sequence. In this chapter these items are specific policies adopted by governments with regard to the political system itself (party revitalization, the introduction of a one-party system, and major governmental reorganization), and to other subsystems of society (nationalization and control of foreign and domestic commercial and manufacturing enterprises, measures aimed at reducing differences among social strata, and ideological-educational-linguistic innovations). Even when items as relatively specific as these are involved, it must be recognized that they may not be exactly equivalent. Hopefully, this exploratory study will make a contribution toward the development of equivalent items of this type.

Issues raised by Verba's final question include the regularity with which stages in a sequence follow one another and the causal relationship between these stages, and these are issues to which this chapter is addressed. Analysis of a nonrandom sample of five polities can only produce tentative answers to these questions. Thus, in this respect we will again fail to measure up to Verba's standards, but we hope to take a meaningful step toward eventually attaining them.

Many of the propositions presented in Chapter 1 were utilized in the original analysis to explain the effects of the sequential ordering and timing of policies designed to implement the development goals articulated by African party state leaders. Those explanations will now be summarized. Propositions (B2, C1) suggest that African polities are likely to find themselves adopting new roles and accepting general values without having yet developed the full set of structuress which would most effectively link new values and roles together into well integrated new political, economic, or stratification systems. While the borrowing of values can only be controlled to a limited extent, it is much easier to control the introduction of new roles. Rather than fight against the implications of this proposition by attempting to create fully integrated new structural complexes all at once, African polities seeking to attain the development goals specified above should accept new roles and use them as building blocks for creating such integrated structures over a period of several years, or even two or three decades. Sufficient time intervals between the introduction of one set of roles and the next will allow linking structures to develop, and selecting for early introduction those roles most likely to contribute significantly to the creation of such links will reinforce this effect. Political roles are particularly useful in this respect for reasons which will be discussed in the explication of subsequent propositions. Thus it can be argued that the political aspects of development, as articulated by African leaders, should have first priority in countries in which the level of national unity is low, and in which the elite desires to make major changes in the other subsystems of society.[5]

Within the political system, both political party and bureaucratic roles can lead to the creation of new integrated system structures, and there has been extensive debate among political scientists concerning which of these types of roles should be introduced first.[6] The five polities discussed in this chapter all inherited many bureaucratic roles from the colonial period, although these roles have been modified since independence. There has been greater variation among these polities in decisions concerning party roles, and it will be argued that the attempt to introduce and/or strengthen these roles even a short time before major cultural, economic, or especially stratification changes are attempted will greatly facilitate development. Party roles seem uniquely well placed to contribute to the creation of structures linking the polity to other subsystems of society.[7]

African political leaders seeking to bring about developmental change as defined above will want to maximize change-oriented mobilization at the time when it is most likely to be effective, and to minimize countermobilization at all times, but especially at crucial moments. Those who desire to develop more slowly and who are less concerned about equality-producing stratification changes will have less need for mobilization, but they may need it occasionally, and they too will want to minimize countermobilization. Although the conditions facilitating or hindering mobilization specified in propositions (C2) and (C3) cannot be completely controlled by political elites, they can be affected by sequential ordering and timing. Samuel Huntington recommends a combination of "Fabian strategy and blitzkrieg tactics."[8] Making strategic moves one by one, even if several major moves take place within a period of a few years (Fabian strategy), allows change-oriented mobilization to take place for each move while minimizing the number of groups engaging in countermobilization at any one time. On the other hand, implementing each move rapidly and thoroughly (blitzkrieg tactics) minimizes the opportunity for countermobilization against its implementation.

Proposition (C3b) points to the need for consistency in the acceptance of change, especially those changes demanded by mobilized groups. Once a sequence of change is underway, political leaders should be prepared to continue it, and the strategies of sequential ordering suggested by other propositions should maximize such preparation. The political aspects of development as defined above involve an increase in the supply of power, and this will allow the subsequent facilitation of other changes, especially if power is exercised dramatically at the right moment (A3, C4, E3a). Given the established traditions of most African political systems, a major danger is that the elite will become fixated in its quest for greater and more concentrated power and will indefinitely postpone attempts to solve other problems. This is why the early establishment of political party or other roles linking the political system to other subsystems of society is so important. If these linkages eventually become very strong, a more equal distribution of power, and perhaps more general changes toward equality in the stratification system as well, will come to have both high utility (for elites as well as nonelites) and strong organizational support.[9]

As stated above, it is difficult to control the borrowing of values without first changing other structural levels. Ideologies separated from the structures connected to them in their society of origin are easily diffused to other societies (B2a), but in this form they are not likely to be effective in controlling the behavior of significant numbers of people. Once political capacity, institutionalization, and participation are sufficiently developed, they can facilitate an imported ideology and help bring about broader societal changes which are in accord with its tenets (A2c).

Sequential ordering and timing can also influence utility calculations (C5). Individuals often perceive greater utility in relatively small increments of change than in larger ones. Furthermore, if changes which have a high utility for many people are made initially, these individuals are more likely to accept subsequent changes. If the initial changes lead to the creation of linking structures, the existence of these structures can alter subsequent utility calculations in favor of further change. Once again development in the political system itself, especially political party development, seems to be a useful first step in the overall development of African societies, as parties (and in a more limited way, bureaucracies as well) can be used very effectively to alter the utility calculations of large numbers of people.

Setting the maximum pace of change and establishing a climate of change expectation may represent important contributions of sequential ordering and timing to the development of African societies (A4, C7). If the first changes attempted are successful, people are likely to anticipate the success of future changes. There then will be a bandwagon effect, as many people expect a high utility to be gained from participating in the soon-to-be dominant structures. Mobilization will be fostered, and structural linkages will be more likely to develop.

Incompatibilities can be reduced (D1) if changes are introduced sequentially over even a very limited period of time. Compatibility is primarily a matter of perception, and small changes are more likely to be perceived as compatible than large ones, even if the small changes follow one another in rapid sequence. A change that is accepted then becomes a pre-existing element with which subsequent changes will be judged as more or less compatible. The sequence in which changes are attempted can also reduce the problems of incompatibility if the earlier changes are closely compatible with some highly valued aspects of the present or past political system or society. The strengthening of political parties is compatible with the tradition of the nationalist movement in most African countries. New structures which are more compatible with pre-existing ones are likely to develop linkages more rapidly.

Reinterpretation of new elements of structure introduced into society through politically induced change (D2) is crucial for successful development in any subsystem because it provides for the emergence of integrated structures after change has taken place. Reinterpretation, however, takes time and occurs more easily if major changes are broken up into smaller changes introduced sequentially. The short time intervals between changes which are the maximum intervals that it is possible for African polities to attain are sufficient for considerable reinterpretation to take place, especially when the favorable conditions specified in discussing previous propositions are also present. These time intervals will be easier to create because elements introduced by diffusion are likely to be given a trial before they are either accepted or rejected (D4).

Proposition (E1) indicates a strong but variable association between change and increased conflict, which is unlikely to be dissolved entirely by any strategic or tactical manipulations. As the level of conflict is increased by the absence of linking structures, perceived incompatibility and disutility of innovations forced on various categories of society's members, and high levels of mobilization and countermobilization, it is possible to reduce conflict by the sequential ordering and timing moves that affect these variables.

Change is an ongoing process in which every stage influences those subsequent to it. Thus the influence of sequential ordering and timing, as explicated by the propositions which have been presented and discussed up to this point, will be manifested over and over again as changes in the various subsystems of society and polity engender reactions in other subsystems. Over time, even those small differences in the sequential ordering and timing of specific policy decisions which are possible in Africa can make a significant difference in the probable success or failure of developmental change as defined by leaders of African party states.

The original analysis then applied this explanation of the possible effects of sequential ordering and timing to a comparison of the five party states. It was concluded that Tanzania and possibly Zambia had done relatively well in employing sequential ordering and timing to foster developmental change in ways indicated by the propositions, especially in comparison to the poor utilization of these strategies by Ghana and Uganda. It was further concluded that Kenya's differing interpretation of the broad developmental goals listed above made it more difficult to compare that country's sequential ordering and timing strategy to the strategies of the

James R. Scarritt

other four countries.

More specifically, it was found that the Obote regime in Uganda adopted a sequential ordering of major policy changes which placed the attempt to create new party roles after attempts at ideological, stratification, and economic changes, and allowed virtually no time interval between changes in the course of the 1969-70 "Move to the Left." Consequently, the regime maximized perceived incompatibilities, negative utility calculations, eventual countermobilization (in 1971 coup), conflict, and reinterpretation of its proposals for change in directions which it considered undesirable, while at the same time it minimized positive utility calculations, the creation of linking structures, change-oriented mobilization, anticipation and momentum of change, and the effective use of power to change economic conditions and role perceptions.

In spite of its initial strengths compared to the Obote regime in Uganda, the Nkrumah regime in Ghana was largely, although not entirely, unsuccessful in engendering developmental change because linking roles were allowed to weaken and even disintegrate, negative utility calculations on the part of many groups in the society became very high, covert countermobilization was extensive, conflict reached very high levels, and thus power was not used effectively to change conditions and role perceptions. A developmental sequence giving higher priority to party development and the scheduling of longer time intervals between the introduction of new policies could have greatly reduced all of these problems.

Tanzania had the initial advantages of greater national unity and less inequality, and Tanzanian leaders have effectively exploited those initial advantages. They made strengthening the party their first priority, and followed this with greater ideological specification and more reinforcing governmental reforms (i.e., decentralization) than were found in Uganda or Ghana. Furthermore, they have allowed time for each change to gain some degree of acceptance before introducing the next one. They have thus fostered developmental change by more effectively building and maintaining linking structures; limiting the number of people for whom changes have had high negative utility; stimulating change-oriented mobilization and minimizing countermobilization and conflict; maintaining some degree of momentum, anticipation, and compatibility of change; avoiding major undesired reinterpretations of policies; and using power more effectively to change economic conditions and role perceptions.

Zambia did not have the same initial advantages as Tanzania, and its leaders have not engaged in party building or ideological specification to the same extent. They have enacted policies in sequence over a period of time, however, although this sequential ordering and timing were only partially deliberate. Given the greater degree of inequality in Zambia,

Sequential Ordering and Timing

President Kaunda has wisely postponed stratification changes among Africans until after considerable political change, cultural integration, and economic nationalization have taken place. The danger in this sequence is that a societal elite or dominant class will get into a position to prevent restratification from taking place at all, but Kaunda is now vigorously attempting to enforce restratification policies.

A Reconsideration of the Original Analysis

Much of the literature on the sequential ordering and timing of societal changes has been criticized for adopting the perspective of governing elites or dominant classes, ignoring the influence of economic dependency, and having little explanatory power.[10] An important aspect of the elitist perspective is said to be the assumption that leaders really desire to attain the goals they have publicly articulated. Some commentators believe that the vast majority of leaders articulate these goals only to pacify their peoples while leaders vigorously pursue their own interests, or those of the class, ethnic groups, or interest-based collectivities to which they belong.[11]

Full utilization of all aspects of the control and facilitation framework invalidates these criticisms by conceptualizing the interaction among leaders, other role players, and various collectivities in the processes of selecting and interpreting developmental goals. Explanatory power is provided by the propositions associated with the framework. If adequate data are available, the goals actually sought by various individual and collective actors, and the influence of these actors in the attainment of actual goals, can be determined. Both international and internal constraints on goal attainment can be taken into account. As was pointed out in Chapter 1, economic dependence involves substantial foreign control over the economic subsystems of African countries, which leads to varying degrees of foreign control or influence on other subsystems, especially the political. The degree of such control or influence needs to be specified for each subsystem.

Interchanges of media among functional subsystems within African societies, and among structural units in the same subsystem, determine the extent to which a societal elite or a dominant class able to control the processes of goal selection and definition develops. As indicated in Chapter 1, a societal elite agglomerates control of a disproportionate share of all media for itself; such an elite becomes a dominant class if it engages in conscious, concerted action utilizing these media to further its corporate interests. Studying the values and norms of members of a societal elite or dominant class will reveal which goals they really support, and which ones they are articulating merely to pacify other members of society. While it is reasonable to assume that the values and norms of the dominant class will favor their objective interests at the expense of other classes, the extent to which this is the case will vary among collectivities and role players within the class, and among situations. Furthermore, a dominant class or societal elite does not control the total supply of any medium of exchange; thus it does not completely determine the goal selection and interpretation processes, and must interact with other elements of society to attain societal goals effectively. Collectivities and role players outside the dominant class or societal elite will affect goal attainment to the extent that they control sufficient media to withhold the legitimacy, political support, and material resources necessary to attain societal goals.

Goal selection and interpretation are continuous processes, and the pattern of participation in them undergoes frequent changes of varying magnitude and speed. Hierarchies of control and facilitation operating among societies, among functional subsystems of a society, among structural levels within a subsystem, and among media of exchange, as described in Chapter 1, are operative throughout these processes, and the direction and extent of change in goal attainment will be determined by the relative effectiveness of these various hierarchies.[12]

While the original analysis of sequential ordering and timing in Anglophone African party states took some of these factors into account, it did not treat any of them fully, and it ignored some of them entirely. The ways in which the conclusions of that analysis can be enhanced and modified by full utilization of the control and facilitation framework can now be explored. The data necessary to analyze the five party states in these terms are not all available, and even a partial analysis based on available data would require many pages. Thus we can only summarize the major points of view regarding dependence, class formation, equality, and participation which are found in the existing literature, and briefly discuss changes in the original analysis which would incorporate all of these viewpoints and provide a test of some of their assumptions.

There is a strong consensus among observers with varying political convictions that the five party states under consideration have a high level of economic dependence on western capitalist countries, although Tanzania is less dependent than the others. There is less consensus on the exact nature of the political, stratification, and cultural implications of this economic dependence, although the existence of such consequences is beyond dispute.[13] There are also significant differences among observers regarding the extent of class formation in these countries. Few would disagree that political elites and private sector owners, managers, and professional employees closely associated with these elites control sufficient media to form societal elites. Many would say that societal elites are well into the process of forming a dominant class, and some would say that other classes are also in the process of formation.[14] The dominant class being formed has been given various labels, but is usefully depicted as a managerial bourgeoisie.[15] Those who see such a class as relatively solidified tend to see its existence as stemming from international dependency, or at least benefiting from it, and thus tend to assume that this class strives to preserve that dependency.[16] Most observers, whether they speak of societal elites or dominant classes, are deeply skeptical of the commitment of privileged strata in African party states to either equality or participation, although there is disagreement about whether they oppose these goals in order to protect their political power or their overall privileges.[17]

Thus, the assumption of shared commitment to a set of broad development goals should be subjected to closer examination. Certain goals may not have been attained in some party states in large part because powerful or influential actors did not want them attained. Which actors supported or failed to support which goals should be specified, along with the exact interpretations they placed on these goals. The amounts of power and influence exercised by actors in support of and opposed to each goal should then be measured. African party state presidents have been primarily responsible for articulating the developmental goals discussed in this chapter, and it is generally agreed that Obote, Nkrumah, Kaunda, and Nyerere of Tanzania have or had a real commitment to these goals. Jomo Kenyatta of Kenya clearly lacked a commitment to reducing international dependence or increasing equality, and in this respect the contrast drawn in the original analysis between Kenya and the other party states is quite valid. In spite of their great power relative to other political actors, however, presidents cannot easily impose goals on reluctant elites or classes. When the balance of power and influence within elites for and against equality and self-reliance is examined, Ghana, Uganda, and even Zambia may be closer to Kenya than to Tanzania, where the formation of a dominant class is least advanced.[18]

There is considerable evidence that commitment to equality and self-reliance are not widespread among members of strata outside the elite or dominant class, and that only small amounts of legitimacy, political support, and material resources are being withheld in response to elites' failure to pursue these goals. Both peasants and workers have been thoroughly exposed to values and norms of achievement and acquisitiveness, and frequently act in terms of ethnic rather than class interests.[19] Tanzania, the only one of the countries under consideration which has seriously attempted to implement a program of rural socialism, has modified that program to de-emphasize cooperative production in the face of stiff resistance from poor as well as wealthy peasants.[20] Trade unions in all five countries have attempted to increase the wages and benefits of their relatively skilled and well-paid members, and have not demonstrated any marked concern for overall equality, although the considerable variations which exist among these countries with regard to the extent of worker privilege create significant differences in the extent to which union activities are equalitarian.[21] Among both workers and peasants, there appears to be little understanding of or support for short-term sacrifices necessary to increase self-reliance.

While elites and dominant classes certainly favor increasing the capacity and institutionalization of the political system, they favor only those forms of participation which increase the legitimacy or political support of the existing regimes. Participation through patron-client networks is usually the form most acceptable to elites in African party states. Other actors tend to hold instrumental orientations toward political participation: if there are specific benefits to be gained, they participate; if not, they refrain from participating.[22] It is easier for the relatively privileged segments of the population or dominant class to perceive the benefits of participation than it is for the less privileged segments or exploited classes. Thus expanding participation by the latter requires greater mobilization efforts. Organized or mobilized participation by the underprivileged is crucial for increasing equality.[23] While the desire to limit participation appears to be universal among African elites, there are great variations in the degree and types of participation viewed as undesirable or actually prohibited. Among the party states under consideration, Tanzania gives the greatest encouragement to participation, even though firm limits are placed on the nature of that participation, and Zambia ranks next in this regard.[24]

This more detailed examination of goal selection and interpretation processes demonstrates the need for some refinements in the original application of our propositions to the sequential ordering and timing of societal changes. The suggestions that roles be borrowed sufficiently gradually to allow linking structures to develop (B2, C1), and that political roles, especially party roles, should be created at an early date because they facilitate such linkages should be refined to specify the types of linkages to be developed. Will these early linkages increase or decrease mass participation? Will they foster or retard greater equality and self-reliance?[25] The proposition that party roles will foster these developmental goals remains valid, but some types of party roles will do so more than others. Participatory party roles should be introduced and institutionalized prior to, or at least along with, centralizing and bureaucratic party roles.[26] Early introduction of participatory governmental roles is necessary to reinforce participatory party roles. If this sequence is followed, change-oriented mobilization, expansion of the societal supply of power, and dramatic exercises of power (C2, C4, E3a) will be more likely to foster greater participation, equality, and self-reliance because those in control of the preponderance of media will wish them to do so (E4).

A complete control and facilitation analysis of the effects of sequential ordering and timing on utility calculations, the pace of change and the climate of change expectation, perceived incompatibility, and reinterpretation (C5, A4, C7, D1, D2) must examine effects for various categories of actors. A change which has high utility and compatibility for a societal elite or a dominant class will be very likely to have low utility and compatibility for other members of society. The original analysis suggested that intitial changes having a high utility for many people would foster acceptance of subsequent changes; it is now suggested that the control of media exercised by those for whom initial changes have utility must also be taken into account. The same type of analysis must also be made of those who perceive incompatibility, expect change, and reinterpret new structural elements.

Over time, the multiple effects of numerous situations in which many people controlling few media conflict with a few people controlling substantially more media can greatly influence the course of developmental change. The direction of change resulting from these conflicts will depend on who wins most frequently (E1, E4). If the sequence of change favors those who initially control small amounts of media, the various hierarchies of control and facilitation will probably operate to redistribute media over time in favor of those who seek equality, self-reliance, and institutionalized participation (E3, E4). Given time to adjust to this redistribution, elites or dominant classes may change their values and norms to be congruent with those contained in the ideologies which they have articulated, even where these ideologies were initially articulated only to pacify other members of society (E3).[27] More data would be needed to specify the exact conditions under which media redistribution and elite acceptance of it will actually occur.

This reconsideration has not altered the principal conclusions reached in the original analysis: that even those small differences in the sequential ordering and timing of specific policy decisions which are possible in African party states can make a significant difference in the probable success or failure of developmental change; and that increased political participation, accompanied or followed by increased political capacity and institutionalization, will facilitate later changes in the economic, stratification, and cultural subsystems of sociey. Reconsideration has instead provided a more complete analysis of crucial differences in the ordering and timing of various changes and some suggestions for possible modifications in the original comparison of the five party states in light of this analysis.

James R. Scarritt

Footnotes

1. James R. Scarritt, "The Significance of Sequencing and Timing of Cultural, Economic, Stratification, and Political Change in Similar Polities: Anglophone African Party States," paper presented at the 9th World Congress of the International Political Science Association, Montreal, August 1973; published in Spanish with minor revisions as "Importancia de las estrategias de ordenación y ritmo para lograr el cambia: los Estados africanos de habla inglesa," *Revista Mexicana de Sociología* 38 (July-September 1976): 559-78. A part of this thesis was presented in James R. Scarritt, *Political Development and Culture Change Theory: A Propositional Synthesis with Application to Africa*, Sage Professional Papers in Comparative Politics 3, 01-029 (Beverly Hills and London: Sage Publications, 1972), pp. 49-51.

2. Michael F. Lofchie, "Observations on Social and Institutional Change," in *The State of the Nations: Constraints on Development in Independent Africa*, ed. Lofchie (Berkeley, Los Angeles, and London: University of California Press, 1971), p. 261. Pessimism is also expressed, from a variety of theoretical and political viewpoints, in most of the other contributions to that volume; and in David E. Apter, *Choice and the Politics of Allocation: A Developmental Theory* (New Haven and London: Yale University Press, 1971); Thomas M. Callaghy, "Implementation of Socialist Strategies of Development in Africa: State Power, Conflict, and Uncertainty," paper presented at the 72nd Annual Meeting of the American Political Science Association, Chicago, September 1976; Richard L. Harris, "The Political Economy of Africa: Underdevelopment or Revolution," in *The Political Economy of Africa*, ed. Harris (New York, London, Sidney and Toronto: Schenkman Publishing Co., Halsted Press Division, John Wiley & Sons, 1975), pp. 1-47; James O'Connell, "The Inevitability of Instability," *Journal of Modern African Studies* 5 (September 1967): 181-91; Immanuel Wallerstein, "Dependence in an Interdependent World: The Limited Possibilities of Transformation Within the Capitalist World Economy," *African Studies Review* 17 (April 1974): 1-26; and Aristide R. Zolberg, "The Structure of Political Conflict in the New States of Tropical Africa," *American Political Science Review* 62 (March 1968): 70-87.

3. These propositions are stated most clearly in Gabriel A. Almond and G. Bingham Powell, Jr., *Comparative Politics: A Developmental Approach*, 1st ed. (Boston and Toronto: Little, Brown & Co., 1966), p. 331; Eric A. Nordlinger, "Political Development: Time Sequences and Rates of Change," *World Politics* 20 (April 1968): 500, 503-4; Lucian W. Pye, *Aspects of Political Development* (Boston and Toronto: Little, Brown & Co., 1966), pp. 66-67; and Dankwart A. Rustow, *A World of Nations: Problems of Political Modernization* (Washington: Brookings

Institution, 1967), pp. 126-28.

4. Sidney Verba, "Sequences and Development," in Leonard Binder et al., *Crises and Sequences in Political Development* (Princeton: Princeton University Press, 1971), p. 285.

5. This argument for the primacy of political development is also made in William G. Fleming, "American Political Science and African Politics," *Journal of Modern African Studies* 7 (October 1969): 502; Samuel P. Huntington, *Political Order in Changing Societies* (New Haven and London: Yale University Press, 1968), pp. 8-32; and Rustow, *A World of Nations*, p. 128.

6. This debate is carried on in Joseph LaPalombara, ed. *Bureaucracy and Political Development* (Princeton: Princeton University Press, 1963); and Michael F. Lofchie, "Representative Government, Bureaucracy, and Political Development: the African Case," *Journal of Developing Areas* 2 (October 1967): 37-55. Huntington, *Political Order in Changing Societies*, pp. 398-402, argues strongly for the primacy of party development.

7. Indirect evidence of this is provided by a number of aggregate data studies linking various aspects of party strength, but not government strength, to political stability. See Walter L. Barrows, "Ethnic Diversity and Political Instability in Black Africa," *Comparative Political Studies* 9 (July 1976): 162-64; Raymond Duvall and Mary Welfling, "Social Mobilization, Political Institutionalization, and Conflict in Black Africa: A Simple Dynamic Model," *Journal of Conflict Resolution* 17 (December 1973): 691-92; Robert W. Jackman, "The Predictability of Coups d'etat: A Model with African Data," *American Political Science Review* 72 (December 1978): 1262-75; Roberta E. McKown, "Domestic Correlates of Military Intervention in African Politics," *Journal of Political and Military Sociology* 3 (Fall 1975): 203-4; McKown and Robert E. Kauffman, "Party System as a Comparative Analytic Concept in African Politics," *Comparative Politics* 6 (October 1973): 64-68; Donald G. Morrison and Hugh Michael Stevenson, "Integration and Instability: Patterns of African Political Development," *American Political Science Review* 66 (September 1972): 906-7, 916-26; Dani B. Thomas, "Political Development Theory and Africa: Toward a Conceptual Clarification and Comparative Analysis," *Journal of Developing Areas* 8 (April 1974): 387-88; and Mary B. Welfling, *Political Institutionalization: Comparative Analyses of African Party Systems*, Sage Professional Papers in Comparative Politics 4, 01-041 (Beverly Hills and London: Sage Publications, 1973), pp. 43-44.

8. Huntington, *Political Order in Changing Societies*, pp. 344-56.

9. Ibid., p. 145; and Taketsugu Tsurutani, "Stability and Instability: A Note in Comparative Political Analysis," *Journal of Politics* 30 (November 1968): 932.

10. Egil Fossum, "Political Development and Strategies for Change," *Journal of Peace Research* 7, 1 (1970): 17-22; Mark Kesselman, "Order or Movement? The Literature of Political Development as Ideology," *World*

Politics 26 (October 1973): 139-54; and Richard Sandbrook, "The 'Crisis' in Political Development Theory," *Journal of Development Studies* 12 (January 1976): 165-85.

11. A strong statement of this position is found in Claude Ake, "The Congruence of Political Economies and Ideologies in Africa," in *The Political Economy of Contemporary Africa*, ed. Peter C.W. Gutkind and Immanuel Wallerstein (Beverly Hills and London: Sage Publicaitons, 1976), pp. 206-11.

12. The ways in which propositions presented in Chapter 1 can be used to analyze dependence, inequality, and revolutionary change are discussed in James R. Scarritt, "Culture Change Theory and the Study of African Political Change: Some Problems of Relevance and Research Design," *The African Review* 2, 4 (1972): 563-67.

13. For points of consensus and dissensus with regard to dependence and its consequences in the African context, see Samir Amin, "Underdevelopment and Dependence in Black Africa—Origins and Contemporary Forms," *Journal of Modern African Studies* 10 (December 1972): 503-24; John D. Esseks, "Economic Dependence and Political Development in New States of Africa," *Journal of Politics* 33 (November 1971): 1052-75; Harris, "The Political Economy of Africa," pp. 2-18; Patrick J. McGowan, "Economic Dependence and Economic Performance in Black Africa," *Journal of Modern African Studies* 14 (March 1976): 25-40; Joel Samoff, "Class, Class Conflict, and the State: Notes on the Political Economy of Africa," paper presented at the 20th Annual Meeting of the African Studies Association, Houston, November 1977, pp. 1-4; Barbara Stallings, *Economic Dependency in Africa and Latin America*, Sage Professional Papers in Comparative Politics 3, 01-031 (Beverly Hills and London: Sage Publications, 1972); Richard Vengroff, "Neo-colonialism and Policy Outputs in Africa," *Comparative Political Studies* 8 (July 1975): 234-50; Vengroff, "Dependency and Underdevelopment in Black Africa: an Empirical Test," *Journal of Modern African Studies* 15 (December 1977): 613-30; Immanuel Wallerstein, "The Three Stages of African Involvement in the World Economy," in Gutkind and Wallerstein, *Political Economy of Contemporary Africa*, pp. 30-57; and Wallerstein, "Dependence in an Interdependent World."

14. These various viewpoints are expressed in the sources cited in footnotes eighteen and thirty-one of Chapter 1; and in Harris, "The Political Economy of Africa;" and Onésimo Silviera, *Africa South of the Sahara: Party Systems and Ideologies of Socialism* (Uppsala: Political Science Association in Uppsala, 1976), pp. 83-87.

15. Richard L. Sklar, "Postimperialism: A Class Analysis of Multinational Corporate Expansion," *Comparative Politics* 9 (October 1976): 81.

16. Ibid., pp. 83-84, provides a good critique of this assumption.

17. The former position is taken by Claude Ake, "Explaining Political Instability in New States," *Journal of Modern African Studies* 11 (September 1973): 357-59; Samuel P. Huntington and Joan M. Nelson, *No Easy Choice: Political Participation in Developing Countries* (Cambridge and London: Harvard University Press, 1976), p. 40; Nelson Kasfir, *The Shrinking Political Arena: Participation and Ethnicity in African Politics, with a Case Study of Uganda* (Berkeley, Los Angeles, and London: University of California Press, 1976), pp. 227-86, esp. p. 270; and Norman H. Keehn, "Building Authority: A Return to Fundamentals," *World Politics* 26 (April 1974): 335. Fred M. Hayward, "Political Participation and Its Role in Development: Some Observations Drawn from the African Context," *Journal of Developing Areas* 7 (July 1973): 604-6, and most class analysts, take the latter position.

18. There is a heated debate over the nature and extent of class formation in Tanzania. See Lionel Cliffe and John S. Saul, eds., *Socialism in Tanzania: An Interdisciplinary Reader*, 2 Vols. (Dar es Salaam: East African Publishing House, 1973); Colin Leys, "The 'Overdeveloped' Post Colonial State: A Reevaluation," *Review of African Political Economy* 5 (January-April 1976): 39-48; Samuel Stephen Mushi, "Revolution by Evolution: The Tanzanian Road to Socialism" (Ph.D. dissertation, Yale University, 1974), pp. 202-38; Cranford Pratt, *The Critical Phase in Tanzania 1945-1968: Nyerere and the Emergence of a Socialist Strategy* (Cambridge, London, New York, and Melbourne: Cambridge University Press, 1976), pp. 215-26; Joel Samoff, *Tanzania: Local Politics and the Structure of Power* (Madison: University of Wisconsin Press, 1974); Samoff, "The Bureaucracy and the Bourgeoisie: Decentralization and Class Structure in Tanzania," *Comparative Studies in Society and History* 21 (January 1979): 30-62; Joel and Rachel Samoff, "The Local Politics of Underdevelopment," *Politics and Society* 6, 4 (1976): 397-432; John S. Saul, "African Socialism in One Country: Tanzania," in *Essays on the Political Economy of Africa*, ed. Giovanni Arrighi and Saul (New York and London: Monthly Review Press, 1973), pp. 237-335; Saul, "The State in Post-Colonial Societies: Tanzania," in *The Socialist Register 1974*, ed. Ralph Miliband and John Saville (London: Merlin Press, 1974), pp. 349-72; Saul, "Tanzania's Transition to Socialism?," *Canadian Journal of African Studies* 11, 2 (1977): 313-39; Issa G. Shivji, *Class Struggles in Tanzania* (New York and London: Monthly Review Press, 1976); and Michaela von Freyhold, "The Post-Colonial State and Its Tanzanian Version," *Review of African Political Economy* 8 (January-April 1977): 75-89.

19. Behavior in terms of ethnic interests is explained in Robert H. Bates, "Ethnic Competition and Modernization in Contemporary Africa," *Comparative Political Studies* 6 (January 1974): 457-84; and Robert Melson and Howard Wolpe, "Modernization and the Politics of Communalism: A Theoretical Perspective," *American Political Science Review* 64 (December 1970): 1112-30. Evidence on peasant and worker

reactions to government policy in Zambia is summarized in James R. Scarritt, "The Decline of Political Legitimacy in Zambia: An Explanation Based on Incomplete Data," *African Studies Review* 22 (September 1979). An excellent case study of peasant reactions to government policy in Ghana is Björn Beckman, *Organizing the Farmers: Cocoa Politics and National Development in Ghana* (Uppsala: Scandinavian Institute of African Studies, 1976).

20. Michael F. Locfchie, "Agrarian Crisis and Economic Liberalisation in Tanzania," *Journal of Modern African Studies* 16 (September 1978): 451-75, esp. 472; Dean E. McHenry, Jr., "Peasant Participation in Communal Farming: The Tanzanian Experience," *African Studies Review* 20 (December 1977): 43-63; and Mushi, "Revolution by Evolution," pp. 409-12.

21. On the contrast between the privileged status of union members in Zambia and Kenya and their lack of privilege in Ghana, see Robert H. Bates, *Unions, Parties, and Political Development: A Study of Mineworkers in Zambia* (New Haven and London: Yale University Press, 1971); Michael Burawoy, *The Colour of Class on the Copper Mines: From African Advancement to Zambianization*, Zambian Papers No. 7 (Manchester: Manchester University Press for the Institute for African Studies, University of Zambia, 1972); Richard Jeffries, *Class, Power and Ideology in Ghana: the Railwaymen of Sekondi* (Cambridge, London, New York, and Melbourne: Cambridge University Press, 1978); and Richard Sandbrook, *Proletarians and African Capitalism: The Kenyan Case, 1960-1972* (Cambridge: Cambridge University Press, 1975).

22. Robert H. Bates, *Rural Responses to Industrialization: A Study of Village Zambia* (New Haven and London: Yale University Press, 1976); Huntington and Nelson, *No Easy Choice*, pp. 116-22, 151-66; Kasfir, *The Shrinking Political Arena*, pp. 275-78; and Marc Howard Ross, *Grass Roots in an African City: Political Behavior in Nairobi* (Cambridge and London: MIT Press, 1975), pp. 117-37.

23. Huntington and Nelson, *No Easy Choice*, pp 17-27, 35-36, 75-78, 89-95, 117-22, 151-70. Their concept of mobilized participation, pp. 7-10, is somewhat different from ours.

24. On Tanzania, see Kasfir, *The Shrinking Political Arena*, pp. 251-63. Electoral participation in that country is described in detail in Lionel Cliffe, ed., *One Party Democracy: The 1965 Tanzania General Elections* (Nairobi: East African Publishing House, 1967); Election Study Committee, University of Dar es Salaam, *Socialism and Participation: Tanzania's 1970 National Elections* (Dar es Salaam: Tanzania Publishing House, 1974); and Denis Martin, "The 1975 Tanzanian Elections: the Disturbing Six Percent," in *Elections Without Choice*, ed. Guy Hermet, Richard Rose, and Alain Rouquié (New York: Halstead Press, John Wiley & Sons, 1978), pp. 108-28. Trends in participation in Zambia are discussed in Margaret Rouse Bates, "UNIP in Postindependence Zambia: The

Development of an Organizational Role" (Ph.D. dissertation, Harvard University, 1971); Robert Bates, *Rural Responses to Industrialization*, pp. 65-100, 202-60; Michael Bratton, "Peasant and Party-State in Zambia: A Study of Political Organization and Resource Distribution in Kasama District" (Ph.D. dissertation, Brandeis Universtiy, 1978); Robert Molteno and William Tordoff, "Conclusion: Independent Zambia: achievements and prospects," in *Politics in Zambia*, ed. Tordoff (Berkeley and Los Angeles: University of California Press, 1974), pp. 363-85; Patrick E. Ollawa, "Political Participation in a Developing Society: Theoretical Considerations and the Case of Zambia," *Journal of Commonwealth and Comparative Politics* 16 (July 1978): 169-89; Scarritt, "The Decline of Political Legitimacy"; and Ian Scott, "Middle Class Politics in Zambia," *African Affairs* 77 (July 1978): 321-34.

25. Fossum, "Political Development and Strategies for Change," pp. 23-26, suggests that in a development model emphasizing participation, equality, and self-reliance, mobilization must precede bureaucracy, distribution must precede accumulation, and autonomy must precede cooperation.

26. Gabriel Ben-Dor, "Institutionalization and Political Development: A Conceptual and Theoretical Analysis," *Comparative Studies in Society and History* 17 (July 1975): 321-23; Hayward, "Political Participation and Its Role in Development," pp. 605, 608; Nordlinger, "Political Development," p. 515; and Dennis A. Rondinelli, "Administration of Integrated Rural Development Policy: The Politics of Agrarian Reform in Developing Countries," *World Politics* 31 (April 1979): 402-5, 412-14. For a discussion of TANU's attempt to develop participatory roles, see Bismarck U. Mwansasu, "Commentary on *Mwongozo wa TANU*, 1971," *The African Review* 1,4 (1972): 9-27.

27. Ake, "The Congruence of Political Economies and Ideologies," p. 211.

8

Revolutionary Change in Mozambique: Implications for the Emerging Postindependence Society

Walter C. Opello, Jr.

Although the now-successful guerrilla wars in Portuguese-speaking Africa generated a plethora of literature on their various aspects, very few books or articles appeared which explained them with conceptual tools from the social sciences.[1] This chapter will fill that lacuna by employing the control and facilitation framework to explain revolutionary change in one of these newly independent states: Mozambique. Before turning to the data, it might be useful to explore briefly how this approach will enhance our understanding of this important example of African political change.

The first academic work dealing specifically with the Mozambique revolution, written by Ronald Chilcote, argues that two reasons explain the apparent contradiction between Portugal's low level of economic development and the capacity of the Portuguese to have maintained hegemony, until recently, in Mozambique as well as two other African colonies, Angola and Guinea (Bissau). One factor was

> fervent Portuguese nationalism based on historical traditions, symbols, and experience. Pervading that nationalism [was] a mystique of imperial destiny that for centuries...caught the imagination of Portuguese policymakers. Accordingly, Portugal's mariners not only discovered the world but fulfilled a special mission to transmit Catholicism and other Portuguese values to the tropical world. Nationhood was conceived as a pan-Lusitanian community stretching around the world and embracing many races into a cultural unity.

Chilcote goes on to say, however, that the second and

> more important and fundamental reason for Portugal's continuity in Mozambique and elsewhere...[was] attributable to economics and the influence of England in the underdevelopment of Portugal.[2]

Employing a three-fold typology of imperialism—"exchange," "extractor," and "transformer"—Chilcote endeavors to show how the modern nationalist movement evolved from historical wars between various indigenous tribal societies in combination with these manifestations of Portuguese imperialism. For Chilcote, the modern nationalist revolution is simply an extension of tribal resistance to conquest and economic exploitation by English capitalists via their Portuguese proxies.[3]

It is doubtful that categorizing the recent guerrilla war together with historical tribal resistance to Portuguese military conquest and imperialism adequately explains the genesis of the modern nationalist movement. Although Chilcote presents an impressive array of empirical data to show the importance of economic factors, nowhere does he attempt to explain why they have been "more important and fundamental" than the belief by the Portuguese that they were transmitting Portuguese-Catholic values to the tropical world. Chilcote, it seems, assumed *a priori* that economic interests were more important than values and then proceeded to compile evidence in support of his assumption.[4] Dismissing out of hand other variables such as values obscures more than it enlightens, simplifies the complex, and leaves a host of unanswered questions.

In the following interpretation of revolutionary change in Mozambique, no prior assumption is made concerning the relative importance of any single factor. The effort is made to avoid over-simplified, single-factor determinism by giving equivalent consideration to economic, social stratification, political, and cultural factors, and examining the complex interrelationships among them. The control and facilitation approach is particularly useful for this endeavor because it draws attention to the full complexity of societies without reverting to the notion that everything influences everything else. This will allow us to explore the way Portuguese values and economic interests have codetermined the rise of African nationalism and successful political revolution in Mozambique.

The chapter proceeds in three stages: the first breaks down the preindependence social system of Mozambique into its constituent functional subsystems and analyzes the interchanges and the hierarchy of control and facilitation among them. The second stage shows how systemic dissynchronization, African collectivity formation, cognitive dissonance among Mozambique's African elite, and the influence of variant values and norms combined in giving rise to the nationalist movement and the organization of an alternative social system. It also deals with the effects of racial, ethnic, and class cleavages among Africans on the mobilization of political power. Finally, the third stage brings the threads together to indicate the directions and extent of change to be expected in the emerging social system of independent Mozambique.

The Preindependence Social System

Mozambique has been historically a meeting ground for three broad cultural currents: Portuguese, Bantu, and Swahili. During the first decades of European contact in the fifteenth and early sixteenth centuries, the Portuguese met the Swahili trading culture of the East African littoral, especially north of what is today Mozambique Island. Contact in this period with the Bantu cultures of the interior was minimal, being limited to occasional meetings in the vicinity of coastal forts and *feitorias* (trading depots). Later, after losing suzerainty over the Indian Ocean mercantile complex and subsequently penetrating the interior, the Portuguese came into direct contact with indigenous Bantu-speaking peoples. Throughout the initial stages of their contact, especially along the Zambezi River where the *regime dos prazos* (land baron system) developed, the relationship between these two cultural currents resulted most often in the acculturation of the Portuguese by indigenous peoples.[5] By the end of the nineteenth century, however, the boundaries and interrelationships of a national society dominated by Portuguese-organized adaptive, goal attainment, integrative, and pattern socialization and control structures had emerged in Mozambique.

In the preindependence period, the pattern socialization and control subsystem was dominated by the belief held by many Portuguese in their unique ability to create multiracial societies. They claimed that certain historical experiences and social practices gave the Portuguese a unique ability to coexist with peoples of color which set them apart from other European colonial powers. Multiracial society represented for the Portuguese the fulfillment of a sacred, historical mission for which they believed they alone were qualified. Only Portugal, they claimed, was in the process of creating societies in the tropical areas of the globe where white, black, and brown could live together in peace, harmony, human brotherhood, and contentment. They claimed that no serious conflicts or racial tensions existed in these societies because their inhabitants lived according to the humanistic values and norms of Portuguese-Catholic culture. Racial tolerance, hard work, religious faith, devotion to home and family, assimilation of indigenous cultures, miscegenation, and respect for the authority of the Church and state were the behavioral norms which the Portuguese claimed were widespread throughout their African colonies and were creating multiracial societies in the image of Brazil. The Portuguese even envisioned the formation of a pan-Lusitanian community comprised of such societies sprinkled around the globe, spiritually linked together by feelings of solidarity and identity derived from the Portuguese "insular provincial personality and [its] celebrated sense of *saudade*."[6]

Contradiction between this multiracial ideal and the realities of Portugal's African colonies is not patent evidence that the Portuguese did not really hold these sentiments. It

> is necessary to realize that this faith in the rightness of the Portuguese way of colonial life is a deep and pervasive force in the Lusitanian consciousness. No matter how absurd these claims may sound to foreign ears, the Portuguese, perhaps the majority, believe what they say. On this point conservative and liberal Portuguese have usually agreed, and it is therefore not surprising to know that the most violent critics of the regime, and of its policies in Africa...share the view that Portugal's history in Africa is a unique experience...[7]

This is not to say that there was a universal consensus on the values and norms of the multiracial ideal among the Portuguese. These values and norms did, however, receive a substantial amount of commitment, and there was an effort to inculcate, reproduce, and maintain them. The Portuguese attempted to socialize and perpetuate adherence to the multiracial ideal primarily through the Church and schools.[8]

From the earliest contact with Africans, the Portuguese granted to the Catholic Church the right and duty to "Christianize and educate, to nationalize and civilize"[9] the indigenous peoples they encountered. After the anticlerical years of the Republic, this responsibility was formalized with the Estado Novo (New State) in 1940, when the Portuguese signed an accord with the Vatican granting the Church the right to establish schools in the African colonies with Portuguese as an obligatory course. Exclusive responsibility for the education of rural Africans was given to the Church, and was to be carried out primarily by Portuguese priests. Foreign missionaries were admitted to the colonies only upon approval of the Portuguese government and the Vatican, and on the condition that their activities be integrated into the Portuguese missionary program.[10]

This accord formally recognized a dualistic system of education that had evolved in Mozambique. For children of Europeans and *assimilados* (Africans acculturated to Portuguese-Catholic values and norms), education was provided by a system called *ensino oficial* (government education), which was the responsibility of the colonial government and duplicated education in the metropole. For rural, unacculturated Africans, education was provided by a system called *ensino de adaptação* (education for adaptation), which was the responsibility of the Catholic missions. In 1961, however, this dualistic system was abolished, and a unified system was established which endeavored to extend the *ensino oficial* to all children in order to eliminate discrepancies between urban and rural systems. Under this reorganization, children began school at the age of six, attending a *posto escolar* (preprimary school) where they were introduced to Portuguese. This was followed by four years of primary school and two cycles of postprimary education. The first cycle was designed to prepare students for the second, which could be taken in a *liceu* (lyceum) for three years or in an *escola industrial* (industrial school) for three or four years.[11]

Instructional emphasis, especially at the primary level, was on acculturating rural African students to the values and norms of Portuguese-Catholic culture. In the preprimary year, the curriculum stressed learning the rudiments of the Portuguese language in classes on personal hygiene, discipline, courtesy, the home and family, and the use of basic agricultural implements. In the primary years, devotion to the school, home, and family; respect for authority and the Church; and the ideal of Portugal as a multiracial and multicontinental nation were emphasized. In the fourth and final primary year, emphasis was put on the peoples, geography, and political organization of this Portuguese multiracial and multicontinental nation.[12]

In spite of these efforts to inculcate and maintain the values and norms of Portugese-Catholic culture, only about 300,000 Africans were assimilated in Mozambique in a very long colonial history, and the unification of the educational system in 1961 did not change that figure significantly. In most rural areas, where enrollments were predominantly African, inadequate facilities and poorly trained teachers often precluded offering the full primary curriculum. Frequently, these schools functioned no differently than their *ensino de adaptação* predecessors; and the full course, including secondary education, was available only in urban areas.[13]

In the preindependence period, the Portuguese were almost totally unsuccessful in actualizing and implementing the Portuguese-Catholic multiracial ideal in "lower" functional subsystems. This failure was due to the inadequacies of the pattern socialization and control structures as well as the presence in Mozambique of contrary behavioral norms in the integrative, goal attainment, and adaptive subsystems. The historical record shows that the alternative belief in the inherent inferiority of peoples of color and the related norms and structures of discrimination, segregation, and racial intolerance were common throughout the Portuguese colonial empire. Portugal's colonial history is replete with

Revolutionary Change in Mozambique

edicts promulgated by Lisbon, such as the celebrated but ineffective decree of 1761, which sought to bring colonial behavior into conformity with the multiracial ideal.[14] This situation was greatly exacerbated when, at the end of the nineteenth century, racialist values and norms achieved world-wide prominence and many adherents among Lisbon's policy makers.[15] Importantly, this happened during the period of imperial revival when most of the modern adaptive, integrative, and goal attainment structures were taking formal shape as the Portuguese established effective occupation and administrative centralization in Mozambique.

In the integrative subsystem, resistance to the implementation of the multiracial ideal came from the configuration of the social stratification system, which divided Mozambicans along the ethnolinguistic, racial, class, and regional lines of cleavage that were present in the society. There are two major ethnolinguistic types in Mozambique. One of them consists of the predominantly patrilineal peoples living south of the Zambezi River. The most numerous group in this area, and the second largest in Mozambique, is the Thonga (1,460,000),[16] who live to the south of the Save River. The Shona (1,115,000), the third largest ethnolinguistic group, are located to the north of the Thonga in the area between the Save and the Zambezi.

The second main ethnolinguistic type consists of the predominately matrilineal peoples living north of the Zambezi. Among them is found the largest ethnolinguistic group in Mozambique, the Makua-Lomwe (2,293,000) three quarters of whom are Makua. The heavily Islamized Makua also make up the majority of the Swahili-speaking inhabitants of the coastal region north of Quelimane. The next largest ethnolinguistic group in the north, the Makonde (136,000), inhabit an isolated plateau in the north-east of Mozambique in the province of Cabo Delgado bordering on Tanzania. Their geographical location, distance from foreign settlements, and traditional distrust of outsiders have acted to preserve Makonde culture in spite of long contact with Arabs and Europeans. The Yao (119,900), on the contrary, became completely Islamized through prolonged contact with Arabs during the East African slave trade in which they acted as middlemen.

The valley of the Zambezi forms the boundary between these two major ethnolinguistic types. The valley has for many centuries been an access route into Mozambique for invasions and migrations of various African peoples, and there has consequently been a considerable mixing of peoples there which has produced a high degree of cultural heterogeneity.

The uneven impact of Portuguese colonialism has given southern ethnolinguistic groups living near Maputo (formerly Lourenço Marques) and in the areas adjacent to Zimbabwe (Rhodesia) and South Africa a head start on northern groups in receiving socioeconomic and educational advantages. It is in this region that nonAfricans were most in evidence in the preindependence period. Thus, a kind of stratification has developed among the country's Africans. Groups from the northern and central regions such as the Makonde and Yao are sometimes considered by southerners as "backward," "primitive," and "traditional," while groups in the south like the Thonga are sometimes considered by northerners to be "aggressive," "domineering," and "corrupt." Ethnolinguistic differences have been simplified into a perception of regional differentiation. In some cases, notably among the Islamic Yao and Makua-Lomwe, religious differences exacerbate a sense of separation.

Superimposed on these ethnic cleavages was a "vertical" system of stratification based upon socio-economic, educational, cultural, and racial factors.[17] At the highest level was a small minority, perhaps 2.5 percent of the whole population, which consisted of Portuguese, Asians, mulattos, and some assimilated Africans, who lived in the major urban centers and were engaged in the money economy in activities such as the civil service, commerce, manufacturing, transportation, and large- scale agriculture.[18] In the preindependence period it was possible to distinguish several categories within this minority. At the top were Portuguese owners of large plantations and various large business enterprises, top-level civil servants and military officers, and successful professionals. This group, which was well-educated and almost exclusively white, considered itself an economic, political, and social elite. Family connections were important; members felt they knew one another, and favors in employment were often given to friends and relatives. Below them were middle-level civil servants, salaried white collar employees, and small farmers, who could be thought of as a "middle class." Although they were by and large white, many members were mulattos, and a few were assimilated Africans. Finally, the lowest level of this minority consisted almost entirely of African assimilants who worked as skilled or semi-skilled wage-earners.[19]

This social structure was the result of the convergence of distinctions made among individuals on the bases of race and culture. The racialist values and norms that pervaded the colonial empire, especially at local levels far from Lisbon, combined with the metropole's official policy of the assimilation of indigenous peoples who were thought to be culturally inferior. The tendency to blur the distinction between racial equality and cultural inequality was formalized in the *regime do indigenato* (native system).[20]

The Portuguese *missão civilizadora* required Africans to divest themselves of what the colonizers considered to be their "inferior" culture, and all Africans not officially recognized as assimilants were classified as *indigenas* (natives). This latter status group was legally without citizenship and civil rights. In 1961, when the *regime do indigenato* was abolished, only about 7,000 Africans had been allowed to change their status, even though perhaps as many as 250,000 qualified. For Africans granted assimilated status there was theoretically freedom to advance in any endeavor, but Portuguese racism, the *assimilados'* still comparatively low levels of education, and the relative paucity of economic and political opportunities militated against widespread social or economic mobility. Mulattos, by contrast, were automatically considered to be assimilated because of their mixed parentage, and their color gave them an ascriptive advantage in the competition for the relatively scarce educational and socio-economic opportunities available.[21]

There were two main reasons for the presence of relatively few *assimilados* in Mozambique. First, some Africans who qualified preferred not to exercise their option because it was to their economic advantage to remain as *indigenas*. Retaining such status allowed them to use reserved tribal lands, to receive free medical care, and to pay lower taxes. Second, and by far the most important, a large number of qualified Africans were simply denied *assimilado* status. The most frequently rejected applications came from skilled blue collar and managerial white collar employees in urban areas who, had they been permitted to exercise their option, would have been in competition with Europeans in the same occupations, and would have been entitled to equal wages because of their newly acquired "civilized" status.[22]

In the goal attainment subsystem, resistance to the implementation of the multiracial ideal came from the extremely unequal distribution of power and influence between Africans and Europeans, and the prevailing norms governing legitimate political activity. In Mozambique, as in Portugal, interest-based politically oriented collectivities were permitted only within the framework of the corporate state. Briefly, the corporate principle holds that national societies are tightly integrated communities knitted together by structures based on the primary units of social life. Corporations grounded in these units were organized vertically within a particular activity, encompassing both ordinary rank and file members and elites. They were organized to cross-cut class cleavages in order to prevent divisive class conflicts, and all collectivity organizing along class lines was strictly forbidden.[23]

Before independence, the organization of the inhabitants of Mozambique into interest-based collectivities had taken place almost exclusively in the uppermost stratum of the social stratification system. *Grémios* (guilds) functioned as consulting groups which presented the views of certain businesses and promoted their economic and social interests. In addition to fostering workers' interests, *sindicatos*, which were organized vertically within a trade, functioned to provide social services and medical insurance to members.[24] In Mozambique, as in the metropole, many industrial, commercial, professional, and agricultural interest-oriented collectivities outside of the official corporate structure assumed a certain economic preponderance in the direction of their representative activities, and despite their purely private character, their functions [were] considered in the public interest, the government using them as "connecting links" between its own services and organs and individual activities.[25]

The only political organization allowed to function outside of these corporate collectivities in the preindependence period was the official government party, the Acção Nacional Popular (ANP), known during the Salazar years as the União Nacional. Although highly structured in a descending hierarchy from its Lisbon headquarters to local units in Mozambique, the ANP did not aggregate and articulate a broad range of interests, nor did it function to mobilize the population—European and African—for mass political action. Its main functions were to advertise government policy and to approve candidates standing for elections.[26]

Although the entire African population of Mozambique theoretically acquired the full political rights of Portuguese citizens in 1961 when the *regime do indigenato* was repealed, almost all of them were still excluded from participation in elections because of the educational and economic requirements set forth in the voting law promulgated in 1963, and the imprecise definition of certain of its key phrases. Two elections were held in Mozambique for Portugal's National Assembly under the terms of this law; only .9 percent of the entire population voted in 1965, and only 1.2 percent in 1969.[27]

The exclusion of the bulk of the African population from government decision making can also be seen in the make-up of the Legislative Council, which was the elected body assisting the Governor-General in the governance of Mozambique in the preindependence period. The Council was comprised of thirty *vogais* (members), of whom two were ex-officio, nine were elected by direct suffrage, and eighteen were elected by the following collectivities: three by individual taxpayers returning at least 15,000 *escudos* (about $750) in direct taxes; three by corporate groups representing employers and economic interests (*grémios*); three by corporate groups reprenting workers' interests (*sindicatos*); three by groups representing religious and cultural interests (one of whom had to be a Catholic missionary); three from native authorities; and three from administrative bodies.[28]

Thus, politics in Mozambique in the preindependence period was an almost exclusively European activity. Collectivity organizing among Africans was limited to apolitical cultural, mutual-aid, and sports associations which were not part of the corporate structure and played no direct role in aggregating and articulating African interests. As participation in the officially sanctioned interest-oriented collectivities and the suffrage were restricted by educational and income requirements, as well as by imprecise definitions of the law, Africans were without even the modicum of power and influence afforded by the legitimate political process and, therefore, had virtually no impact on government policy.

Finally, in the adaptive subsystem, resistance to the implementation of the multiracial ideal was provided by the extreme dualism of Mozambique's economy. The sector of greatest Portuguese concern, the money economy, had been influenced by dependent relationships with the metropole and a geographic position between the Indian Ocean and the highly productive industrial and agricultural areas of the southern African hinterland. These factors, coupled with extensive control and regulation from Lisbon, encouraged the development of commercial agriculture and the expansion of port facilities and rail lines to South Africa, Swaziland, Zimbabwe (Rhodesia), and Malawi.[29] The subsistence sector, which produced the bulk of the food consumed by the African population, was of little concern to the Portuguese.

Greater productivity in commercial agriculture was promoted by wage and price controls which exploited Africans, the improvement of transportation and marketing facilities, the direct supervision of the main export crops, and some research. It was not until the late 1950s that the government began to direct some attention to the subsistence sector as well. This included several settlement projects for Europeans and Africans, the distribution of higher quality seeds, and technical assistance for crop improvement.[30]

The three full six year development plans and one supplemental plan (Plano de Fomento I, 1953-58; Plano de Fomento II, 1959-64; Plano Intercalar de Fomento, 1965-67; Plano de Fomento III, 1968-73) drawn up and carried out by the old regime allocated the bulk of their monies and credits to the development of basic infrastructure, the improvement of commercial agriculture, and the settlement of Portuguese on agricultural lands. These plans allocated about two-thirds of their funds to the development and improvement of railway lines and harbor facilities. The goals were to expand the transit trade with South Africa, a major source of revenue, and to open up new areas for settlement along the line of rail. A substantial majority of the remaining one-third was allocated for irrigation projects and soil preparation in the areas of European settlement. Social services and subsistence agriculture, which were of primary importance to the African population, received scarcely 10 percent of the total investment.[31]

Although the bulk of the African population was primarily integrated into the subsistence sector, many young men ventured into the money economy as laborers for various periods of time, or sold their own cash crops to raise money for taxes or to purchase manufactured goods. In the south of Mozambique it was common for as much as 50 percent of the men to be working in the urban areas or on the South African Rand at any one time.[32] Africans were overwhelmingly employed as miners, stevedores, laborers, and domestic servants. On the average, Africans earned very poor wages which left, after deductions for taxes and room and board, little money for anything more than the bare essentials. Europeans received much higher wages and, legal prohibitions notwithstanding, there were often great differences in the wages paid to Europeans and Africans performing similar tasks.[33]

Portugal began officially regulating the labor supply in Mozambique in the late 1890s. These laws, which forbade the use of the *shibalo* (forced labor) for private businesses, gave the government the right to enlist for work on public projects such as road and bridge construction any African male who did not fulfill the requirements of self-sufficiency and economic contribution to society. There were, however, many abuses of this law because of past practices, lack of administrators, and collusion between some officials and private businesses. Reforms ending these abuses and making the plight of the *shibalo* less difficult did not come until the 1960s.

The supply of labor going to the Rand was controlled by the Transvaal Convention of 1909 and a series of subsequent conventions which allowed labor recruitment in Mozambique for South African gold and coal mines in return for the guaranteed passage of 47.5 percent of all transit traffic from the Johannesburg-Pretoria-Krugersdorp industrial region through Maputo over the Portuguese railroad. Mozambique also received lucrative railway traffic rates, charges on each worker recruited, and the influx of wages.[34]

Now that the functional subsystems of preindependence Mozambique have been briefly described in terms of our conceptual framework, it is time to examine the interchanges among them. In the political support interchange, demands and supports emanated almost exclusively from interest-based collectivities organized primarily among Europeans. The prevailing procedural norms of the corporate state restricted legitimate input to demands from *grémios, sindicatos,* and "independent" industrial, commercial, and agricultural associations. These collectivities had almost unfettered access to important governmental decision making structures such as the Legislative Council, and articulated demands for government decisions and policies to meet their economic and social interests. These inputs were successfully exchanged for policies and programs which met most if not all of their demands. Africans had no significant membership in these collectivities, and had been prohibited by procedural norms from organizing alternative collectivities (except apolitical mutual-aid and cultural associations) around their interests *per se*. In addition, Africans were denied access to even the modicum of political power and influence authorized by the franchise because of suffrage requirements they could rarely meet. Furthermore, the ANP did not function to aggregate or articulate the demands and interests of Africans (or Europeans for that matter) who were not members of the legitimately organized collectivities. Africans were, then, almost totally powerless, and played no role in the legitimate political process.

In the resource mobilization interchange, government regulation and stimulation of the economy was exchanged for African labor and some of the financial resources needed to attain the major goal of the Portuguese government: the development of the money economy primarily for the benefit of the metropole and local European-dominated interest-based collectivities. To this end, the government kept African wages low; regulated the supply of African labor to the mines on the Rand and to Mozambique's urban areas, plantations, and transit trade facilities; and forced Africans to work on public projects and raise cash crops. The government stimulated the cash sector with three development plans covering a twenty year period which allocated the bulk of their monies and credit for the expansion of the transit trade. The burden of developing the money economy fell disproportionately on Africans, whose share of the benefits of this development was extremely low, while the cost to them was very high indeed.

In the legitimation interchange, in contrast, the relationship between the goal attainment and pattern socialization subsystems was highly incompatible, as political support for a single set of values was not being exchanged for legitimation of the pattern of political authority by such values. In fact, the multiracial ideal was not only nonsupportive of the institutionalized procedural norms and distribution of political power in the corporate state, but also taught that such an arrangement was unjust and illegitimate. Power was exercised by European collectivities, not for the attainment of a multiracial society, but rather for development of the cash sector and perpetuation of the unequal distribution of those rewards which the society had to offer. Moreover, the Portuguese were never able to generate widespread support for this unequal distribution of power among Africans, especially the assimilated and mulatto elites, by means of appeals to the multiracial idea.

The relationship between the integrative and pattern socialization subsystems in the loyalty, solidarity, and commitment interchange was also highly incompatible. The unequal stratification system and interest-based collectivity structure which effectively divided the society along racial lines contradicted the multiracial ideal. This incompatibility was exacerbated by the general lack of support for the multiracial society from European-dominated collectivities, and the incapacity of the adaptive subsystem to provide the resources required to meet the needs of Europeans and Africans equally.

The compatibility among the adaptive, goal attainment, and integrative subsystems, and the incompatibility between the pattern socialization and control subsystem and the other three, as shown in Figure 8.1, meant that the hierarchy of control and facilitation among functional subsystems was dissynchronous. The economy was providing facilities to the political system which, in turn, was regulating the economy for the development of

Walter C. Opello

FIGURE 8.1
Incompatible Hierarchy of Control and Facilitation in Preindependence Mozambique

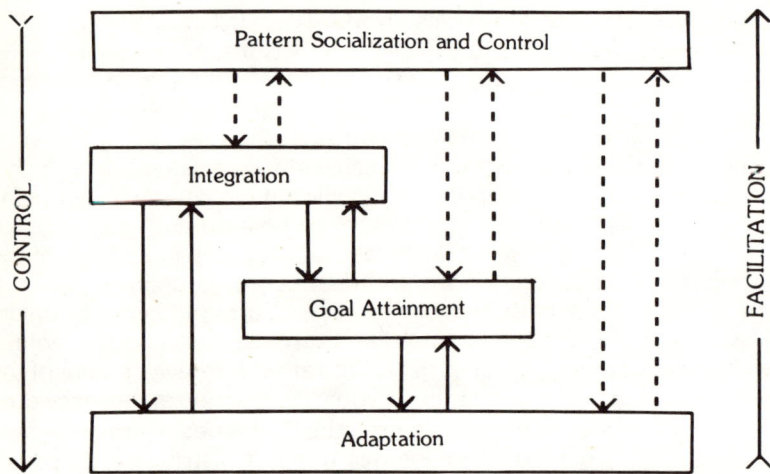

the money sector. This was in response, *inter alia*, to demands and supports coming from European interest-based collectivities in the integrative subsystem. However, the dominant system-legitimating values and norms produced in the pattern socialization subsystem were not controlling the other subsystems, nor were these subsystems providing facilitation for the actualization of these legitimating values.

Now that preindependence colonial society has been discussed, propositions dealing with the state of the pre-existing social system and the likelihood of significant change occurring within it can be examined. We saw that in Mozambique innovative values and norms were almost totally absent in the pattern socialization and control subsystem, which was dominated by such values as respect for authority, unquestioning obedience, discipline, and hard work. These values and norms of Portuguese-Catholic culture and the belief in the multiracial ideal militated against changes in response to new demands emanating from Africans

(A1). However, we also observed that the social system was in a state of dissynchronization and not well integrated, which meant that change was more likely to take place (A2). The subsystem most susceptible to change was the one least compatible with the others: pattern socialization and control (A2a). This lack of synchronization tended to retard the implementation of the multiracial ideal in lower subsystems (A2b). On the other hand, as we shall see, it paved the way for fundamental changes in the decades after World War II when a well-differentiated set of variant values and norms provided a highly dissatisfied and frustrated African and mulatto elite with a positive model of a more integrated social system (A2c). The driving energy or facilitation for this change came from the expansion and concentration of power among Africans through collectivity organization (A3).

The Expansion of African Power and the Alternative Nationalist Social System

The first interest-based collectivity mobilization significant for the expansion of African power began in the 1920s and 1930s, based upon the incipient class, tribal, regional, and racial cleavages mentioned earlier. During these years, a small elite of "urban intellectuals and wage-earners, of individuals essentially detribalized, mostly assimilated Africans and mulattos"[35] began to organize regional, welfare, sports, ethnic, and social clubs and associations. In 1920, the Liga Africana was established in Lisbon by João Albasini, an African journalist from Mozambique, with the avowed aim of defending the rights of Africans within the context of the social system obtaining at that time.[36] However, as the Liga was small and remote from the colonies, it soon disappeared.

More important for the expansion of power among Africans and the development of the independence movement was the Grémio Africano. The Grémio, like the Liga, sought to defend the interests of all Mozambique Africans. In the early 1930s however, the main body of the Grémio became the Associação Africana, while a splinter group, initially called the Instituto Negrofilo, became the Centro Associativo dos Negros de Mocambique. The former became primarily an organization of mulattos, whereas the latter became an association of predominately black membership.[37]

In the early decades of the twentieth century, various mutual-aid associations were established representing labor, regional, and ethnic groups. The Associação dos Carpinteiros, the Associação dos Motoristas, and the Associação dos Alfaiates brought together Africans of the same occupation to provide solutions to problems concerning working conditions, to aid in the provision of social necessities, and to organize holiday and other kinds of celebrations. The Associação do

Inhambaneses and the Associação dos Muchopes only admitted to membership Africans from a particular region or ethnic group in Mozambique.[38]

These early interest-based collectivities, especially those organized by mulattos and assimilated Africans, developed an African press, the best known example of which was the weekly newspaper, *O Brado Africano* (*The African Cry*). The organ of the Associação Africana, this newspaper sustained for many years a journalistic campaign against the specific injustices and inequalities mulattos and assimilated Africans experienced in Mozambique. An editorial from the 27 February 1932 edition was typical:

> We've had a mouthful of it. We've had to put up with you, to suffer the terrible consequences of your follies, of your demands....We can no longer put up with the pernicious effects of your political and administrative decisions. From now on we refuse to make even greater and even more useless sacrifices... Enough!...We insist that you carry out your fundamental duties not with laws and decrees but with acts...We want to be treated in the same way that you are...And we demand something...we demand bread and light...We repeat that we do not want hunger or thirst or poverty or a law of discrimination based on colour...[39]

Such editorials are suggestive of the high level of dissatisfaction and extreme evaluative and cognitive dissonance which existed among mulattos and *assimilados* concerning the preindependence social system. It is important to note that during these early decades protesters did not yet speak of nor seek fundamental change in Mozambique's prevailing social system. Their critique was aimed at specific behavioral norms and government policies such as racial discrimination, poor wages, forced labor, and the like. Mulattos and assimilated Africans felt the impact of these norms and policies most intensely because frequent contact with Europeans sharpened their perception that such behavior diverged from the professed humanitarianism and multiracialism of Portuguese-Catholic culture. In general, then, before World War II, collectivities tended to be organized around specifics, their claims to represent all Africans notwithstanding. Since these collectivities lacked significant power, owing to insufficient organizing efforts among nonelite Africans, internal cleavages, corruption, and manipulation by the Portuguese authorities,[40] they failed to overcome the incompatibilities among Mozambique's functional subsystems. These protests were still not revolutionary, because assimilated Africans and mulattos valued the Portuguese-

Catholic way of life and its professed multiracialism, and lacked a fully articulated set of variant antiPortuguese values and norms to which they could adhere.[41]

After World War II, a second-generation elite of assimilated Africans and mulattos began to express dissatisfaction with and experience cognitive dissonance concerning the incompatibilities in the Mozambican social system, which, by this time, had become very severe. This time, however, their protest had a significantly radical "political consciousness and a new national dimension."[42] It began among artists and writers, such as the painter Malangatana Gowenha Valente; the poets José Craveirinha, Rui Nogar, and Noemia de Sousa; and the writers Rui de Noronha and Luis Bernardo Honwana. Malangatana was inspired by traditional African sculpture and mythology; Honwana used the African parable to convey the deeper political meaning of the story; and in the poetry of Craveirinha, Nogar, de Sousa, and others, the themes of Africa as the mother country, the rise of blacks throughout the world, and the hardships suffered by Africans under the *shibalo* and in the mines of the Rand became significant themes.[43] Protest and dissatisfaction were not confined to African and mulatto elites. In 1947 discontent with working conditions produced a series of strikes on the docks of Maputo which culminated in the deportation of several hundred workers to the island of São Tome. In 1956 another series of strikes took place, resulting in the death of forty-nine of the strikers. Again in 1963, strikes broke out in Maputo and spread to Beira and Nacala. In the countryside dissatisfaction was manifested in numerous peasant protests, especially in the north. The most important of these took place near Mueda in the northeastern district of Cabo Delgado in 1960, resulting in the deaths of about five hundred African protestors.[44]

Important traditional African themes articulated by this new dissatisfied elite were supplemented with a set of variant, essentially Marxist, values and norms which promised to end the incompatibilities in the Mozambican social system and, therefore, relieve the psychic tension of the cognitive and evaluative dissonance elite members were experiencing. These variant values were sufficiently antiPortuguese to motivate this new elite to foment fundamental change by increasing African power through organizing others. The source of this set of variant values and norms has been labelled the "revolutionary international milieu,"[45] a more or less coherent body of revolutionary ideas and historical examples. The "transmission belts" of these variant values and norms were the personal experiences, travels, and meetings of elite members, and their direct contacts with revolutionaries from other societies. Men of similar ideological persuasion met, shared ideas, organized for mutual aid, and developed channels for disseminating ideology, programs, and resources. A number of countries in Africa (e.g., Algeria, Tanzania, Zambia, and Zaire) acted as havens for exiles, provided sites for meeetings, and assisted in organizing efforts. The same values and norms were espoused by many third world members of the United Nations, and by private political groups in the United States, Canada, and Europe, such as the American Committee on Africa, the Vancouver-based Liberation Support Movement, and the London-based Committee for Freedom in Mozambique, Angola and Guine. In Portugal, these values and norms were manifested among students, professionals, intellectuals, and many military men, who supported various clandestine political and paramilitary organizations such as the Partido Comunista Português (PCP) and its activist wing the Acção Revolucionária Armada (ARA), the Partido Socialista Portugues (PS), the Brigadas Revolucionárias, the Peking-oriented Acção Revolucionária Comunista (ARCO), and the Comité Anti-Colonista.[46]

In Mozambique, the central idea which emerged from this milieu of alternative values and norms and made the interest-based collectivities in the post-war years significantly different from those of the 1920s and 1930s was:

> the idea of anti-colonialism, of national self-determination. This is an idea of transnational origin and influence which manifests itself in the world political milieu; it became a motivating idea for a small number of Mozambicans after their exposure to it in that milieu. When their nationalist aspirations were frustrated by Portuguese intransigence, these individuals became attracted to radicalized or ideological versions of the anti-colonial idea, which they likewise encountered in their exile milieu. As before they had become an elite of self-conscious Mozambican nationalists, so now they began to think of themselves as Mozambican revolutionaries. They discovered and began to circulate in international revolutionary circles, acquainting themselves with certain major works of revolutionary theory [Marx, Lenin, Mao Tse-Tung, Che Guevara, Ho Chi Minh, etc.] and with recent historical examples of successful revolutions [China, Vietnam, and Cuba]. They discovered and were exhilarated by a diverse body of ideas which included contributions from revolutionaries from many parts of the world, and they perceived that many of the tenets of this theory were applicable to Mozambique.[47]

As a consequence of the penetration of values and norms from the revolutionary international milieu, the interest-based collectivities organized by Mozambique's postwar African and mulatto elite assumed a new form: organized collectivities could "best be distinguished as primarily socio-cultural before World War II and either openly political or political but camouflaged by a socio-culture cover after the war."[48]

One of the most important of these postwar collectivities was the Núcleo dos Estudantes Africanos Secundárias de Mocambique (NESAM), which was linked to the Centro Associativo. Under the guise of social and cultural activities, NESAM spread values and norms from the revolutionary international milieu among Mozambique's African and mulatto elite. NESAM's program stressed a mixture of traditional African values and Marxist values and norms from the world revolutionary milieu. Although NESAM came under close surveillance by the Portuguese secret police, it survived until the early 1960s, and even managed to publish a magazine called *Alvor (Dawn)*. In 1964 NESAM was banned by the authorities, and many of its members were arrested or forced into exile.[49]

In Portugal during this period, a small group of *assimilado* and mulatto intellectuals attending metropolitan universities gathered at the Casa dos Estudantes do Imperio (CEI). They advocated independence for their respective territories, and established a link with the Clube dos Maritimos, an organization of sailors from the overseas territories. In 1961 CEI members formed the Centro de Estudos Africanos which, until its dissolution in 1965, sought to transmit variant values and norms from the revolutionary international milieu among students and intellectuals in the metrópole. Another organization which emerged about this time was an association of Africans and mulattos exiled in Paris, the Movimento Anti-Colonista, which was the forerunner of later cooperative efforts among the various nationalist movements from Portugal's African colonies.[50]

The major thrust for independence and self-determination, however, emerged among some one-half million Mozambicans working in neighboring countries. There they "were exposed to the then politically more permissive environments of South Africa and Southern Rhodesia." In Southern Rhodesia, where young Mozambican men sought work, education, and asylum from the Portuguese authorities, expatriates began to organize their own social and mutual aid associations. In October 1960 a group working in and near Bulawayo organized the União Democatica Nacional de Mocambique (UDENAMO), led by Hlomulo Chitofo (Adelino) Gwambe, who claimed to have founded a nationalist group inside Mozambique previously. In February 1961 he moved UDENAMO to Dar es Salaam because cooperation between Rhodesian and Portuguese authorities made it impossible for the group to function in Rhodesia. In Dar es Salaam Gwambe contacted other exile groups.[51]

One of these organizations was the Mozambique African National Union (MANU). Established in Februrary 1961 with the East African Goan League's help, MANU had grown out of an ethnically based mutual aid association, the Tanganyika Mozambique Makonde Union, founded in

Walter C. Opello

1954 by Makonde tribesmen from Mozambique living in Tanganyika. Many MANU leaders, such as its President, Mathew Mmole, and its Secretary-General, Lawrence M. Millinga, spoke English and had been involved in the Kenya and Tanganyika nationalist movements. In the early days they were supported by the Kenya African National Union (KANU) and the Tanganyika African National Union (TANU).[52]

Another organization was the União Nacional Africana de Moçambique Independente (UNAMI), led by José Balthazar de Costa Chagong'a. Chagong'a, formerly a medical orderly in Zumbo, Mozambique, had been briefly jailed in 1960 for allegedly criticizing the Portuguese government's treatment of students and workers. That year he fled to Blantyre. As the Portuguese secret police were then free to arrest Mozambicans in Nyasaland, Chagong'a left Blantyre in 1961 and headed for Dar es Salaam. Before leaving Mozambique, he organized the Associação Nacional Africana de Moçambique in Moatize. the precursor of UNAMI.[53]

Under pressure from Ghanaian President Kwame Nkrumah, and with the aid of Julius Nyerere and TANU, Gwambe of UDENAMO, Mmole of MANU, Chagong'a of UNAMI, and Eduardo Mondlane met in late June 1962 at the Conference of Freedom Fighters held in Winneba, Ghana, with the purpose of forming a unified nationalist movement. Upon returning to Tanganyika they held five days of meetings, at the conclusion of which they announced the creation of a single nationalist organization, the Frente de Libertação de Moçambique (FRELIMO).[54] The formation of FRELIMO culminated the process of the elite's rejecting the values and norms of the Portuguese-Catholic way of life and substituting a set of variant values and norms which promised fundamental change in Mozambique. The organizers of FRELIMO were highly motivated by the desire to bring independence and self-determination to Mozambique, and replace its adaptive, goal attainment, integrative, and pattern socialization and control structures with new ones compatible with the alternative values and norms they now held. FRELIMO represented a quantum jump in the amount of political power among Africans, and provided the energy for fomenting revolutionary change.

At the First FRELIMO Party Congress, held in Dar es Salaam during September 1962, delegates elected Eduardo Mondlane president, and passed a series of resolutions which presented the goals of the movement and its program for effecting revolutionary change in Mozambique. The resolutions, to be executed by the Central Committee, called for developing and consolidating the organizational structure of FRELIMO; promoting unity among Mozambicans; achieving maximum utilization of the energies and capacities of every FRELIMO member; encouraging the organization of trade unions, students, youth, and women's organizations; cooperating with other nationalist groups in Angola and Guine; and procuring diplomatic, moral, and material aid for the movement.[55]

Although FRELIMO immediately encountered problems organizing "a cohesive, purposeful force out of an ethnically, educationally, and ideologically dissimilar group of ambitious men,"[56] of which more later, it survived and developed before independence a well-established alternative social system in areas of Mozambique wrested from Portuguese control. Two phases of this development may be identified. The first phase lasted from September 1962 to September 1964. It marked the founding of FRELIMO and the start of combat operations in northern Mozambique,[57] and was characterized by politico-military organization and consolidation. An underground network inside Mozambique was established utilizing **UNAMI, MANU, and UDENAMO** contacts, as well as NESAM's organizational apparatus. Members were recruited and cells organized. Outside Mozambique, an army was started. In 1963 about two hundred men departed to Algeria for training. The education of Mozambican exiles and refugees in Tanzania was begun with the founding of the Instituto Moçambicano in Dar es Salaam in 1963 under the direction of Mondlane's American wife, Janet. The Institute provided secondary education and procured scholarships abroad for qualified Mozambicans.[58] Finally, during this phase, a program of diplomacy and propaganda was launched with the twin objectives of rallying world opinion to FRELIMO's side and countering Portuguese propaganda and diplomacy. FRELIMO members attending international conferences presented the nationalist point of view; articles were written; information bulletins in English and Portuguese called *Mozambique Revolution* and *A Voz da Revolução*, were published; and propaganda offices were opened in Cairo, Algiers, and Lusaka.[59]

The second phase began in September 1964, after FRELIMO had achieved considerable success in liberating areas of northern Mozambique. The void left by the withdrawing Portuguese had to be filled. In Mondlane's words, a

> population of some 800,000 had to be served. First and foremost, their material needs had to be satisfied, an adequate food supply assured, and other important articles such as clothes, soap or matches provided; medical and educational services had to be established and administrative and judicial systems organized.[60]

FRELIMO was thus compelled to organize pattern socialization, integrative, goal attainment, and adaptative structures in certain areas of northern Mozambique and adjacent regions of southern Tanzania.

In the preindependence period, the dominance of Portuguese-Catholic values and norms and the Portuguese belief in their superiority led to a denigration of almost all aspects of traditional culture. Although nearly all purely traditional values and norms had been lost among certain ethnolinguistic groups, much still existed in what Mondlane called an "underground culture." Out of the remnants of this traditional underground culture, which had survived in idealized form through the efforts of African and mulatto painters, writers, and poets, FRELIMO began creating an alternative national culture. In this new culture there was an attempt to synthesize the elements of a number of traditional cultural strains from the various ethnolinguistic groups and regions of Mozambique, to be mixed with elements drawn from the revolutionary international milieu:

> In the camps, the young people are not only practicing the songs and dances of their own tribe, but learning those of others, while in the fields of production new ideas and techniques are being introduced both from different areas of Mozambique and from outside...in the camps militants may learn the songs of the Russian revolution, read magazines from Cuba, see pictures of life in Vietnam. At the Mozambique Institute...documentary films are shown from all over the world...student militants are sent to a wide variety of countries, from the United States to the People's Republic of China, and to some extent spread their knowledge among their companions when they return.[61]

Schools were established to insure that the new alternative national culture was transmitted to the membership, and to train cadres for political, military, and economic activities. In 1965 FRELIMO started its first primary school in one of the areas wrested from Portuguese control in northern Mozambique. By 1970 it claimed more than twelve thousand students in 120 bush schools. The curriculum consisted of four grades in which pupils learned to read, write, and speak Portuguese. History and geography courses emphasized the place of Mozambique as an independent national society in the African and third world contexts. In this regard, FRELIMO created new textbooks which presented the history of Mozambique from their point of view.[62] Arithmetic, elementary science, civics, and practical arts were taught; civics classes were oriented toward political training, teaching who was the enemy, and presenting the political structure of FRELIMO. FRELIMO political documents were often used as "textbooks."

Before independence, secondary education was not provided by FRELIMO inside Mozambique. Secondary schools had come under the aegis of the Mozambique Institute in Dar es Salaam until 1968, when it was closed by a student strike. The Institute provided residency and training in the Portuguese language, while other academic subjects were offered at a secondary school in Korisini. In addition, FRELIMO established a program of intermediate education designed to socialize middle-level cadres and train them in the areas of production, political and military affairs, and health. An adult education program was only partially successful because of high illiteracy among refugees.[63]

FRELIMO had placed a major emphasis on the equality of all persons regardless of race, religion, ethnicity, region, occupation, or sex. The party attempted to create in the integrative subsystem a new system of social stratification free from the inequalities that existed in Mozambique. One thrust in this direction was the effort to reduce differences based on wealth and educational attainment. A second was the simple distinction made within the organization between "comrades" and "responsible comrades." Responsible comrades occupied key roles in FRELIMO's political, military, and economic structures. Although responsible comrades were comparatively better off than ordinary ones, they generally enjoyed modest and frugal life styles.[64] A third thrust in the direction of a more equalitarian social stratification system was FRELIMO's attempt to change the social position of women. In traditional African societies women were subservient to men. The need for the total mobilization of both men and women; the influence of Mondlane's American wife, Janet; and values and norms from the revolutionary international milieu led to an improvement in the status of women within FRELIMO's alternative social system.

Before independence FRELIMO established alternative adaptive structures based on a subsistence economy, which sustained not only the civilian members of the nationalist movement, but the guerrillas as well. The fighting, coupled with the low level of technological skills among the population living in the FRELIMO areas inside and outside Mozambique, dictated an emphasis on self-sufficiency. Some FRELIMO members were taught to spin and weave cotton, make cloth, and render soap. Surpluses were exchanged for goods which could not be produced locally. In northern Mozambique, where the Portuguese withdrew when fighting started, the inhabitants had to be furnished with matches, clothes, lamp paraffin, salt, and other products formerly supplied by Portuguese merchants. To meet these needs, FRELIMO established "people's shops" where Africans exchanged agricultural produce for consumer goods.[65]

Reflecting the influence of both tradition and values from the revolutionary international milieu, as well as the need for an efficient utilization of the available arable land and implements, FRELIMO organized a collective agricultural system. Production was accomplished in three ways. In military camps guerrillas cultivated crops for their own provisions. "National camps" in each of the three northern provinces of Mozambique produced food crops that FRELIMO earmarked for redistribution. One part would go to the army, another to civilians, and the third would be put up for sale. "Peoples' camps," usually abandoned cashew or coconut plantations, were turned into cooperatives, where peasants organized and decided what was to be produced and how it was to be used. These camps retained some of the produce; the rest was sold or exchanged for consumer items.[66]

Before independence, FRELIMO exercised sovereign rights in areas without Portuguese physical presence. A number of alternative goal attainment structures were created to govern the liberated zones. These structures, like the adaptive and integrative, were strongly influenced by values and norms from the revolutionary international milieu. The Congress, elected by the party's membership, was established as the supreme policy making body of FRELIMO. A Central Committee of forty-two members (twenty-two until expanded at the Second Congress in 1968), organized into several administrative departments, had overall responsibility for the direction of FRELIMO and the implementation of party programs.[67]

At the Second Congress the Central Committee was expanded, bringing in not only department heads and their deputies, but also provincial secretaries, members elected by the provinces (then the three northern districts of Mozambique) and the Congress, and representatives of "mass" organizations. The Central Committee was limited to legislative responsibilities, and a new structure, the Executive Committee, composed of the President, Vice-President, and the secretaries of the various departments, was created and given executive responsibilities. A political and military committee comprising the President, Vice-President, Provincial Secretaries, and the Secretary of Defence and Security was also established, charged with the responsibility of taking care of urgent problems that might arise between meetings of the Central Committee.[68]

At the local level, the smallest units of the party were the cells, membership in which was open to every local resident. Above the cells were the District Councils, composed of representatives elected from the cells in each district. The District Councils in turn elected representatives to the Provincial Councils, and the Provincial Councils sent delegates to the Party Congress. According to Mondlane, decisions were reached through discussion at each level. If a consensus was not feasible, the issue was resolved by vote.[69]

The interchanges among these alternative functional subsystems have generally been highly compatible. In the legitimation interchange between the pattern socialization and control and the goal attainment subsystems, the values and norms of the revolutionary international milieu are highly supportive of the distribution of political power, institutionalized procedural norms, and form of governmental structure within the FRELIMO goal attainment subsystem. Power has been exercised in accordance with the ideals of the alternative national culture, and FRELIMO has been highly successful in generating widespread support among Africans, and some Europeans, for the alternative goals of independence and self-determination by appeals to the idea of an independent African society. In the loyalty, solidarity, and commitment interchange between the alternative pattern socialization and integration subsystems, the relationship has likewise been highly compatible. The alternative stratification system created by FRELIMO is harmonious with the values and norms of their alternative national culture. This new stratification system has received considerable support from the party's membership, and there is a strong commitment to maintaining and spreading it throughout Mozambique. The resource mobilization interchange between the alternative adaptive and goal attainment subsystems has also been highly compatible. The economic structures organized by FRELIMO are harmonious with the primary goals of self-determination and independence and the values and norms of the alternative national culture. The new distribution of the rewards and costs of achieving these goals is also consonant with alternative values and norms. Except for a period in the early stages of organizing in the 1960s, when FRELIMO suffered considerable elite conflict, the political support interchange between the integrative and goal attainment subsystems has on the whole been compatible.

The incompatibility in the political support interchange experienced by FRELIMO from 1962 to 1969 was primarily the result of competition among elite factions for the highest power and prestige roles within the structure of the party. During this period, different elites used appeals to ethnic and class cleavages as they vied for these relatively few high level positions. The linkage between societal cleavages and elite behavior was their perception of the importance of regional, racial, class, and ethnolinguistic differences, which were often irrelevant for the actual levels of support various factions were receiving. These perceptions derived from the pyramidal social structure of Mozambique, which tended to produce among Mozambicans a general readiness to perceive the finest distinctions among themselves. Unacculturated Africans were inclined to see both *assimilados* and mulattos as representing Portuguese colonialism, while *assimilados* contrasted themselves with mulattos, who were seen as its direct agents. These varied perceptions, in addition to distinctions made between northern and southern ethnolinguistic groups, together with personality clashes and generational differences, structured the competition for office within the nationalist movement during the 1960s, when victory seemed far distant.

The schisms, expulsions, and resignations among the leadership during this period produced a number of rival nationalist parties. In 1962 an expellee from FRELIMO organized the Comité Secreto de Restauração da UDENAMO in Kampala. Some time later he reformed UDENAMO under the name União Democrática Nacional de Monomotapa (UDENAMO-Monomotapa). The expulsion of others in 1962 led to the formation of the União Democrática Nacional de

Moçambique (UDENAMO-Moçambique) in Cairo. MANU was also reorganized. In Kampala in 1963, UDENAMO-Monomotapa, MANU, and the Mozambique African National Congress (MANC) came together to form the Frente Unida Anti-Imperialista Popular Africana de Moçambique (FUNIPAMO). Additional FRELIMO expulsions led to the creation of the Mozambique Revolutionary Council (MORECO) in early 1964. Later, in June of that year, MORECO, UDENAMO-Moçambique, MANU, and UDENAMO-Monomotapa coalesced to form a new party called the Comité Revoluncionário de Moçambique (COREMO), which was based in Lusaka.

With the exception of COREMO, which initially attracted a fairly substantial following of dissatisfied Africans from northern ethnolinguistic groups, the elite conflict of the 1960s did not result in the formation of viable, alternative nationalist movements drawing significant support from groups within Mozambique. In most cases, the alternative organizations formed by dissatisfied elites had little substance beyond the paper on which their constitutions were written.

Elite conflict was a result of the special circumstances in which FRELIMO found itself. Independence seemed remote; the Portuguese control of Mozambique was backed by overwhelming force and apparant determination; the movement had to survive outside Mozambique or, even more precariously, in the perilous environment of an "occupied" country; and there were relatively few power and prestige positions available for men of ability. Under these circumstances, FRELIMO provided the sole structure in which Mozambique's exiled political elites could appropriately compete. This tended to focus elite conflict within FRELIMO, and intensified perceived differences among factions. In a sense, the politics of the movement became a zero-sum game, with racial, ethnolinguistic, regional, and class cleavages providing the major categories which elites, especially those in the minority, used as they competed for the scarce economic and political resources available within the nationalist movement.[70]

In marked contrast to the dissynchronous hierarchy of control and facilitation in the preindependence social system of colonial Mozambique, control and facilitation in FRELIMO's alternative social system, as shown in Figure 8.2, has been harmonious and balanced. The economy has been organized according to the values and norms of the revolutionary international milieu, and has been providing facilities to the political structures, which, in turn, have been regulating the economy for the achievement of self-determination and independence. This was in response to demands coming from a significant number of Africans who had been organized into interest-based collectivities in the integrative subsystem. Systemic legitimating values and norms produced in the pattern socialization subsystem were controlling the goal attainment, integration, and adaptive subsystems, and those subsystems were

FIGURE 8.2
Compatible Hierarchy of Control and Facilitation in the FRELIMO Alternative Social System

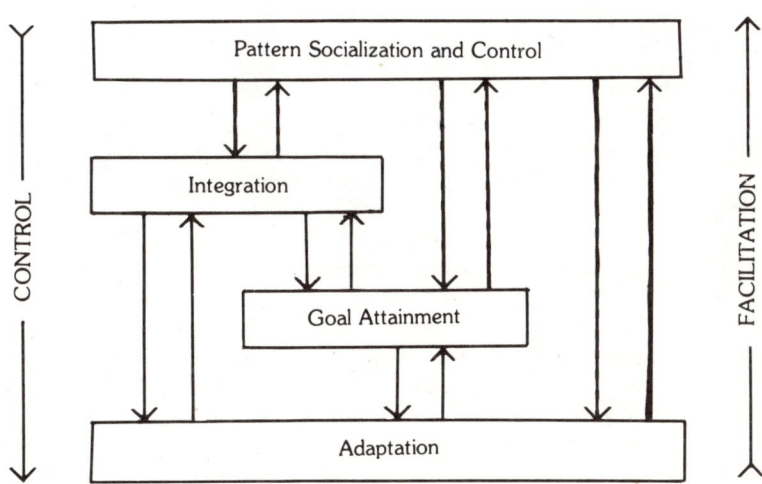

facilitating the actualization of these legitimating values.

Let us return to our propositions to sum up the argument thus far. As Africans began to organize legitimate mutual aid and work associations and, later, proto-nationalist groups, and their political power began to increase, proposals for change in the social system began to increase. However, the power of these collectivities was not sufficient to get the change they wanted accepted, nor did increasing concentrations of power in the hands of the nationalist movement, brought about by the coalescing of the three proto-nationalist movements, push the Portuguese to immediately accept African demands for self-determination and independence as a possible solution to Mozambique's societal incompatabilities (A3). Power was insufficient because, initially at least, regional, class, racial, and ethnolinguistic differences which had developed among Africans acted as barriers by spawning elite conflicts in early African interest-based collectivities as well as in the nationalist movement, FRELIMO (A2d). Although the Portuguese responded with some changes in lower functional subsystems (e.g., abolition of forced labor and the *regime do indigenato*) which reduced dissynchronization, they did not reduce it significantly. Such minor adjustments were the only responses the Portuguese could make because of the paucity of innovative values and norms in the dominant subculture, the presence of conservative values and norms which demanded conformity, and the high level of resistance to the complete implementation of the multiracial ideal encountered in lower functional subsystems. The threshold for the kind of change that was possible in the system was reached quickly. Change beyond the threshold (e.g., a significant and rapid realization of—or at least commitment to—the multiracial ideal) was simply not possible because both control by variant values and facilitation of power by organized collectivities were absent among the Portuguese (A4). This led to stiff resistance to alternative values and norms from the revolutionary international milieu and African power concentrating in support of them.

As we observed, important sources of change were both internal and external to the Mozambican social system. The most important external sources were those societies and like-minded groups comprising the revolutionary international milieu which provided an alternative set of values and norms to act as a positive model for change. The major internal sources of change were the incompatabilities between the pattern socialization and control subsystem and lower functional subsystems (B1). This lack of integration allowed change to occur at all levels in the hierarchy of control and facilitation, including the importation of variant values and norms (B2,B2a). Contrary to expectations based on relatively well-integrated social systems, a crucial impact point of change was the pattern socialization and control subsystem (C1). The incompatibilities between this and "lower" functional subsystems and the combined compatibilities among "lower" ones allowed change to impinge most easily on the pattern socialization subsystem and to be resisted by subsystems lower in the hierarchy (C1a).

The mobilization of collectivities among Africans developed primarily around work-related groups, social clubs, and ethnic associations in the integrative subsystem, and led to a significant increase in the exercise of power and influence when such organizing became sanctioned by variant values and norms which differed significantly from those held by the dominant Portuguese elite (C2a,b). Such mobilization was viewed by an African and mulatto counterelite as leading to a significant increase in African power, and was seen as the only means available for the implementation of variant values and norms (C2c). This mobilization of African power stemmed from the desire of the emerging African and mulatto counterelite to control and redistribute the scarce resources available in Mozambique (C2d).

The mobilization of African collectivities for the exercise of power and influence for change met with countermobilization by the Portuguese elite to resist change (C3). This defensive countermobilization was quite intense, involving large numbers of military troops and the commitment of vast amounts of material resources, because the values and norms of Portuguese-Catholic culture were substantially different from the variant, essentially Marxist values and norms controlling African collectivities organizing for change (C3a[2]); the supply of power and influence of the Portuguese elite was small enough to be challenged by change-oriented mobilization but not so small that defensive countermobilization would seem impossible (C3a[3]); and elites on both sides were in competition for scarce resources (C3a[4]). The intensity of the conflict which was produced through countermobilization was abated, however, because the values and norms of Portuguese-Catholic culture did not particularly sanction aggressiveness (C3a[1]).[71] Within the structure of the colonial social system, rapid and extensive change was postponed by the policy of repression (C3b). The mobilization and countermobilization of both elites was relatively successful, resulting in a stalemate. However, the coup in Portugal sharply increased the rapidity of change by dramatically decreasing the power available for countermobilization in Mozambique (C4).

Change in the original social system was also fostered because an African and mulatto elite, who were able to communicate through prose, poetry, and painting, exerted pressure for change (C6). Although early African and mulatto elites tended to share the dominant values and norms of Portuguese-Catholic culture, later postwar elites did not. Nor did they participate effectively in institutionalized interest-based collectivities or high prestige roles in significant numbers. It was these elites who introduced new values and norms into the system (C6a). Their ability to create an alternative social system indicated that they were intimately knowledgeable of the dynamics of Mozambican society and were able to predict with great accuracy the consequences of their actions (C6c). This African and mulatto counterelite used both the application of power through organizing (FRELIMO) and the invocation of variant values and norms to increase the probability that change would be successful (C6d). The unification of three proto-nationalist movements into one unified organization called FRELIMO greatly enhanced African power and influence, and increased proportionately the likelihood that change would be successful (C6e).

It was inevitable that the changes demanded by the nationalist movement would be unacceptable to the Portuguese because the elements the nationalists wanted to introduce were highly incompatible with existing ones. The mixture of traditional and Marxist values and norms and the demand for African self-determination were totally antithetical to the idea of a multiracial and multicontinental Portugal and the values and norms of Portuguese-Catholic culture (D1). In the preindependence social system, the values and norms of multiracial, Portuguese-Catholic society were not widely shared; therefore, more well-established racialist norms controlled behavior in lower functional subsystems (D3). This dissynchronization in the hierarchy of control and facilitation was the major cause of revolutionary political change from within the social system.

The most important immediate consequence of the importation of variant values and norms in the postwar period was increased conflict manifested in terms of dissension on values and norms and competition between African and European collectivities (E1). During the postwar period, dissonance between cognitions and evaluations of the conditions of Africans in the preindependence society was developing among Mozambique's African and mulatto elite (E2). As the discrepancies between the professed multiracial ideal, the professed values and norms from the revolutionary international milieu, and the realities of life in Mozambique for Africans increased, dissonance increased (E2a). The African and mulatto elite resolved this conflict by attempting to change the configuration of the social system to make their cognitions congruent with their evaluations (E2b). Synchronization was pursued by replacing the preindependence system by a new one conforming to variant values and norms from the revolutionary international milieu. In this process of change, during the early postwar years, there was considerable ambivalence for many *assimilados* and mulattos about which norms to follow—those of the Portuguese-Catholic way of life or those from the revolutionary international milieu. The latter, however, eventually came to control their behavior, and change proceeded in a recognizable direction (E3). Control of the media of power, influence, commitments, and money by the African nationalist elite, in direct consequence of the organization of FRELIMO, gave them a high degree of control over the life conditions of ordinary Africans in areas wrested from Portuguese control and was used to implant change in the direction specified by variant values from the revolutionary international milieu (E3a). Finally, change made by the new elite in the liberated zones was the minimum necessary to integrate new values, norms, collectivities, and roles into a new social system. There did not occur vast disruptions of traditional patterns of life and radical reorganization of communities. The alternative structures were unobtrusively blended with traditional patterns, especially in the adaptive subsystem. Similarities between them were stressed, and they sometimes merged (E4).

The Emerging Social System of Independent Mozambique

Now that the process of revolutionary change in Mozambique has been mapped out, what can the control and facilitation framework and the incorporated propositions tell us about the direction and extent of change and the degree and type of synchronization to be expected in the emerging social system? Is Mozambique, because of its birth in armed conflict against the colonial power and its values and norms from the international revolutionary milieu, significantly different from older African states such as Tanzania proclaiming a similar revolutionary ideology?[72] The analysis which has preceded suggests that, notwithstanding revolutionary values and norms and a relatively high degree of mobilization, there are barriers and constraints on change which will dampen its extent and modify its direction. Our framework, which considers a host of variables, allows us to identify these barriers and constraints and to pinpoint the locus of possible disequilibrium which could lead to future breakdown and stagnation in the social system of independent Mozambique.

Since gaining full independence on 25 June 1975,[73] FRELIMO has taken steps to generalize its alternative social system to the whole of Mozambique. Most of the adaptive, goal attainment, integrative, and pattern socialization and control structures left behind by the Portuguese are being dismantled and replaced by structures organized by FRELIMO during the struggle for independence in accordance with values and norms from the international revolutionary milieu.

In terms of pattern socialization and control, great efforts are being made to transmit these values and norms throughout the society. At FRELIMO's Third Party Congress, held in February 1977, a decision was made to create a national culture and give it a revolutionary content. To achieve this goal, the Congress made four concrete policy decisions. The first was to create *Casas de Cultura* (Houses of Culture) throughout Mozambique which would serve as centers for the generation and diffusion of the new revolutionary culture. The second was to launch a general "Cultural Offensive of the Working Classes" by organizing cultural groups in all sectors of society (schools, factories, communal villages, government offices, etc.) which would foment the expression of Mozambique's new revolutionary culture through plays, songs, dance, wall murals, and the like. The third was to organize "Cultural Brigades," to be dispatched throughout Mozambique to collect and preserve the oral history, songs, and artistic traditions of the country's various ethnic groups. Finally, the Ministry of Education and Culture was reorganized to include a National Office of Culture to direct and administer the Cultural Offensive and a National Institute of Culture to develop and implement new programs and modes of artistic expression.[74]

Within a month of independence, all private schools were nationalized and reorganized. All of the most advanced students (those in their final two years of secondary school) were put into government service, where the majority are being trained as teachers. These students are to become a new cadre of revolutionary teachers who will act as the agents of Mozambique's educational and cultural transformation. Most will be posted to rural areas where they will be expected to transmit revolutionary values and norms, build educational structures, and develop communal villages.[75]

The primary unit within Mozambique's reorganized schools is the *turma* (teaching unit) which is composed of twenty-five to thirty students. Within each *turma* there are five or six leaders, one of whom is elected to serve as the *turma's* representative to higher bodies and chair its discussions. Each *turma* elects its own director from among the teachers at the school. The director is responsible for organizing and mobilizing the *turma*, dealing with disciplinary problems, and carrying out routine administration. Within the *turma* students organize their own productive and cultural activities. Teachers elect from their numbers a Comissão Directiva (Steering Committee) and representatives to the school's seven *secções* (sections). These sections deal with social and disciplinary matters, teaching, cultural activities, health and hygiene, administration, production, and sports. At the apex of this new organizational schema sits the *Conselho da Escola* (School Council) which is composed of representatives from the *turmas*, the steering committee, and the school's *grupo dinamizador* (consciousness raising group).[76]

With respect to goal attainment, FRELIMO has continued to generate energy for change through the mass mobilization of the population. In all regions and sectors of life the people of Mozambique are being organized and involved in the development and implementation of revolutionary political structures. Although in the preindependence phase FRELIMO encompassed all political, administrative, and social activity, Mozambique's new elite has begun to make a clear distinction between party structures and state structures. The key party structure is the *grupo dinamizador*, or GD as it is called in Mozambique, and the key state political structure is the elected assembly.

Established during the period of transition from colonial rule in the southern regions of the country where FRELIMO's contact with the people had been minimal, the GDs were initially designed to educate the population about the party's political and social philosophy and policies. As the need arose, however, because of the withdrawal of large numbers of Portuguese managers and technicians, the GDs initially also performed a wide range of economic and administrative tasks such as reorganizing and managing agricultural and industrial production. Now that the state's administrative and political apparatus is more fully organized, these broader social and economic tasks are being carried out by state structures, and the GDs have become FRELIMO cells. Organized in neighborhoods, schools, factories, states farms, the bureaucracy, and communal villages, the GDs are the primary link between the party and the population.[77]

During 1977, national elections were held for Mozambique's assemblies. All adults residing in towns and cooperative and communal villages elected more than 22,000 men and women to 894 local assemblies throughout the country. Deputies serve for two and one half year terms, and the local assemblies are the primary political organization of the state. Also during 1977, elections were held for provincial and district assemblies, as well as for a 226 member national representative body called the Popular Assembly. In the days preceding the vote, notices were disseminated urging people to participate. Although lists of candidates were proposed by the GDs, the final judgement was left to the local community. By the time the elections had been completed, over 2,200 candidates had been rejected. These rejected aspirants were usually either traditional authorities who sought to maintain their positions of power and prestige or former members of the colonial regime.[78]

Relative to adaptation, the alternative economic structures developed in the preindependence phase are being extended throughout Mozambique. First, the peasant cooperatives organized in the liberated zones are being set up in all rural areas. This policy has been most successful in the north of the country where the Portuguese had already resettled more than one million people into *aldeamentos,* over which the communal villages have been superimposed. As in the liberated zones, these villages are organized around the principles of collective participation in decision making and collective labor.[79]

Second, Mozambique's new elite has established a network of state farms. These are the nationalized estates which formerly belonged to Portuguese planters who abandoned their holdings after independence. Although labor is somewhat differently organized from farm to farm, the basic principles are the same as in the communal villages: collective decision making and collective labor. The primary units of organization on the state farms are *brigadas* (brigades), each of which is assigned a specific task. Each brigade elects a *responsável* (responsible person) who directs its activities, and a representative to the farm's *conselho* (council) which oversees day-to-day operations.[80]

Third, all businesses and factories have been nationalized and reorganized. When Portuguese owners abandoned their factories, FRELIMO organized *comissões administrativas* (administrative committees) to manage them. These committees, which receive instructions from the Ministry of Commerce and Industry, are composed of workers who are elected from among their fellows, and are empowered to deal with day-to-day management. In October 1976 *conselhos de produção* (Production Councils) were established in factories. These structures explain the production process to the individual worker, explore ways of increasing production, set production quotas, and maintain discipline and morale.[81]

Walter C. Opello

With respect to integration, the major policy has been a continuation of FRELIMO's long-standing effort to change the traditional status of women. The Organization of Mozambican Women (OMW), which is the primary group responsible for this policy, holds consciousness-raising sessions, attacks any manifestations of unequal work load or status for women, and lobbies against polygamy, the *lobola* (bride price), and female initiation rites.[82]

FRELIMO is also insisting on a new life style and "mentality" among the people. Emphasis is being placed on the norms of "community," "collective action," "participation," and "consultation." The new elite is openly hostile to "decadent" western behavior such as "individualism" and "competition," as well as to popular culture which seeps in from South Africa.[83]

The success of the transfer of new revolutionary structures to the whole of Mozambique will depend, in part, on the power and prestige of the new governing elite (C6b). Getting the people to accept these new structures and policies will require the invocation of revolutionary values and norms as well as the application of force (C6d). This can be seen from events that occurred when a cashew plant in Maputo was nationalized. When the Portuguese staff left, FRELIMO put the management of the plant into the hands of an administrative committee composed of workers. This polarized the factory's work force and provided a target for some of the workers who were still dissatisfied with their wages despite the fact that these had been doubled when the plant was nationalized. After several wildcat strikes, FRELIMO instituted an intensive campaign of "political explanation" among the workers, and, at the same time, sent eight recalcitrant "reactionary" workers to a rehabilitation camp.[84]

There will be no vacillation by Mozambique's new political elite between accommodation and repression, nor will countermobilization by dissidents be tolerated (C3,C3b). FRELIMO has organized a secret police force called the Serviço Nacional de Segurança Popular (SNASP-People's National Security Service) which has been empowered to detain "reactionary forces" in rehabilitation camps.[85] Some countermobilization took place immediately following the cease fire in August 1974, when a number of African political groups emerged and coalesced to challenge FRELIMO dominance. The most important of these was the Partido de Coligação Nacional (PCN), situated in Beira. PCN's president was Uria Simango, and its vice-president was Paulo Gumane, both of COREMO. Joana Simião, an erstwhile COREMO member and the vice-president of the Portuguese sponsored Grupo Unido de Moçambique (GUMO), and Narcissa Mbule of FUMO were key members of the PCN executive committee. The leaders of PCN were subsequently arrested and taken into Tanzania where they confessed their "crimes" against the Mozambican people and were "reeducated."[86]

Although the new elite's power and economic resources within

Mozambique give it a high degree of control over the life conditions of ordinary Africans (E3a), there are constraints and barriers to the extent of change and the amount of synchronization that can be accomplished in the postindependence social system. Resistance to change will emerge when the threshold of tolerance for change is reached (A4). This threshold has been reached in those areas where FRELIMO has attempted to replace the most deeply rooted structures of the preindependence social system (D5). Available evidence suggests that the most deeply rooted structures are those associated with traditional life, and it is from these that FRELIMO is encountering the stiffest resistance to change. For example, strong resistance to the formation of communal villages came from traditional chiefs who had enjoyed the benefit of work on their *shambas* (African family farms) donated by their villagers. Because of the *shamba* tradition, FRELIMO was also forced to provide opportunities for the cultivation of private family plots within the communal villages.[87]

In addition, despite the Organization of Mozambican Women's campaign to change the status of women, traditional sex roles have been difficult to change. Even in the communal villages, where behavior is most controlled, much of the division of labor is yet based on traditional sex-assigned roles. Women still do an unequal share of work: they still pound the grain, work the fields, and look after children. Men refuse to do inferior "women's work." Furthermore, attempts to eradicate female initiation rites have not proved successful, and the majority of fathers still insist on the *lobola* and arranged marriages.[88]

The most resilient structure left behind by the Portuguese is proving to be the Catholic Church. Despite FRELIMO's attacks on the Church and religious behavior as "reactionary" and "counter-revolutionary," Mozambique's new elite has not and cannot abolish this institution. Although its schools have been nationalized and religious instruction within them forbidden, the Church's religious and instructional activities outside of the educational sphere have not been curtailed. Furthermore, the clergy is proving to be a force to be dealt with, as is evinced by their active protest against alleged "inhuman conditions" in FRELIMO's reeducation camps.[89]

In the transformation process, it is most likely that new structures which are most compatible with pre-existing traditional elements will be more readily accepted than alien ones (D1), and new structures will be reinterpreted and modified to make them more compatible with extant structures, especially those that are more resistant to change (D2). For example, "People's Courts" are being partially staffed with tribal elders, which combines aspects of FRELIMO's new revolutionary courts with traditional patterns of adjudication.[90]

The extent of change has been the minimum necessary to integrate new structures and modify old ones to establish a workable level of harmony between revolutionary values and norms and the organization of new structures (E4). Thus, factories are nationalized and their management put in the hands of workers' committees, but, as before, strikes are forbidden, wages are controlled, and productivity is emphasized. The Church's schools are taken over and religious instruction forbidden, but the Church is allowed to continue its religious activities. Communal villages are organized, but the people living in them are permitted to cultivate private plots. Efforts are made to reduce sexism, but sex discrimination, female initiation rights, arranged marriages, and the *lobola* continue.

Even though the subsystem which is least well integrated with the rest of the social system—pattern socialization and control—has been most susceptible to widespread structural change (A2a), the low level of overall system integration will hinder much purposive change-oriented activity (A2b). In other words, FRELIMO, not unlike the Portuguese colonizers before them, runs the risk of disequilibrium between pattern socialization and control and "lower" functional subsystems. The gap between ideal "revolutionary" behavior and the reality of the bulk of the population living according to modified traditional values and norms cannot and will not be closed unless FRELIMO can mobilize sufficient power to harmonize the latter with the former (C1a). If disequilibrium continues over a long period of time, disillusionment with the revolution could develop. Such disillusionment could lead to support for an alternative elite, and could cause a schism within FRELIMO itself between its "idealists" and "realists."[91]

In FRELIMO's favor on this point, however, is the fact that postindependence dissynchronization will not be as severe as that which existed during the colonial period because the national level goal attainment, adaptive, and pattern socialization and control structures that have been organized are harmonious with revolutionary values and norms. The departure of 95 percent of Mozambique's Portuguese population has removed support from most colonial structures and drastically altered the social stratification system, making it more harmonious with pattern socialization and control. Moreover, when compared to the Portuguese, FRELIMO has generated significantly higher levels of power and influence behind the new structures it supports. Whether or not it can generate sufficient power to extirpate deeply entrenched modified traditional structures or prevent class cleavages among Africans from increasing remains to be seen.

Such structures and cleavages, as well as Mozambique's ethnic and regional cleavages, could become significant barriers to change (A2d). This will be especially true now that independence and FRELIMO's policies have brought about mass participation. It is not unlikely that perceived differences in the application of these policies along the cleavage lines that precipitated elite conflict during the early days of the nationalist movement will cause these cleavages to become politicized beyond the elite level.

Finally, a dramatic act of power exercising such as the intervention of Cuba or the Soviet Union on the side of FRELIMO, or South Africa on the side of exiled Portuguese and/or African elites opposed to FRELIMO, could either speed up or retard change (C4). Neither of these contingencies seems likely, however. The absence of significant overt opposition to FRELIMO eliminates the rationale that has led to Cuban military action in Angola. Although there is evidence that South Africa is providing support and a sanctuary for Portuguese and African elites opposed to FRELIMO, overt intervention is not likely because FRELIMO has not discontinued the transit trade or the recruitment of labor for the mines on the Rand.[92] In the case of Zimbabwe (Rhodesia), however, FRELIMO has been less accommodating. Since March 1976, rail lines with Zimbabwe have been cut, the frontier sealed, and Mozambique has been providing training and sanctuary for the Zimbabwe Liberation Army.

In conclusion, it can be said that revolutionary change in Mozambique did not derive simply from class contradictions within its social structure, nor was it an extension of traditional tribal resistance to Portuguese colonialism. As has been shown, it was, instead, the result of the complex interaction and disequilibrium among specific economic, political, social, cultural, and psychological factors within the Mozambique social system, and the importation of values, norms, power, and material assistance from without. Its future success will depend not upon the resolution of class conflict alone, but on the ability of its leaders to overcome various structural barriers to change in the society, especially traditionally based ones. As more fundamental restructuring is attempted, the greater will be the resistance and the need to mobilize political power. Despite FRELIMO's fairly successful building of political power, however, the various constraints may prove to be too great. If so, the future could be one of stagnation and political repression, and perhaps a cyclical pattern of military intervention, as has been the case in much of Africa.

Walter C. Opello

Footnotes

1. See Perry Anderson, *Le Portugal et la Fin de l'Ultra-Colonialisme* (Paris: Françoise Maspero, 1963); Gérard Chaliand, *Armed Struggle in Africa* (New York: Monthly Review Press, 1969); Ronald Chilcote, *Portuguese Africa* (Englewood Cliffs, N.J.: Prentice-Hall, 1967); Basil Davidson, *The Liberation of Guine* (Baltimore: Penguin Books, 1969); Richard Gibson, *African Liberation Movements* (New York: Oxford University Press, 1972); John Marcum, *The Angolan Revolution* (Cambridge: M.I.T. Press, 1969); Eduardo Mondlane, *The Struggle for Mozambique* (Baltimore: Penguin Books, 1969); Thomas Okuma, *Angola in Ferment* (Boston: Beacon Press, 1962); William Minter, *Portugal and the West* (New York: Monthly Review Press, 1973); Maina Kagombe, "African Nationalism and Guerrilla Warfare in Angola and Mozambique," in *Southern Africa in Perspective,* ed. Christian P. Potholm and Richard Dale (New York: Free Press, 1972), pp. 196-204; David M. Abshire and Michael Samuels, eds., *Portuguese Africa: A Handbook* (New York: Praeger Publishers, 1969); James Dodson, "Dynamics of Insurgency in Mozambique," *Africa Report* 12 (November 1967): 52-55; John Marcum, "Three Revolutions," *Africa Report* 12 (November 1967): 9-22; Paul Whitaker, "The Revolutions in 'Portuguese' Africa," *Journal of Modern African Studies* 8 (April 1970): 15-35; I. William Zartman, "Guinea: The Quiet War Goes On," *Africa Report* 12 (November 1967): 67-72; and Donald H. Humphries, *The East African Liberation Movements*, Adelphi Paper No. 16 (London: Institute for Strategic Studies, 1965). Kenneth Grundy, *Guerrilla Struggle in Africa* (New York: Grossman, 1971), utilizes social science concepts, but does not deal specifically with Mozambique, Angola, or Guinea (Bissau).

2. Ronald Chilcote, "Mozambique: The African Nationalist Response to Portuguese Imperialism and Underdevelopment," in Potholm and Dale, *Southern Africa in Perspective,* pp. 184-85. An early historical piece on Mozambique is Douglas L. Wheeler, "The Portuguese in Mozambique: The Past Against the Future," in *Southern Africa in Transition,* ed. John A. Davis and James Baker (New York: Praeger Publishers, 1966), pp. 180-96. The general theoretical framework for Chilcote's analysis follows that of Anderson, *Le Portugal*, as does Minter, *Portugal and the West*, except that in the latter England has been replaced by the United States.

3. On the putative linkage between tribal resistance to the Portuguese military conquest of Mozambique and the modern nationalist revolution, see Allen F. Isaacman, "The Tradition of Resistance in Mozambique,"*Africa Today* 22 (July-September 1975): 37-50.

4. This is to be expected as he employs a neo-Marxist framework. For studies which devalue the importance of economics as the central determinant of Portuguese continuity in Africa see Richard J. Hammond,

"Economic Imperialism: Side-lights on a Stereotype," *Journal of Economic History* 21 (December 1961): 582-98; Hammond, "Uneconomic Imperialism: Portugal in Africa Before 1910," in *Colonialism in Africa 1870-1960*, Vol. 1, ed. L:H. Gann and Peter Duignan (New York: Cambridge University Press, 1969), pp. 352-82; Hammond, *Portugual's African Problem: Some Economic Facets,*Occasional Paper No. 2 (New York: Carnegie Endowment for International Peace, 1962), esp. pp. 12-14; and Thomas Henricksen, "Portugal in Africa: A Noneconomic Interpretation," *African Studies Review* 16 (December 1973): 405-16.

5. Allen F. Isaacman, *Mozambique, The Africanization of a European Institution: The Zambezi Prazos, 1750-1902* (Madison: University of Wisconsin Press, 1972). On the history of Portugal in South-east Africa, consult Eric Axelson, *Portuguese in South East Africa, 1600-1700* (Johannesburg: Witwatersrand University Press, 1967); Raymond W. Bixler, "Anglo-Portuguese Rivalry for Delagoa Bay," *Journal of Modern History* 6 (December 1934): 425-40; James Duffy, *Portuguese Africa* (Cambridge: Harvard University Press, 1959); Mabel V. Jackson-Haight, *European Powers and South East Africa* (New York: Praeger Publishers, 1967); Richard J. Hammond, *Portugal and Africa 1815-1910* (London: Longmans, Green, 1962); Douglas L. Wheeler, "Gungunhana the Negotiator: A Study in African Diplomacy," *Journal of African History* 9,4 (1968): 585-602; and Wheeler, "Gungunhana," in *Leadership in Eastern Africa*, ed. Norman R. Bennett (Boston: Boston University Press, 1968), pp. 167-220.

6. Duffy, *Portuguese Africa*, p. 271. This claim to uniqueness as a colonizer spawned in the Luso-Brazilian world an influential branch of sociology called "Lusotropicology." See, by its propounders, Gilberto Freyre, *Portuguese Integration in the Tropics* (Lisbon: Agencia-Geral do Ultramar, 1961); António Alberto de Andrade, *Muitas Raças Uma Nação* (Lisbon: Agencia-Geral do Ultramar, 1968); and Oscar Soares Barata, *A Cultura Portuguesa e os Fenómenos de Contacto das Raças*(Lisbon: Instituto Superior de Ciencias Sociais e Politica Ultramarina, 1963).

7. James Duffy, *Portugal's African Territories: Present Realities,*Occasional Paper No. 1 (New York: Carnegie Endowment for International Peace, 1962), p. 10. See also his "The Dual Reality of Portuguese Africa," *Centennial Review* 4 (Fall 1960): 450-64; "The Vice of History—Portuguese in Africa,"*Texas Quarterly* 3 (Summer 1960): 77-89; and "Portugal's Colonies in Africa," *Foreign Affairs* 39 (April 1961): 481-93.

8. It is precisely on this point that our approach reveals its superiority as an explanatory tool. The difference between the multiracial ideal and the actual situation in the colonies has been pointed out by almost all analysts. Usually, the discrepancy is resolved by arguing that the multiracial ideal was a "myth," or was propaganda designed to rationalize or cover over the "real" underlying motive for Portuguese colonialism: economic

exploitation. We make no such assumption, nor do we deny that exploitation existed. As will be shown below, we suggest that the juxtaposition of these two *realities* was an important determinant, not only of Portugal's continuity in Africa, but of the start of revolutionary change as well.

9. James Duffy, *Portugal in Africa* (Cambridge: Harvard University Press, 1966), p. 172.

10. Allison Butler Herrick et al., *Area Handbook for Mozambique* (Washington: U.S. Government Printing Office, 1969), p. 106.

11. See Michael A. Samuels and Norman A. Bailey, "Education, Health, and Social Welfare," in Abshire and Samuels, *Portuguese Africa,* pp. 178-79, for details of this development.

12. Ministério do Ultramar, *O Ensino no Ultramar* (Lisbon: Agencia-Geral do Ultramar, 1966), pp. 49-59.

13. Samuels and Bailey, "Education, Health, and Social Welfare," pp. 180-82.

14. See C.R. Boxer, "The Colour Question in the Portuguese Empire, 1415-1825," in *Proceedings of the British Academy, 1961* (London: Oxford University Press, 1962), pp. 113-38; and Boxer, *Race Relations in the Portuguese Colonial Empire 1415-1825* (Oxford: Clarendon Press, 1963).

15. Richard J. Hammond, "Race Attitudes and Policies in Portuguese Africa in the Nineteenth and Twentieth Centuries," *Race* 9 (October 1967): 205-16. Hammond suggests that such racialist sentiments were legitimized by Social Darwinism and the then nascent discipline of physical anthropology which claimed to have demonstrated the inferiority of blacks empirically through the measurement of cranial capacities.

16. The statistics on the size of each ethnolinguistic group are from the 1950 census, and therefore are a serious underestimation of present figures. The relative sizes of the ethnolinguistic groups, however, remain largely unchanged. See A. Rita-Ferreira, "Mozambique Ethnic Characterizations and Groupings," *South African Journal of Science* 55 (1959): 201-4; and Michael A. Samuels and Norman A. Bailey, "African Peoples," in Abshire and Samuels, *Portuguese Africa,* pp. 123-27.

17. Junta de Investigacoes do Ultramar, *Promoção Social em Moçambique,* Estudos de Ciencias Politicas e Sociais No. 71 (Lisbon: Centro de Estudos de Serviço Social e de Desenvolvimento Comunitário, Junta do Instituto Superior de Ciencias Sociais e Política Ultramarina, 1964), pp. 21-22.

18. Assimilated status was theoretically to be granted upon application to any African who demonstrated that he was eighteen years old, employed, and able to read, write, and speak Portuguese fluently.

19. Herrick, *Area Handbook for Mozambique,* pp. 86-87.

20. Duffy, *Portuguese Africa,* pp. 298-99.

21. On the *assimilado* see the works of Marvin Harris: "The Assimilado

System in Portuguese Africa," *Africa Special Report* 3 (November 1958): 7-10; *Portugal's African "Wards,"* Africa Today Pamphlet No. 2 (New York: American Committee on Africa, 1958); and "Race, Conflict, and Reform in Mozambique," in *Transformation of East Africa,* ed. Stanley Diamond and Fred G. Burke (New York: Basic Books, 1966), pp. 158-59.

22. Harris, "The Assimilado System in Portuguese Africa"; and Norman A. Bailey, "Native and Labor Policy," in Abshire and Samuels, *Portuguese Africa,* pp. 165-77.

23. On Portugal's corporate state see F.C.C. Egerton, *Salazar: Rebuilder of Portugal* (London: Hodder & Stoughton, 1943); and Hugh Kay, *Salazar and Modern Portugal* (New York: Hawthorn, 1970), esp. Chapter 4.

24. Norman A. Bailey, "Local Community Power in Angola," *Western Political Quarterly* 21 (September 1968): 400-408.

25. Vincente Loft as quoted by Norman A. Bailey in "The Political Process and Interest Groups," in Abshire and Samuels, *Portuguese Africa,* p. 152.

26. United Nations, General Assembly, Special Committee on the Situation with Regard to the Implementation of the Declaration on Granting of Independence to Colonial Countries and Peoples, Territories under Portuguese Administration, *Working Paper Prepared by the Secretariat* (A/AC.109/L.625/Add. 2 [Part 1]), 12 May 1970, p. 13. It should be noted that a modicum of European opposition did exist in Mozambique in the preindependence period. This opposition, based on and drawing support from a small group of young professionals and businessmen born in Mozambique, educated in South African universities, and experienced in the relatively free South African political climate, tended to view control from Lisbon as despotic and stifling for Mozambique's economic and political development. Many were sympathetic to the African nationalist movements and thought that Mozambique's future would be best served by independence under African majority rule. The primary formal organization for this opposition was a group known as the Associação dos Naturais de Moçambique.

27. United Nations, General Assembly, Special Committee..., *Working Paper* (A/AC.109/L.625/Add.2 [Part 2]), 15 May 1970, p. 12. Franchise requirements are given in United Nations, General Assembly, Special Committee..., *Working Paper Prepared by the Secretariat* (A/Ac.109/L.126), 9 June 1964, pp. 20-21.

28. United Nations, General Assembly, Special Committee..., *Working Paper* (A/AC. 109/L. 625/Add. 2 [Part 1]), 12 May 1970, p. 3.

29. William A. Hance, "Three Economies," *Africa Report* 12 (November 1967): 23-30; and Frank Brandenburg, "Transport Systems and Their External Ramifications," in Abshire and Samuels, *Portuguese Africa,* pp. 320-44.

30. Irene S. van Dongen, "Agriculture and Other Primary Production,"

in Abshire and Samuels,*Portuguese Africa*, pp. 268-77. For details on one of these schemes see R.J. Harrison Church, "The Limpopo Scheme," *Geographical Magazine* 37 (July 1964): 212-27. Several agricultural schemes had been started primarily for Africans. The most successful was located on the flood plain of the lower Limpopo. The Inhamissa marsh was drained, and several African cooperatives were organized for the production of rice. See Ralf von Gersdorff, "Endeavor and Achievement of Cooperatives in Mozambique," *The Journal of Negro History* 45 (April 1960): 116-25.

31. United Nations, General Assembly, Special Committee..., *Mozambique: Background Paper Prepared by the Secretariat* (A/AC.108/L.8), 16 October 1962, p. 48; and *Working Paper* (A/AC.109/L. 538/Add. 2), 15 April 1969, p. 8.

32. Bailey, "Native and Labor Policy," pp. 165-77; Marvin Harris, "Labour Emigration Among the Thonga: Cultural and Political Factors," *Africa* 29 (January 1959): 23-30; and A. Rita-Ferreira, "Comments on a Study by Marvin Harris," *Africa* 30 (April 1960): 141-52.

33. The inequalities of wages can be seen in the following figures: In 1962 the average industrial wage was 4,104 *escudos* ($205) for Africans, but 47,541 *escudos* ($2,377) for Europeans. Moreover, Europeans, who comprised only 10 percent of the power supply workers and 2 percent of the miners received 64 and 19 percent, respectively, of the wages paid in those industries. Even in agricultural work, where wages were low for both Europeans and Africans, the former received 5,837 *escudos* ($291) per annum and the latter 2,151 *escudos* ($107) per annum. See United Nations, General Assembly, Special Committee..., *Working Paper* (A/AC.109/L.625/Add.2 [Part 1]), 12 May 1970, p. 13.

34. James Duffy, *A Question of Slavery: Labour Policies in Portuguese Africa and the British Protest, 1850-1920* (Cambridge: Harvard University Press, 1967), pp. 154-55.

35. Mondlane, *Struggle for Mozambique*, p. 105.

36. Frente de Libertacao de Mocambique (FRELIMO), *Curso Político* (Dar es Salaam: Escola de Formação de Quadros Políticos Militares Revolucionarios, n.d.), p. 72.

37. Ibid., p. 72. Although the precise cause of the split will never be known, competition for leadership positions probably took place along racial lines and caused the group to divide as these positions came to be occupied by mulattos over Africans.

38. Ibid., p. 73.

39. Quoted in Mondlane, *Struggle for Mozambique*, pp. 106-107. See also FRELIMO, *Curso Político*, p. 72.

40. Ibid., p. 73, indicates that in spite of the importance of these collectivities for the development of the nationalist movement, their effectiveness was curtailed by: 1) the bourgeois mentality of the members; 2) their location in the cities, which effectively excluded the great majority

of Africans who lived in rural areas; and 3) their Portuguese-recognized legality, which left them open to manipulation.

41. See Walter C. Opello, Jr., "Cognitive Inconsistency Among Some Mozambican Revolutionaries," *Journal of Social Psychology* 102 (June 1977): 73-77. For corroborating evidence on this point from Angola, see Douglas L. Wheeler, "An Early Angolan Protest: The Radical Journalism of José de Fontes Pereira (1823-1891)," in *Protest and Power in Black Africa,* ed. Robert I. Rotberg and Ali A. Mazrui (New York: Oxford University Press, 1970), pp. 854-74.

42. Chilcote, "Mozambique: The African Nationalist Response," p. 189.

43. Ibid.; FRELIMO, *Boletim Nacional* 21 (June 1965): 10, reports that Craveirinha, Honwana, Nogar, Malangatana, and others were arrested by the Portuguese in 1965. Many of those detained were members of the Centro Associativo dos Negros da Província de Moçambique, the Núcleo dos Estudantes Africanos Secundárias de Moçambique, and the Associação Africano. The Centro Associativo is reported to have been a front for the nationalist movement which was just being organized in Tanzania. For details see "Portuguese Seize 14 in Mozambique," *New York Times,* 31 May 1965; Virgílio de Lemos, "La Persécution des Intellectuels et des Artistes au Mozambique," *Vie Africaine* 58 (May 1965): 16-18; and "O Tribunal Militar Condenou Sete dos Novo Reus Acusados de Actividades Subservisas," *Diário* (Lourenço Marques), 11 November 1966.

44. Mondlane, *Struggle for Mozambique,* pp. 115-17.

45. Frederick G. Whelan, "The Rationale of Revolution: Origins of Insurgency in Mozambique" (senior thesis, Department of Government, Harvard College, 1969).

46. On dissension over colonial policy and clandestine revolutionary activity in Portugal see Marvin Howe, "Portugal at War: Hawks, Doves, and Owls," *Africa Report* 14 (November 1969): 18; Douglas L. Wheeler, "Anti-Imperial Traditions in Portugal Yesterday and Today," *Boston University Graduate School Graduate Journal* 12 (Spring 1964): 125-37; and United Nations, General Assembly, Special Committee..., *Working Paper* (A/AC.109/L.388), 21 March 1967, pp. 13-14; and *Working Paper* (A/AC.109/L.690) 26 March 1971, pp. 23-25.

47. Whelan, "The Rationale of Revolution," p. 172.

48. Brenden F. Jundanian, "The Mozambique Liberation Front," Memoire Présenté pour la Diplome de l'Institut, Institut Universitaire de Haute Études Internationales, Geneva, July 1965, pp. 15-16.

49. Mondlane, *Struggle for Mozambique,* pp. 113-14; see also FRELIMO, *Boletim Nacional* 21 (June 1965): 10, for a list of detainees.

50. Mondlane, *Struggle for Mozambique,* pp. 113-14. Among the students who met at the Casa dos Estudantes do Império were the future top leadership of the various nationalist movements in the colonies:

Walter C. Opello

Amílcar Cabral of the Partido Africano da Independencia da Guiné e Cabo Verde (PAIGC), Mário Andrade and Agostinho Neto of the Movimento Popular de Libertação de Angola (MPLA), and Eduardo Mondlane and Marcelino dos Santos of FRELIMO.

51. Marcum, *The Angolan Revolution*, pp. 195-96. Eduardo Mondlane, "The Struggle for Independence in Mozambique," *Presence Africaine* 20 (Fourth Quarter 1963): 36, says that Gwambe had been an agent of the Portuguese secret police sent to spy on his fellow Mozambicans in Southern Rhodesia, but later decided to throw in his lot with the exiles.

52. Marcum, *The Angolan Revolution*, p. 196; Chilcote, *Portuguese Africa*, p. 119, however, says that MANU was founded in Mombassa. George M. Chilambe, "The Struggle in Mozambique,"*East African Journal* 4 (July 1966): 3-8; and Uria T. Simango, "The Liberation Struggle in Mozambique," *The African Communist* 32 (First Quarter 1968): 54, suggest that MANU was established in 1959 in Tanganyika, probably in Dar es Salaam. *New York Times*, 20 February 1961, reports that the conference establishing MANU was headed by Michael Chockwe.

53. Marcum, *The Angolan Revolution*, p. 198. In addition to UDENAMO, MANU, and UNAMI, a number of small movements reportedly existed during this period. See "Mozambique Prepares for Revolution," *Africa Today* 9 (November 1962): 8; Chilcote, "Mozambique: The African Nationalist Response," p.190; and United Nations, General Assembly, Special Committee.... *Mozambique* (A/AC.108/L.8), 16 October 1962, p. 11.

54. Marcum, *The Angolan Revolution*, pp. 216-44.

55. Mondlane, *Struggle for Mozambique*, pp. 122-23.

56. Marcum, "Three Revolutions," pp. 20-21.

57. On the fighting, see Walter C. Opello, Jr., "Guerrilla War in Portuguese Africa: An Assessment of the Balance of Force in Mozambique," *Issue: A Quarterly Journal of Africanist Opinion* 4 (Summer 1974): 29-37.

58. On the work of the Institute see Janet Rae Mondlane, "The Mozambique Institue (Instituto Maçambicano)," Dar es Salaam, 1963; and "Mozambique and the Mozambique Institue," Dar es Salaam, 1972.

59. Mondlane, *Struggle for Mozambique*, pp. 129-30.

60. Ibid., p. 167.

61. Ibid., pp. 183-84.

62. Michael A. Samuels, "The FRELIMO School System," *Africa Today* 18 (July 1971): 69-73. See also "National Reconstruction," *Mozambique Revolution* 40 (September 1969), pp. 38-39. For an example of FRELIMO's educational publications, see their textbook for the 4th level, *História de Moçambique, Livro de História para 4a Classe* (Dar es Salaam: Departmento de Educação e Cultura de Frente de Libertação de Moçambique, August 1971).

63. "National Reconstruction," pp. 40-41; and "Education in Free

Mozambique: Report on Tete's First Pilot School," *Mozambique Revolution* 46 (January-April 1971): 4-7.

64. Rev. Edward A. Hawley, "Refugees in Kenya Formerly Affiliated with Liberation Movements," Joint Refugee Service of Kenya, Nairobi, 1971, p. 4.

65. Mondlane, *Struggle for Mozamibique*, p. 186.

66. "National Reconstruction," pp. 47-48.

67. Ibid., 50. See also Samora M. Machel, *Produzir e Aprender, Aprender para Produzir é Lutar Melhor* (Dar es Salaam: FRELIMO, Departmento de Informação e Propaganda, Colocção "Estudos e Orientações," October 1971).

68. Details on these administrative departments can be found in Mondlane, *Struggle for Mozambique*, pp. 168-70.

69. Ibid., p. 171. The President and Vice-President were elected by the Congress on the recommendation of the Central Committee. They held office from Congress to Congress. A Congress was supposed to be held every four years.

70. For more details, see Walter C. Opello, Jr., "Pluralism and Elite Conflict in an Independence Movement: FRELIMO in the 1960s," *Journal of Southern African Studies* 2 (October 1975): 66-82.

71. There is very strong circumstantial evidence, however, that toward the end of the fighting, incidents of torture by both sides increased, and that special units of Portugal's army massacred innocent civilians at several locations in Mozambique, especially at the village of Wyriamu. *Manchester Guardian Weekly*, 18 May 1974; *New York Times*, 11 May 1974; and Adrian Hastings, *Wyriamu* (Nairobi: Transafrica Publishers, 1974).

72. John Saul, "African Peasants and Revolution," *Review of African Political Economy* 1 (August-November 1974): 41-68.

73. During the interim between the coup in Portugal and full independence, Mozambique was governed by a provisional government comprised of FRELIMO and Portuguese personnel.

74. Barbara Barnes, "Creating A National Culture: An Overview," *Issue: A Quarterly Journal of Africanist Opinion* 8 (Spring 1978): 36-37.

75. Chris Searle, " 'Escola Nova': The New Secondary School in Mozambique," *Issue: A Quarterly Journal of Africanist Opinion* 8 (Spring 1978): 33-34. See also Delegation from Maputo to the Conference of Ministers of Education of African Member States of U.N.E.S.C.O., Lagos, 27 January to 4 February 1976, "Education Policy in the People's Republic of Mozambique," *Journal of Modern African Studies* 14 (June 1976): 331-39.

76. Searle, "Escola Nova," p. 32.

77. Carole Collins, "Mozambique: Dynamizing the People," *Issue: A Quarterly Journal of Africanist Opinion* 8 (Spring 1978): 12-16.

78. Allen Isaacman, "Mozambique Since Independence," *Africa Report*

23 (July-August 1978): 6.

79. Allen Isaacman, "Transforming Mozambique's Rural Economy," *Issue: A Quarterly Journal of Africanist Opinion* 8 (Spring 1978): 19-21.

80. Ibid., pp. 21-22.

81. Collins, "Mozambique," pp. 15-16.

82. Stephanie Urdang,"'Precondition for Victory': Women's Liberation in Mozambique and Guinea-Bissau," *Issue: A Quarterly Journal of Africanist Opinion* 8 (Spring 1978): 29-30.

83. René Lefort, "Liberated Mozambique," *Monthly Review* 28 (December 1976): 32-35.

84. Ibid., pp. 33-34.

85. "African Update," *Africa Report* 20 (January-February 1975): 33, and 21 (May-June 1976): 33.

86. An army mutiny of about four hundred soldiers was put down within twenty-four hours. *New York Times,* 19 and 20 December 1975.

87. See Isaacman, "Transforming Mozambique's Rural Economy," p. 20.

88. Urdang, "Precondition for Victory," p. 30.

89. *Africa Research Bulletin,* Political, Social, and Cultural Series 14 (15 June 1977): 4428.

90. Robin Wright, "Spreading the Revolution," The Alicia Patterson Foundation, 12 May 1975.

91. Lefort, "Liberated Mozambique," pp. 36-39.

92. Charles L. Geshekter, "Independent Mozambique and Its Neighbors: Now What?," *Africa Today* 22 (July-September 1975): 21-36.

9

Prospects for Reactionary and Revolutionary Change in Zimbabwe

Kevin Maguire

In this chapter the processes and prospects of reactionary versus revolutionary change in Zimbabwe-Rhodesia will be assessed in an analysis of the state of the goal attainment system of that society, including its legitimation, integrative, adaptive, and goal attainment subsystems. The political support and legitimation interchanges will also be analyzed; included in this analysis is a presentation of survey findings relevant to some of my conclusions concerning control factors in the patterns of political legitimation and support. Limited space prohibits an analysis of the resource mobilization interchange. My discussion will focus on an assessment of the forces operative in each subsystem and interchange for and against a system dominated and directed by three types of governing coalitions: settler dominant, Zimbabwean neo-colonial, and Zimbabwean revolutionary. Analysis of the settler system will focus on an explantion for the Rhodesian Front (RF)'s failure to secure racial supremacy. A Zimbabwean neo-colonial coalition would be a Zimbabwean nationalist government dependent on international capital and therefore devoted to forestalling revolutionary outcomes; while a revolutionary coalition would strive for socialist self-reliance and therefore would be necessarily directed toward the overthrow of the settler regime or a neo-colonial system evolved from that regime.

The settler dominant system is represented by the newly formed internal settlement, Rhodesia-Zimbabwe government led by Prime Minister Bishop Abel Muzorewa. Since this new "constitutional" order serves to perpetuate the Rhodesian racial supremacy system and is wholly dependent upon Rhodesian (European) support for its existence, we continue to refer to this system as "Rhodesia." It is conceivable, but not probable, that Muzorewa's government might attempt to articulate more authentically the Zimbabwean nationalist cause by aligning with one of the two nationalist groups. With an almost nonexistent structural basis (mobilized military and political collectivities) for exercising power and influence, Muzorewa would have little to offer in exchange for an alliance with either of the Zimbabwean nationalist movements. As the Rhodesian power bases continue to erode, Muzorewa might seek such an alliance; however, his willingness to accept South African aid would suggest that the Bishop would be more likely to fill the European gap through a South African intervention. It is also conceivable, but equally improbable, that the settlers might facilitate, over a period of years, the transformation of the Rhodesian racial supremacy system into a Zimbabwean neo-colonial system. My conclusion on the basis of the analysis that follows is that Rhodesia will continue to fail to secure a viable racial supremacy. Only massive intervention could maintain the settler system. I do not analyze such an eventuality because predicting the outcome of an escalated, internationalized conflict in Southern Africa is beyond the purview of this chapter and the capabilities of its author.

An authentic neo-colonial Zimbabwe does not exist, but it could be facilitated by a governing coalition between the Zimabawe African People's Union (ZAPU), led by the popular nationalist, Joshua Nkomo, and the newly created settlement regime. According to my definitional criteria, ZAPU would have to be the dominant partner in a Zimbabwean neo-colonial outcome. Even though the patterns of resource mobilization in Zimbabwe would continue to benefit international and domestic European capital, the establishment of a Zimbabwe national regime requires at least the capacity to exercise some control over the society's goal attainment subsystem. In short, some degree of political, if not economic, independence is stipulated by definition. I conclude that such a Zimbabwean neo-colonial coalition is unlikely, and that even if it were to eventuate, it would not be a viable system.

Revolutionary Zimbabwe is potentially represented by the Zimbabwe African National Union (ZANU), led by Robert Mugabe. ZANU exercises power and influence throughout the Eastern regions of Zimbabwe in a structure apparently based on revolutionary, Marxist-Leninist principles. Since I do not have access to either actual ZANU operations in the liberated areas or primary documents on organizational, policy, and ideological principles, my empirical reference points are derived from secondary sources, while my analysis is based on statements about the necessary conditions for revolutionary change. These statements also represent an agenda for development and indicate concrete obstacles to revolutionary transformation. Revolutionary transformation would involve a fundamental change in all functional subsystems, structural levels, and media of exchange that would commit Zimbabweans to the values of democratization, equalization, and communal self-sufficiency.

The division of the Zimbabwean nationalist movement into two armed, mobilized collectivities, even though they are loosely and tensely aligned within the Patriotic Front, remains the single greatest obstacle to the facilitation of a revolutionary outcome. However, I conclude that factors facilitating and controlling for a revolutionary Zimbabwean outcome outweigh factors facilitating and controlling for either the perpetuation of the settler supremacy system or a Zimbabwean neo-colonial outcome.

The central issue dividing the Rhodesian government and the Zimbabwean nationalists revolves around who will govern. The fragile alliance between ZAPU and ZANU, the Patriotic Front, is cemented by a common nationalist stance on the governance issue. The central issue dividing ZAPU and ZANU, however, is whether capital accumulation occurs as a continuation of economic dependency and internal inequality derived from growth without development, or by means of economic self-reliance and the equality derived from a socialist plan of growth for development. Thus revolutionary change is the process of transforming the system of privilege and *all* of its political, economic, social, and cultural manifestations. Reactionary change involves the slight expansion of privileged status to co-opted and incorporated African nationalist elites (settler dominant), or the actual displacement of the settler class by an indigenous comprador class (Zimbabwean neo-colonialism).

Historical Development of the European Dominant System

Settler legitimating options have been played out through successive stages that have vacillated between not very distant poles of exclusion and inclusion (C3b). The exclusionary two-tiered, parallel development stage (1923-1948) would not suffice in an age of anticolonialism. The partnership stage (1948-1962) was too much of a dangerous solution for the European electorate, and too little too late to satisfy Zimbabwean nationalists. The RF's initial strategy of establishing a secure settler base in an exclusionary, preemptive police state (1962-1978), while holding out for opportunities to win external recognition, has been modified. Now government and society are to be based on an inclusive formula that goes far beyond the earlier version of partnership, but still falls far short of Zimbabwean expectations.

The 1962 electoral victory of the RF gave them control of an autonomous but not a sovereign state system. They shared with the former United Federal Party (UFP) government a fundamental commitment to achieving settler sovereignty in order to protect European privileges; however, their techniques differed radically. While the UFP government temporized and negotiated the independence issue with Britain, the RF dallied only briefly, issued a unilateral declaration of independence (UDI), and then negotiated the independence issue. The UFP government had expanded on an authoritarian colonial system with the addition of some internal security legislation, the suppression of overt dissent, and the courting of black bourgeois partners. The new RF regime immediately set about establishing an extensive and elaborate police state, a super-exploitative corporate capitalist economy, and a preemptive political economy involving a conscious and systematic combination of political, economic, strategic, and administrative policies aimed at preempting any African challenge. While the former governments engaged in preventive reactionary responses to African nationalist initiatives, the RF took preemptive reactionary measures to preclude all African initiatives (C3, C3b).

The emergence of the RF was fostered by the UFP's attempts to facilitate changes under the rubric of "partnership" between the races. This caused increasing value-normative dissonance among the European electorate and an incongruence between this electorate and the government party's policies, a dissonance that would take on more significance as the Zimbabwean challenge appeared more threatening (E2, E4). The UFP lost European and African support because of weaknesses endemic in its established elitist mechanisms of political integration. The RF's mobilization of the European electorate through the apparatus of an active, differentiated political party proved to be superior to the UFP's mobilization capacities (C3a), and the shift of African politicization from reformism to militant nationalism deprived the former government of critical African votes (C2). Evidence for the integrative weakness and decline of support for UFP policies emerged by the 1958 election, although the UFP's electoral success in the 1961 constitutional referendum obfuscated the political change that would emerge in the 1962 election. However, it should be recognized that the UFP very nearly won the 1962 election, and that it was not until after the RF gained political power and effectively manipulated public opinion (primarily in terms of fostering a seige mentality and raising questions about racial solidarity and survival) that the near totality of European support for the RF was achieved.

Thus the Rhodesian Front's countermobilization represented more than the presentation of policy alternatives on the independence and race issues. By parlaying these issues into questions about the capacity of the old elite to preserve basic racial values, and by effectively mobilizing the electorate, the RF successfully challenged and replaced the manner in which governmental decisions were made.

The RF's failure to facilitate an exclusionary legitimating strategy forced them to adopt the latest, more "liberal" version of the partnership legitimating strategy, which obfuscates the most extreme form of coercive oppression ever experienced by Zimbabweans. The settler regime has escalated the overtly violent and terroristic dimensions of its formerly less militarized political-administrative strategy of preempting Zimbabwean mobilization. Thus the Muzorewa government represents a last ditch effort to rationalize a settler system so wholly devoid of authority that it can only be precariously maintained by warring against most of its own subjects.

Because the RF had not succeeded in building a secure power foundation for a preemptory police state, they were pressured into an internal settlement in which political control over the settler police state is symbolically shared in a coalition with moderate black "nationalists." Factors inhibiting the regime's attempts to facilitate an exclusionary racial supremacy system came from several sources:
1. The elusiveness of settler sovereignty based on exclusionary constitutional formulae.
2. The radically changed geo-political regional situation resulting from the collapse of the Portuguese empire and the establishment of a revolutionary regime in Mozambique (B1).
3. The success of African nationalist movements in establishing a military challenge to the settler regime (C2).
4. The diplomatic efforts of transnational and South African capitalists and their respective governments, who preferred a negotiated settlement once they realized that a neo-colonial, or what is commonly called a Kenyan solution, was more amenable to producing profits on investments and more efficacious in avoiding revolutionary confrontations than the continuation of an undiluted settler supremacy (B1).

The pursuit of settler sovereignty has been constantly frustrated by its lack of legitimacy. Rhodesia's illegitimacy is the necessary controlling condition for:
1. The mobilization of Zimbabwean dissent and its gradual translation into outright warfare (C2).
2. The continuous failure to achieve international recognition and legitimation.
3. The reversal of the RF's exclusionary policy and return to a "partnership" type of legitimating strategy to cover for ever more extreme forms of oppression.
4. The erosion of the European will to resist.

Power is controlled by legitimacy; but no legitimating formula can logically reconcile the integrity of settler supremacy with the goals of Zimbabwean nationalism. Numerous deceptive and projective formulations have been put forward that would appear to reconcile these contradictory forces, the latest being the internal settlement.

The Political Subsystems

Our discussion of the political or goal attainment system is analytically divided into four internal functional subsystems: pattern socialization and control, adaptive, integrative, and goal attainment. The political system developed by the RF and the internal settlement regime and the constraints inhibiting its further development will be discussed according to these analytic categories. Parallel analyses of neo-colonial and revolutionary outcomes will be organized within the same format.

The Legitimation Subsystem

Legitimation by the pattern socialization and control subsystem within the political system is achieved either through the operation of institutionalized decision making rules for politically relevant actors, or in more tenuous ways through charismatic leadership. An institutionalized constitutional order regulates and directs political and governmental activities. For the European sector, former Prime Minister Ian Smith's charisma may be as important as any codified constitutional order, especially in light of the tenuous, short life span of the products of Rhodesia's prolific constitutional engineering. Constitutionalism as a normative order applies loosely to the operation of the civil service (except for the Ministry of Interior which operates as a paramilitary apparatus in the Tribal Trust Lands). It also applies in some general ways to the judiciary and to representative institutions such as Parliament and elections, and legitimizes the form, if not the substance, of other civil and procedural rights. European property rights derived from the expropriation of Zimbabwean land and labor are sacrosanct; Africans have no security in land tenure anywhere in Rhodesia. As a matter of fact, Rhodesian constitutionalism has never inhibited the governmental exercise of power over its Zimbabwean subjects. Now that martial law officially sanctions the army's unrestrained, terroristic attacks on the indigeneous people, Rhodesian constitutionalism is wholly devoid of meaning for Zimbabweans (C5). Since Rhodesian constitutions have always served as legal instruments of entrenched racial privilege, they have failed as mechanisms for institutionalizing conflict resolution between blacks and whites (C5a and b).

The 1969 constitution, and two other constitutional enactments of 1969—the Electoral Act and the Land Tenure Act—provide clear evidence of the RF's intentions to reverse the direction of political change from partnership and multiracialism to undiluted racial supremacy, separate development, and the establishment of a preemptory rather than reacting police state. Rhodesia's foremost constitutional scholar, Claire Palley, indicates that the above-mentioned constitutional instruments were based on a systematic, coherent theory of power maximization designed for controlling every facet of African life. They were aimed at the establishment of a separate development system contained within a phony devolution of authority to chiefs and other traditional leaders, labeled euphemistically as community development and provincialization; these instruments were a return to the earlier policy of parallel development elaborated along lines that were principally an imitation of South Africa's apartheid system without, however, any hope of even a

Bantustan status (C3a).[1] The distance between the *baaskap* constitutional principles of 1969 and the "majority rule" principle of the 1978 internal settlement constitution obviously demonstrates the government's incapacity to achieve a racially exclusive preemptive police state. Even though the new constitution guarantees the preservation of European political and economic power for another ten years, the new provisions represent a reversal in direction, a clear concession that neither the settlers' power nor their manipulation of legitimating facades prevented a Zimbabwean mobilization against the class of privileged Rhodesians (E4).

The settlement constitution serves several purposes besides winning international recognition and maintaining the support of powerful allies in South Africa, Britain, and the United States. Most obviously, it provides legal assurance of both continued European control of the state and the perpetuation of their privileged status. The latter is accomplished by the absolute inviolability of property rights, which freezes property and class relationships. With at least a quarter of the Cabinet posts ensured for at least five years, control over all major state institutions (civil service, military, police, and the judiciary) for ten years, and a veto over constitutional amendments, the Europeans will continue to run the country. A corollary objective is to provide a democratic facade that is designed for paralysis. Historically, ruling elites have usually fragmented and thereby emasculated decision making institutions before making them accessible to broader sectors of the society: it is a simple and obvious application of the divide and rule principle. Finally, the constitution serves as a dilatory tactic for a dependency regime attempting to assure its international capitalist sponsors that progress is being made toward a neo-colonial solution, while simultaneously holding out for a favorable shift in the political climate in those patron, capitalist countries. All three principal settlement leaders, former Prime Minister Smith, "Prime-Minister" Muzorewa, and the former nationalist leader, the Reverend Ndabaningi Sithole, have visited the United States to contribute to that shift.

Finally, the constitutional principles of civilian control of the military and state monopoly over the use of "legitimate" force are purposely violated by Smith's support of private armies for both Muzorewa and Sithole (C3). This ploy fosters violent conflict among Zimbabwean groups and alienates the population from the struggle for freedom, consequently debilitating that struggle as it did during the initial mobilization of the Zimbabwean challenge in the early 1960s (A2a). It also provides plenty of grisly material for the western news media, most of which keenly and consistently distort and debase the liberation struggles in Africa. Worst of all, it provides a blue print for the structural fission of a disintegrating state. As violence escalates in this staged pandemonium, the propensity for the military to stage a coup increases, as does the probability of foreign intervention to protect European lives and property and to facilitate stability and security for foreign investments. With increased use of mercenaries and the deterioration of civil order, the military may well become a praetorian guard and/or disintegrate altogether as a coherent state institution (E1).

As long as the Patriotic Front remains united on rejecting participation in a "settlement" deal, no African political group, least of all Muzorewa's United African National Council (UANC), will be capable of forming a government with any semblance of legitimacy. The only combination of factors that could keep a UANC "government" reigning for any time would be Anglo-American recognition, substantially more overt support by core capitalist states, and probably South African intervention.

A neo-colonial Zimbabwe would initially adopt a written constitution, perhaps even the "settlement" constitution, as a democratic facade that would hide its real nature as a self-serving dependent client of external capital, just as past and present Rhodesian constitutions have been attempts to conceal the fact that narrow race and class interests were served at the expense of general interests. The constitutional myth that confuses personal and productive property rights is a critical liberal mechanism for rationalizing wide disparities in material well-being. For a brief while, principles of representative government, political equality, and civil and procedural rights might be espoused; but on the periphery of capitalism, in a society with an effective revolutionary movement, it will not work. These institutions would so blatantly serve the interests of the few, and would be so remote from the needs of the masses, that legitimacy would be denied to them because they would not be credible. Consequently, repressive instruments of state power (bureaucratic and coercive) would be elaborated while legitimation and support institutions atrophied (C5).

A revolutionary Zimbabwean outcome (i.e., the establishment of a regime serving the needs and interests of the proletariat and the peasants) directed by ZANU would be less concerned initially with formal constitutional principles, since its legitimating charter would be the maximization of economic and social equality. Revolutionary ideology clearly recognizes that bourgeois rights may be guaranteed to the individual, but that the power to exercise and make meaningful such rights derives from control over the means of production, the work process, and the product. The major difficulty with establishing a new socialist democratic order on the foundation of a producers' democracy is that the revolutionary party may succumb to an elitism that increasingly expropriates the social product and reverses the process toward social democratization (C5, D2, D5, E3, E4). Only general adherence to revolutionary values and norms can prevent this from happening in the long run.

The Integrative and Adaptive Subsystems

Integrative and adaptive functional subsystems within the Rhodesian political system—the governmental, party and bureaucratic mechanisms, respectively—will be discussed as the failure of the RF to facilitate an effective preemptory police state. Palley, in the works cited above, mentions that the RF possessed a coherent scheme of power maximization, and her analysis of the RF constitution characterizes many components of such a scheme. However, she neither identifies what this RF theory of power was, nor systematically relates it to her exegesis of RF legal instruments. I suggest that this theory was a strategy of political development by inversion, an exercise in preemptive politics (C3).

The principle of this strategy was no more complex than strengthening yourself by weakening your enemy, although the RF developed this simple principle into a rather elaborate combination of programs aimed at systematically preempting the development of dissident African capabilities rather than just weakening their opponents through the repression of overt dissent. The latter strategy would not distinguish the RF from previous administrations; the former clearly did. If power means the capacity to take action, to initiate, to generate motion in order to achieve collective goals, then obviously preemptive power is used to deny the target group the capacity to act collectively on behalf of group goals. The choice of separate "development" may have been, as Palley indicates, natural enough for the RF given its electoral mandate, settler race attitudes, and ideological proximity to South Africa, from which this political formula was borrowed (B2, C1, D1).[2] More important motives and critical objectives were involved in dumping and encapsulating Africans in "traditional," impoverished settings: separate development was a significant component of preempting African dissidence, an inverted development strategy. A regime that so consciously pursues "growth without development" economically must pursue a corollary political strategy of "the development of underdevelopment."

Some preemptive pay offs result from simply repressing overt dissent: killing or incarcerating Zimbabwean leaders, particularly bridge elites, taxes the training capacity of a dissident organization, and represents, at least temporarily, what might be metaphorically characterized as an organizational decapitation (C6d). A government's use of informers sows the seeds of distrust, which in turn breaks down political communication, fragments the scope of loyalties, undermines socio-political organization, and stifles overt political dissidence (C6e). Other preemptive effects do not require any conscious, concerted effort by the ruling elites; they are the logical consequences of the social stratification and conditioning which the regime supports. For example, the ruling class in the United States generally does not have to conspire in an overt way to repress dissident free speech because: ideological hegemony precludes the necessary consciousness; lack of democratic praxis in most institutions and organizations precludes the personal atributes (efficacy, verbal skills, etc.) necessary for exercising such individual rights; the wide disparity in the distribution of resources, particularly in this case mass media resources, precludes the nonelite's effective access to the public and to governmental decision makers; and the control over life opportunities by dominant class interests encourages conformity rather than confrontation. Conflict and confrontation constantly emerge, yet under most circumstances the aforementioned controls suffice to contain dissidence without repression. In the super-exploititive periphery, allocative processes provide such meager benefits to so few that a regime cannot count on the natural suppressive workings of social stratification. It must rely on overt repression to divide, demobilize, and depoliticize its opposition.

The RF has found it rather easy, given the smallness, the homogeneity, and the increasing desperateness of the European community, to crystalize settler solidarity in support of the most drastic and harsh measures to secure their privileges. Despite class, linguistic, or particularistic interests operating occasionally at cross purposes, the leadership of these divergent groups recognized a common interest in a strategy that diminished the Zimbabwean challenge (C5). The settler society possesses all the ingredients of nation-class consciousness: with an apparent common interest as the beneficiaries of an exploitive economy and a shared, distinct conquest culture, they have been politically mobilized to protect against the common threat to their privileged status (A2, A5).

The RF, having initially crystalized and fostered this class consciousness to gain control of the settler state, has in turn used this class identity to achieve a high level of political integration. The RF has advanced its electoral strength among Europeans in each election since 1962. Intraparty opposition from the right has neither threatened the leadership within the party nor challenged its electoral supremacy through significant splinter parties. Opposition from the center or "left" has posed even less of a challenge. Ian Smith's leadership has continually grown more preeminent and predominant. High levels of political integration expand the flexibility and the authority of the political elite to discover a political formula that best serves settler interests. For example, 85 percent of the vote in the January 1979 "internal settlement" referendum supported constitutional proposals diametrically opposed to the undiluted racial supremacy system formerly fostered by the RF. The RF's manipulation of a siege mentality has paid off in European electoral support, but as the Zimbabwean revolutionary mobilization increasingly challenges the regime, these manipulated feelings of fear and anxiety are more likely to be translated into white flight than into a long, hard fight for a system no longer capable of providing a secure base for the enjoyment of privileged racial status (C5).

Thus separate development, in either its apartheid or provincialized version, is a strategy of preemptive power for neo-colonial or settler societies. Separate development is not a theory of race relations, except in the sense that all such theories of human relations (racist, sexist, elitist, etc.) are rationalizations for exploitive human relations. The "development of underdevelopment" has both political and economic dimensions: separate development is a preemptive power strategy designed as a solution to the problem of super-exploitation. European integration is political growth, while Zimbabwean disintegration is the development of underdevelopment.

The RF's failure to facilitate an effective preemptive system cannot be attributed to a lack of effort; even the more extreme second stage version of the preemptive strategy (strategic hamlets, free fire zones, and preemptive strikes against external bases) has failed to achieve the regime's purposes. The following factors provide some explanation of the government's failure:

1. Revivalism or retraditionalization, which is the basis of separate development and critical to the accomplishment of preemptive incapacitation, is based on the fundamentally flawed "Sambo" assumption that most Africans are either encapsulated in backward, traditional village life, or are so slightly removed from such a condition as peasant workers that they are easily returned to it.[3] Rural Africans are not "country bumpkins"; peasants can and are being mobilized for revolutionary guerrilla warfare; and communication networks linking the dispersed Zimbabwean population are relatively immune to both the regime's control over modern media and its attempts at rupturing communication channels through population concentration and dispersal (C2). In this case the settlers were victims of their own racial stereotyping.

2. For provincialization to work, the chiefs had to serve as the critical link, the bridge elites, between the rural population and the governmental bureaucracy (D1). But as a number of government reports and scholarly works have indicated,[4] chiefs could not reconcile their conflicting roles as both petty administrators of an oppressive regime and leaders of their people; chiefs possessed little authority for significant segments of the rural population; they were not respected by the government; and they had not been granted any real administrative power, since the exercise of officially invested powers was always in reality limited by the discretion of the local District Commissioner. In fact, a chief's status was enhanced greatly by opposition to the regime.

3. The Zimbabwean nationalists have been able to escape the full thrust of the regime's preemptive strategy in training and operational bases

which are protected from the regime's constant disruptive tactics, if not beyond the regime's capacity for occasional preemptive strikes. With only a brief respite for the development of their organizational integrity, the Zimbabwean cause was rejoined in political and military guerrilla operations launched by ZANU in the east and more conventional military raids and acts of sabotage by ZAPU in the north and west. Existence of such levels of mobilization meant that the regime's strategy had failed the critical test of preventing the mobilization of Zimbabwean dissidence; consequently, the Rhodesian government faced what they knew they had to avoid: a general dispersed rebellion that overextended their military and intelligence resources, a large part of the land and people liberated by a revolutionary movement, and a high attrition rate among Europeans (A2, C2, C5, C6, E1).

Party, government, and bureaucratic institutions in a neo-colonial Zimbabwe would represent the dominant economic interests combined in a coalition consisting of white capital (domestic and international), the African and Asian bourgeoisie (service employees of the public and parastatal sector, small capital operative/owners in industry, commerce, agriculture, and services), and perhaps the leadership of a few favored "tribal" groupings. Political integration would deteriorate as a consequence of an allocative process that would reflect and promote dominant economic interests, perpetuate inequality and super-exploitation, and provoke increasing resistance (C5). Regime stability would require preemptive outcomes aimed at demobilization, depoliticization, and deliberate division of the population, which would be reflected in the decline of popular institutions. To the extent that popular institutions like the nationalist party and representative assemblies would continue to exist, their functions would be focused exclusively on consensus formation (C3, A1-4). Governmental and bureaucratic institutions would become increasingly centralized, personalized, and coercive. Public policy would be produced through cynical and corrupt bargains, struck at the expense of the virtually powerless masses. Assuming that the Zimbabwean revolutionary forces would survive the capture of state power by an "anti-revolutionary reformist" regime, they would increasingly recover whatever mobilizing momentum they had lost as alienation spread to all sectors of the society. The military, if it maintained its organizational integrity, would be inclined to carry out a coup. As the military's capacity to maintain the integrity of the state declined, military and coercive functions would be internationalized. More than likely, arrangements with the South African police and military would be retained by a neo-colonial government, so the possibilities for internationalizing the military could begin directly with the transfer of power. The Rhodesian government would transfer intact a bureaucratic system monopolized by European staff and an army dominated by Europeans in command positions with Africans trained and indoctrinated by a reactionary regime.

ZAPU's more conventional internal structure and ideology would be more compatible with such a system than ZANU's revolutionary, guerrilla structure and ideology (C1). Nevertheless, both ZANU and ZAPU would be faced with a critical decision whether to "smash," "integrate," or "absorb" the remnants of the state's apparatus. To smash the system, the Europeanized bureaucracy would be sent packing, ideally after accounting for appropriate records, assets, and accounts. The European and mercenary military command would be immediately supplanted (hopefully, again under controlled exit terms) by Zimbabwean nationalists (C6). African troops, some of whom would have already deserted and joined the ranks of either ZANU or ZAPU, would have to be immediately disarmed. That could pose quite a problem. The integration option would be risky, as gradual Africanization would leave control of the state in the hands of essentially antagonistic forces. Absorption of the European administrative personnel would not be an option, since rapid Africanization would be forced upon either type of regime by the large number of well-educated and trained Zimbabweans. Absorption of the Rhodesian African troops by ZAPU would at best be the culmination of a long and careful integrative process. Who would be absorbing whom would not be predictable at outset of the precess. ZANU would have to screen, supervise, detoxify, and reindoctrinate these troops carefully before admitting them to the ranks of the revolutionary army.

A neo-colonial Zimbabwean regime would probably inherit some of the settler regime's intelligence and security resources, which would be used for the same preemptive purposes. So while a capitalist, outward oriented regime would engage in most of the same preemptive techniques the settler regime is using, it would be even less likely to succeed in facilitating preemptive outcomes. The new regime would lack the level of political integration and the organizational and coercive capacities of the former regime. Neo-colonial regimes rely more on political and institutional decay and the debilitating effects of extreme deprivation and neglect than do settler regimes, which are more capable of reactionary thrusts against potential and actual dissident countermobilization.

The patterns for neo-colonial allocative processes would be similar to the settlement government's substitution of financial discrimination for racial segregation. Abolishing the Land Tenure Act and other segregative enactments and replacing them with "ability to pay"criteria would presumably provide legal equality to all. But where legal equality exists in a nonrevolutionary Zimbabwe, it will function, as some sage once observed, to prohibit equally the beggar and the rich man from sleeping under the bridge. Unequals will be treated in apparently equal ways in order to guarantee the logical, predictable unequal outcomes. As in the historical development of other capitalists countries, the political system would overtly support exploitive processes that would create great inequalities, and then would concede, under sufficient pressure, a primarily symbolic legal equality that has virtually no substantive effect on the structure of inequality.

If a neo-colonial Zimbabwe would represent and reflect the interests of a relatively small indigenous and international elite, while suppressing the mechanisms facilitating collectivity mobilization from below, a revolutionary Zimbabwe would do just the opposite: it would maximize the (political, governmental, administrative, and military) institutional mechanisms available for mobilizing and actively involving the nonelite masses of peasants, workers, and women, while suppressing the privileged power position of the elite. Reactionary regimes integrate the masses by demobilizing, depoliticizing, and denying them the collective capacities to create power and influence. Revolutionary regimes integrate the masses by mobilizing, politicizing, and expanding collective capacities to create commitments, material resources, power, and influence. Reactionary regimes pursue a preemptive strategy of political growth without development; revolutionary regimes pursue a facilitating strategy of political growth for development.

Revolutions are continuous processes; they neither begin nor end with the capture of state power. Although revolutionary principles must be embedded in all human institutions, revolutionizing the relations of production (the resource mobilization interchange) is most critical for the transformation of society. In zones liberated by ZANU, productive units, both industrial and agricultural, must be organized so that productivity is rationalized through maximizing producers' and consumers' control over the processes. Workers organized into various collectivities—cooperatives, communes, unions, women's organizations, etc.—must have maximum control over all party and state institutions. ZANU may serve as the vanguard in providing ideological and organizational leadership, but it must avoid self-serving functionaries independent of the masses(E4). If ZANU belongs to the peasants and proletariat and unites them through institutions that facilitate workers acting as a class for itself, then institutionalized elitism will be an impossibility. The party performs its revolutionary functions if party members are deeply committed to the principle of "politics in command": all collective activities are informed by the revolutionary goal of abolishing the domination, coercion, exploitation, and alienation produced by private, profit-oriented property relations and replacing them with a producers' democracy, free association, justice, and empowering labor. Once peasants and workers have recaptured their labor power, the economic foundation for a classless society will have been established; consequently, domestic counterrevolutionary forces will be incapable of sustaining themselves.

Obviously if productive·processes are to be revolutionized, the Zimbabwean revolutionary party and state must be organized according to principles that are compatible with the democraticization of production

(D1). If not, the party and the state will themselves become reactionary societal forces: the resource mobilization process will be directed away from serving broad societal needs and towards the self-serving interests of a dominant bureaucratic petty bourgeoisie.

Revolutionary organizational values and norms are against elitism and for equality; against specialization within occupations, and for personal growth and diversification; against passivity and dependence, and for activism, initiative, and collective self-reliance. Revolutionary party and state organizations struggle against artificial divisions of labor separating mental and manual labor, superordinates and subordinates, elites and masses, urban and rural, center and periphery, educated and uneducated. These struggles are not aimed at homogenization of society; diversity and pluralism find genuine expression where they are not institutionalized into strata possessing a privileged claim to societal resources. Since a revolutionary regime is not protecting an exploitive system, it does not need to depend on divisive strategies. Finally, since exploitive, profit-oriented motives are no longer the dominant principle of collective effort, alienating and exploitive practices such as "scientific management," wage slavery, and the continuous debasement of labor skills (the "Babbage Principle") are no longer necessary.[5] As work becomes more meaningful and less alienating, incentive structures based on intrinsic rather than extrinsic motivations become dominant. A revolutionary Zimbabwe's developmental strategies would value the processes of resource mobilization nearly as much as the outcome of material production. In short, revolutionary organizational principles provide institutional environments conducive to eroding the conditions and dispositions that support the tendency toward the "iron law of oligarchy," replacing them with social democratic environments conducive to a revolutionary iron law of democracy.

Under settler and neo-colonial domination, the principle of decentralization is basic to the strategy of fragmentation. Decentralization under these systems, involving no real devolution of authority, is a political-administrative formula for depoliticization and demobilization. Under a revolutionary regime, decentralization, involving authentic devolution of authority, would accomplish the regime's purpose of integration if rural and urban populations were united through a revolutionary party, government, and administration which were accountable and responsive to the people. Effective control from below requires a combination of centralized planning and decentralized, relatively autonomous productive, political, and administrative units. The incubators of democratic dispositions and skills are these local governing units that make participation meaningful through collective self-management. A vast amount of knowledge and experience with radical decentralizaiton and self-management in various countries, which could be adapted and applied to local conditions, is available to

Zimbabwean revolutionaries (A2c).[6]

The success of Zimbabwean revolutionary forces against settler and neo-colonial outcomes will depend on their capacity to forge organizational structures that match these principles within the areas they already control and in those areas where they are attempting to penetrate politically or maintain their influence. Besides providing a moral example that lends an aura of credibility and feasibility to the ideological vision, revolutionary praxis is the most effective mechanism for the generation of collective power.

In the short run, major obstacles to facilitating revolutionary political integration and administration would stem from the difficulties in overcoming the economic devastation of a protracted war and a flight of white capital and skills. These obstacles would also limit a revolutionary regime's immediate capacity to mobilize material resources that would improve the quality of life for the Zimbabwean people. However, revolutionary control over the distribution of resources would be facilitated by the Rhodesian government's tremendous expansion of state financed and state owned enterprises.

In the short run it also would be difficult to surmount the divisiveness perpetuated by colonialism and neo-colonialism. Factions, subclasses, and regional-ethnic collectivities would have a tendency to revert to the capitalist mode of behavior. Prerevolutionary regimes of both the settler and neo-colonial varieties encourage such competitive behavior because the ruling class, given their predominant power and influence, are assured that their interests remain dominant under unequal competitive conditions (E3a). A revolutionary party state obviously does not create homogeneity and end all factional conflicts. However, the rules of the game of a revolutionary regime provide competitive advantages to those least benefited under the old regimes. Moreover, given a more egalitarian distribution of resources and more effective participatory mechanisms, a more genuine pluralist politics prevails, preventing the emergence of dominant factional interests. Thus, the determination of proletariat and peasant class interests remains a political, not a dogmatically prescribed, process. However, revolutionary decision making rules differ from nonrevolutionary in that they are enlightened and informed by an ideological vision, a continuous critical analysis, and a reservoir of revolutionary praxis. Despite such guidance, difficult but fundamental developmental policy decisions, such as achieving a balance between growth, participatory, and welfare needs, must be worked out.[7] Over the longer run, revolutionary ideology, organizations, and institutions can only be sustained by transforming the pattern socialization and control subsystem so that revolutionary conciousness, critical perspectives, and radical behavior are universally distributed (D2a-c).

Change in Zimbabwe

The Goal Attainment Subsystem

The goal attainment subsystem for each type of regime will be analyzed in terms of goals, external support systems, leadership roles, and governing coalitions.

The following statement by Cecil Rhodes provides the most perceptive grasp of the primary purpose of any colonial or neo-colonial system:

> I was in the East End of London yesterday, and attended a meeting of the unemployed. I listened to the wild speeches, which were just a cry for "bread," 'bread!" and on my way home I pondered over the scene and I became more than ever convinced of the importance of imperialism. . .My cherished idea is a solution for the social problem, i.e., in order to save the 40,000,000 inhabitants of the United Kingdom from a bloody civil war, we colonial statesmen must acquire new lands to settle surplus population, to provide new markets for the goods produced in factories and mines. The Empire, as I have always said, is a bread and butter question. If you want to avoid a civil war, you must become imperialists.[8]

In short, the periphery must pay tribute to the center; otherwise the center itself may succumb to revolution. The elites within the periphery are allied with and benefit from dependence upon external capital support. International finance is in turn dependent, although not equally so, on the local elite to provide conditions favorable to the profitable exploitation of human and material resources. Consequently, settler and neo-colonial regimes have some latitude in preserving their own race and class interests, but always within the confines of a dependency relationship. Smith may have declared UDI in the face of initial opposition from the multinationals in 1962, but his regime's dependency upon international capital has deepened since that time.[9]

By contrast, the goals of a revolutionary regime are socialist self-reliance and the destruction of world-wide imperialism. The flow of benefits (all four media) under a revolutionary regime would be internal and egalitarian, the opposite of a dependency outcome. External support for revolutionary Zimbabwe comes from their natural allies in Angola, Mozambique, Tanzania, and Cuba, with both the Soviet Union and the People's Republic of China competing for influence. If Zimbabwe remains within the South African and thereby the world capitalist orbit, Angola, Mozambique, and the South West African People's Organization (SWAPO) in Namibia will be isolated, with Zimbabwe carved out as the neo-colonial spearhead. A revolutionary Zimbabwe would turn the spearhead toward South Africa by linking SWAPO, Angola, Mozambique, and Tanzania to each other, perhaps drawing Zambia and

Malawi within the revolutionary wake.

Smith's leadership role in perpetuating a settler-dominated regime is congruent with a leadership style required to preserve a dying colonial order. He is a cunning negotiator and a master in the craft of dilatory tactics. He has succeeded in the strategy of delay, exhausting every opportunity for drawing out the process of change, putting off whatever can be put off, and maximizing the time available for getting the right break. The overwhelming electoral support for the internal settlement in the January 1979 referendum suggests that Smith possesses considerable latitude in obtaining the best deal possible for the settlers. However, Smith may be too cunning and crafty for his own good: he can humiliate Muzorewa in dismissing his minister of justice, Byron Hove; he can fleece Muzorewa at the negotiating table; but he cannot gain the African support he needs for regime viability through such tactics. While it is true that Smith's shabby treatment of his African allies demonstrates how the settlers' racist stereotyping can come back to haunt them as blinders to the political sophistication of the Zimbabwean population, it is more significant to note that Smith is probably not counting that much on African support. Apparent African support, as indicated by the high voter turnout in the April 1979 elections for the internal settlement government, will be used in obtaining more Western support and possible direct South African intervention. But the latter objective would be gained primarily through a rerun of the 1962 techniques of controlled terror. Armed followers of Sithole and Muzorewa have already been unleashed on the African population, and the internal conflict will be allowed to escalate as the Rhodesian collapse approaches. The "atrocities" and general chaos will be duly reported by a sympathetic Western press to a suitably gullible and outraged public.

These conditions would provide a justification for South African intervention on a scale more massive and permanent than Pretoria's 1975 invasion of Angola. South Africa, of course, may not be willing to play such a direct patron role, particularly since the Ministry of Information scandals hamper bold initiatives by the present government. They may insist that Smith establish a neo-colonial system through an accommodation with Nkomo. Whatever decision South Africa makes, it is likely that they would intervene if such action were necessary to forestall a military victory by radical ZANU forces.

The United States government, as a matter of consistent foreign policy support for neo-colonial outcomes, and because of strategic and economic interests, will be increasingly drawn into a more active and interventionist role in the emerging Southern African confrontation. British investments in Rhodesia and South Africa, their strategic interest in the area, and their complicity in the sanctions-breaking oil deliveries to Rhodesia suggest that they, like the Americans, will facilitate either a perpetuation of the settler system under the guise of the existing internal settlement government or, more to their liking, a neo-colonial system under a ZAPU-RF coalition. Zambia has encouraged the latter form of accommodation, and has hosted, with American and British diplomatic support, several secret meetings between Nkomo and Smith. These diplomatic maneuverings exacerbate tension between the "moderate" ZAPU and the radical ZANU nationalist movements that have been nominally allied within the Patrotic Front, and split the leaders of the Front Line States. The pursuit of this divisive strategy by the United States and Britain represents a betrayal of their commitment to a negotiated settlement that includes both wings of the Patriotic Front.

Nkomo could play the neo-colonial leadership role easily, naturally, and comfortably, as is apparent from his early years as an activist in the more accommodationist African trade associations rather than with the more militant trade unions, in his attempt to secure nomination as a UFP candidate for the (Rhodesia and Nyasaland) Federal Parliament in 1953, in his now repudiated accommodationist stance during the negotiations over the 1961 constitutional proposals, in his close personal contacts with the bosses of international capital such as Roland "Tiny" Rowland of Lonrho, and in his eagerness to meet with Smith to work out a deal. He has called for the protection of private enterprises, which he considers to be, along with public efforts, major mechanisms of modernization. Nkomo is widely known for not having any radical or ideological convictions. Any shift to a radical role would be out of necessity, not inclination; it would be an uncomfortable, ingenuine, and probably brief role performance. Nkomo's personal biography and his viability as a populist leader fit the script written for a neo-colonial leader. If there were auditions for a Zimbabwean Jomo Kenyatta, Joshua Nkomo would get the part.

Despite Nkomo's proclivities, talents, and credentials as a neo-colonial leader, there are controlling factors that seriously hamper his opportunity to play this role. The events surrounding and subsequent to the 14 August 1978 Nkomo-Smith meeting in Zambia are instructive for understanding the factors that control Nkomo's options.[10] Smith evidently offered Nkomo the "golden handshake": Nkomo would be president, and joint ZAPU-Rhodesian forces would attack and demolish ZANU. Evidently, Nkomo was not inclined to an open attack on ZANU, but he was more than happy to accept a diplomatic offensive that would catapult him into a political preeminence unsustained by the power of an internal military and organizational apparatus. Consequently, Nkomo did come to terms with Smith on the idea of giving Mugabe a figure-head position in an integrated government. Mugabe and the ZANU executive rejected this arrangement despite strong pressures from the Nigerian, British, and American principals. With Mugabe's rejection of the proposal, one might have expected Nkomo to have reconsidered Smith's offer of a joint attack on ZANU. However, Nkomo is a practical and cautious man. He had already come dangerously close to being discredited as nationalist spokesperson in his negotiating stance over the 1961 constitutional proposals. As a junior partner within a future RF coalition government, he might salvage the pomp and ceremony of a "founding father," but if he became an agent of Smith and international finance at a point when the revolutionary challenge reached its peak, he could become the Zimbabwean equivalent to Benedict Arnold. The analogy with a neo-colonial Kenyan solution ignores the fact that Kenyatta was not confronted by a revolutionary guerrilla movement in control of half the countryside. Kenyatta could both reign and rule; Nkomo's options will probably be limited to reigning over either a reactionary or a radical government that is not of his own making. As long as Nkomo and ZAPU do not have a significant internal politico-military operational base, they cannot dictate terms of alliance, whether it is with Smith or Mugabe.

ZANU's rejection of this imposed political solution was compatible with their long-standing public commitment to the destruction of the settler system and capitalism through armed, revolutionary struggle. Once it was clear that ZANU was not going to be detracted from its revolutionary goal by diplomatic and economic pressures, Nkomo was faced with severely limited options. He probably knew that any overt alliance with Smith against ZANU would split his own ranks. Moreover, he may have realized that a confrontation with Mugabe which was in any way associated with the purposes of the settler regime would cost him dearly in public esteem. Finally, Nkomo might have realistically calculated that the military outcome of an attack on ZANU, even in conjuction with the Rhodesian armed forces, would be dubious. Even with a successful military outcome against ZANU, ZAPU would at best remain dependent upon Rhodesian troops; at worst, ZAPU would be demolished by the Rhodesians once they were freed from the internal military and political challenge posed by ZANU.

The failure of the 14 August diplomatic offensive to draw Nkomo into an alliance with Smith against Mugabe, or even to split the Patriotic Front, does not mean that further diplomatic efforts along these lines will not be attempted again, particularly as Smith's manpower base erodes. But ZAPU's downing of a Rhodesia Airlines' Viscount and Smith's reprisals against ZAPU since the fall of 1978 make a negotiated deal less likely *for now*. The effects of the air strikes against ZAPU bases in Zambia are more likely to harden ZAPU against negotiations and strengthen the postion of those within ZAPU who have been pushing for a more active deployment of troops to the battlefield. The integration of ZAPU and ZANU would represent the fusion between the nationalist and revolutionary wings of the Zimbabwean mobilization, and would tremendously advance the revolutionary cause in Zimbabwe. Since ZANU's control of power, influence, and commitments (although not necessarily material resources) is superior to ZAPU's, I assume that ZANU would be capable of giving a solidified Patriotic Front a revolutionary direction. In any case, some political formula for resolving differences between these two collectivities would have to be worked out in order to establish a revolutionary, nationalist Zimbabwean government.

Robert Mugabe's leadership of ZANU is unequivocally committed to revolutionary socialism. Eric Wood argues that Mugabe's ideas have been influenced by Presidents Julius Nyerere of Tanzania, Agostinho Neto of Angola, and Samora Machel of Mozambique. Mugabe articulates a clear understanding of and opposition to imperialism in the following statement quoted by Wood: "We distinguish our enemies from our political opponents. Britain as the Colonial power is our enemy, rather than the settler regime which is merely temporary and [an] extension of the British occupation."[11] Mugabe's critical consciousness concerning socialist transformation is expressed in his statement: "We are not intending to replace the white bourgeois property owners with a black bourgeois class. We are fighting against the system in that country. The system has to go."[12]

One could argue that equally radical rhetoric has been expressed by Ndabaningi Sithole, but Sithole's actions contradict his rhetoric, and he does not lead a revolutionary movement (C2). Smith has written the script for him, Muzorewa, and Chief Jeremiah Chirau, leader of the conservative coalition of chiefs and rural, African bourgeoisie, the Zimbabwe United People's Organization (ZUPO). Their primary function is to legitimate the perpetuation of settler dominance. Chief Chirau, by suggesting that no viable settlement can be achieved without the participation of ZANU and ZAPU, is the only one of the three who has demurred in enthusiastically performing his appointed legitimating role.

The accommodationist roles that Muzorewa and Sithole play for Smith highlight the fractionized nature of the Zimbabwean nationalist mobilization. The Zimbabweans are divided by issues of strategy, leadership, ideology, and ethnicity. These divisions exist between and within the major and minor mobilized Zimbabwean collectivites. Muzorewa and Nkomo are not ideologically inclined, while Sithole sounds radical but acts like a collaborationist. Mugabe and ZANU are officially committed to Marxist-Leninism. ZAPU must contain overlapping leadership and ideological divisions, in which Nkomo's own conservative inclinations and those of the old guard (e.g., Vice-President Josiah Chinamano) are balanced against the more radical, younger, middle level military leaders like Dumiso Dabenja and Akim Ndlova. The political preeminence of the Kalanga does not always appease the Ndebele factions within ZAPU, while the Shona resent their underrepresentation in higher ZAPU councils.

ZANU likewise must contain divisive forces. The revolt against Mugabe in early 1978 was in part motivated by those who pushed for closer relations with ZAPU. ZANU lacks a political and military Ndebele base, while ZAPU's Kalanga-Ndebele leadership dominance makes it difficult for ZAPU to bridge the historical differences between the Ndebele and the Shona. Zezuru and Manyika Shona factions are reputed to exist within ZANU. The settlers have obviously not created all these divisions, but they have done their best to exacerbate the rivalries and reap the benefits from them (A2b).

Another factor defining the present and future shape of the Zimbabwe polity's goal attainment subsystem is the external dependency of all three principal actors in the Zimbabwean-Rhodesian drama. Zimbabwean-Rhodesian collectivities are dependent upon patron states, which are in turn dependent upon international centers of finance capital or communism. The West holds the purse strings on Pretoria and could, if they were able to act out of character, stop the bloodshed in Zimbabwe in short order.[13] Likewise, ZAPU is dependent on Zambia, which in turn is also dependent upon international finance capital. Zambia has a continually bad foreign trade balance and a shortage of foreign currency, which, along with its dominant bureaucratic and parastatal petty bourgeoisie, tie Zambia into the world capitalist system.[14] Zambia's reopening of its border with Rhodesia under pressure from the International Monetary Fund demonstrates the nature of its dependency. ZAPU is also dependent on the Soviets for military supplies and training. ZANU is dependent upon Mozambique and Tanzania, both of whom are economically weaker, even if less vulnerable to external pressures than Zambia. Considerable pressure could be brought to bear on Mozambique if its economic situation is not bolstered considerably by communist aid. ZANU's dependence upon Chinese military support has reaped somewhat meager and declining benefits in comparison with Soviet support for ZAPU. However, the Soviets are moving to a more balanced position vis-a-vis ZAPU and ZANU. Zambia and Mozambique are also vulnerable militarily; they are obviously not capable of providing a safe haven for either Zimbabwean nationalist group.

To conclude our discussion of the internal political subsystems, short term objectives of the three regime types will be derived from an analysis of the most pressing problem confronting each of the protagonists: Smith, Nkomo, and Mugabe. Smith's most pressing need is for Anglo-American recognition of the internal settlement government produced by the April elections. Recognition would give Smith badly needed weapons and foreign exchange. It would also give a boost to sagging settler morale, which might temporarily stem the exodus of whites and diminish the potential for rebellion from black troops. Another benefit of recognition would be that international sovereignty would confer a legitimating facade for obtaining a military intervention from an ally. This would be a useful asset when the manpower crunch forces Smith and his African ministers to call for external help. Outright recognition now appears likely, because there are sufficient pressures and interests within both the U.S. and

Britian to find some alternative to Mugabe. Recognition and external support for either the settlement government or some kind of Smith-Nkomo accommodation will not suffice for long run viability, however.

Of course that which would rectify Smith's most pressing problem is at the same time that which would be most problematic for the nationalists. Nkomo's interests would be more damaged by recognition than Mugabe's. Assuming that recognition would be combined with Western pressure on Zambia to bring Nkomo to the negotiating table again, Nkomo would find himself in a more disadvantageous position than he was in August 1978. His major problem then, now, and in the immediate future stems from his lack of an internal power base that would strengthen his hand in negotiating either a settlement with Smith or a coalition government with Mugabe. Mugabe's most urgent problem is a shortage of weapons, but his greatest tactical need is for continued ZAPU cooperation in dispersing Rhodesian military capacities. He also needs ZAPU, or at least part of it, in order to politically integrate the Ndebele.

The Political Support and Legitimation Interchanges

The thesis of this section is that the prevailing Zimbabwean political orientations, with regard to both regime legitimacy and specific support, exert control through the legitimation and political support interchanges in favor of a revolutionary regime and against either a settler-dominant or Zimbabwean neo-colonial regime, while prevailing Rhodesian orientations provide legitimacy to a settler dominant regime only to the extent that it provides specific benefits for them. I first state some general conclusions which elaborate on this thesis and explain why it is valid; I then present data from a survey I conducted in Zimbabwe in 1971 which provide evidence in support of most of these conclusions.

General Conclusions

Rhodesian (European) political orientations are more specific than diffuse, more support for a system because of the benefits supplied by its allocative processes than commitment to a moral order (C5). Their orientations are specific because the dominant modes are charismatic authority, performance orientation, and self-serving racist ideology. The tenuous and shallow Rhodesian (European) support for the regime is vulnerable to the guerrilla strategy of attrition. Additional support for this interpretation of the data is supplied by the ever-increasing rate of white flight in the face of increased advances by ZANU's liberation forces, particularly as they have encroached upon the European urban centers. Some twenty thousand left in 1977; and now flight is reaching a crescendo, particularly among the professional and technical classes who represent the most critical manpower gap for the settler regime. If it were not so true to character for capitalists' behavior, it would be ironic that the sanctions "busting" Rhodesian exporters are now using their skills and contacts in clandestine trade to withdraw their wealth from Rhodesia, and are thereby undermining the regime whose survival they had formerly facilitated by the accumulation of wealth through sanctions "busting." The most immediate effects of white flight will be critical manpower and capital shortages, demoralization, and probable desertion or rebellion among African troops. White flight is the death knell of the settler regime; if continued unabated, it will force Smith and Muzorewa into either a compromise with Nkomo or intervention from an ally. While it is possible that Anglo-American recognition of the internal settlement government could stem the tide of settler emigration, my evidence suggests that the flow of emigration could be diminished only temporarily as long as the liberation forces can sustain a threat to European material well-being and physical security.

Finally, my findings on the extensiveness of charismatic authority for Smith are supported by newspaper accounts of Rhodesians perceiving him in "Churchillian" proportions. We have already concluded that Smith, given his capacity to win overwhelming electoral support for a "constitutional" solution diametrically opposed to everything the RF has stood for, will have considerable discretion in negotiating the best deal for the European remnants. My data give credence to this interpretation. However, I predict that attrition effects will continue to erode Smith's population base and his negotiating strength as a number of Europeans conclude, as those who have already departed have concluded: "It was a nice time and place for a party, but who wants to stick around for the tab?" Charismatic authority is inadequate as a basis of allegiance to a political system that is no longer capable of preserving privileges.

The depth and the extensiveness of Zimbabwean alienation manifested in my findings suggest that any attempt to facilitate a settler outcome through the internal settlement regime or a Zimbabwean neo-colonial outcome through a Nkomo-Smith accommodation would be negatively controlled by the contamination of settler illegitimacy, and would therefore ultimately fail (E3, E4). I have already referred to the incapacity of traditional leaders to reconcile their role as representatives of both an oppressive regime and a traditional collectivity. This incapacity and the rapid decline in popularity of Sithole and Muzorewa since the beginning of their collaboration with the settler regime provide supporting evidence for the potency of the poisoning effect Smith and his regime possess for Zimbabweans. My data alone demonstrate that, during a period of *relative* political quietude, the moral authority of the regime was so impoverished in terms of Zimbabwean values and norms that it could not have transferred or generalized any legitimacy to an ostensibly African regime serving its purposes. Assuming that ZANU can sustain its internal guerrilla bases, it will enjoy the benefit of recruits from the ranks of those alienated from any regime facilitated by the morally bankrupt settler power structure.

A settler or neo-colonial Zimbabwean regime that suffers from a lack of legitimacy can obtain some specific support from Zimbabweans by expanding the scope of benefits allocated by the system, and by demobilizing a substantial majority of Zimbabwean workers, peasants, and intellectuals (C2, C5). Because the purpose of a settler or neo-colonial regime is to allocate benefits to the privileged few, there are logical limits to the egalitarianism of such regimes. The contamination effect would limit the number of Zimbaweans willing to be bought off and co-opted (E3). Massive infusions of Anglo-American aid, as initially envisioned by the former U.S. Secretary of State, Henry Kissinger, might attract some Zimbabweans, but even this is dubious conjecture. The Zimbabwean students who were recruited as part of the Kissinger plan and enrolled in Carnegie Mellon University withdrew once they realized that their personal career advancement would serve the purpose of perpetuating the settler regime.

Demobilization of the population could only be accomplished through the destruction of ZANU as an effective revolutionary guerrilla movement and either the destruction or the co-optation of ZAPU. As long as these two movements are committed to the liberation of Zimbawe, they will continue to be mechanisms for the articulation of Zimbabwean alienation. Regardless of the fortunes of these nationalist movements, I predict that the facilitation of political dispositions compatible with demobilized collectivities would be extremely difficult to accomplish. This is true because, first, virtually the whole Zimbabwean population has been mobilized and politicized to some extent by one or more of the many political, military, and economic forces operative in a highly charged revolutionary situation. Political consciousness emerges for a villager herded into a "protected village" or just dodging bullets after curfew, and for a resident of Harare and other urban areas listening to illicit broadcasts or avoiding Sithole's henchman. Secondly, the data analyzed below demonstrate that the respondents are politicized, efficacious, and militant by both disposition and behavior. On a summary index of politicization, operationalized by comparing Zimbabwean and Rhodesian scores on political knowledge, efficacy, and participation, the Zimbabwean respondents consistently scored higher than Rhodesian respondents. Another pattern that stands out in the survey responses and in discussions with Zimbabweans is confidence in the Zimbabwean future. None of these dispositions is compatible with the stability needs of either a settler or a neo-colonial regime, but they are compatible with the transformation needs of a revolutionary regime (C5,C7,E3,E4).

My research findings do not measure for the existence, depth, or breadth of revolutionary, critical consciousness. If we distinguish between necessary and contingent consciousness, I can say that my Zimbabwean respondents, and probably all Zimbabwean intellectuals, are at least at the contingent level of consciousness defined as a "disenchantment primarily preoccupied with short-run and superficial contradictions of the system which can be resolved within the system." My survey does not address the issue of necessary consciousness defined as "a disenchantment with a social, economic, and political system resulting from an appreciation of the basic and long run contradictions within the system and ... directed at a structural transformation of social, economic and political relations."[15] I would conjecture that most Zimbabwean intellectuals would find the resonant chord of revolutionary ideology more appealing than the dissonant chord struck by those who would forego economic self-determination for their own selfish interests. I can say with greater confidence that Zimbabwean political orientations are not dependency orientations.

My survey is even further removed from testing for revolutionary consciousness among Zimbabwe's peasants and proletariat. However, without going into a detailed analysis of emergent class and radical consciousness, an analysis that has been admirably begun by several authors,[16] I can provide a brief interpretation of the literature which lends support to my belief that Zimbabwean peasants and workers are more susceptible to revolutionary than to reactionary ideological appeals. It can probably be assumed that ZANU has succeeded, through its indoctrination programs, in raising the critical, necessary consciousness of its cadres and many of its supporters, especially in the areas of its control and influence. It can also be assumed that those ZAPU members exposed to the radical ideology espoused by their communist-radical trainers are capable of some level of radical analysis. The commitment of the Zimbabwean workers and peasants to the liberation struggle is measured daily by very risky but widely practiced acts of rebellion in supplying the critical material and behavioral support prescribed for guerrilla warfare.

I would also assert that the remnants of traditional culture to which many peasants adhere are most compatible with a socialist outcome (D1). The communal mode of production is likely to produce values and norms that are more congruent with socialist than with capitalist developmental programs. A. Lerumo aptly characterized the socialist potential of traditional culture in the following way: "the forms of primitive communism existing in Africa before European conquest embodied cultures, values and traditions in many ways far superior to those of the representatives of capitalism who invaded and destroyed them. . ."[17] Although the penetration of capitalist values and norms into the countryside, and exploitative traditional cultural elements such as sexism pose real control obstacles to the social transformation envisioned by socialist ideology, capitalist penetration of the Tribal Trust Lands is self-defeating in two ways: 1) the creation of markets simply creates dissatisfaction to the extent that induced consumerism must remain unsatisfied for impoverished peasants; 2) the exploitation of labor and natural resources by large-scale agribusiness enterprises simply expands the proletarian base available for recruitment into the revolutionary movement. In addition, the settler government has facilitated the alienation and radicalization of those peasants who have been uprooted and herded in "protected" village concentration camps.

Research on the revolutionary consciousness of Zimbabwean workers has only recently begun. The central issue is whether a significant proportion of Zimbabwean workers represent a labor "aristocracy," as Giovanni Arrighi's pioneering study contends,[18] and are therefore more susceptible to reactionary than to revolutionary appeals. I would contend that the rich empirical evidence and careful analysis of specific historical collectivities supplied by two former University of Rhodesia economists, Peter Harris and Duncan Clarke, wholly demolish the myth of a Zimbabwean labor aristocracy.[19] Although the general applicability of the "labor aristocracy" thesis is still hotly debated,[20] I concur with Harris and Clarke that the objective conditions for a privileged, reactionary proletariat do not yet exist in Zimbabwe because of racial stratification in the labor force. It is difficult to determine what significance an impoverished, semi-proletariat or lumpen proletariat has for the advancement of a revolutionary Zimbabwean consciousness; revolutionary theorists disagree on how easy it is for revolutionary leaders to involve this class in a constant, conscious struggle against oppression (C6). The revolutionary struggle does not end with political or even economic transformation; time gaps exist between facilitating the revolution in the principal political-economic institutions and other secondary group relations and actually changing the life conditions, consciousness, and behavior controlled by primary group relations functioning as pattern socialization and control mechanisms (E3). This is especially true for the least privileged peasants and lumpen proletarians.

Survey Findings

A straightforward report of my findings is presented here in support of the conclusions I have made above.[21] The reader may judge the adequacy and the accuracy of my interpretations by comparing the findings with these conclusions.

In order to test for the amount of support for the most visible and salient political authority in Rhodesia, (former) Prime Minister Ian Smith, the following item was included in the survey:[22] "The Prime Minister of Rhodesia is doing a good job," with a modified Likert response scale of "Agree Strongly, Agree, Disagree, Disagree Strongly." Given the constraints under which the survey was conducted, the item was necessarily innocent looking and disarming: a polling type question which gauged the public mood regarding the popularity of its leading politician rather than a test for the more general evaluation of the country's leading authority. However, the singularity, salience, and symbolic significance of the incumbent of the top political leadership post is well demonstrated in the literature of political socialization, and the prominence of Ian Smith's role in establishing and leading the Rhodesian Front party, as well as his role in declaring UDI and conducting numerous subsequent settlement negotiations provide satisfactory *prima facie* evidence that this item was an effective measure of allegiance to or alienation from systemic authorities (C6). Moreover, responses to the question provided sufficiently clear discriminatory patterns to give some confidence in the validity of the test.

As expected, orientations toward the Prime Minister varied strongly with race. Table 9.1 provides strong evidence that the Prime Minister elicited strong and opposing emotional responses along racial lines, and the data suggest that the Prime Minister did and still does represent and perform the functions of what Murray Edelman has termed a condensation symbol:[23] for the white respondents Smith was more than a symbol of partisan politics and policies, he was a symbol of white nationalism, patriotism, and security; while for the black respondents, he epitomized white exploitation, oppression, and the frustration of black nationalism.

TABLE 9.1
Authority Orientations by Race

The Prime Minister is doing a good job	Zimbabweans (Africans)%	Rhodesians (Europeans)%
Strongly Disagree	79.9	8.4
Disagree	16.5	13.2
Agree	2.4	50.0
Strongly Agree	1.2	28.4
Total %	100.0	100.0
N	(334)	(296)

$X^2 = 400.82$, $p < .001$, Cramer's V = .80, Contingency Coefficient = .62.

Comparable data from surveys conducted in other countries will provide "benchmarks" or points of comparison for further gauging the amount of alienation and allegiance in Rhodesia.[24] Daniel Goldrich in his study of Costa Rican and Panamanian high school students found that 32 percent of the relatively alienated Panamanians endorsed negative responses to an evaluation of their President,[25] an alienation score considerably lower than the 94.7 percent of Zimbabwean high school students who endorsed the negative responses to an evaluation of their Prime Minister. These Zimbabwean respondents were also apparently more alienated than the high school seniors in the alienated subculture of Appalachia where Dean Jaros *et al.* found that 31 percent endorsed the statement that "the President is not a good person."[26] Since this statement is more extreme than the response choices used in my study, this comparison is only suggestive; yet it is useful to note that fully 78 percent of the Zimbabwean high school students endorsed the most negative option in the structured responses. On the other hand, Rhodesian high-school students were more positively oriented toward authority than the generally allegiant Costa Rican high school students— 82 percent and 39 percent respectively.[27]

For the purposes of this study, the summary concept of regime support was divided into five component variables: regime performance, political trust, regime ideology, political obligation, and political efficacy (C5,C6). The following discussion involves a definition, a presentation of data, and a brief analysis of the significance of the findings on each variable.

The concept of regime performance is considered to be an indicator of specific support for the regime. Three items measuring the respondents' evaluation of the Rhodesian government's past, present, and anticipated future performance were included in the survey in order to operationalize the concept of specific support. The measurement instrument is a test for general, overall evaluations of regime performance rather than a test for attitudes toward particular policies.[28]

Table 9.2 provides striking evidence that for these respondents there was no shared perception that the Rhodesian government operated in such a way as to represent a common national interest; to the contrary, it indicates that racial interests were perceived as dominating to the advantage of the privileged whites and to the exclusion of the blacks. Rhodesian identification with the regime met the minimal test of expected satisfaction of collective needs through the allocation of public goods; identification with the regime was predicated on the perceived congruence between white nation-caste interests and regime performance. For the Zimbabwean respondents the opposite was true, indicating that governmental attempts at disseminating the myth of a Rhodesian regime representing a common national interest fell on many deaf black ears.

The next component of regime orientations, political trust, has become an increasingly central concept in the literature relevant to legitimacy and alienation, political stability, and political change. According to Talcott Parsons, Samuel Huntington, and others, political trust is a determining factor in the amount of power a political system has at its disposal for the achievement of collective goals.[29] Table 9.3 would indicate that the

TABLE 9.2
Regime Performance Evaluation by Race

Evaluation of Regime Performance	Zimbaweans %	Rhodesians %
Low	75.6	2.9
Medium	17.0	13.9
High	7.4	83.2
Total %	100.0	100.0
N	(340)	(310)

$X^2 = 440.65$, $p < .001$; Cramer's $V = .80$; Contingency Coefficient = .62.

Rhodesian government's power base did and does not readily extend much beyond the limits of the racial barrier. Confidence in generalizing from these data to the black population as a whole was supplied by the finding of the Pearce Commission, appointed by the British Government to test public support for constitutional proposals which would have perpetuated settler rule, "that 'mistrust of the intentions and motives' of the Smith regime 'transcended all other considerations.'"[30]

TABLE 9.3
Political Trust by Race: Rhodesian, Zimbabwean and Detroit Respondents[31]

Political Trust	Zimbabweans% (Detroit Blacks)	Rhodesians% (Detroit Whites)
Low	75.0 (52)	8.4 (33)
Medium	23.6 (13)	55.9 (24)
High	1.5 (35)	35.7 (43)
Total %	100.0 (100)	100.0 (100)
N	343 (186)	311 (327)

$X^2 = 350.77$, $p < .001$, Cramer's $V = .72$, Contingency Coefficient = .59.

Since the operational indices and samples employed in the Detroit Study were quite different from those used in my survey,[32] they are included only to suggest that the degree of alienation and legitimacy may be more widespread in the two Rhodesian subpopulations than in somewhat comparable populations elsewhere. Further evidence of this generalization can be derived from the following data:

1. Jeffrey Paige's finding that 38 percent of black respondents from a

sample of the July 1967 Newark, New Jersy riot area "felt they could almost never trust the government," considerably below the 75 percent of Zimbabwean respondents who gave a similar response.[33]
2. Rhodesian high school students were about equally trusting (39.7 percent) as the most supportive (working) class of Jamaican students (40 percent), while Zimbabwean high school students were considerably more alienated (74.7 percent) than the most alienated (upper) class of Jamaican students (17 percent).[34]
3. Low political trust was much more widespread among Zimbabwean high school students (75 percent) than among relatively alienated Appalachian high school students (48 percent).[35]
4. The least alienated Zimbabwean respondents, the seminarians, were consistently and significantly less trusting than any of the above comparison groups.

The regime ideology variable was defined as the articulated rationalizations and justifications that regime spokesmen manipulate in order to legitimize the uneven allocation and distribution of political power. Regime legitimacy ideologies are distinguished from partisan ideologies, which are aimed at winning support for a particular party rather than at the development of moral convictions about the propriety of the regime structure. The extent to which a regime ideology functions as a *source* of legitimacy is defined by the amount of control a regime can exert through the manipulation of expressive symbols and beliefs, as determined by the degree to which they actually serve as mechanisms of self-expression. For the purposes of this study, ideology was conceptualized and operationalized as negative and positive evaluative statements justifying racial supremacy; utopian ideas and political myths, often considered to be basic elements of ideology, were not included as part of the survey design.[36]

Table 9.4 illustrates the consistent pattern of cleavage along racial lines. Justifications for racial dominance struck a consonant chord in the cognitive and emotional predispositions of the Rhodesian respondents and provided the government with a potent instrument for mobilizing diffuse support for the institutional expressions of racial supremacy. In sharp constrast, Zimbabwean respondents almost universally rejected the often used rationalizations for their political subservience.

For the Rhodesian respondents, material benefit fused with moral conviction to supply the regime with caste-nationalistic support. The fact that so many Rhodesian respondents, representing a presumably more skeptical educated elite, subscribed to blatantly propagandistic appeals of racial domination would suggest that deep emotional needs were being tapped, possibly basic needs for a positive personal identity and role taking which link an individual's self-acceptance to the rationalizations of regime ideology. Such individual-public linkages are particularly potent in the confusing and anxiety-arousing context confronting young white

TABLE 9.4
Regime Ideology by Race[38]

Regime Ideology Score	Zimbabweans %	Rhodesians %
Low	92.4	7.0
Medium	6.9	29.3
High	0.6	63.8
Total %	100.0	100.0
N	(344)	(301)

$X^2 = 492.64$, $p < .001$, Cramer's $V = .87$, Contingency Coefficient $= .66$

Rhodesians.

The political obligation variable was an attempt to measure regime legitimacy from the perspective of obedience dispositions toward the law. Obedience dispositions are divided into three dimensions:[37] 1) compliance—obedience stems from instrumental motives (i.e., to avoid negative sanctions or to reap benefits) without regard for the content of the law or identification with those who perpetrate and obey it; 2) identification—obedience is elicited out of a sense of self-defining role relationships, the maintenance of a socially defined desirable self-image, without regard for the content of the law and without necessary consideration of instrumental reinforcement; 3) internalization—obedience occurs because the laws are compatible with the individual's value system, and is not only instrumental or self-defining. Internalization represents the highest mode of legitimacy disposition and provides a sense of moral obligation to obey that underpins diffuse support. Identification is a somewhat lower order of legitimacy disposition, more susceptible to change but nevertheless a potent basis for diffuse support; while compliance is a substitute for legitimacy orientations, and constitutes a type of specific support, in this case an avoidance of sanctions. As expected, a high percentage of Zimbabwean respondents (see Table 9.5) endorsed the compliance mode of obedience, expressing, in effect, their belief that the regime was morally bankrupt and its laws were without moral sanction. Zimbabwean obedience, then, was simply a recognition of superior force.

The final dimension of regime legitimacy involves the variable of political efficacy. Unlike the previous variables of regime legitimacy, which were measures of orientations toward what the regime produces, political efficacy is a measure of how the individual perceives himself in relation to the regime's responsiveness to his influence. In contrast to some conceptualizations and operationalizations of political efficacy which

TABLE 9.5
Modes of Political Obligation by Race

Reason for Obeying Laws	Obedience		Rejection of Disobedience	
	Zimbawean %	Rhodesian %	Zimbawean %	Rhodesian %
Compliance	83.8	29.9	62.2	10.2
Identification	14.3	40.5	3.5	4.9
Internalization	1.9	29.6	34.4	84.8
Total %	100.0	100.0	100.1	99.9
N	(306)	(284)	(259)	(283)

For obedience and race, X^2 = 185.90, p $<$.001, Cramer's V = .56, Contingency Coefficient = .49.

define it as a combination of political understanding and evaluation of the political system's responsiveness, my survey distinguished between the perceived intelligibility of the political world and the perceived responsiveness of the political system to one's needs and will.[39] This distinction was necessary in analyzing legitimacy orientations in Rhodesia, where the government attempted to win African support by providing only symbolic and expressive instruments of participation and representation. In short, the more politically sophisticated a Zimbabwean student was the more realistically he would evaluate the responsiveness of the political system. Moreover, this distinction was necessary for an evaluation of the potential to participate in antiregime or revolutionary activities, which would require a high degree of alienation due to the unresponsiveness of the regime, combined with a high political action propensity produced by a strong sense of political competence (measured here by perceived intelligibility of the political world).

Thus it was hypothesized not only that perceived regime responsiveness would vary significantly with race, but also that Zimbabwean respondents' sense of regime responsiveness would decline with education, while perceived intelligibility of the political world would increase. Tables 9.6 and 9.7 provide support for these hypotheses. In addition to demonstrating sharp racial differences, Table 9.6 indicates that Zimbabwean respondents became increasingly realistic about regime unresponsiveness with increased education, as contrasted with the increased sense of political efficacy with increased education found in other surveys. Table 9.7 shows not only that the perceived intelligibility of the political world increased with educational level for the black respondents, but that the black respondents possessed a higher sense of personal political competence than the white respondents possessed.

TABLE 9.6
Perception of Regime Responsiveness by Race and Education

Regime Responsiveness	Zimbabweans %			Rhodesians %	
	H.S.	Sem.	Univ.	H.S.	Univ.
Low	44.4	48.0	66.7	20.0	11.7
Medium	43.8	45.2	29.9	63.0	78.3
High	11.7	6.8	3.5	16.9	10.0
Total %	99.9	100.0	100.1	99.9	100.0
N	(153)	(114)	(73)	(249)	(60)

Test 1: Regime responsiveness by race, $X^2 = 38.92$, $p < .001$, Cramer's V = .24, Contingency Coefficient = .24.

Test 2: African perception of regime responsiveness by education, $X^2 = 25.53$, p .01 for one tailed test, Cramer's V = .19, Contingency Coefficient = .26.

TABLE 9.7
Perceived Intelligibility of the Political World by Race and Education

Intelligibility of Political World	Zimbabweans %			Rhodesians %	
	H.S.	Sem.	Univ.	H.S.	Univ.
Low 0	10.5	13.5	.9	10.0	4.9
1	26.1	28.4	25.6	57.2	32.8
2	30.7	36.5	35.0	29.2	45.9
High 3	32.7	21.6	38.5	3.6	16.4
Total %	100.00	100.0	100.0	100.0	100.0
N	(153)	(74)	(117)	(250)	(61)

Test 1: Intelligibility of political world by race, $X^2 = 85.53$, $p < .001$, Cramer's V = .36, Contingency Coefficient = .34.

Test 2: African intelligibility of political world by education, $X^2 = 16.41$, $p < .01$ in one tailed test, Cramer's V = .15, Contingency Coefficient = .21.

Some comment on the apparently low level of political efficacy scores for the Rhodesian respondents is in order. Given the educational level of these students, as well as the privileged status of political access every white Rhodesian enjoys, it was surprising to find a relatively widespread sense of powerlessness. Any number of explanations could be put forward for this phenomenon: the traditional heritage of deferential political orientations,[40] especially when combined with the Rhodesian tradition of an imperial and elitist political order; the lack of party competition; and the youthfulness of the Rhodesian sample. The survey data could mean that the relatively low Rhodesian sense of political efficacy combined with high legitimacy orientations had and still has the systemic effect of increasing the decision making discretion of the government; while the opposite pattern of scores on both these variables for Zimbabwean respondents represents potential political dynamite (C2, C5). For example, Paige has found that high political information combined with low political trust is strongly related to riot participation.[41] The relatively high level of political competence among Zimbabwean respondents would provide the attitudinal basis for expressing alienation from the political system through modes of revolutionary activism, rather than through apathy and political withdrawal.[42] Finally, even though the Rhodesian internal settlement government is expanding the symbolic participation opportunities of its Zimbabwean subjects, there will probably not be a corresponding decrease in alienation for reasons discussed above. In addition, Ada W. Finifter has found that increased political participation decreases the sense of powerlessness but does not decrease the sense of political alienation.[43]

In order to provide an overview of the pattern of systemic support orientations revealed in the preceding data, a rank order display of legitimacy and alienation scores is presented in Table 9.8. In this table the dimensions of systemic support are ranked according to the extent of Zimbabwean alienation and Rhodesian legitimacy, as determined by their respective percentages of low and high scores (not by the individual respondent's ranking of these dimensions). The degree of Zimbabwean alienation from the Rhodesian political system, evident throughout the preceding analysis, is brought into high relief here. It is not surprising that the Prime Minister symbolized and focused Zimbabwean feelings of hostility toward the entire Rhodesian political system. Nor is it surprising that such widespread Zimbabwean consensus existed on rejecting the ideological props of racial supremacy. The hierarchy of Rhodesian response patterns was apparently less predictable, and will be analyzed now in more detail.

Table 9.8 demonstrates that for these Rhodesian respondents widespread positive support orientations did extend across most of the dimensions of systemic legitimacy; but the scope of positive support was broadest on the most tenuous types of legitimacy orientations: regime

TABLE 9.8
Rank Order of African Alienation Scores and European Legitimacy Scores

Degree of Zimbabwean Alienation			Degree of Rhodesian Legitimacy		
Rank	Dimensions	% of Low Scores	Rank	Dimensions	% of High Scores
1	Authority	96.4	1	Performance	83.2
2	Ideology	92.4	2	Authority	78.4
3	Obligation*	83.8	3	Obligation*	70.1
4	Performance	75.6	4	Ideology	63.8
5	Political Trust	75.0	5	Political Trust	35.7
6	Efficacy	33.8	6	Partnership	6.4
7	Partnership	22.2	7	Efficacy	3.2

*The obligation score is a combination of the internalization and identification scores on the first test as described in footnote 38.

performance and political authority.

The patterns of systemic support among these Rhodesian students can be characterized as subordinate dispositions toward the regime, with loyalty to the systemic order predicated upon the relatively narrow foundations of rational self-interest, charismatic authority, and ideological rationalizations. The category of subordinate dispositions is defined by the low political efficacy score combined with the high political obligation score, which, when combined with a widespread disposition to obey the laws, provides the government with increased decision making discretion. The relatively high level identification with the regime ideology of racial supremacy indicates that specific support for the regime is translated into "moral convictions about the validity of the regime."[44] When this observation is linked to the highest ranking given to regime performance *plus* the broad rejection of racial partnership, one can conclude with some confidence that the primary basis for regime support is a realistic evaluation of the congruence between individual and racial self-interests and the prevailing political order. For Rhodesian respondents, diffuse support is dependent on specific support. There is also the large percentage endorsement of obligation orientations, indicating another element of diffuse support. However, here again there is some mixture of specific support, since it is distinctly to the advantage of Rhodesian Europeans to endorse and propagate a belief in obedience to a legal order that defines and perpetuates their own privileged status.

Given the limitations of the data at hand, it is impossible to separate the operation of charismatic legitimacy orientations, manifested in the high percentage endorsement of former Prime Minister Smith, from the operation of specific support based on self-interest. Since Rhodesian settler nationalism is a fusion of racial-class interests and nationalistic pursuit of self-determination fired by primordial fears of self-survival, Smith is simultaneously a symbol of both.

The crucial question for determining how committed elite European youth are to the Rhodesian political system can be posed colloquially: "What happens when the going gets tough?" If my thesis that European systemic support is narrowly based on material advantage rationalized by a racial supremacy ideology and symbolically represented by charismatic authority is correct, the answer to the above question is "emigrate" (C5). Specific support is inherently tenuous because it is dependent on material, social, or psychological gain. Charismatic authority is also tenuous because it is tied to the continued impression that the leader possesses an exceptional capacity to master the environment, and in a secular, materialistic society such an impression cannot be maintained for long without substantial supporting evidence. The relative deprivation of insecurity and anxiety arising from an armed camp, state of siege condition would be the highest and the least tolerable for those Europeans possessing the greatest skills and resources, because the relief of emigration is the most readily at hand and the status loss the least profound for them. Charismatic authority, self-justifying racial supremacy ideology, and the obligation to obey become inoperative when regime performance can no longer guarantee privilege or even survival. Rhodesian Europeans, especially the elites, are not in the same league as committed Zimbabwean nationalists when it comes to suffering for nationalist-ideological causes.

If the systemic significance of white legitimacy orientations revolves around the question of sustained commitment in the face of adverse conditions, the systemic significance of African alienation lies in whether it will be channeled into political withdrawal and apathy or into revolutionary activities which will contribute to white discomfort, anxiety, and departure (E3). My evidence clearly demonstrates that Zimbabwean alienation is not translated into acquiescence or passivity. Zimbabwean respondents scored high on measures for militant attitudes and behavior. On an index measuring militant political attitudes, 57 percent of the Zimbabwean respondents scored in the highly militant category, with males and university students scoring appreciably higher: 70 percent of the university students were highly militant. An even higher percent of these Zimbabwean respondents claimed to have engaged in the militant behavior of demonstrating: for the whole sample 70 percent claimed to have done so; and even 45 percent of the consistently less-alienated seminarians said they had demonstrated. Even if these respondents were exaggerating their participation in demonstrations (and while I have no way of validating such participation, impressionistically their claims do not seem very distorted), the broad scope of these responses would indicate that protest behavior was a normative expectation. Engagement in ad hoc, although not necessarily spontaneous, demonstrations is not a measure of involvement in sustained revolutionary activity; but it certainly indicates that these Zimbabwean students were not inactive, acquiescent, or subordinate.[45] To engage in protest behavior which often evokes immediate violent countermeasures, detention, and/or surveillance and harassment, as well as lasting opportunity-deprivations, constitutes a type of political activity which seems to be determined more by political than by personality factors. Experiencing such sanctions is often an important factor in the formation of revolutionary commitment.

It must be recognized that my data are too outdated and incomplete to provide a full and clear portrayal of the Zimbabwean-Rhodesian legitimation and political support interchanges today. If western foreign policy makers were serious about determining the legitimacy of the newly formed Murzorewa government, they should fund an expanded research design replicating and improving on my survey. A project of this magnitude is a cheaper and more valid test of regime legitimacy than the April 1979 elections.

I have concluded throughout the foregoing analysis that factors of facilitation and control favor a revolutionary Zimbabwean outcome rather than either perpetuation of the Rhodesian system through the internal settlement regime or the establishment of a neo-colonial Zimbabwe. Predicting such an outcome provides a useful test of the control and facilitation model and my application of it to the assessment of revolutionary potential in Zimbabwe.

Footnotes

1. Claire Palley, "Law and the Unequal Society: Discriminatory Legislation in Rhodesia under the Rhodesian Front from 1963 to 1969," Parts 1 and 2, Race 12, 1 and 2 (1970): 11-47, 139-67.
2. Ibid., Part 2, p. 162.
3. Charles van Onselen, "Black Workers in Central African Industry: A Critical Essay on the Historiography and Sociology of Rhodesia," *Journal of Southern African Studies* 1 (April 1975): 228-46.

4. A.K.H. Weinrich, *Chiefs and Councils in Rhodesia: Transition from Patriarchal to Bureaucratic Power* (London: Heinemann, 1971); and J. F. Holleman, *Chief, Council and Commissioner: Some Problems of Government* (London: Oxford University Press, 1969). Holleman reports on the failure of human relations training exercises to change District Commissioners' racist, authoritarian, and condescending attitudes toward Africans.

5. Harry Braverman, *Labor and Monopoly Capital: The Degradation of Work in the Twentieth Century* (New York: Monthly Review Press, 1974).

6. See, for example, Charles Bettelheim, *Class Struggle in the USSR: First Period: 1917-1923*, trans. Brian Pierce (New York: Monthly Review Press, 1976), pp. 484-96.

7. See John R. Nellis, "Socialist Management in Algeria," *Journal of Modern African Studies* 15 (December 1977): 529-54.

8. Quoted from William Eckhardt and Christopher Young, *Governments Under Fire: Civil Conflict and Imperialism* (New York: HRAF Press, 1977), p. 65.

9. See Michael Bratton, "Structural Transformation in Zimbabwe: Comparative Notes from the Neo-Colonisation of Kenya," *Journal of Modern African Studies* 15 (December 1977): 605.

10. Information about the 14 August 1978 Lusaka meeting and subsequent events given by Edgar Tekere, secretary general of ZANU, and reported by Jim Hoagland and David B. Ottaway, "Strategy to Halt War in Rhodesia at a Dead End," *Washington Post*, 3 December 1978, p. A1.

11. Eric Wood, "Community Action, Urban Protest and Change in Zimbabwe and South Africa," *African Affairs* 77 (April 1978): 184.

12. Quoted in *Africa Research Bulletin*, Political, Social, and Cultural Series 15 (15 March 1978): 4755.

13. Compare Yash Tandon, "The Role of Transnational Corporations and Future Trends in Southern Africa," *Journal of Southern African Affairs* 2 (October 1977): 391-402; and Timothy M. Shaw, "International Stratification in Africa: Sub-Imperialism in Southern and Eastern Africa," ibid., pp. 145-66.

14. Stephen A. Quick, "Bureaucracy and Rural Socialism in Zambia,"

Journal of Modern African Studies 15 (September 1977): 379-400.

15. The definitional distinction between contingent and necessary consciousness is taken from Guy C. Z. Mahone, "Factor Combinations and the Distribution of a Product in a Dominance-Subjugation System," *Journal of Southern African Affairs* 2 (January 1977): 52.

16. For a penetrating historical analysis, see Charles Van Onselen, "Worker Consciousness in Black Miners: Southern Rhodesia, 1900-1920," *Journal of African History* l4, 2 (1973): 237-55.

17. Quoted in Dialego, *Philosophy and Class Struggle* (London: Inkululeko Publications). Reprinted from *The African Communist 67-70 (1976-1977)*.

18. Giovanni Arrighi, "The Political Economy of Rhodesia," in *Essays on the Political Economy of Africa,* ed. Arrighi and John S. Saul (New York: Monthly Review Press, 1973), pp. 336-77.

19. Peter Harris, "Industrial Workers in Rhodesia, l946-1972: Working Class Elites or Lumpenproletariat?" *Journal of Southern African Studies* 1 (April 1975): 139-61; and D. G. Clarke, *Agricultural and Plantation Workers in Rhodesia: A Report on Conditions of Labor Subsistence* (Gwelo, Rhodesia: Mambo Press, 1977).

20. Richard Sandbrook and Robin Cohen, *The Development of An African Working Class: Studies in Class Formation and Action* (Toronto: University of Toronto Press, 1975).

21. I am indebted to the University of Rhodesia and Shimer College for supporting the research for this survey, and to the Laboratory for Political Research, University of Iowa, for making computer facilities available. I am particularly grateful to Marshall Murphree, Professor of Race Relations at the University of Rhodesia, and to Mrs. Joan May of the same institution's Sociology Department for their assistance in conducting the survey. Finally, I wish to thank Joel Barkan of the University of Iowa for his help in the analysis of data.

22. The data used in this chapter are taken from a larger study of political socialization and revolutionary potential in Rhodesia. The survey was conducted from April 1971 to February 1972. In order to minimize problems of equivalence of meaning, the research instrument was carefully pretested by a panel of experts and a panel of students. The subjects interviewed in this survey did not constitute a representative sample of the universe of Rhodesian students; in fact, there was a definite elite bias in the survey design. Access to government schools was not granted, which meant that the European high school students surveyed were from the wealthier families who could afford to send their children to private schools. Moreover, although the University of Rhodesia respondents were selected by random sample methods, more than half of all European university students study abroad, mostly in South Africa. Given the lack of educational opportunities for African students, the African respondents were very definitely part of the educated elite;

however, the inclusion of the consistently more conservative African seminarians provided some measure of control.

23. Murray Edelman, *The Symbolic Uses of Politics* (Urbana: University of Illinois Press, 1967), p.6.

24. There is considerable difficulty in finding such points of departure or "benchmarks" because a variety of survey items and combinations of items are used in operationalizing the same concept; because the display of data is usually presented in an explanatory rather than, as for our purposes, a descriptive way; and finally, because sample structures differ.

25. Daniel Goldrich, *Sons of the Establishment: Elite Youth in Panama and Costa Rica* (Chicago: Rand McNally and Co., 1966), p. 107. Goldrich's questionnaire items are the same as mine, and his sample of high school students is similar. This makes his data highly comparable.

26. Dean Jaros et al., "The Malevolent Leader: Political Socialization in an American Sub-Culture," in *The Learning of Political Behavior*, ed. Norman Adler and Charles Hurrington (Glenview, Ill.: Scott, Foresman, and Co., 1970), p. 67.

27. Goldrich, *Sons of the Establishment,* p.107.

28. Space does not permit a complete description of the items used in the survey. A limited number of questionnaires can be made available upon request. The regime performance index consisted of six items which asked for: 1) evaluations of the country's progress since U.D.I. and anticipated future progress; 2) evaluations of central and local governmental activities; 3) an evaluation of "public officials"; and 4) an evaluation of how well the government was doing in resolving basic problems. Questions under number one were constructed by the author; those under number two were taken from Gabriel A. Almond and Sidney Verba, *The Civic Culture: Political Attitudes and Democracy in Five Nations* (Princeton: Princeton University Press, 1963); and the remainder were taken from Goldrich, *Sons of the Establishment,* pp. 107-8.

29. Talcott Parsons, "The Political Aspect of Social Structure and Process," in *Varieties of Political Theory,* ed. David Easton (Englewood Cliffs, N.J.: Prentice-Hall, 1966), pp. 71-104; and Samuel P. Huntington, *Political Order in Changing Societies* (New Haven: Yale University Press, 1968),pp. 140-47.

30. Reported in *African Diary* 12 (17-23 June 1972): 6010.

31. The figures for Detroit are taken from Joel D. Aberbach and Jack L. Walker, "Political Trust and Racial Ideology," *American Political Science Review* 64 (December 1970): 1204. Their black sample was taken in part from the area of the July 1967 riots in Detroit.

32. My trust index was derived from a combination of two questions: one asking how often the government can be trusted, the other asking how honest the government has been.

33. Jeffrey M. Paige, "Political Orientations and Riot Participation,"

American Sociological Review 36 (March 1971): 810-19. Paige's questionnaire item is the same as one of the two in my study, but his sample is not skewed toward an elite bias as mine is, which probably explains some of the differences in the amount of alienation.

34. Kenneth P. Langton, *Political Socialization* (New York: Oxford University Press, 1969), p. 128.

35. Jaros, "The Malevolent Leader," p. 169.

36. Five items were combined for the construction of the index. They included evaluative statements about "the system of government," "European rule [and] continued progress and prosperity," the Land Tenure Act precluding racial exploitation, incapacity of "European rule" to make necessary changes (rejection equaled a positive score), and the performance of "African governments to the north of us."

37. The three dimensional analysis of obligation was derived from Herbert C. Kelman's analysis of behavior change. See his "Processes of Opinion Change," *Public Opinion Quarterly* 25 (Spring 1961): 57-78.

38. The first test provided three reasons for obeying the "Rhodesian government and its laws": 1) "the government stands for what I believe in," 2) "I am a Rhodesian," 3) "I will get caught and punished if I don't obey." The second test involved a rejection of disobeying the "Rhodesian government and its laws": 1) "it is proper to obey the government in power in order to avoid lawlessness and chaos," 2) "people would think that I am not a loyal Rhodesian," 3) "People would make life miserable for me." For each test, number one was categorized as internalization, two as identification, and three as compliance.

39. The political efficacy items are the same as the Survey Research Center efficacy items with the exclusion of the question on voting. Political efficacy is also distinguished from a sense of personal competence. It should also be noted that the perceived intelligibility of the political world can be measured subjectively as was done in this survey, or it can be measured objectively by a political information test. See Almond and Verba, *The Civic Culture*.

40. There is some evidence that Rhodesian Europeans are even less participant than the British: for example, Colin Leys concluded after analyzing registration figures in Rhodesia between the years 1924-1954 that "only about a third of the European population is registered, as compared with over two-thirds in Britain." *European Politics in Southern Rhodesia* (Oxford: Clarendon Press, 1959), p. 195. However, one should take into consideration that it is more difficult to register in Rhodesia than in Great Britain.

41. Paige, "Political Orientations," p. 815.

42. For a conceptualization of this, see Ada W. Finifter, "Dimensions of Political Alienation," *American Political Science Review* 64 (June 1970): 406-9.

43. Ibid. The same discovery is made by Alex Inkeles, "Participant

Citizenship in Six Developing Countries," *American Political Science Review* 63 (December 1969): 1120-41.

44. David Easton, *A Systems Analysis of Political Life* (New York: John Wiley and Sons, 1965), p. 287, provides an excellent conceptual scheme for the analysis of ideology and systemic support.

45. Compare Kenneth Prewitt, "University Students in East Africa: A Case of Political Quietude," in *Education and Political Values: An East African Case Study,* ed. Prewitt (Nairobi: East African Publishing House, 1971), pp. 141-70.

10

Conclusion: From Case Studies to Systematic Hypothesis Testing

James R. Scarritt

It was asserted in Chapter 1 that the complexity of the control and facilitation framework fosters more adequate explanation of various types of political change than that provided by alternative frameworks, and all of the case studies presented in subsequent chapters support this assertion explicitly or implicitly. The relationship between religion and politics, the diffusion of legislative and poitical party structure, the failure of development planning, the effects of the sequential ordering and timing of policy innovations, the process of regime change through revolution, and the subsequent revolutionary transformation of society are all most adequately described and explained by utilizing propositions involving the concepts of society and environment, functional subsystems and interchanges, structural levels, and media of exchange, related to one another in terms of control and facilitation. Progress toward hypothesis testing should not sacrifice this conceptual complexity, but should rather guarantee that all aspects of the framework are taken into account fully in the analysis of any specific change, something that is not possible with interpretive case studies.

As pointed out in Chapter 1, however, there are too many propositions by any reasonable standards of theoretical parsimony, and many propositions are too imprecise to be converted into testable hypotheses. These problems are reflected in the explanations given and the predictions made in the case studies. Lockard's analysis of the causes of increased political interference in religious affairs in Uganda indicates that the recent overthrow of Amin is unlikely to reverse that trend, although it is very likely to change the specific nature of political intervention. But her analysis is insufficiently precise to predict either the exact nature of polity-religion relationships under the new regime or the exact conditions under which the trend toward increased political intervention in religious affairs would be reversed. Scarritt describes and explains differences as well as similarities in the norms, collectivity structures, and roles borrowed or invented by legislatures and political parties in formerly British African countries, and in the functional performance of these legislatures and parties. But his analysis is insufficiently precise to predict whether specific legislatures and parties will increase their power, institutionalization, and functional effectiveness, or to specify the exact conditions under which such changes would occur. Dubnick delineates the variety of ways in which planning systems in African countries inhibit successful planning, and suggests a number of changes in these systems which would be likely to increase planning effectiveness. But his analysis is insufficiently precise to predict the exact planning system reforms which would be sufficient to produce specific planning policy outcomes in various countries. Scarritt's conclusions about the effects of sequential ordering and timing of policy innovations are imprecise in a number of ways which he notes in the course of his discussion, and his original analysis failed to utilize the control and facilitation framework fully. Even when he uses it fully in his reconsideration, he cannot predict the exact sequence of change or time intervals between changes which would produce specific components of development in various Anglophone African party states.

Koehn, Cohen, and Opello demonstrate the complex balance of forces involved in the process of successful revolutionary regime change in Ethiopia and Mozambique, although Koehn places special emphasis on collectivity mobilization, Cohen on elite resistance, and Opello on functional dissynchronization. Cohen's original analysis failed to predict that fundamental change would occur in Ethiopia because he failed to anticipate potential control and facilitation linkages among the values and role behavior of progressive individuals and groups at the national center. All three authors suggest that revolutionary regimes, once in power, are likely to encounter substantial difficulties in bringing about societal transformation, although Koehn stresses the necessity to share power with popular local authorities and Opello stresses the need to overcome resistance from precolonial and religious values and norms. But these authors' analyses are insufficiently precise to predict the exact combination of conditions under which revolutionary regime change would occur, exactly which role players and collectivities would resist societal transformation, exactly what tactics they would utilize, or the specific measures which would overcome this resistance. Maguire predicts that revolutionary regime change will occur in Zimbabwe-Rhodesia, and utilizes various propositions in combination with data on Zimbabwean (African) and Rhodesian (European) political values, norms, and role behavior to support this prediction. Given the absence of sufficient data on revolutionary organization and ideology, and the imprecise nature of many of the propositions utilized, Maguire's prediction may be persuasive, but it is no more than that. Furthermore, he cannot predict the exact conditions under which revolutionary regime change or societal transformation would succeed.

James R. Scarritt

A more parsimonious list of precise testable hypotheses is necessary for the more powerful explanation and prediction of the complex processes of African political change which these interpretive case studies cannot provide. Such hypotheses could be developed by refining the existing propositions if a systematic set of data on African political change on which they could be tested was available. In their present form, some propositions refer to shared orientations (values and norms) or preceptions (preceived utility and compatibility); others to attributes of societies, political systems, or subsystems thereof; and yet others to events. Because the kinds of orientation-perceptual and system attribute data called for would be extremely difficult to collect, and because change is comprised of events, an events data set would be most appropriate for testing these propositions. In addition, it is easier to be comprehensive in covering a broad scope of relevant actions with an events data set.[1] Where possible, concepts which refer to other types of data would be rephrased to refer to events; where this was not possible, limited amounts of perceptual or attribute data would be collected, or certain propositions employing these concepts would not be refined through testing. For example, compatibility could be measured in terms of similarity of structures, functions, or policies before and after an event, while perceived utility or the presence of innovative values and norms would have to be measured with perceptual data if they were to be measured at all. Propositions involving attributes of a pre-existing system could not be tested because events data provide measurement only of change and not of initial attributes.

Procedures which could be used to construct a valid and reliable African political change events data set and to test and refine our propositions on it will now be outlined to provoke from readers both constructive criticism and expressions of interest in cooperative research. The tentative nature of the following suggestions should be emphasized. Given the complexity of the problems involved, it would be most fruitful to work initially with a small number of similar countries with which the researchers are familiar.[2] If the initial analysis of these countries proved to be successful, the data set could then be expanded to include all African countries, and perhaps even a more global population of nations, in order to test the general validity of the refined hypotheses developed in the initial analysis.

The vast majority of events data collection has been in the areas of foreign policy and international interaction—especially international conflict.[3] Some internal events data have been collected on global samples of countries, mostly involving conflict events.[4] The major existing African attribute data set includes some events data, and a related project has collected primarily events data on African political party institutionalization, but in published analyses from both of these projects, these events have been aggregated into time periods of a year or more.[5]

The definition of an event for the proposed political change data set could be borrowed from the international events literature with only relatively minor modifications, even though different types of events would be analyzed and different propositions would be tested. "An event can be loosely defined as an action enclosed in some kind of boundaries."[6] Action may be verbal or nonverbal. An actor, an action, a target, an issue area, and a time period have been specified as the components of an international event, and variation in any one of these components signifies the presence of another event.[7] Internal political change events differ most significantly from international events in the absence of a specific target. Thus boundaries between such events would have to be determined in terms of actors, types of action, and time periods. Very tentatively, it might be fruitful to code all events in which the actors are government, political party, or other politically relevant, interest-based collectivity officials, holding some precisely defined set of national and regional positions in their respective organizations, or are precisely specified segments of the societal population; and in which the action is to propose, enact, implement, accept (with or without modification), or reject a nonroutine change in political structure, functions, or policy content. It is hoped that the printed sources from which events would be recorded would identify nonroutine changes in an unambiguous manner. Each event should occur within a time period of a few days at most, and a maximum time period would be established for each type of action, beyond the limits of which a separate event would be coded.

Each event would also be coded in terms of the direction and extent of change it entailed. Relevant directions of change would include creation or elimination of structural units, increase or decrease in various components of structural institutionalization, increase or decrese in functional effectiveness, increase or decrease in the supply of various exchange media, greater or lesser equality in the distribution of media, and increased or decreased dependence of the society or political system on its environment. Scales of the extent of change in each of these directions would be developed by procedures described below.

Finding the most satisfactory combination of data sources would be extremely important. It has been shown that multiple data sources yield more events, and thus a more valid sample of events, and that regional sources are more adequate than global sources.[8] Thus coding of events would begin with a regional news source, probably *Africa Research Bulletin*, which has a broad coverage of events and categorizes them in a useful manner for the analysis of political change. Following the strategy described by Edward Azar, additional news sources, laws, and major secondary monographic sources would be coded one at a time for a sample of countries and time periods, until the addition of a new source made no significant contribution to the data set.[9] Monographic sources might reveal significant changes which were too gradual and/or unpublicized to be picked up by news summaries, but which could be validly and reliably coded as events. Once the population of events was established by the procedure just described, a variety of other sources, including African newspapers, would be examined to see if they could contribute to more valid coding of the events already identified.

Many variables contained in the propositions to be refined through testing, such as compatibility, reinterpretation, collectivity mobilization, and conflict would be measured in terms of trends or patterns of events, since they refer to relationships among events rather than to individual events. Causal relationships among events and patterns of events could be examined through quasi-experimental, interrupted time-series analysis if certain events were followed by marked changes in the pattern of other events.[10] It would be crucial, however, to measure the extent of change in various directions entailed in each event, since this would determine its significance as part of a larger pattern. Events data sources would be of limited usefulness in this task.

The possibility of using expert judges to determine the extent of change involved in individual events and patterns of events through the construction of scales should therefore be explored. Judges might also be asked to validate causal relationships found in the data analysis and to estimate whether these relationships could be projected to remain constant in the near future. Expert judges have been used to code and validate the coding of political attributes, and have been used by international events analysts to scale events, primarily in terms of the degree of conflict involved.[11] These uses of expert judges have been criticized on several grounds, including their possible lack of expertise, their unarticulated biases, and their differing conceptions of the tasks they are asked to perform.[12] To minimize lack of expertise, judges would be selected carefully and encouraged to scale only those events with which they were thoroughly familiar. To minimize bias, serious consideration would be given to the use of modified Delphi procedures to increase agreement among judges.[13] Scaling the extent of change involved in an event is a much more specific task than scaling a society or collectivity on some attribute, and judges would be given specific instructions for scaling events. Thus differing conceptions of the judgmental task should also be minimized.

The road from interpretive case studies to systematic hypothesis testing is long and difficult when dealing with a set of phenomena as complex as African political change. Events data may provide a vehicle for moving down that road without sacrificing the conceptual richness of the control and facilitation framework and the associated propositions.

Conclusion

Footnotes

1. The second of these points is made in Gary D. Hoggard, "An Analysis of 'Real' Data: Reflections on the Uses and Validity of International Interaction Data," in *Theory and Practice of Events Research: Studies in Inter-Nation Actions and Interactions,* ed. Edward E. Azar and Joseph D. Ben-Dak (New York, London, and Paris: Gordon and Breach Science Publishers, 1975), p. 20. The third point is made in Charles F. and Margaret G. Hermann, Maurice A. East, and Barbara G. and Stephen A. Salmore, *CREON: A Foreign Events Data Set,* Sage Professional Papers in International Studies 2, 02-024 (Beverly Hills and London: Sage Publications, 1973), p. 16.

2. This strategy is advocated by Edward E. Azar, "Analysis of International Events," *Peace Research Reviews* 4 (November 1970): 8; and Joseph D. Ben-Dak, "Some Directions for Research Toward Peaceful Arab-Israeli Relations," *Journal of Conflict Resolution* 16 (June 1972): 291-92.

3. Major international events data sets are described in Philip M. Burgess and Raymond W. Lawton, *Indicators of International Behavior: An Assessment of Events Data Research,* Sage Professional Papers in International Studies 1, 02-010 (Beverly Hills: Sage Publications, 1972), pp. 28-58. See also Raymond W. Copson, "Foreign Policy Conflict Among African States, 1964-1969," in *Sage International Yearbook of Foreign Policy Studies,* Vol. 1, ed. Patrick J. McGowan (Beverly Hills and London: Sage Publications, 1973), pp. 189-217.

4. Ivo K. and Rosalind L. Feierabend, "Aggressive Behaviors within Polities, 1948-1962: A Cross-National Study," *Journal of Conflict Resolution* 10 (September 1966): 249-71; Ted Gurr, "A Causal Model of Civil Strife: A Comparative Analysis Using New Indices," *American Political Science Review* 62 (December 1968): 1104-24; Kenneth Janda, "Comparative Political Parties: A Cross-National Handbook," Department of Political Science, Northwestern University, Evanston, 1974; R.J. Rummel, *The Dimensions of Nations* (Beverly Hills: Sage Publications, 1972); and Charles Lewis Taylor and Michael C. Hudson, *World Handbook of Political and Social Indicators,* 2nd ed. (New Haven and London: Yale University Press, 1972).

5. Donald G. Morrison, Robert C. Mitchell, John N. Paden, and Hugh M. Stevenson, *Black Africa: A Comparative Handbook* (New York: Free Press, 1972); Morrison and Stevenson, "Integration and Instability: Patterns of African Political Development," *American Political Science Review* 66 (September 1972): 902-27; and Mary B. Welfling, *Political Institutionalization: Comparative Analyses of African Party Systems,* Sage Professional Papers in Comparative Politics 4, 01-041 (Beverly Hills and London: Sage Publications, 1973). Internal conflict data on African countries have also been analyzed in Robert W. Jackman, "The

Predictability of Coups d'etat: A Model with African Data," *American Political Science Review* 72 (December 1978): 1262-75; and John N. Collins, "Foreign Conflict Behavior and Domestic Disorder in Africa," in *Conflict Behavior and Linkage Politics*, ed. Jonathan Wilkenfeld (New York: David McKay Co., 1973), pp. 251-93.

6. Charles F. Hermann, "What is a Foreign Policy Event?," in *Comparative Foreign Policy: Theoretical Essays*, ed. Wolfram F. Hanrieder (New York: David McKay Co., 1971), p. 301.

7. Hermann et al., *CREON*, p. 19; and Edward E. Azar, Stanley H. Cohen, Thomas O. Jukam, and James McCormick, "Making and Measuring the International Event as a Unit of Analysis," in *International Events Interaction Analysis: Some Research Considerations*, ed. Edward E. Azar, Richard A. Brody, and Charles A. McClelland, Sage Professional Papers in International Studies 1, 02-001 (Beverly Hills and London: Sage Publications, 1972), p. 62.

8. The first of these points is made in Edward E. Azar, Stanley H. Cohen, Thomas O. Jukam, and James M. McCormick, "The Problem of Source Coverage in the Use of International Events Data," *International Studies Quarterly* 16 (September 1972): 373-87; Robert Burrowes, "Mirror, Mirror on the Wall...: A Comparison of Event Data Sources," in *Comparing Foreign Policies*, ed. James N. Rosenau (New York: John Wiley and Sons, 1974), pp. 383-406; Gary D. Hoggard, "Differential Source Coverage in Foreign Policy Analysis," in ibid., pp. 353-82; and Hermann et al., *CREON*, p. 18. The second point is made in Ben-Dak, "Some Directions for Research Toward Peaceful Arab-Israeli Relations," p. 291; and Timothy M. Shaw and Douglas G. Anglin, "Alternative Sources of Zambian Foreign Policy Events Data," paper presented at the 18th Annual Meeting of the International Studies Association, St. Louis, March 1977. Robert W. Jackman and William A. Boyd, "Multiple Sources in the Collection of Data on Political Conflict," *American Journal of Political Science* 23 (May 1979): 434-58, doubt that use of multiple sources in the analysis of political conflict within African countries is worth the added cost, or that conclusions will differ significantly if regional rather than global sources are utilized. Since the use of a systematic events data set to analyze change is a new venture, and since change can take a greater variety of forms than conflict, use of multiple and regional sources would be important for the proposed project.

9. Edward E. Azar, "Ten Issues in Events Research," in Azar and Ben-Dak, *Theory and Practice of Events Research*, p. 4.

10. Descriptions and examples of this research design are found in Donald T. Campbell, "From Description to Experimentation: Interpreting Trends as Quasi-Experiments," in *Problems in Measuring Change*, ed. Chester W. Harris (Madison: University of Wisconsin Press, 1963), pp. 220-30; Campbell and Julian C. Stanley, *Experimental and Quasi-Experimental Designs for Research* (Chicago: Rand McNally, 1963), pp.

37-43; and James A. Caporaso, "Quasi-Experimental Approaches to Social Science: Perspectives and Problems," in *Quasi-Experimental Approaches: Testing Theory and Evaluating Policy,* ed. Caporaso and Leslie L. Roos, Jr. (Evanston: Northwestern University Press, 1973), pp. 18-22.

11. Judges have been used to code or validate the coding of attributes by Russell H. Fitzgibbon, "Measuring Democratic Change in Latin America," *Journal of Politics 29* (February 1967): 129-66; Kim Quaile Hill and Fred R. von der Mehden, "Data Reliability in Cross-National Research: A Test Employing Black African Country Experts," Paper No. 83, Program of Development Studies, Rice University, Houston, 1978; Janda, "Comparative Political Parties"; and Lars Schoultz, "U.S. Policy Toward Human Rights in Latin America: A Comparative Analysis of Two Administrations," in *Developing Human Rights: Public Policies, Comparative Measures, and NGO Strategies,* ed. Ved P. Nanda, James R. Scarritt, and George W. Shepherd, Jr. (Boulder: Westview Press, forthcoming). Descriptions of their use in scaling events are found in Azar et al., "Making and Measuring the International Event," pp. 64-73; Azar and Ben-Dak, *Theory and Practice of Events Research,* pp. 29-39, 46-50; Burgess and Lawton, *Indicators of International Behavior,* pp. 35, 38-39, 52, 67-68; and Hermann et al., *CREON,* pp. 46-50.

12. Ted Robert Gurr, *Polimetrics: An Introduction to Quantitative Macropolitics* (Englewood Cliffs, N.J.: Prentice Hall, 1972), pp. 83-84; and John F. McCamant, "A Critique of Present Measures of 'Human Rights Development' and An Alternative," in Nanda, Scarritt, and Shepherd, *Developing Human Rights.*

13. See Norman C. Dalkey, with Daniel L. Rourke, Ralph Lewis, and David Snyder, *Studies in the Quality of Life: Delphi and Decision-Making* (Lexington, Mass., Toronto, and London: Lexington Books, D. C. Heath and Co., 1972); Harold A. Linstone, ed., special issue on the Delphi method, *Technological Forecasting and Social Change* 7, 2 (1975): 111-222; and Linstone and Murray Turoff, eds., *The Delphi Method: Techniques and Applications* (Reading, Mass : Addison-Wesley, 1975).

Index of Authors Cited

Aberbach, Joel D., 341
Abshire, David M., 292, 294, 295, 296
Addis Hiwet, 101, 102
Adler, Norman, 341
Agyeman, Opoku, 187
Ake, Claude, 34, 150, 180, 252, 253, 255
Alderfer, Harold, 138
Almond, Gabriel A., 31, 37, 181, 250, 341, 342
Amin, Samir, 252
Anderson, Perry, 292
Andrade, Antonio Alberto de, 293
Andreas Eshete, 99
Anglin, Douglas G., 350
Apter, David E., 181, 183, 185, 186, 188, 192, 222, 223, 228, 235, 250
Apthorpe, Raymond, 233, 234
Aquio, Belinda, 143
Arnold, Guy, 186
Arrighi, Giovanni, 100, 253, 327, 340
Asmelash Beyene, 98
Asmerom Legesse, 100
Atkinson, Dick, 31
Austin, Dennis, 188, 191, 192
Axelson, Eric, 293
Ayres, Robert L., 236
Azar, Edward E., 347, 349, 350, 351

Bailey, Norman A., 294, 295, 296
Baker, James, 292
Baker, Pauline H., 189
Baldwin, David A., 36
Banfield, Edward C., 224, 235
Banks, Arthur S., 210, 234
Barata, Oscar Soares, 293
Barber, Bernard, 33, 36
Barkan, Joel D., 184, 185, 189, 191, 340

Barnes, Barbara, 299
Barrows, Walter L., 188, 193, 251
Bates, Margaret Rouse, 185, 187, 188, 191, 193, 254
Bates, Robert H., 192, 253, 254, 255
Bauer, P. T., 232
Baum, Rainer C., 33, 34
Beckman, Björn, 192, 254
Ben-Dak, Joseph D., 349, 350, 351
Ben-Dor, Gabriel, 255
Bennett, Norman R., 293
Benveniste, Guy, 196, 197-198, 217, 221, 222, 233, 234, 235, 236
Berg, Elliot J., 192
Berger, Peter L., 233
Bershady, Harold J., 33, 36, 37
Bettelheim, Charles, 339
Bienen, Henry, 98, 149, 179, 185, 186, 187, 188, 189, 190, 191, 193
Binder, Leonard, 251
Bixler, Raymond W., 293
Blalock, Hubert M., 39
Blau, Peter M., 35, 37
Boskoff, Alvin, 37, 38
Boulding, Kenneth, 201, 233, 234
Bourricaud, François, 34
Boxer, C. R., 294
Boyd, William A., 350
Boynton, G. R., 181, 183
Bradshaw, Kenneth, 182
Braibanti, Ralph, 236
Brandenburg, Frank, 295
Bratton, Michael, 255, 339
Braverman, Harry, 339
Braybrooke, David, 234
Bretton, Henry L., 186
Brody, Richard A., 350
Buckley, Walter, 31, 32, 34, 37
Burawoy, Michael, 254
Burgess, Philip M., 349, 351

Burke, Fred G., 295
Burns, Sir Alan, 178
Burrowes, Robert, 350
Butler, Jeffrey, 187, 192

Cain, Leonard D., 32
Callaghy, Thomas M., 250
Callaway, Barbara, 191
Calvez, Jean-Yves, 179
Cameron, David R., 38
Campbell, Donald T., 350
Caporaso, James A., 351
Carter, Gwendolen M., 191, 193
Cartwright, Bliss C., 35
Cartwright, John R., 186, 188, 193
Castagno, A. A., 187
Chaliand, Gérard, 292
Chilambe, George M., 298
Chilcote, Ronald, 256, 257, 292, 297, 298
Chockwe, Michael, 298
Chodak, Szymon, 32, 36
Church, R. J. Harrison, 296
Clapham, Christopher, 100, 106
Clarke, Duncan, 327, 340
Cliffe, Lionel, 187, 188, 190, 191, 253, 254
Cohen, Dennis L., 185, 186, 187, 188, 189, 191, 193
Cohen, John M., 28, 97, 98, 99, 101, 102, 104, 106, 138, 139, 140, 142, 143, 345
Cohen, Robin, 34, 340
Cohen, Stanley H., 350
Coleman, James S., 149, 179, 192
Collier, Ruth, 151, 181, 186
Collins, Carole, 299, 300
Collins, John N., 350
Cook, Robert M., 37
Copson, Raymond W., 349
Coser, Lewis A., 44, 71
Crotty, Wiliam J., 181-82
Crummey, Donald, 97

Dahl, Robert A., 179, 236
Dale, Richard, 292

Dalkey, Norman C., 351
Davidson, Basil, 292
Davies, James C., 99
Davis, John A., 292
Diamond, Stanley, 295
Dirlam, Joel B., 219, 235, 236
Dodge, Dorothy, 178
Dodson, James, 292
Dror, Yehezkel, 221, 235
Dubnick, Melvin J., 29, 232, 233, 234, 345
Dudley, B. J., 188, 192
Duffy, James, 293, 294, 296
Duignan, Peter, 138, 178, 293
Dunning, H. C., 140
Duvall, Raymond, 180, 251
Duverger, Maurice, 182, 186
Dye, Thomas R., 232

East, Maurice A., 349
Easton, David, 31, 35, 341, 343
Eckhardt, William, 339
Edelman, Murray, 328, 341
Edinger, Lewis J., 38
Effrat, Andrew, 33, 35
Egerton, F. C. C., 295
Eisenstadt, S. N., 235
Ellis, Gene, 140
Engholm, G. F., 182, 183, 184
Esseks, John D., 252
Evers, Hans-Dieter, 102

Fanon, Frantz, 97
Fecadu Gedamu, 105
Feierabend, Ivo, 99, 349
Feierabend, Rosalind L., 99, 349
Festinger, Leon, 38, 202, 233, 234
Filmer, Paul, 32
Finer, S. E., 180
Finifter, Ada W., 335, 342
Finucane, James R., 185, 189, 190
First, Ruth, 178
Fitzgibbon, Russell H., 351
Flanagan, Scott C., 31, 37
Fleming, William G., 251
Foltz, William J., 179, 192

Foss, Daniel, 31
Fossum, Egil, 251, 255
Foster, Philip, 185
Freyre, Gilberto, 293
Friedland, William H., 192
Friedmann, John, 217, 234

Galanter, Eugene, 233
Gamst, Frederick C., 97, 139
Gann, Lewis H., 138, 178, 293
Gee, T. W., 71
Gertzel, Cherry, 182, 183, 184, 185, 189, 191, 192
Geshekter, Charles L., 300
Ghai, Yash P., 183
Gibson, Richard, 292
Giddens, Anthony, 32, 35
Gilkes, Patrick, 100, 101
Gingyera-Pinycwa, A.G.G., 186, 187, 192
Ginzberg, Eli, 99
Glass, Ruth, 233
Gluckman, Max, 38
Goddard, Ian, 104
Goldman, Sheldon, 142
Goldrich, Daniel, 328, 341
Goldsmith, Arthur A., 143
Goldsworthy, David, 179
Goldthorpe, J. E., 178
Good, Kenneth, 188
Gould, Mark, 34
Gouldner, Alvin W., 13, 32, 35, 36, 37
Grant, James, 104
Green, Reginald H., 232
Gross, Bertram M., 217, 221, 234, 235
Gross, Neal, 141
Grundy, Kenneth, 292
Guessous, Mohammed, 37
Guilbaud, G. T., 36
Gupta, Anirudha, 192
Gurr, Ted R., 99, 349, 351
Gutkind, Peter C. W., 252

Haas, Michael, 182

Haberland, Eike, 138
Hah, Chong-do, 38
Hakes, Jay E., 151, 181, 182, 183, 184, 188, 191
Hammond, Nancy, 38
Hammond, Richard J., 292, 293, 294
Hance, William A., 295
Hanreider, Wolfram F., 350
Hanson, A. H., 182
Harries-Jones, Peter, 189
Harris, Chester W., 350
Harris, Marvin, 294, 295, 296
Harris, Peter, 327, 340
Harris, Richard L., 180, 250, 252
Hastings, Adrian, 299
Hastings, Philip K., 234, 236
Hatch, John, 186, 187
Hawley, Edward A., 299
Hayes, Louis D., 98, 100
Hayward, Fred M., 253, 255
Heeger, Gerald A., 137
Helgerson, John Leonard, 182, 183, 184, 185, 188
Helleiner, G. K., 196, 233
Henricksen, Thomas, 293
Hermann, Charles F. 349, 350, 351
Hermann, Margaret G., 349
Hermet, Guy, 189, 190, 254
Herrick, Allison Butler, 294
Hess, Robert L., 138, 143
Hill, Kim Quaile, 351
Hines, Samuel M., Jr., 181
Hinnant, John, 105
Hirsch, Walter, 37
Hirschman, Albert O., 236
Hoagland, Jim, 339
Hoben, Allan, 98, 101, 103, 138, 139, 143
Hodgkin, Thomas, 179, 186
Hofferbert, Richard I 232
Hoggard, Gary D., 349, 350
Holleman, J. F., 339
Holmberg, Johan, 97, 104
Homans, George C., 32

Hopkins, Raymond F., 183, 184, 185, 191
Horowitz, Irving Louis, 234
Howe, Marvin, 297
Hudson, Michael C., 349
Huffnagel, H., 137
Humphries, Donald H., 292
Huntington, Samuel P., 38, 97, 99, 100, 179, 236, 241, 251, 253, 254, 329, 341
Hurrington, Charles, 341
Hydén, Goran, 190

Ilchman, Alice Stone, 234, 236
Ilchman, Warren, 203, 234, 236
Ingle, Clyde R., 189, 190, 193
Inkeles, Alex, 33, 36, 342
Isaacman, Allen F., 292, 293, 299, 300
Isajiw, Wsevolod W., 38

Jackman, Robert W., 251, 349, 350
Jackson, R. H., 36
Jackson-Haight, Mabel V., 293
Jacobson, Michael, 104
Jahnige, Thomas P., 142
James, Jeffrey A., 184
Janda, Kenneth, 186, 191, 193, 349, 351
Jaros, Dean, 329, 341, 342
Jeffries, Richard, 254
Jewell, Malcolm E., 148, 178, 184
Johnson, Benton, 31, 37
Johnston, Bruce F., 137
Jones, Charles O., 232
Jones, Trevor, 184, 185, 186, 187, 188, 189, 191, 192
Jukam, Thomas O., 350
Jundanian, Brenden F., 297

Kagombe, Maina, 292
Kamarck, Andrew M., 195, 232
Kanter, Rosabeth Moss, 35
Kaplan, Harold, 32
Kariel, Henry S., 182
Kasfir, Nelson, 150, 180, 190, 253, 254
Kauffman, Robert E., 150, 180, 251
Kay, Hugh, 295
Keehn, Norman H., 38, 253
Keller, Suzanne, 141, 142
Kelman, Herbert C., 342
Kermode, D. G., 183
Kesselman, Mark, 97, 106, 251
Kilby, Peter, 137
Kilson, Martin L., 179, 188, 189, 191, 192
Kim, Chong Lim, 181, 183, 184
Kingsley, J. Donald, 225
Kitching, Gavin N., 36
Kjekshus, Helge, 182, 183, 184, 185, 190
Klineberg, Otto, 80, 100
Knipp Thomas R., 100
Koch, Sigmund, 33
Koehn, Eftychia, 105
Koehn, Peter, 28, 97, 98, 99, 100, 102, 104, 105, 106, 136, 140, 143, 345
Kornberg, Alan, 181, 183, 184
Kraus, Jon, 182, 185, 189
Kritzeck, J., 72
Krupp, Sherman, 234
Kuhn, Thomas S., 233
Kuper, Leo, 34, 236

Langlands, B. W., 71
Langton, Kenneth P., 342
LaPalombara, Joseph, 31, 179, 182, 236, 251
Lawrence, J.C.D., 140
Lawson, Kay, 182, 186
Lawton, Raymond W., 349, 351
Lee, J. M., 178, 182, 183, 185
Lefort, René, 300
Legum, Colin, 72, 73, 143, 196, 232
Leiserson, Avery, 186
Lele, Uma J. 137
Lemos, Virgilio de, 297
Lerner, Daniel, 138
Lerza, Catherine, 104

Levine, Donald N., 98, 101, 139
Levine, Katherine, 190
Levy, Marion J., 140, 141
Lewis, Ralph, 351
Lewis, W. Arthur, 232
Lewis, William, 72
Lexander, Arne, 138, 139
Leys, Colin, 179, 253, 342
Lidz, Victor Meyer, 33
Lijphart, Arend, 2, 31
Lin, Nan, 39
Lindblom, Charles E., 218, 234, 235, 236
Linstone, Harold A., 351
Lipset, Seymour Martin, 37
Lockard, Kathleen G., 28, 344
Loewenberg, Gerhard, 181
Lofchie, Michael F., 34, 72, 149, 179, 250, 251, 254
Loft, Vincente, 295
Lopreato, Joseph, 32
Loubser, Jan J., 33, 34, 35, 36, 37
Low, D. A., 71
Lowenkopf, Martin, 72
Luckham, Robin, 188
Luckmann, Thomas, 233

Macartney, W.J.A., 185
Machel, Samora M., 299
Mackintosh, John P., 184, 185, 191, 192
Maguire, Kevin, 30, 345
Mahone, Guy C. Z., 340
Maitland-Jones, J. F., 178
Mann, H. S., 140
Marcum, John, 292, 298
Marcus, Harold G., 105, 138
Marenin, Otwin, 36
Markakis, John, 75, 97, 99, 100, 101, 102, 103, 104, 106, 140, 143
Martel, Marvin U., 32
Martin, C. J., 196, 233
Martin, Denis, 190, 191, 254
Martin, Jeffrey, 38
Mason, Ward S., 141

Masotti, Louis H., 98
May, Joan, 340
Mayhew, Leon H., 33, 37, 38
Mazrui, Ali A., 178, 183, 297
McAuslan, J.P.W.B., 183
McCamant, John F., 351
McClelland, Charles A., 350
McClelland, David C., 137
McCormick, James, 350
McEachern, Alexander, 141
McFarlane, Bruce, 102
McGowan, Patrick J., 252, 349
McHenry, Dean E., Jr., 254
McKenzie, R. T., 186
McKinney, John C., 35
McKown, Roberta E., 150, 180, 251
McLennan, Barbara, 191
Meier, Gerald M., 235
Meier, Richard L., 220, 234, 235
Mellor, John W., 137, 143
Melson, Robert, 253
Menzies, Ken, 32, 36, 37
Merkl, Peter H., 138, 182
Merton, Robert K., 138
Miliband, Ralph, 33, 34, 38, 253
Milkias, Paulos, 99, 100
Miller, George A., 233
Miller, Norman H., 190, 193
Miller, Robert A., 36
Mills, C. Wright, 141
Minter, William, 292
Mitchell, Robert C., 349
Mitchell, William C., 31, 33
Mittelman, James H., 73, 187
Mlinar, Zdravko, 38
Mohammed, Duri, 99
Molteno, Robert, 183, 185, 188, 191, 255
Mondlane, Eduardo, 292, 296, 297, 298, 299
Mondlane, Janet Rae, 298
Moore, Clement Henry, 179
Moore, Wilbert E., 37, 236
Morgenthau, Ruth Schachter, 179
Moris, Brian, 35

356

Moris, Jon R., 190
Morrison, David R., 36
Morrison, Donald G., 251, 349
Mueller, Suzanne D., 192
Mujaju, Akiki B., 186, 187, 188, 191, 192
Mulford, David C., 187
Mulkay, M. J. 32, 33, 34, 35, 36
Mundt, Robert J., 31, 37
Murphree, Marshall, 340
Murphy, Robert F., 32
Mushi, Samuel Stephen, 253, 254
Musolf, Lloyd D., 181, 183
Mwansasu, Bismarck U., 190, 255
Myrdal, Gunner, 233

Nadel, S. F., 141
Naegele, Kaspar D., 31
Namirembe, G., 71
Nanda, Ved P., 351
Nayak, Sanjeeva, 192
Nega Ayele, 100, 103, 104, 106, 140, 143
Nekby, Bengt, 139
Nellis, John R., 339
Nelson, Joan M., 38, 253, 254
Neuberger, Benyamin, 180
Nordlinger, Eric A., 250, 255
Nsibambi, Apolo, 71
Nwabueze, B. O., 178, 182, 183, 184
Nye, Joseph S., Jr. 187, 188

O'Barr, Jean F., 190
O'Connell, James, 250
O'Connell, M. J., 179
Odumosu, Oluwole Idowu, 184
Okuma, Thomas, 292
Okumu, John J., 184, 189, 191
Ollawa, Patrick E., 255
Opello, Walter C., Jr., 30, 297, 298, 299, 345
Osherson, Samuel, 31
Ossowski, Stanislaw, 34
Ottaway, David B., 103, 104, 143, 339
Ottaway, Marina, 101, 103, 140, 143
Owusu, Maxwell, 189, 191

Packenham, Robert A., 181
Paden, John N., 180, 349
Paige, Glenn D., 38
Paige, Jeffrey M., 330, 335, 341, 342
Pajestka, Jozef, 195, 232, 235
Palley, Claire, 306, 309, 339
Pankhurst, Richard, 99
Park, Sang-Seek, 151, 181
Parson, J., 187
Parsons, Talcott, 4, 15, 31, 32, 33, 34, 35, 36, 37, 138, 329, 341
Patterson, Samuel C., 181
Pettman, Jan, 186, 187, 191, 193
Phillipson, Michael, 32
Pierce, Brian, 339
Pitts, Jesse R., 31
Plotnicov, Leonard, 101
Polanyi, Michael, 138
Post, K.W.J., 188, 189, 192
Potholm, Christian P., 292
Powell, G. Bingham, Jr., 181, 250
Powelson, John P., 235
Pratt, Cranford, 186, 187, 188, 191, 253
Prewitt, Kenneth, 343
Pribram, Karl H., 233
Pring, David, 182
Proctor, J. Harris, 184, 185, 190
Provizer, Norman W., 187
Punnett, R. M., 182
Pye, Lucian W., 234, 250

Quick, Stephen A., 339

Ranney, Austin, 232, 236
Ranney, David C., 233
Rasmussen Thomas, 193
Reid, Escott, 236
Rhoads, John K., 35
Rhodes, Cecil, 317

Richards, Peter G., 182
Riggs, Fred W., 181
Rita-Ferreira, A., 294, 296
Robertson, Roland, 36
Rocher, Guy, 31, 37
Rogin, Michael, 193
Rondinelli, Dennis A., 255
Roos, Leslie L., Jr., 351
Rosberg, Carl G., Jr., 149, 179, 192
Rose, Richard, 183, 186, 189, 254
Rosenau, James N., 350
Rosenberg, Milton J., 38
Rosenthal, Donald, 106
Ross, Marc Howard, 254
Rostow, W. W., 235
Rotberg, Robert I., 179, 297
Rothchild, Donald, 193
Rouquié, Alain, 189, 254
Rourke, Daniel L., 351
Rueschemeyer, Dietrich, 37
Rummel, R. J., 349
Rustow, Dankwart A., 224, 235, 250, 251
Ryan, Selwyn, 187, 188, 190, 191

Salmore, Barbara G., 349
Salmore, Stephen A., 349
Samoff, Joel, 33, 34, 186, 189, 190, 191, 192, 193, 252, 253
Samoff, Rachel, 191, 193, 253
Samuels, Michael A., 292, 294, 295, 296, 298
Sandbrook, Richard, 252, 254, 340
Sartori, Giovanni, 150, 180
Sathyamurthy, T. V., 187, 191
Saul, John S., 100, 190, 191, 253, 299, 340
Savage, Stephen P., 35
Saville, John, 34, 253
Scarritt, James R., 29, 31, 37, 72, 183, 250, 252, 254, 255, 344, 345, 351
Schaffer, B. B., 178
Schoultz, Lars, 351
Schumacher, E. F., 236

Scott, Ian, 186, 187, 188, 189, 191, 193, 255
Scott, James C., 149, 180
Scott, John Finley, 32
Searle, Chris, 299
Seleshi Sisaye, 97, 143
Seymour, Tony, 190, 193
Shapiro, Miriam, 143
Shaw, Timothy M., 339, 350
Shepherd, George W., Jr., 351
Shils, Edward, 31, 138
Shivji, Issa G., 253
Sidjanski, Dusan, 192
Sills, David L., 35
Silverman, David, 32
Silviera, Onésimo, 178, 252
Simango, Uria T., 298
Simon, Herbert A., 199, 233
Simpson, Richard L., 32, 35
Singer, Norman J., 105
Sjoberg, Gideon, 32
Sklar, Richard L., 34, 101, 186, 187, 188, 189, 191, 192, 252
Smelser, Neil J., 31, 34
Smith, Anthony D., 32, 33, 35, 37
Smith, Donald E., 65, 66, 73
Smith, Herbert A., 99
Smith, Joel, 181
Smith, M. G., 34, 236
Smith, N. D., 232
Smock, Audrey C., 189, 190, 192
Snyder, David, 351
Soja, Edward W., 180
Spengler, J. J., 236
Spiegelglas, Stephan, 235
Stacey, Frank, 182
Stahl, Michael, 101, 143
Stallings, Barbara, 252
Staniland, Martin, 179
Stanley, Julian C., 350
Stein, Maurice, 31
Stevenson, Hugh Michael, 251, 349
Stren, Richard, 102
Stuart, Mary, 71

Stultz, Newell M., 147, 148, 164, 178, 183, 185

Tamarkin, M., 184, 185
Tandon, Yash, 339
Tansey, S. D., 183
Taylor, Charles Lewis, 349
Taylor, John V., 47, 71
Tegagne Yeteshawork, 102
Tekere, Edgar, 339
Tekle Mariam Wolde Michael, 100
Teune, Henry, 38
Thio, Alex O., 38
Thomas, Dani B., 251
Tinbergen, Jan, 198, 232, 233
Tiryakian, Edward A., 35
Toby, Jackson, 33
Todaro, Michael P., 137, 233, 235
Tordoff, William, 183, 185, 186, 187, 188, 189, 191, 192, 193, 255
Tsurutani, Taketsugu, 251
Tuden, Arthur, 101
Turk, Herman, 32, 35
Turner, Jonathan H., 32, 33, 35
Turoff, Murray, 351
Twumasi, Yaw, 188, 192

Uphoff, Norman Thomas, 236
Urdang, Stephanie, 300

Vallier, Ivan, 35
Valtos, Henry, 100
Van Dongen, Irene S., 295
Van Onselen, Charles, 339, 340
Vengroff, Richard, 252
Verba, Sidney, 239, 240, 251, 341, 342
Vergener, Zdeneka, 235
Vickers, Michael, 189, 192
Vidich, Arthur, 32
Vignad, V. C., 233
von der Mehden, Fred R., 351
Von Freyhold, Michaela, 253
Von Gersdorff, Ralf, 296

Wahlke, John C., 181
Waldron, Sidney R., 104, 105
Walker, Jack L., 341
Wallerstein, Immanuel, 33, 149, 179, 192, 250, 252
Walles, Malcolm, 182
Walsh, Annmarie H., 106
Walsh, David, 32
Walton, John, 98
Warner, R. Stephen, 35
Warwick, Donald P., 31
Waterston, Albert, 106, 195, 218, 232, 235
Watson, Andrew, 219, 235, 236
Watson, Goodwin, 37
Weiner, Myron, 179, 182
Weinrich, A.K.H., 339
Weintraub, Dov, 137, 138, 140, 142, 143
Welbourn, F. B., 71
Welfling, Mary B., 150, 151, 180, 181, 186, 251, 349
Welsh, Charles J., 235
Werlin, Herbert H., 189
Wetterhall, H., 140
Wheeler, Douglas L., 292, 293, 297
Wheelwright, Edward L., 102
Whelan, Frederick G., 297
Whitaker, C. S., Jr., 188, 189, 192
Whitaker, Paul, 292
Wiener, Norbert, 234
Wilkenfeld, Jonathan, 350
Willetts, Peter, 187
Williams, Robin M., Jr., 36, 37, 38
Wolf, E. R., 142
Wolfe, Marshall, 235
Wolpe, Howard, 253
Wood, Eric, 321, 339
Wriggins, W. Howard, 182
Wright, Robin, 300

Young, Christopher, 339
Young, Frank W., 137
Young, M. Crawford, 72, 178, 179, 180, 187

Young, Roland, 182
Young, Ruth C., 137

Zaltman, Gerald, 37, 39
Zartman, I. William, 292
Zavalloni, Marisa, 80, 100
Zolberg, Aristide R., 149, 150, 179, 180, 185, 250
Zollschan, George K., 37